General Speech Communication

McGraw-Hill Series in Speech

Glen E. Mills, Consulting Editor in General Speech
John J. O'Neill, Consulting Editor in Speech Pathology

Armstrong and Brandes: *The Oral Interpretation of Literature*
Baird: *American Public Addresses*
Baird: *Argumentation, Discussion, and Debate*
Baird and Knower: *Essentials of General Speech*
Baird, Knower, and Becker: *General Speech Communication*
Black and Moore: *Speech: Code, Meaning, and Communication*
Carrell and Tiffany: *Phonetics*
Gibson: *A Reader in Speech Communication*
Hahn, Lomas, Hargis, and Vandraegen: *Basic Voice Training for Speech*
Hasling: *The Message, the Speaker, the Audience*
Kaplan: *Anatomy and Physiology of Speech*
Kruger: *Modern Debate*
Ogilvie: *Speech in the Elementary School*
Ogilvie and Rees: *Communication Skills: Voice and Pronunciation*
Powers: *Fundamentals of Speech*
Reid: *Teaching Speech*
Robinson and Becker: *Effective Speech for the Teacher*
Wells: *Cleft Palate and Its Associated Speech Disorders*

General Speech Communication

A. Craig Baird, 1883 -
Department of Speech and Dramatic Art
University of Iowa

Franklin H. Knower
Department of Speech
Ohio State University

Samuel L. Becker
Department of Speech and Dramatic Art
University of Iowa

Fourth Edition

McGRAW-HILL BOOK COMPANY

New York   St. Louis   San Francisco   Düsseldorf   Kuala Lumpur   London
Mexico   Montreal   New Delhi   Panama   Rio de Janeiro   Singapore
Sydney   Toronto

GENERAL SPEECH COMMUNICATION

Library of Congress Catalog Card Number 71-140953

07-003268-8

1 2 3 4 5 6 7 8 9 0   HDMM   7 9 8 7 6 5 4 3 2 1

This book was set in Medallion by York Graphic Services, Inc.,
printed on permanent paper by Halliday Lithograph Corporation,
and bound by The Maple Press Company. The designer was
Richard Paul Kluga; the drawings were done by BMA Associates,
Inc. The editors were Cheryl Kupper and Timothy Yohn. Robert
Fry was the sponsor. Matt Martino supervised production.

ACKNOWLEDGMENTS

Pp. 386–392: Richard M. Nixon, "Campus Revolutionaries." Reprinted with the kind permission of the office of President of the
United States.

Pp. 392–399: John E. Swearingen, "Environmental Pollution: A
National Problem." Reprinted with the kind permission of John E.
Swearingen.

Pp. 399–404: Benjamin E. Mays, "Eulogy on Dr. Martin Luther
King, Jr." Reprinted with the kind permission of Benjamin E. Mays.

Pp. 404–408: Neil Armstrong, Col. Edwin E. Aldrin, and Lt. Col.
Michael Collins, "Moon Rendezvous." Reprinted with the kind
permission of Neil Armstrong.

Pp. 412–418: Walter Lippmann, "On Understanding Society." Reprinted with the kind permission of Walter Lippmann.

contents

part seven
Bases for Evaluation

part eight
Speech Types

part nine
Special Speech Types

preface

The first three editions of *General Speech Communication* were written in an attempt to unify the basic principles of communication as developed in traditional rhetoric and in today's behavioral sciences. Since the appearance of the third edition, there has been a tremendous leap forward in the clarification and development of communication theory. This fourth edition of *General Speech Communication* is written not only to update our original goals, but also to supplement them with greater attention to current communication theory.

Not only has there been the inescapable development of a new vocabulary with which students must become acquainted, but also refinements of old concepts have taken place which cannot be ignored today. In this book we have tried as much as possible to deal with these problems in everyday language. We do believe that an understanding in depth of the principles of communication can be attained only by leading the beginning student from where he is to where we want him to go. We have tried to accomplish this by writing about what we want to teach him in the language he knows.

In the bibliography for each chapter, we have a set of relevant readings in the field, ranging from the elementary and simple to the quite advanced and complex. The instructor can assign those readings which are most appropriate for each student.

In this edition, we have tried to bridge the gap between the traditional approach to the study of speech with its emphasis on practice and the growing interest in a communication ideas–centered introductory course. The book can be used in either type of course, as well as a course with a greater number of total hours in which the two approaches are integrated.

This edition of the text maintains its threefold goal in speech communication education. We believe that communication students need to develop a concern for significant ideas which they communicate about. The message system as influenced and influenceable in many ways by all the other communication variables must be seen as the important focus.

The study of speech as well as other forms of communication often has been and continues to be a study of one or more of the subprocesses which enter into the whole. Thought, language, cultural compatability, and adaptation to other persons are examples of such processes.

The study of communication as process focuses upon types of communication behavior adapted to purposes, people, and situations. We have included chapters devoted to representative types of communication situations. A significant aspect of the study of both communication processes and communication as social process is a concern for relevant impact or effect.

As our knowledge of each variable in communication has expanded, it has become more and more difficult for the student to experience his study of communication as a unified whole. We believe overcoming this difficulty to be one of the most important educational goals of our time. It is our hope that the references included will supplement the text in giving the student a richer appreciation of the "many roads to truth" in this field today.

A. Craig Baird
Franklin H. Knower
Samuel L. Becker

PART ONE

General Processes and Aims

Adlai Stevenson campaigns for the Presidency.
Cornell Capa, Magnum.

introduction

Twentieth-century man lives in a pressure cooker of communication; everyone and everything is pushing him in a different direction. The media are telling him to buy a car, cigarettes, and deodorants, to wear an auto seat belt, to vote for the party of his choice, to support our military efforts, and to demonstrate against war. His children are asking him to play with them or to give them money for the movies or to buy them a car, while his wife is pushing him to mow the lawn but to take it easy and to fix his tie. Those above him at the office are telling him to work harder, and those below him are telling him to stop making *them* work so hard. All of this pushing is done through communication.

We are pushed by our television sets, radios, newspapers, magazines, billboards, handbills, memoranda and, most of all, by the old-fashioned open mouth which is often so uncomfortably close to our ear. We are pushed not only through verbal communication, but through nonverbal communication as well. We are attacked not only at supraliminal levels, but also at the barely liminal and even at the subliminal. We cannot escape this barrage of communication; our wives or husbands, parents or friends, wonder why we are not more communicative in the evening when they demand, "Talk to me. Why don't you ever talk to me?" As one writer put it, the world is a "blooming, buzzing, confusion." The problem for you in all this is how to make your own messages stand out in this busy field of stimuli and how to pick out the messages you need to notice. Actually, when you look at the world this way, it is amazing that any effective communication takes place at all.

Even what we have just mentioned does not hint at the complexities of our tasks as communicators. We are constantly developing new media of communication which have far-reaching effects—on other media, on senders, on receivers, and even on the nature of our society which, in turn, affects the way our communication processes work. Our channels of communication have grown extremely rapidly in the last few decades, both within the United States and between this country and others. To consider the latter alone, twenty-five to thirty years ago international communication was severely limited. Some undependable radiotelephone circuits and a few telegraph cables existed, but relatively few messages could be transmitted at once, and the probability of any given message coming through ungarbled was not high.

Nowadays we have transistorized underseas cables and an ever-increasing number of channels with constantly increasing reliability available via communication satellites hovering over various parts of the earth. In fact, our supply of channels for international communication appears to exceed the demand. Within this country, the opposite seems to be the case. Though intranational channels have increased even more rapidly than international ones have, demand has far outrun supply. The demand for space in the broadcasting spectrum has grown so great that the United States government has even considered the abolition of broadcasting as we now know it, switching this service over to a type of closed-circuit system. Though you might wish at times you could simply erect a dam against the flood of communication, you cannot.

Communication As Social Mold and Bond

Communication both shapes society and holds it together. Ours is a social world: whatever you do, you are involved with other people. Extremely rare is the individual who lives in total isolation. You live among your families, your friends, and your coworkers. You need to understand and be understood by them. You need to shape your behavior to some extent because of others, and you need to help others to shape their behavior because of you. In other words, society can exist only through interaction and mutual adjustment among people. Conflicts arise and society tends to disintegrate when there is a breakdown in this interaction—when adequate adjustments do not occur. That is to say, only adequate communication can create and maintain the sort of society that we must have.

The more skilled at communication are the people whose goal is a just and good society, the greater the chances that we will have that sort of society. As one, presumably, with that goal, you have the responsibility to develop to the maximum your abilities to communicate in order to help your society toward that goal. This is true whether your society is made up of two persons, of the persons in a college, of a total community, or of an entire nation. It is only through the various and continuing processes of communication that men are able to adjust to each other and to work together for individual or mutual goals. Even the effects of the mass media are mediated in large part by interpersonal communication, as we point out in a later chapter.

If you should keep a diary of all the communication situations in which you are involved during a single day you would be amazed at both the number and variety. Just the instances of your talking, listening, writing, and reading would fill a fair-sized book. To be complete, you would also have to note many instances of nonverbal communication—the perception of the moods or reactions of others simply from their facial expressions, their gesture, posture, or what they were doing. You can probably tell whether you ought to joke with your roommate simply by the way he walks into the room and puts his books down on the desk. You can often predict the kind of time you are going to have for the evening by the expression on your date's face when you meet.

The Goals Are Understanding and Skill

In order to have some control of your communication environment, and its effects upon you, you must learn to understand as completely as possible how it works, and you must develop maximum skill at affecting it.

Though you have been talking and listening, saying things with facial expression and gesture and watching the facial expressions and gestures of others for a good part of your life, it is a safe bet that the communication which went on was often not as efficient or effective or satisfactory as it might have been. Shakespeare may well have been commenting upon our feeble efforts in *Romeo and Juliet* when he had Romeo say, "She speaks, yet she says nothing." The sad fact is that we, like Juliet, usually go right on in our usual way unaware of what is going on about us—unaware of our failures as sources and receivers of messages. Though most of us learned to talk and to hear the talk of others just about as easily as we learned to walk, the difference between normal talking or hearing and skillful communication is as great as the difference between walking and accomplished ballet dancing. Effective communication requires sensitivity and skill that can only come from careful study of communication processes and an awareness of what you and others are doing as you communicate. It also requires a great deal of understanding of other people. As a matter of fact, learning to communicate effectively in large part means learning to understand what causes other people to behave as they do. Whenever we talk in this book about choosing a subject, finding materials, organizing your message, or using appropriate language, we are really talking directly and indirectly about factors which affect human behavior. You do not ordinarily select a subject, choose materials, organize your message, or deliver it in a certain way solely because of your personal needs; you do these things as you do partly because of the needs of those with whom you are communicating.

Social Goals Are Most Important

The best communicator is the one who is most sensitive to the needs of those with whom he communicates, who is trying to serve their needs rather than his own. For example, in a discussion, it is essential that you be concerned more with achieving the group goal and helping others in the group to make their maximum contribution than with displaying your superior knowledge. In teaching, it is more important to discover what each learner already knows and what he needs to learn to reach or surpass the course goals and to help him to learn it than to deliver a series of preset lectures, no matter how perfectly organized and beautifully delivered. In other words, the art of communication is "other directed," not "inner directed."

If you consider the truly great speeches of recent times—Franklin Delano Roosevelt's speeches during the depths of the Depression, Winston Churchill's speeches during the darkest days of World War II, Martin Luther King's speeches at the height of the civil rights movement that he led—you will see that the speakers did not begin with their personal needs or purposes; they began rather with the needs and purposes of their audience and the larger society. Thus, to improve your communication skills, not only is it important to get a good background in history, economics, natural science, and literature, it is extremely important to get as sound an understanding of human beings as possible—the elements that affect their learning, their attitudes, their values, and their behaviors.

Excellent Communication Is Complex

One factor which makes communication more difficult and skill at communication more essential is that many of the messages or ideas with which we must deal today are far more complex than they were in the past, while the human organism has stayed pretty much the same. Thus, to increase our skill at communicating, we must learn to use more and more abstract symbols effectively—relatively simple stimuli which carry a great deal of information. Symbols help us to communicate more efficiently; they also help us to organize—to put into perspective—the fragmented, almost random flow of data by which any man is bombarded. Symbols help man to structure and make "sense" out of his environment, whether that "sense" has any relationship to "reality" or not. If he does not structure these data from his environment, he cannot operate. As a skilled communicator, you can learn to organize data in fruitful ways for your purposes and help others to do so; in a very real sense, you can provide key symbols for others.

You can also help in ensuring more systematic—less random—diffusion of critical information. Clearly, among the many serious problems faced by this and any other country are the diffusion of information which people need to vote intelligently on local, state, or national issues; the diffusion of information about new ideas, such as new ways of teaching, farming, raising children, or operating a college or university; convincing people of the need to do something about the population explosion—whether it is a question of health and food distribution in a more crowded world or one of adopting some means of limiting the size of families; causing people to eliminate prejudice toward minority groups.

Democracy Demands Participation

Another problem which communication skill can help resolve is the need in our society for indigenous leadership and widespread participation by individuals in the various groups and communities in this country. It is generally recognized, for example, that many of the problems of minority groups in the ghettos cannot be resolved until such leadership and participation develop. Similar problems and needs exist in many other countries. Participatory democracy is essential to the kind of society that most of us want, and widespread communication must occur between and among all the people in a society before such a condition can exist.

You may think that, as a single individual, you can have little impact on these widespread national or international problems. However, ample evidence from recent history shows that a single person can have a great impact. Consider Senator Eugene McCarthy, who in 1968 had a major impact in bringing foreign policy questions to the attention of the American public, or Ralph Nader, who in the late sixties focused the nation's attention on automobile safety. These men, in different ways, spoke to the entire nation. However, not all communication, to have an impact, need be directed at or involve the so-called "mass public." Sociologist David Riesman has noted that if we are to live long enough to imagine and, hopefully, to create a utopian society, our imperative need "is for ideas and for small audiences for them—ideas which are not immediately cut short or truncated by the need to make them appealing to a mass audience. . . . We must have the courage to experiment with ideas among ourselves and within each of us—ideas which cannot be immediately sloganized or sold."[1]

Communication As Social Interaction

Up to this point, we have been talking in a very general way about communication. Let's stop now and ask ourselves what we mean by the term. What does "communication" mean to you? Is any sort of talk, any sort of writing, or any sort of display of signs communication? We suggest that the answer to that question is no. We suggest also that one of the problems that many people have communicating results, at least in part, from too simplistic a conception of communication. Too many people define communication as something akin to shooting spitballs. Shooting spitballs requires only some sort of material that can purposefully be changed through wetting and wadding—and then shot out. If there is someone to aim it at, that's fine; but whether he is hit or not has little effect on whether one is shooting spitballs. (As a matter of fact, if our spitball misses, we can always say our target moved.) In communication, too, one begins with some sort of material whose form can be purposefully changed through some manipulation or translation. Again, you shoot it out. However, if it fails to hit the target, there is no communication. If there is no perception by a receiver, there has been no communication. And, most important, if the message decoded by the receiver has little similarity to the message intended by the sender, there is communication, but the sender has failed. Whether the message is verbal or nonverbal, whether it is a radio commercial, a poem, a poster, a speech, or a piece of sculpture, the problem is the same.

An analogy may help convey how communication influence is multidirectional, rather than unidirectional. If you examine the way most of us in the United States look at international communication, you will note that we tend to consider it a one-way circuit. When we hear the term "international communication," most of us think of the effect of Voice of America or other forms of American propaganda on other countries, or the effect

---

[1]David Riesman, "Private People and Public Policy," *Shenandoah*, 10:63–64, Autumn 1958.

of Russian or Chinese propaganda on other countries. We seldom think about the equally important effect of stimuli from other countries on us. Yet, one of the world's critical problems today is the image held by people in the United States of what is going on in Southeast Asia, or China, or Russia. Our policy and the chances of our going to war depend in large part on those perceptions. Closely related to this distinction between the effects of the messages coming into this country and the effects of those going out is the interaction between these effects. For example, our perceptions of another nation affect the sort of information we send to them. This is a dynamic process. As the other countries respond, our perceptions change, which affects additional information that we send, and so on.

The process of communication between two or more individuals is closely analogous to that between nations. What you say to others and what they say to you are affected by the constant change in the set of perceptions which you have of each other.

The Speech Situation

To understand communication, and to be an effective communicator, you must recognize that the particular speech situation in which you participate is not an isolated event. What happens in the situation depends in large part on forces outside the situation, and what follows the speech event also depends on an ongoing stream of forces. Your message will never be the first influence on anyone else's behavior or knowledge. It is not truly possible to pick an initial influence, because all prior experiences interact with the stimuli in your speech to affect each member of the audience, and your speech becomes part of that process of change and development. So it is important for you to think of communication as a process or set of processes in which there is constant change of each involved individual; where each individual's responses of any sort affect each of the other individuals in the situation; and where perceptions of these responses interact with all of each individual's other experiences in the past and present.

If you look at speaking or any other form of communication in this way, you will learn to be sensitive and respond more fruitfully to the fact that a great deal beside speech is going on while one is speaking—that the speaker is changing in the process of speaking, the audience is changing, the situation is changing—and much will go on afterward. To some extent, once we say or do something, we lose control of it, just as scholars who have studied the diffusion of ideas or practices have found. The extent to which you are directly responsible for the nature of the changes your speaking brings about is limited.

Communication, in other words, is an interaction process which, when successful, involves a constant adjustment among the parties to the process.[2] You must learn to adjust your communication behaviors not because it is "correct" to do so, but because, by doing so, you can increase the probability of influencing your environment. By developing your communication skills, you will increase your leadership ability, including your ability to work with various types of individuals and groups in the solution of problems.

Social Purpose in Communication

We hope that this book will help you to learn what sort of communication processes are fruitful for various sorts of purposes. For example, evidence is clear that formal public speeches have little likelihood of changing votes in a national political election. Informal communication among friends, on a one-to-one basis, is more effective for this purpose. On the other hand, the enthusiasm of party workers is apparently best created with the mass meetings and speeches to the party faithful; the informal conversations are less useful for this purpose. The mass media are most effective at introducing new ideas; interpersonal communication seems essential for most people to change "knowledge of" to "practice of."

This book is not prescriptive. Our purpose is not to help you learn a set of rules on the "correct" way to communicate. Rather, it is to give you some methods for analyzing any communication situation and making intelligent decisions about the communicative behaviors you should adopt for that occasion. We will remind you that, in most communication situations, there is an audience of one or more persons in a state of need or drive (which either existed before or is induced by a communicator through his structuring of stimuli) and the goal of the communicator is to suggest responses the audience can make that will reduce that state.

As regards the needs of the audience and the demands of the situation, we will remind you that there are many functions which communication can serve:

1. Reinforcement of existing attitudes or tendencies to behave in certain ways. Whipping up the enthusiasm of the already persuaded is an extreme example of this phenomenon.
2. Dissonance reduction. When members of the audience are torn between conflicting attitudes or between a particular attitude and contradictory

---

[2]Since we shall use the words "process" and "processes" frequently, their meaning and significance may warrant a brief note. Among their more important meanings are: a continuity in time, from eternity to eternity with related antecedents and consequences; a slice of time with a beginning and an end; an operation or procedure, a function, an activity; a dynamic system with subsystems. The words are used somewhat differently in various parts of the text, and we hope that the context will make these differences clear. For a discussion of the concept of process, see W. J. Kobb and J. Gould, *A Dictionary of the Social Sciences,* The Free Press, New York, pp. 538–540, 1964.

knowledge, communication can help to direct the way in which people will reduce that dissonance—whether they will move in one direction or the other, or bring both attitudes or the attitude and the cognition toward each other.

3. Providing information or ideas for opinion leaders to use in their interpersonal communication.

4. Increasing salience for an issue so that it is talked of more, or so that people are more aware of it.

5. Self-adjustment—testing one's position. As someone has said, "How can I know what I think if I don't say it?" More important, how can one know how sound or useful his opinion or knowledge is unless he tries it out on others and sees how it works? In this way, communication is not only a means of influencing others, it is also a means of adjusting oneself to others. That is to say, it is a type of testing—one speaks, notes the responses, adjusts, speaks, notes responses, etc.

6. Social functions—making and keeping friends and acquaintances; maintaining one's position within a group of friends or acquaintances.

Clearly a speech or any other communication form functions differently when it concerns an issue on which an audience has received no or few other messages than when it concerns one for which the audience has gotten many other messages.

We will also remind you that communication takes place in some sort of social milieu which affects our interaction. People in any given social milieu have certain expectations about their behavior and the behavior of others.

Those involved in a communication situation have varied knowledge of the substance or content of the messages, the others involved in the communication situation, and communication processes. They vary also in their attitudes toward the content of the messages, the people, and communication. And they vary in their sending and receiving communication skills.

All of these affect the processes occurring in any communication situation. An effective communicator must be sensitive to them all. An effective communicator, above all, is one who has acquired the ability to place himself in the shoes of those with whom he is interacting—one who understands their needs and the other forces acting upon them and who can, therefore, predict the responses they will make. An effective communicator is sensitive to the conflicting needs and purposes of the various individuals in the communication situation. An effective communicator assumes major responsibility for the "success" of any given communication encounter. He does not shift blame onto others if he is misunderstood, and he does not shift blame onto others if he does not understand them. He assumes major responsibility for both being clear to others and understanding what others are saying, no matter how complex or confused their messages. (As a student, have you ever found yourself blaming the teacher when you failed to understand something? As a member of a family or group, have you ever thought others were stupid because they did not understand you?)

The sort of communication with which we are primarily concerned in this book is purposive communication. People become involved in a communication situation for a reason—they want to find out something or they want to decide what to think or what to do or, perhaps, they want to be entertained. On the other hand, their purpose may be to help someone else learn something, decide something, or be entertained. In order to achieve any one of these goals, each individual involved must be constantly making decisions or predictions about the best thing to do next. In a very real sense, the processes of communication are largely a continual set of predictions and testing of predictions. When you seek information or advice, whether conscious of the process or not, you are predicting where or from whom you can get it. As you listen to a person, you are constantly making predictions about what he means by what he is saying and what he will say next. As you give information or advice to another person, you make predictions about the information he already has, about the language with which he is familiar, and about the order in which to present the material which will be easiest for him to understand or which will influence him most. Both seeker and giver constantly check their predictions through observation of the responses of the other. Thus, there is mutual effect. In this sense, all who are involved in a communication situation are both senders and receivers of messages and, sometimes more important, one is doing both simultaneously. Therefore, some theorists consider it somewhat inaccurate to categorize some people in a situation as sources and others as receivers. In many communication situations, each individual is simultaneously source and receiver most of the time.

Though we are concerned primarily with oral communication in this book, it is important to recognize that oral communication works within a context of all forms of communication, nonoral as well as oral, nonverbal as well as verbal. Though we will not go into these other aspects in as great detail, we hope that we can give you enough knowledge about what they are and how they operate so that you can continue to develop further sophistication on your own or in other courses.

As a communicator, we assume that you have no special wisdom that will enable you alone to set the goals for society, but you do have a responsibility to help in setting them and acquire a sophisticated knowledge of existing goals and needs and to make your communication consistent with them. This is not to say that your responsibility is necessarily to serve the status quo or to aid your society to achieve goals which you believe to be destructive. But it is to say that your responsibility is to help in the development and attainment of those societal goals which are just and which serve mankind.

Projects and Problems

PROJECT 1:   An introduction to what you know about communication:
Plan a three-minute report to the class on what you know about communication. Discuss such topics as what instruction you have had on the subject, what books you have read about it, what experiences you have had as a communicator, what types of communication especially interest you, in what kinds of communication you like to participate, what variable in the process of communication you consider important, or how you believe others react to your attempts at communication.

PROJECT 2:   Readings about communication:
Read the introductory chapter in one of the references suggested at the end of this chapter and report to the class on what you have read. Try to relate your own thinking about what communication is to the explicit or implied definition of communication that you find in your reading. Invite and answer questions from the class.

PROJECT 3:   Class discussion about communication:
Hold a class discussion about personal experiences in communication which were successful or unsuccessful, or communication experiences in which you encountered difficulty. Consider what generalizations you can make about communication as a result of the experiences which various members of the group have had.

References

Barnlund, Dean C. (ed.), *Interpersonal Communication: Survey and Studies.* Boston: Houghton Mifflin Co., 1968.

Berlo, David K., *The Process of Communication.* New York: Holt, Rinehart and Winston, Inc., 1960.

Borden, George A., Richard B. Gregg, and Theodore G. Grove, *Speech Behavior and Human Interaction.* Englewood Cliffs, N.J.: Prentice-Hall, Inc., 1969.

Campbell, James H., and Hal W. Hepler (eds.), *Dimensions in Communication.* Belmont, Calif.: Wadsworth Publishing Co., 1965.

Ellingsworth, Huber W., and Theodore Clevenger, Jr., *Speech and Social Action.* Englewood Cliffs, N.J.: Prentice-Hall, Inc., 1967.

Monroe, Alan H., and Douglas Ehninger, *Principles and Types of Speech,* 6th ed. Glenview, Ill.: Scott, Foresman and Co., 1967.

Schramm, Wilbur, *The Science of Human Communication.* New York: Basic Books, Inc., 1963.

Sereno, Kenneth K., and C. David Mortensen (eds.), *Foundations of Communication Theory.* New York: Harper and Row, 1970.

the social and cultural setting for communication

No one can tell you what communication is. All anyone can tell you is what the word means to him. The word has so many meanings that some are confused. One of the attributes your authors deem worthy of emphasis is the social nature of communication. Though the first stages of communication occur within the family, one continues to learn about communication all his life. When we succeed at communicating there is always some commonality—some common ground between the communicator and those he communicates with. Yet, a gap exists between them. A speaker does not transmit his message. He does not deliver it. He stimulates the receiver in such a way that the receiver correctly interprets, even creates, the meaning. Some communication analysts write of intrapersonal communication, a person talking to himself, for example. Others of us prefer not to use the word "communication" for such events; we would call it "thinking out loud." Because the social variable may make or break communication events—and this is our main concern—we limit our use of the word "communication" to the symbolic interaction achievements of two or more people.

Social Attributes of Communication

If communication is to occur, some stimulus must be *received*. If you don't get the letter, no communication can occur. If the voice on the other end of the wire is too faint to be audible, meaning is obscured. If the sign by the road is hidden by the branch of a tree, one cannot get its message. Messages are sent by and to people. Only interacting people can communicate in the most useful meaning of this word.

The potential receiver of the message must give it his *attention*. In speaking, this attention is to the total context-speaker-message system. By attending to the message the listener increases the probability of his understanding. Even very young children soon learn that they cannot communicate unless father or mother pays attention.

The message must be *intelligible*. It may or may not be correctly understood, but it must make sense. If, in order to make sense, the communicatee must fill in or even distort the manifest intent of the message, this may be done. Again the intelligibility of the message is really the intelligibility of   **15** the context-speaker-message system. Intelligibility then is largely a social phenomenon.

The success of communication behavior in achieving the event is influenced by the way the participants perceive each other. Perceptions determine and are determined by *set and expectations*. If *A* expects *B* to ignore or oppose his statement, he may send a different message system than he would if *B* is expected to approve and support his statement. If *A* expects *B* to understand what is said he may say something different from what he would say if he expects that *B* may have difficulty understanding.

Speech involves direct and personal *confrontation*. Radio speech is perceived as direct. The human organism is so structured that interaction is facilitated when participants face each other. The word "confrontation" has in some circumstances a somewhat specialized connotation. An old edict at law is that an accused person has the right to confront his accuser. Apparently justice is aided by this practice. In modern times, demonstrations to attract some special attention to one's cause are often called confrontations. This kind of symbolic show of support or power need not be involved in the confrontation of two or more people reacting in communication. Here the presence of the other in person seems to exercise personal influence in increasing the effectiveness of the message.

Communication often works best when the participants experience some *involvement* with each other. To communicate with another is in some way to have an *encounter* with him, to carry out a *transaction* with him, to have commerce in the give and take of ideas. Brainstorming is an example of this process in which people working together on a problem may sometimes be more creative in problem solving than the same individuals would be if they worked alone. Here again, the ability to understand and to work with people is one important basis for success in communication.

The ultimate test, the very existence of communication, depends upon some *response* to the communicative stimulus. The response may be immediate or delayed; it may be partial, complete, or inconsistent with the speaker's intentions; it may be in the form of understanding, feeling, or overt action. But without response there is no interaction; without a response event there is no communication.

The failure to achieve some response may be attributed to a communication *barrier*. The inability of two people to communicate with each other may be due to such physical limitations as lack of sight or hearing, the failure to have learned a common language, or the language peculiar to a particular age, interest, or occupation. It may also be a product of strong emotional reactions, attitudes, or value systems in such conflict that they inhibit normal interaction. When one switches off a radio, it goes dead. When the communication processes are terminated or so distorted by emotions, disturbances, or disabling events that the message does not get through, we say there has been a *breakdown* in communication. Barriers to and breakdowns in communication are social phenomena.

Social Levels of Communication

- *Interpersonal* or *person-to-person communication* is the simplest and basic level of communication. It may be called the prototype of all communication. Even mass communication is basically a process in which a person perceives a message formulated by a news reporter or a broadcaster. The mass media communicator must know the same basic principles as the participants in the simplest pattern. We are not saying that this is all he needs to know. The person-to-person communicator is direct. The mass media communicator may seem so, even though time and space intervene. The person-to-person communicator may get his feedback and make his adjustments almost instantaneously. In broadcasting the feedback is delayed at best. The person-to-person communicator, depending upon his role in life, may be limited to personal influence. The mass media communicator is more often a professional, supported by the prestige of the medium in which he works. The interpersonal communicator probably has more freedom than communicators at higher levels, who are more bound by the greater number of people involved, as well as the purposes and policies of a group or medium.

- The second level of communicative behavior is the *group* or *organizational*. The group may be informal or formal, the organization small or large. The communication of groups is typified by the committee, the panel, the seminar, the decision-making group such as a jury, a council, or board, the informal conference, or formally organized society. Groups tend to have prescribed tasks. Different members have different roles. What one communicates about and the way he communicates in his role may be largely determined by written policy or custom. Much group communication is routine or ritualistic. These routines may be very important for the health of the organization. What others expect also has a great deal to do with one's communication. Some business organizations have tightly knit structures and procedures, others are more loosely organized. Obviously, an individual has more freedom of communication in the latter. Within any organization some administrators run a tight ship, others operate on the policy that the best administrator is one who administers least. Choices of this type may well depend on the state of the organization. An old and successful concern has men who have worked together for a long time. These men may have less need for a written policy on communication than a young and developing company. There are many patterns or networks for communication in groups. Those seem to work best where the number of links in the chain are kept to a minimum.

- *Public communication* is a third level of numbers of people who are typically involved in communication. Although members of a group may be addressed publicly, public communication transcends limited group boundaries. This type of communication is devoted not only to what the public needs to know and has the right to know but also to what they derive satisfaction from knowing. If people who want to be in the know are not informed, rumors are spawned. They serve the function of giving people some sense of involvement, even when it's false or harmful. Public appearances, public commitments, and public reporting are big business in this country, where democracy functions and public speaking, newspapers, and news broadcasts thrive. Public declaration in our culture is deemed more significant than a statement for a limited number of insiders. Independent public verification is considered by many one of the best tests of "truth" available.

Although the main actors in a culture or their representatives sometimes participate in *mass communication,* those who operate most in the media are professional or third-party participants. The average individual hasn't the time, skill, or financial resources to locate the information he wants or needs or to use his resources to help others. Professional communicators function in both public and mass communication. They are the people who seek out information difficult or impossible for the individual to get on his own, select what is to be passed on, recast it as deemed desirable for mass consumption, and distribute it through available channels. The selections made are deemed fair and necessary by these professionals. But it must be conceded that in a real sense they are gatekeepers of news. Where there is adequate competition for listeners and readers, more seriously conflicting points of view may get a fair hearing in the marketplace of ideas. Unfortunately, the cost of this process is so high that varied and conflicting points of view are not made universally available. While teachers are professional communicators they operate in sufficient numbers to keep education from taking on the gatekeeping nature of the mass media.

Cultural Determinants of Communication

The more social an activity of man becomes, the more it tends to be regulated by and for the group as a whole. Since man's communication is one of the most pervasive of his social achievements, it follows that much of his communication is influenced by his culture. We use the language of our fellows. We accept similar if not identical value systems. We play similar roles. We seek similar goals. Such matters make for stability of a culture. But since meaning is a personal experience, it is always possible for a single stimulus to produce somewhat different reactions from those intended. Because an individual can and does think his own thoughts, it is possible for people to become creative—to be different. Those who are different sometimes become the teachers, the agents of change among us. As the innovation is disseminated among people, the culture itself is changed. So man makes progress, be it ever so slow. If it were not so, we wouldn't know what we could depend upon, what to expect. On the whole, a *culture* operates in a state of *balance* or equilibrium, primarily stabilizing, yet

Library of Congress.

Modes of public communication change as rapidly as means permit. Lincoln and Douglas faced each other in debate before small local audiences. A decade later, Andrew Johnson drew larger crowds from his rear observation-car platform.

New York Public Library.

Library of Congress.

William Jennings Bryan spoke so eloquently from the front porch . . .   *Brown Brothers.*

that McKinley also brought his message directly to the people.   *Brown Brothers.*

Harding, who coined the word "normalcy," used the radio, . . .   Library of Congress.

but Roosevelt developed its use into a warm, personal art.   UPI.

Robert Montgomery coached Eisenhower in the days of early TV, . . .   *Ed Clark,* © *Time, Inc.*

but TV eventually revitalized the hot confrontation of the debate.   *UPI.*

reaching out as in hope for a better world tomorrow. Communication works both to preserve the old and to generate the new. Cross-cultural communication happens when persons of one culture communicate with those of another culture, but the barriers of difference between cultures reduce the probability of attaining the degree of understanding possible within a single culture.

Law and *formal policy* are communicable ideas that stabilize and unify human behavior. Laws, in particular, tell us what we must not do, and what others must not do to us. Some laws are formalized by our governing bodies; others are unwritten but so long established that they are deeply ingrained in our culture. *Rituals* and *ceremonies* are largely reinforcing communication behavior which contribute to its stabilization. Freedom of speech and the press cannot be infringed upon, yet we must not libel or bear false witness. We may be prohibited from using abusive language.

Unwritten law becomes operative as the *mores, customs,* and *norms* of a culture. Mores sometimes express value systems of one period of time which have become out-of-date in a later period giving rise to a generation gap. For example, though we have standards for what is acceptable or unacceptable in our language, the language *does* change. As the change becomes disseminated, new standards are formulated. In addition, there are many negative communication conventions in our culture, which may prevent people from communicating as well as they might otherwise. Some difficulties in communication arise from the fact that ideas about what is acceptable are changing.

Situations, contexts, and *climate* have much to do with the effectiveness of communication. The presence of a number of people in close proximity does not necessarily make for a communication situation. Even an audience of people gathered together to hear a speaker usually includes some persons who are there because they wish to be seen, or merely want to accompany someone to and from the place and don't want to stay outside in the cold, the heat, or the rain. It cannot be safely assumed that all the members of a college class are in attendance because they hunger for the knowledge the professor wishes to share with them. Some will be there because they need two hours credit or for some other reason extraneous to the manifest function of a class. The context not only includes the space, it includes the time of day, what went before or will come after, the general nature of the topic, etc. By climate we mean the spirit of the occasion. Is it one of gaiety, sadness, sternness, anger, optimism and encouragement, or pessimism and discouragement? One cannot expect support for a proposal by introducing it in a spirit of rejection. On the other hand, if you can associate your proposal with something many of your listeners already want, the *social facilitation* of those who approve will be of help in getting your job done. *Reference groups* and *pressure groups* are also social influences upon the acceptance or rejection of a message system.

Subcultures within the dominant pattern of a culture may be shown to have people with vastly different *images* of what is desirable in communication, different *attitudes* toward communication, different *value systems* in some respects, and different *habits* of communication. Differences between subcultures account for such phenomena as the generation gap, conflicts between the North and the South, conservatives and liberals or radicals, and manifest themselves in various religious preferences and different goals in life. Since the same fact, the same communication stimulus may be perceived differently by people with such differences, misunderstanding and misinterpretation are inevitable. But this is not to say that to be different is bad. Maturity in our culture is marked by a tolerance of differences. To condemn others for being different is a mark of provincialism and conceit. And by "provincial," we don't mean that all intolerant people live in remote and rural areas.

A Cultural Operationalism

The most adept communicators among us tend to be the most social in nature. They are socially sensitive; they possess low thresholds of social stimulation and are good people readers; they are concerned about the way others feel and are able to understand why others see the issues as they do. They have a basic respect for people and are sufficiently flexible in adapting resources and the strategies of communication behavior to maximize the probabilities of achieving successful communication.

To be a good communicator one must understand the culture in which he communicates. His message systems must be so organized that they are supported by cultural mores and motivations. The symbol systems must make sense. The forms, types, styles, and strategies should conform to expectations sufficiently to avoid unnecessarily discordant notes. Channels must be found which get the message through. The climate and the time must be appropriate. Resources must be adequate to meet any challenge in feedback. Behavior must be such that standards of evaluation show it to be relatively free from distraction and inefficiency.

Projects and Problems

PROJECT 1:   Discuss the existence of a generation gap in our culture. In what situations is it most apt to occur? What suggestions can you make for reducing the gap? Can you discuss the problem without blaming someone else for the situation?

PROJECT 2:   Read one of the references at the end of the chapter and discuss its application to the problem of understanding cultural influences on communication. Does it help you in clarifying some of the principles of communication?

PROJECT 3:   What level of communication is most influenced by culture?

Try in class to formulate some principles of cultural influences at the various levels discussed in the chapter.

PROJECT 4:   Hold a class discussion on subcultural differences in communication within the United States. How many kinds of cross-cultural differences within our own country can you identify? What can you suggest for overcoming cross-cultural differences between these groups?

PROJECT 5:   Compare and contrast the conception of communication as expression and as social achievement. What differences may this distinction make in the way you would formulate communication principles?

References

Berrien, F. K., *General Social Systems*. New Brunswick, N.J.: Rutgers University Press, 1963.

———, *Human Relations*. New York: Harper and Brothers, Publishers, 1951.

Biddle, Bruce J., and Edwin J. Thomas, *Role Theory*. New York: John Wiley & Sons, Inc., 1966.

Cleveland, Harlan, et al., *The Overseas Americans*. New York: McGraw-Hill Book Company, 1960.

Crane, Edgar, *Marketing Communications*. New York: John Wiley & Sons, Inc., 1965.

Goffman, Erving, *Behavior in Public Places*. New York: The Free Press of Glencoe, 1963.

———, *Encounters*. Indianapolis: The Bobbs-Merrill Company, Inc., 1961.

Heider, Fritz, *The Psychology of Interpersonal Relations*. New York: John Wiley & Sons, Inc., 1964.

Lederer, William J., and Eugene Burdick, *The Ugly American*. Greenwich, Conn.: Fawcett Publications, 1958.

Maier, Norman R. F., *Principles of Human Relations*. New York: John Wiley & Sons, Inc., 1953.

Merrihue, Willard V., *Managing by Communication*. New York: McGraw-Hill Book Company, 1960.

Monane, Joseph H., *A Sociology of Human Systems*. New York: Appleton-Century-Crofts, 1967.

Oliver, Robert T., *Culture and Communication*. Springfield, Ill.: Charles C Thomas, Publishers, 1962.

Raser, John R.. *Simulation and Society*. Boston: Allyn and Bacon, Inc., 1969.

Shubik, Martin (ed.), *Game Theory and Related Approaches to Social Behavior*. John Wiley & Sons, Inc., 1964.

Smith, Henry Clay, *Sensitivity to People*. New York: McGraw-Hill Book Company, 1966.

Toch, Hans, *The Social Psychology of Social Movements*. Indianapolis: The Bobbs-Merrill Company, Inc., 1965.

———, and Henry Clay Smith, *Social Perception*. Princeton: D. Van Nostrand Company, Inc., 1968.

Weick, Karl E., *The Social Psychology of Organizing*. Reading, Mass.: Addison-Wesley Publishing Co., 1969.

PART TWO

The Communicator

Saul Steinberg, from Labyrinth, Harper & Row, 1961.

interpersonal communication

We have characterized communication as a social event. If an event is to be social, at least two people must participate. A communicative interaction limited in general intent to two people has become known as interpersonal communication. In one sense all communication is interpersonal. It is a prototype form. The basic unit, no matter what the form or type, consists of a dyadic, person-to-person relationship. Any basic unit of communication must be an expression of the fundamental principles involved. Much that has been written about all forms of communication is concerned with basic principles. If a reasonably adequate treatment of fundamental principles of communication could be covered at the most elementary level, it would release the scholar at more advanced specialized levels for more adequate treatment of the ways these levels go beyond fundamentals.

You and the other person involved bring to the communication situation *unique* experiences, knowledge, opinions, attitudes, beliefs, needs, and skills of communication. Yet, there must be some *similarity* in what both of you bring or communication is impossible. In this two-person communication situation, as in most communication situations to some degree, you are both a sender and a receiver of messages. Not only are you alternately speaking and listening; you are emitting messages of some sort all of the time and sensing messages from the other person all of the time. While you are speaking, whether you are conscious of the fact or not, you are generally

observing whether the other person's facial expression, posture, or grunts indicate that he is listening or not, understanding or not, agreeing or not. Even when speaking on the telephone, if you hear absolutely no sound from the other end periodically, you will probably stop and ask, "Are you still there?"

It is important for you as a communicator to be aware of the sensing of feedback and to practice at improving your ability to sense and interpret it. Clearly, this means understanding the person or type of person with whom you are talking, for the cues which a listener feeds back to a speaker vary widely. To take an obvious example, you must know the listener well enough to know whether, if his eyes are closed, he is listening carefully or rather is asleep. Awareness of this sensing of feedback and practice at improving your ability to sense and interpret it are essential for optimum communication. The effective communicator is constantly adjusting what he says and does to this feedback. The effective communicator, in his receiving role, is also constantly adjusting the visual and auditory cues he gives the source in order to shape that source's behavior to his needs.

This text is primarily concerned with basic principles, although it also provides an introduction to more specialized communication forms. In this chapter we shall mainly discuss some of the relatively unique characteristics of interpersonal communication behavior.

There are other reasons for the study of interpersonal communication. As its label implies, it is often more personal, that is less public—more private. Directed to an individual, we expect it to be adapted to the individual, not a generalized message trimmed to a leveling average. An expectation of adaptation and the need for flexibility and spontaneity in the process make it more difficult in some ways. It is the form where communication as catharsis is most apt to be appropriate. The agonies and the ecstasies of human experience can find more adequate expression here. Although some interpersonal discussion is primarily for amusement and relaxation, much of it is very serious talk about personal interests and problems. Many shun talk about personal problems because they feel so inadequate at such talk. For example, some people would rather avoid the expression of condolences to a grieving friend and trust that he understands their sympathy than do it ineptly. Because it is the smallest of the social units of communication it must be the most frequent in occurrence.

The type of communication in which you will be engaged most during your lifetime probably will be relatively short, simple interactions between you and one other person. This type of communication is, in a very real sense, the cement of society. It includes the communication between husband and wife through which they attempt to understand and adjust to each other and to plan their life together, the communication between parent and child through which the life styles of both are shaped, the communication between student and teacher, employee and employer, interviewer and respondent, fellow workers, consulter and consultant, casual acquaintances, old friends, and lovers.

Not only is interpersonal communication between you and one other person important for the adjustments that it facilitates, but also because the effects of many other types of communication, including both mass communication and group discussion, are often mediated by some form of interpersonal communication. Though each of us gets much of his information and ideas from those relatively "mass" sources, our attitudes toward the information and ideas and our decisions concerning what to do about them are very often based upon the results of interpersonal communication. We test the information and ideas on other individuals through interpersonal communication, reshape them according to the responses we receive, and try them again. We listen to the information and ideas of those with whom we converse and provide responses which help them to reshape what they know and believe. Thus, there is a mutual adjustment of information and ideas among the individuals to whom we are closest. Interpersonal communication has been found in modern research to be more effective than any other communication type tested.[1]

Reasonable interpretations of the comparative effectiveness of interpersonal communication are to be found in such explanations as the implied recognition of the importance of the individual by the attention given to him. When someone of an opposite view tries to persuade in interpersonal communication, all of the social facilitation is in the direction of change. The virtual anonymity in which many types of work are carried out in modern business and industry tends to reduce motivation to a minimum. Communication can increase this motivation. In most interpersonal communication participants become more personally aware of each other and perhaps more focused on the total message complex and significance.

It takes much more effort to talk to fifty people individually than to talk to all of them at one time. Time is money, but it may be money well spent. Feedback is easier and more direct. If the boss is willing to meet with one personally, he is more apt to take time to consider suggestions. The manager of one of Ohio's largest manufacturing plants once told one of us that his philosophy of management was summed up in four words: "Walk, talk, and act." Each day he made a tour of his plant, stopping frequently to talk to the men. He said he found these conversations useful in keeping production on the move.

■ It may be helpful to look at some of the characteristic forms of interpersonal communication. One is *dialogue,* and dialogue, if anything, must be meaningful. Dialogue is not debate where participants compete for the

[1]Franklin H. Knower, "Experimental Studies of Changes in Attitude: A Study of the Effect of Oral Argument on Changes of Attitude," *Journal of Social Psychology,* 6:343, 1935; and Elihu Katz and Paul F. Lazarsfeld, *Personal Influence,* The Free Press, Glencoe, Ill., 1955.

convictions of others. They do not expect to convince each other. Dialogue is not two intermittent monologues, with each speaker waiting until the other finishes to have his say. Dialogue is not getting something off your chest or "putting someone in his place." The dialogue form of interpersonal communication involves direct confrontation in the traditional sense of direct facing up to the interchange. Dialogue tends to equate the two participants more than situations where the communication stimulus comes largely from one person. The equating process facilitates rapport and reciprocity.

Though interpersonal communication tends to be informal and unstructured, the extent depends upon the subject and situation. In some semiritualistic situations where convention calls for a general kind of communication behavior, it may be formalized; for example, congratulations in a wedding reception line or expressions of thanks at the end of a party. When the climate is informal, interactions are maintained on a light and cheerful level. Where the situation is serious or grave, the mood must be fitting to the occasion. Role expectations and interpretations can influence what is said to whom on an interpersonal level. The greater the role distance between members of an organization, the more formal and standardized interpersonal remarks are apt to be. Those high in role status must accept a greater responsibility for initiating interpersonal communication than those lower in the organizational scale.

- *Rumor* and the grapevine are types of interpersonal communication which can do real harm if allowed to go unchecked. Shibutani has carried out a very interesting study of rumor.[2] He concluded that rumor arises to provide information in a communication vacuum. If the administration of an organization provides information, rumor does not develop. If authentic information is not provided, there is almost always somebody who, liking the power that usually goes with those who are in the know, is willing to develop a guess as to what is happening or about to happen. The rumor given out as an explanation that "makes sense" is passed on without the notation that it is just a guess. Purely personal rumors or gossip often arise in a state of jealousy or as a vendetta for a real or imagined injury. Sometimes they can only be explained as malicious mischief by a completely irresponsible person. A simple principle that every student of communication should come to know well is that words can be dangerous weapons as well as healing medication.

- *Phatic communication* is that type of interpersonal communication carried on to symbolize friendly social interest in the people one is with. It may be verbal, nonverbal, or both. It is often only pseudocommunication in that the idiom isn't intended to be given a realistic interpretation. For

---

[2] Thomatsu Shibutani, *Improvised News,* The Bobbs-Merrill Company, Inc., Indianapolis, 1966.

example, much of the communication between children and parents, between husband and wife, or between lovers, or among members of a gang or a group of close friends is of this type. The manifest content of what is being said may make the communication which occurs appear simply a waste of time, that no information is exchanged or no influence exerted. However, this could be misleading. The participants may very well be revealing their feelings to each other in indirect ways, showing that they share the same or similar feelings, or simply creating through apparently meaningless interactions a warm and sociable atmosphere which provides a sense of security for those involved.

Problems in effective communication which may occur in some more complex types of communication are most apt to crop up at the interpersonal level when one or more of the participants falls into such behavior categories as one following:

The one-track mind with several instant replays in speech
The domineering, monopolizing, compulsive talker
The nit-picking quibbler
The smug, caustic snob critic who knows all the answers
The prophet of doom or the Pollyanna optimist
The narrow, closed-minded, inflexible dogmatist
The grouchy, touchy, defensive introvert
The prying, overzealous busybody
The sadistically inclined innuendo specialist who tries to keep you off guard
The sorehead crybaby who wants to make you his personal psychiatrist
The pusher with no respect for privacy, confidences, and differences
The disrespecter of social norms, ideals, taboos, and the convenience of others
The grating, abrasive, socially insensitive and vindictive egotist
The show-off demanding attention but inattentive to others
The childish, conniving, plotting paranoiac

These types of behavior do not make for constructive social relationships.

You probably have strong social interests and concerns for the welfare of others, but are sometimes hesitant to start a conversation. If this is true, try some such technique as the following:

Ask a question about what you know to be an interest or experience of the person or persons present.
Ask a question about a topic or incident much discussed in the current news.
Make a brief statement about what you consider to have been an interesting recent experience.
Share with someone else a problem which might be of general interest and ask for advice.
Ask for an opinion on a recent statement or event about which people differ.

Projects and Problems

PROJECT 1:   Interview another member of the class to learn as much as you can about him. Ask where he is from. What are his interests? What experiences has he had that he considers significant? What are his hopes and ambitions? What studies have appealed to him? Make a brief report to the class on what reactions you might anticipate from him if you were to talk with him on a subject which you selected.

PROJECT 2:   Prepare and make a brief report on something you have read on a controversial subject. Designate a person to whom you might make this report, and indicate how you would adapt your presentation of the subject to him.

PROJECT 3:   Observe a number of cases in which two people are engaging in interpersonal communication and evaluate the degree to which each pair is engaging in true "dialogue." Report to class on the behavior that facilitated dialogue and the behavior that interfered with dialogue.

PROJECT 4:   Pair off with another member of the class, select two or three subjects you might converse about, and give some thought to something you might say about each. Then meet your partner in class and carry on a short conversation. The other members of the class ·should rate you and your partner as conversationalists.

PROJECT 5:   Hold a class discussion about ideas you generate about interpersonal behavior from reading one or more of the references noted at the end of this chapter.

References

Bach, George R., and Peter Wyden, *The Intimate Enemy*. New York: William Norrow & Company, 1969.

Barnlund, Dean C., *Interpersonal Communication*. Boston: Houghton Mifflin Company, 1968.

Borden, George A., Richard B. Gregg, and Theodore G. Grove, *Speech Behavior and Human Interaction*. Englewood Cliffs, N.J.: Prentice-Hall, Inc., 1969. Section II, pp. 75–176.

Bormann, Ernest G., et al., *Interpersonal Communication in the Modern Organization*. Englewood Cliffs, N.J.: Prentice-Hall, Inc., 1969.

Ginott, Haim G., *Between Parent and Teenager*. New York: The Macmillan Company, 1969.

Goffman, Erving, *Interaction Ritual*. Garden City, N.Y.: Doubleday & Company, Inc., 1967.

———, *The Presentation of Self in Everyday Life*. Garden City, N.Y.: Doubleday & Company, Inc., 1959.

Keltner, John W., *Interpersonal Speech—Communication*. Belmont, Calif.: Wadsworth Publishing Company, Inc., 1970.

Mann, Richard D., *Interpersonal Styles and Group Development*. New York: John Wiley & Sons, 1967.

Matson, Floyd W., and Ashley Montague (eds.), *The Human Dialogue*. New York: The Free Press, 1967.

Wiseman, Gordon, and Larry Barker, *Speech—Interpersonal Communication*. San Francisco: Chandler Publishing Company, 1967.

John F. Kennedy's charm conveyed almost as much as his words.
Cornell Capa, Magnum.

the speaker as a person

Someone always initiates the process of communication. At times one is invited to speak on a designated topic on which he is known to be informed, or one is asked for information or an opinion. In each of these cases the communication process is initiated by one party for some reason. We really don't know whether messages are more frequently volunteered or sought, and comparative frequency may not be very important anyway. Those who want to be known or want to be heard more often than not will volunteer their message. In our society of specialists, fortunate is the one with information sought after by others. Knowledge can be used to gain power, to earn a livelihood, or simply to offer a helping hand to a friend. Here we are primarily concerned with the idea that since all communication is social, there is in every communication event at least one person who can be called the communicator.

The terms *source, transmitter,* and *sender* of messages are sometimes used to designate the person who does the communicating. Because the word *source* is used also to refer to the location of a statement in a document, it is an ambiguous and impersonal label for what may be a very personal variable in communication. Moreover, the communicator of messages is a variable interacting with other variables in a total process. Likewise, the word "transmitter" conjures up the image of a radio. Thus we prefer the more personal word *communicator;* or in speech, the *speaker;* in writing, the *writer.*

The Medium and the Message

In one way the person of the speaker provides a part of the context of a message, even before he has uttered a word. The interpretation and effect of a message are often influenced as much by who speaks as by any other variable. It isn't only in television that "the medium is the message." Is he a man who respects his listeners? Is he sensitive to their interests and reactions? Is he motivated by values the listeners understand and accept? Does he know what he talks about well enough to warrant the time he takes? Is his message helpful and credible? Is he an unknown? Does he show himself worthy of trust? These and similar questions warrant some attention to the personality of the speaker. When we refer to the personality of the speaker we are not implying that the social functions of effective speech **37** call for a unique set of characteristics that we can call a speaker's personality. The personality variables we shall discuss are the variables of people in most walks of life.

Speech and Personality

Our initial reaction to a speaker is often a reaction, to his personality. At times, we like a personality which has characteristics to which we can respond positively. At other times we respond better to a personality which complements our own. Anyone who can collect a large circle of admirers is said to have *charisma*. The "good guy" is one who is perceived as trustworthy or credible in the expression of one's value systems. The classical rhetoricians were essentially talking about personality when they stressed the importance of *ethos* or ethical proof. That speaker with ethos demonstrates that he is a person of intelligence, character, and goodwill. Some people refer to such qualities as *sincerity*. Unfortunately, not all of us are good judges of sincerity. A good actor (not necessarily a professional actor) may well deceive us as to his character, for purposes of exploitation.

What of the factor of *intelligence* in the communicator? Since the development of communication skills is a product of learning, we would expect people of superior intelligence to be more effective communicators. In a large sense this is true. One criterion of mental retardation is weakness in the use of communication processes, but, although the man of genius is usually a better communicator than the less intelligent person, it is not always the case. It depends upon the extent to which the more intelligent man has used his learning capacity to improve his communication processes. Knowledge is power only to the extent that one knows how to use it and apply what he knows. The person who has something less than the topmost capacity to learn but has devoted his talent to the development of his communication processes will be a better communicator than the person of greater capacity who takes this area of learning for granted. The study of communication is thus not only important in learning to talk, it is also a developmental process for the individual.

Since good judgment is so important in the achievement of communication, we must recognize the place of *character* in the personality of the speaker. A speaker of character formulates his judgments on the basis of the value systems of his culture. The exercise of judgment is an aspect of the exercise of responsibility. To be responsible one avoids false pretenses, misrepresentations, and unreliability in both word and deed; he is aware of the existence of bias, prejudice, and injustice and he does what he can to keep these to a minimum. He seeks all relevant available information in making decisions. He is not selfish or abrasive in his relationships with others. He is courageous and firm in his pursuit of what he considers to be right. The speech of a man of character reflects these qualities. If he is a great speaker, to quote Cicero, he is a good man speaking well. Although most excellent communicators do not aspire to be great speakers, they nevertheless strive to accomplish the goals we are discussing.

One approach to the understanding of communication is to seek to understand the motives or value systems of communicators. Since the man speaking is part of the message, the character of the message can be assumed to be no better than that of the man behind the message. The words of the man of shady reputation will be doubted. The stranger will be suspected. The person with vested interest, something at stake, a commitment to ends regardless of means, or one who has been promotionally involved may quite subconsciously reflect some bias in what he says.

In Chapter Two we discussed the social nature of communication. The basis of this variable is found in the *sociality* of good communicators. To be a social person one must first be sensitive to the behavior of others; he must be a good people reader. Can one be "too sensitive"? We don't think so. What is usually meant by this is too low a threshold for emotional responses. It is possible for a person to get "worked up" too easily, but this type of response behavior is not inherent in sensitivity. It is, however, the basis for the type of mental hygiene training designed to "desensitize" people. Industrial psychologists have recently become interested in sensitivity training. Such organizations as the National Training Laboratory are sponsoring "T-group" training to help people become more sensitive to each other. Sociality also involves the ability to perceive social issues as others see them and to experience a sense of concern for others.

Good speaking is hard work. To be a good speaker one must learn to release sufficient energies to be at least moderately aggressive. Neither a shy retiring person nor an aggressive bully is apt to get the fullest response from his audience. The former is simply not given attention; a conversation with the latter is avoided. To be sure, not any single energy level is appropriate for all occasions, but adaptation to many communication situations does call for the ability to speak forcefully when the occasion calls for it. We are talking here of the aggressiveness of enthusiasm, persistence, and painstaking thoroughness. Yet it is possible to be too highly motivated. The communicator who is overanxious, tense, easily angered, or speaks in hate, out of fear, may be less credible than the person who can "keep his cool." There are occasions when time is of the essence and any action to help is needed at once. But at other times a cooling-off period may lead to more rational and more effective communication.

The communication of the adult—young or old—calls for that kind of maturity and stability of personality which enables him to show order and self-control. The mature person is a "pro" at his job. He knows how to do "his thing," and he does it patiently and systematically. Much of the enjoyment of sports spectators comes from watching professionals at work. The good communicator tends to have breadth of interests. This does not mean that he cannot be a specialist. But both the specialist and the common man should know that they must bridge the chasm of their differences. This is difficult for the man who is only a specialist.

The imagination which comes with intelligence is a wonderful asset. It is the heart of art, invention, problem solving, and entertainment. But unbridled imagination can be detrimental. Imagination can create an interesting story, but it can also bankrupt a business or ruin a life. The communicator must live with reality. He must learn to operate the checks by which reality orientation can be maintained; he must distinguish fact from fiction, the probable from the improbable. Who knows what dreams have died in process for want of the means, the skill, or the courage to argue or to fight them through to success.

There can be little doubt that extended discussions are best carried on by pleasant, courteous, and considerate people. Those who are filled with hate, ridicule, and bitterness or are emotionally charged with grief, anger, or resentment will turn off their listeners rather than woo them to their cause.[1] Remarks which have the sole function of getting something off one's chest, of catharsis, are best reserved for the ears of friends and family. Those who can devote their energies to the clarification of issues and the building up of evidence and reasoned discourse rather than merely condemning others are most apt to accomplish their purpose. Members of congressional bodies learn to excel in the art of treating their opponents with courtesy while tearing their arguments apart.

The good speaker practices the principles of good mental hygiene. Not only has he achieved the maturity of emotional self-control, but he also has disciplined his thinking processes and habits of social interaction. Nobody loves a poor loser, and the man who spends too much of his time griping is advertising his weakness. Many people have complexes which are irrational and nonproductive, conflicts which need to be solved, and habits of self-defense which are unhealthy. A little success does not warrant delusions of grandeur. The habit of projecting all of one's difficulties upon others, the tendency to suspect others of bad intentions, fixed ideas which cannot be adjusted to changing conditions, the inability to concentrate one's energies in a productive direction are not uncommon among people who are considered relatively normal. Yet, such states will interfere with many types of communication activity. Being forewarned should enable one to take stock of himself occasionally, and if he cannot initiate corrective procedures, he should seek the help of a professional mental hygiene counselor.

---

[1]Much of the use of force by "activists" in our time is first-order impact rather than symbolic action. Many question whether this type of interaction should be considered communication.

Confidence and Stage Fright

Perhaps the biggest personality problem in communication occurs in that lack of self-confidence we know as stage fright. Some say it should be ignored or considered only a normal desire to act with responsibility in speaking. To ignore it is to ignore a very frequent and serious problem. It can occur even to those who at one time or another say it is not a problem. Even the reported frequency of stage fright may be an inadequate index, for some people are so embarassed about their nervousness that they will not admit it.

Our main concern is that many people do not understand such reactions in themselves or others. They feel confused and upset by such a reaction and even do things about it that are self-defeating and damaging. It does no good to run away and refuse to participate. A person who runs away not only loses the opportunity to serve others, he may also reinforce his negative reactions and make them worse in the future. The first step is to find an acceptable explanation of this nervous reaction. We do know a great many things about it.

Psychologists have found it useful to classify human behavior into subsystems of responses.[2] Some behavior is overt and observable to the naked eye; it is called a motor or conative subsystem in action. Other responses are more covert and have to do with the feelings of pleasantness and unpleasantness, sadness, anger, or fear. This subsystem is called affective behavior or response. A third system of behavior consists of cognitive responses. These are the responses of our sense organs, our "minds," our memories, our perceptions, and our thinking processes. Each of these reaction types functions on both conscious and subconscious levels. When we are consciously aware of our responses and can recognize the relationship between them and stimuli, we may feel that we understand ourselves. At other times we make subconscious responses which we don't understand. The stage fright experience appears to be initiated as a subconscious response. We don't understand it; consequently we are confused and upset.

The motor, affective, and cognitive systems in human behavior, operating as one system, tend to be consistent and support each other. Change is brought about by some stimulus which produces a change in one of these subsystems. Changes such as this occur in learning. The things we learn are not always effective in changing all three of these subsystems equally

---

[2]William J. McGuire, in Gardner Lindzey and Elliot Aronson (eds.), *The Handbook of Social Psychology*, 2nd ed., Addison-Wesley, Reading, Mass., 1969, Vol. 3, p. 155, says: "Philosophers at diverse times and places have arrived at the same conclusion, that there are basically three existential stances that man can take with respect to the human condition: knowing, feeling, and acting."

at the same time. The consequences are a state of dissonance.[3] Dissonance is the awareness of a disturbed state in an organism which is uncomfortable. When dissonance occurs the organism strives to achieve balance or consonance. As a consequence of some learning change in one of these subsystems, the other subsystems in time tend to change as well, to bring the total system back to a preferred balance or consistency. Evidence indicates that the symptoms of stage fright are not equally strong in all of these subsystems. Indeed, the fact that one becomes aware of this condition is the basis for the dissonant reactions. When this dissonant state exists it calls for self-directed response types to speed up the process of achieving balance.

The symptoms of stage fright are all characteristics of typical fear responses. They can be understood as parts of the process of organismic reaction in fright. They apparently have survival value in adapting to physical dangers. The fact that they do not have survival value in speaking is traceable to the dangers which are not readily recognizable. The intensity of the experience does change with time. One can facilitate relief from stage fright by making the following kinds of adjustment. In general, they can be expressed as the law of resolution of cognitive dissonance. *Anything which can be done to reduce the intensity of affective response, or anything which can be done to increase the efficiency of cognitive and motor behavior will tend to reduce stage fright.*

Here's what you can do about stage fright: Study the nature of human emotional behavior; learn what causes the various signs of nervousness, and the typicality of such experiences. Become aware of the functions of the cortical and the autonomic nervous systems. Stop and think about what it feels like to be nervous. James claims that this sometimes causes the nervous feeling to disappear. Delay your physical responses. Talk about your nervousness to family and friends. Don't memorize or just read; have an outline developed with concrete, often personal experience-type materials. Arrange these in a sequence easy to remember. Try to get off to a good start. Use relaxation techniques. Have notes available for self-prompting if they may be needed. Develop attitudes inconsistent with nervousness such as a sense of humor, great concern, vital convictions. It is almost impossible to be nervous and have a sense of humor at the same time. Develop and maintain efficiency of the cognitive responses. Don't let them get frozen with emotional reactions of deep intensity. Prepare carefully. Use cues to stimulate your memory and thoughts. Understand communication well enough so that you know when you are doing reasonably well. Set reasonable goals a step at a time. Watch for and adapt to feedback. Anticipate and plan for the unexpected.

---

[3]For a further discussion of dissonance theory, see Chapter Six; see also Robert P. Abelson, et al, *Theories of Cognitive Dissonance, A Sourcebook,* Rand McNally, Chicago, 1968.

Motor responses can help to develop and maintain a state of consonance. There is a point in the range of motor response called "optimum tonicity." This state is neither highly relaxed nor highly tense. If you are plagued with overtension, you can achieve voluntary relaxation by voluntary production of tension and release. Deep breathing also facilitates relaxation. Learn to use up the energy-producing tension with controlled activity. Let your total physical being reflect and express the ideas of your message.

We have suggested that confidence can be developed by producing some change in one of the three major types of psychological subsystems: the affective, the cognitive, and the motor processes. The same procedures can be used to modify other personality characteristics which are a product of learning.

Many people in our time lack motivation or are mismotivated. They are said to be seeking their identity; they want to know who they are. It may be that they already know who they are and are merely trying to establish a different identity. What one is and becomes appears to be a total product of his native abilities, his experiences with his environment, his projected image of himself in his goals and aspirations, and the constructive marshaling of his energies in working toward his goals. It is important to take long looks ahead. Don't resign from the human race because you lose a battle now and then. To the extent that you can continue to learn and develop as a person, you will have need for and continue to achieve in communication.

Projects and Problems

PROJECT 1:   Make a double list of what you consider to be your achievements and your problems as a speaker. Talk over this list with your instructor.

PROJECT 2:   Discuss the question of the influence of one's sense of values on what he says and how he says it. To what degree does self-interest influence communication? How can one avoid accusation of special pleading in stating a case? Develop a list which shows your judgment of the hierarchy of your values in communication.

PROJECT 3: Develop and make a short report to your classmates on some subject you consider of special interest. Ask your classmates to react to your credibility in this situation.

PROJECT 4: How important is it for a speaker to be sensitive to those with whom he talks? What makes a speaker sensitive? How may he increase his sensitivity? Can he be too sensitive? Might it sometimes be helpful to be desensitized to the social environment.

PROJECT 5: Discuss your nervousness about speaking with your classmates. Discuss the suggestions in class for reducing nervousness.

References

Boorstein, Daniel J., *The Image*. New York: Harper Colophon Books, 1961.

Boulding, Kenneth E., *The Image*. Ann Arbor: The University of Michigan Press, 1961.

Brown, Charles T., and Charles Van Riper, *Speech and Man*. Englewood Cliffs, N.J.: Prentice-Hall, Inc., 1966.

Cattell, Raymond B., *The Scientific Analysis of Personality*. Baltimore: Penguin Books, 1965.

Hall, Calvin S., and Gardner Lindzey, *Theories of Personality*. New York: John Wiley & Sons, Inc., 1957.

Katz, Elihu, and Paul F. Lazarsfeld. *Personal Influence*. Glencoe, Ill.: The Free Press, 1955.

Kelly, George A., *A Theory of Personality*. New York: W. W. Norton & Company, Inc., 1963.

Kretch, David, et al., *Individual in Society*. New York: McGraw-Hill Book Company, 1962.

Maslow, Abraham H., *Toward a Psychology of Being*. Princeton: D. Van Nostrand Company, Inc., 1962.

Milbrath, Lester W., *Political Participation*. Chicago: Rand McNally & Company, 1965.

Rogers, Carl R., *On Becoming a Person*. Boston: Houghton Mifflin Company, 1961.

Sanford, Nevitt, *Self and Society*. New York: Atherton Press, 1966.

Southwell, Eugene A., and Michael Merbaum, *Personality: Readings in Theory and Research*. Belmont, Calif.: Wadsworth Publishing Company, Inc., 1964.

Communication problems can beget more or less problematic solutions.
Alan Copeland, Black Star.

learning and communication achievement

Learning to communicate is what the course you are taking, this text, and the work of your instructor are all about. Of course you have been communicating since you learned to talk. You may ask as many do, "Isn't that all I need to know?" The answer is that the problems of adult communication are so different from those of childhood that the achievement of responsible adult behavior cannot be met by childhood attainments. Your parents, brothers, sisters, and teachers helped you learn to communicate your childhood needs. As an adult you are more on your own, and often in

competition with others. As an adult you must be aware of what you know, what you believe, and what your goals are. You must know more about what you can accomplish with communication, and set your goals accordingly.

In childhood, your speech was, in large part, a conditioned type of vocal play. Now your communication is a much more complex self-managed social achievement in symbolic behavior. Such self-management requires that your information and concepts of communication help you make much finer and more realistic discriminations. You began as a child with a clean slate. You had no bad habits to interfere with your initial learning. As an adult, you may have acquired many habits and concepts which may need to be reexamined and modified if you are to cope with your new world. As a child, you learned to communicate without knowing much about what you were doing or why you were doing it. As an adult, you must learn as much as you can about this complex process in order to manage yourself, to help others, and to solve adult problems.

The study of communication in the modern university is a complex process. We can learn things about communication from many disciplines.[1] Each may even call the part or processes it studies by the name *communication*. In the behavioral sciences, the use of the name of the whole for one or more of its parts is called *reductionism*. Reductionism is rampant in the field of study we call communication today. We cannot afford to ignore the contributions to knowledge about communication from those who study any of its parts, elements, or processes. But the most fruitful study of communication fits the parts together and supplies other pieces to form an integrated whole which can be realistically experienced.

Multidisciplinary Sources

What other studies may help you become a better communicator? Perhaps the most important is a general or liberal education. You will need to communicate with many people whose specialty is different from your own. Ideas from their areas of study may be applicable to yours. Your general education provides a bridge, a basis for reaching them. Moreover, an area of specialization has many facets. There is general agreement among educated people that there are many sources of satisfaction to be derived from a general education. A specialist in communication needs to be a liberally educated man, just as a liberally educated man should have some expertise in communication.

A communication event has physical properties. The human voice and its use in speech is studied by physical scientists, and in departments of

[1]Those who think the multidisciplinary approach to communication is particularly modern should see Charles H. Woolbert, "The Organization of Departments of Speech Science in Universities," *The Quarterly Journal of Speech,* 2:64–77, 1916, for an early discussion of this problem.

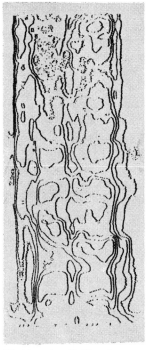 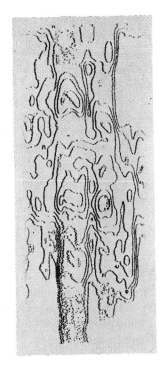

The sonogram invented by Dr. L. G. Kerstar traces contour-form voice prints, below. The print at far left shows a contour tracing of John F. Kennedy's voice; that at the near left, of an actor imitating him.

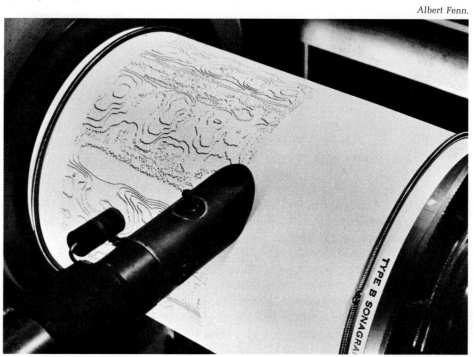

speech by voice scientists and experimental phoneticians. It is known, for example, that your voice is as specific to you as your fingerprints. In all the world there probably is no other voice exactly like it, and it can be identified from "voice printing." There are schools in which the study of speech is almost exclusively the study of voice. Speech has other physical properties, knowledge of which can be useful to you as a communicator.

Most communication involves a language, and communication scholars utilize many disciplines in the study of language, such as linguistics and general semantics. Even the study of mathematics as a special kind of language and the study of nonverbal symbols are relevant if you want to understand some communication processes. When you speak, for example, you may communicate many simultaneous messages. While your words are communicating one meaning, your voice identifies you as the speaker; it reflects your attitude and mood, and it can tell your listener something of the direction and distance from which you speak. You communicate all these ideas simultaneously.

The study of some aspects of psychology is helpful in understanding communication. Psychologists have made contributions to our understanding of learning, our perception of the world under different conditions, our memory, our thinking, our judgments, and our development as personalities in general and as specific human beings. They have taught us about man's motivations, emotions, feelings, moods, and attitudes, and many other variables important in communication.

Sociologists have contributed to our understanding of the social nature of communication and how it works in groups, organizations, and institutions. They are concerned with group norms and variabilities, with mores, social sanctions, and taboos, with the stabilities and changes, and with the diffusion of innovation in society.

The study of communication involves variables also studied in philosophy. Philosophers, as well as psychologists and linguists, have added to our knowledge of the nature of symbolic and related forms of behavior. Philosophers are concerned with the logic of analysis, inference, and reason, the nature of ethics and aesthetics, and the formulation of systems of thought and research.

We can learn things about communication from many other arts, sciences, and technologies. We should note especially the cognate fields specializing in other forms of communicative behavior, the arts such as painting and graphics, technologies such as broadcasting and journalism, management, salesmanship, and teaching. We also need to know something of the ways knowledge of communication is advanced and validated through research. Rhetoric as a humanistic study has been primarily concerned with the history and criticism of formal public address. The behavioral sciences have used descriptive and experimental techniques to examine the broad spectrum of human communication problems from interpersonal and small-group communication to cross-cultural communication and the mass media. They have been especially active in recent years in the development of systematic communication theory.

From the multidisciplinary approach to communication, one learns that communication is more than any one of its parts; indeed it is more than the sum of its parts. One can engage in one or more of the processes and still not communicate. James Winans once said that speech is more than an essay on its hind legs. The same holds true for communication. Communication as an event is best thought of as a social achievement in symbolic behavior. To achieve it we study and integrate human processes as variables in a near total integration of the whole man in transactional behavior with other men.

Problems, Barriers, and Breakdowns

If you are to learn to improve your communication, it may be helpful to give some consideration to situations known as "communication problems," "barriers," and "breakdowns." Of course, communication sometimes occurs in situations where purposes are not clearly accomplished. If your expectations are not accomplished to some reasonable degree, it may be because you have expected too much. If you believe in your argument, but do not state your case, you yourself are remiss even though others disagree with
- you. This is not a communication problem. A *communication problem* exists where social problems occur which might be mitigated, if not solved, by communication, *where* reasonably useful communication activities have been undertaken, and *where* such communication activities have been denied, ignored, or counteracted in the face of the social need for action. Campus protestors, those seeking civil rights protection, and youth experiencing a generation gap complain of this type of communication problem. Sometimes the problem occurs because one has not learned to communicate as well as he might.
- *Communication barriers* exist when one seeks protection from the efforts of others to take up his time and to influence him in ways he has already decided he does not want to be influenced. Top administrators of organizations create line positions to protect them from such confrontations; bureaucrats cultivate an aloof manner to shield them from self-seeking
- patronage. A *communication breakdown* occurs when communication is discontinued because of some event that has diminished the utility of communicating for one or more of the participants. Problems, barriers, and breakdowns in communication can be overcome, but seldom by those who seek to solve their problems by continuing old routines. Such situations, which are best handled by creative communication techniques, constitute a major challenge for the student of communication principles in depth.

Principles of Learning

The study of communication in schools today puts much less emphasis on practice than it once did. This does not mean that we discount the value of practice as a learning procedure. Practice, role playing, rehearsal, and simulation studies are still recognized as valuable experiences in understanding communication. The fact is that most people do get a substantial amount of practice in day-to-day living, but do not get an equal opportunity to think about and advance their understanding of what it is all about, why they fall short, and the principles and procedures which can enhance their probabilities of success. Nevertheless, the alternatives aren't as simple as all theory versus all practice. We can profit from some of both.

Though you may be aware of the value of the best communication achievement of which you are capable, perhaps you haven't had it forcefully brought home to you just how valuable this can be to you. On the other hand, you may have been comparatively successful at communicating up to this point in your life without much effort. Perhaps you've been told you have talent, and you have some trophies or certificates to prove it. Don't let this lull you into complacency. The further along you go in school, the tougher it gets. You will find that the in-depth study of communication is complex, and challenging. To make the grade you have much to learn, and you'll only do it if it's something you want very strongly. *If you can accept and develop the desire to learn you have taken the first step.* At times you will believe you have no ability, that you started the race too far back, but, if it's something you want to do, don't let that worry you.

You as a person are an important part of your learning. In Chapter Four we discussed the place of the communicator as a person in the total process. Take a second look at those suggestions. Don't avoid any chance to demonstrate that you are a person of intelligence, character, and goodwill. Personality can be developed. Though you hear much these days about the problems of finding one's identity, a greater problem arises from the recognition and rejection of your identity as you now perceive it. If you don't like what you see, perhaps you can develop an identity you would prefer. Personality development involves three kinds of learning: developing knowledge, changing attitudes, and developing new skills. If you work at all three, each will reinforce the other. Changes in even one of these directions can go a long way toward bringing the other two around to avoid dissonance and achieve a balance which enhances your success in communicating messages.

Don't let anyone fool you into believing he has simple answers to the problems of communication. If you accept those simple answers, sooner or later you'll learn that you have been misled. Understanding the field of communication means the development of personal insight into a long and complex interacting set of facts, processes, principles, characteristics, types, events, and standards. *The study of communication is a cognitive and intellectual endeavor of the highest order.* You will need to learn how to differentiate communication from noncommunication, how to name, describe, analyze, synthesize, explain, and evaluate areas of your knowledge. When you have achieved these goals, you will have reached a point where you may expect to be creative. If you are, you may find yourself a leader rather than one who has merely tried to keep up.

If you accept the challenge of the study of communication, you will find achievement your greatest reward. To learn simple things requires only elementary motives, conditioning, and reinforcement of that conditioning. To learn those types of behavior which are classified as among the highest achievements of man requires goal clarification and motivation, complex and extensive operations to be performed, self-realization and dedication. If you are able to engage in such behaviors, you may reasonably expect to become an expert in communication.[2]

Projects and Problems

PROJECT 1: Talk with teachers in other departments (disciplines) about the contributions of their field of study to the understanding of communication. Report back to class and have a discussion of the multidisciplinary nature of the study of communication.

PROJECT 2: Develop a list of your experiences with problems, barriers to, and breakdowns in communication. Ask others to share their similar difficult experiences with you. Hold a classroom discussion and make a class list of the apparent reasons for these difficulties. With the help of the instructor, try to find at least one way to work on solving the problem.

PROJECT 3: Compare school or vicarious learning with apprenticeship or first-order experience. List what each has to contribute, and what may be the weaknesses of each. Which is more concrete? Which covers the subject more thoroughly? Decide which you like best and why?

PROJECT 4: Develop your own list of different procedures recommended for the development of learning and apply it to your communication. Which methods do you recognize as having worked for you? Could you make them work better? What methods could you use which you are not aware of having tried? How could you go about trying some of these?

References

Allport, Floyd H., *Theories of Perception and the Concept of Structure.* New York: John Wiley & Sons, Inc., 1955.

---

[2] See Chapter Seventeen for further discussion of variables in learning and behavioral change.

Bandura, Albert, *Principles of Behavior Modification*. New York: Holt, Rinehart, and Winston, 1969.

Bennis, Warren G., Kenneth D. Benne, and Robert Chin, *The Planning of Change*, 2nd ed. New York: Holt, Rinehart, and Winston, 1969.

Berlyne, D. E., *Conflict, Arousal, and Curiosity*. New York: McGraw-Hill Book Company, 1960.

Bloom, Benjamin S., *Stability and Change in Human Characteristics*. New York: John Wiley & Sons, Inc., 1964.

De Cecco, John P. (ed.), *The Psychology of Language, Thought, and Instruction: Readings*. New York: Holt, Rinehart, and Winston, 1967.

De Simone, Daniel V., *Education for Innovation*. New York: Pergamon Press, 1968.

Dixon, Theodore R., and David L. Horton, *Verbal Behavior and General Behavior Theory*. Englewood Cliffs, N.J.: Prentice-Hall, Inc., 1968.

Miller, N. E., and J. Dollard, *Social Learning and Imitation*. New Haven: Yale University Press, 1941.

Mowrer, O. Hobart, *Learning Theory and the Symbolic Process*. New York: John Wiley & Sons, Inc., 1960.

Neisser, Ulric, *Cognitive Psychology*. New York: Appleton-Century-Crofts, 1966.

Richardson, Stephen, B. S. Dohrenwend, and David Klein, *Interviewing*. New York: Basic Books, 1965.

Rogers, Everett M., *Diffusion of Innovation*. New York: The Free Press, 1962.

Solley, Charles M., and Gardner Murphy, *Development of the Perceptual World*. New York: Basic Books, 1960.

Statts, Arthur W., *Learning, Language, and Cognition*. New York: Holt, Rinehart, and Winston, 1968.

PART THREE

Audience Adaptation

Carl Rose. New York Times Magazine

the audience and the occasion

Adaptation to your audience is one of the most important aspects of communication. Communication is a social activity; in general, people do not talk simply to be talking or write simply to be writing; rather they communicate largely to help themselves adjust to each other and to their environment.

There are various ways in which one can adapt to an audience. Too often, though, we adapt by simply finding the arguments which will persuade that audience or the language which will make our ideas most clear so that *our* purposes are served. Although this is clearly important, it is not as important as serving the needs or purposes of the *audience*. To put this another way, in most communication situations which you will encounter, you ought to be thinking not only or primarily of how to move the audience according to your desires, but also of how to change yourself—how to change your communication behaviors to meet the needs and desires of the audience. This means that you must understand those with whom you talk; you must become sensitive to their needs and put yourself in their shoes, because your effectiveness as a speaker will depend on far more than your ideas alone; it will depend to a very large extent on the identification of your listeners with you and your message.

Most of the great speeches in history were not planned to serve the speakers' own needs and purposes, but rather to serve the needs and purposes of their audiences. This was true of President Franklin Roosevelt's speeches in the early 1930s, when the nation was in the depths of a disastrous economic and psychological depression. Roosevelt's "fireside chats" on radio helped to calm the people's fears and start the nation on the road to recovery. It was in one of these speeches that he said, "We have nothing to fear but fear itself." Similarly, during the darkest days of World War II, when the invasion of Britain by Hitler's troops seemed likely, Prime Minister Winston Churchill's ringing speeches to the British people helped them to keep fighting and, ultimately, to turn the tide of the war ("We shall defend our Island, whatever the cost may be, we shall fight on the beaches, we shall fight on the landing grounds, we shall fight in the fields and in the streets, we shall fight in the hills; we shall never surrender."). In more recent times, when young people in the United States were becoming disenchanted with our government and society, and lacked a clear goal beyond their personal or selfish ones, President John Kennedy, in his Inaugural address, offered them that goal in telling them, "Ask not what your country can do for you, ask what you can do for your country." Martin Luther King served yet another need of the people and our society when he gave voice to our hopes and aspirations in his famous "I have a dream" speech. These, of course, were national and international leaders who had opportunities to inspire vast numbers of people through communication. Although most of us will never have such momentous opportunities, we are constantly given the chance in informal as well as in more formal situations, to serve the needs of other people through communication, either to give them information they need or to help them solve problems or determine policy.

If you are to understand fully the processes of communication and learn to adapt to various audiences and occasions—and thereby become an effective communicator—you must understand the forces which cause people to behave as they do, which make them say what they do and respond to what others say as they do. In other words, you should understand some of the laws or generalizations about human behavior that scholars of communication and other forms of human behavior have established.

Below are three major generalizations about human behavior with which you should be familiar. We will state each one briefly and then discuss the way in which each applies in communication situations.

1. When a response is reinforced, it is more likely to recur.
2. Our behaviors are affected by our reference groups—groups to which we look for models of how to behave and groups from which we seek reinforcement.
3. There is pressure within an individual to achieve and maintain consistency among what he knows, what he believes, and what he does.

Reinforcement

The principle of *reinforcement,* often called the "law of effect," is probably the most consistent finding from all educational research. It has been found again and again that if reinforcement—some reward, some satisfaction—accompanies a response which a learner makes, he will learn that response faster than others not accompanied by reinforcement. Thus, in teaching, it is important to find ways to reinforce the responses which you want your audience to make. This reinforcement does not always need to be some sort of reward. It has been found, for example, that simply the knowledge that one is making the "correct" response is reinforcing to most individuals.

An obvious implication of the law of effect is that, when communicating, you must plan your messages, your responses, and the rest of the communication situation in such a way as to give the others involved some sense of satisfaction or other reinforcement if they learn or do what you believe they ought to be learning or doing during or following your speaking with them. At times, it is possible to provide immediate reward or satisfaction. At other times, reinforcement occurs because of future reward of which people are made aware. For example, your audience might be made aware that they can increase the probability of achieving one of their long-range goals—happiness, satisfaction, money, love, or what have you—through learning or doing what you are suggesting.

In short, those with whom you communicate will not be moved simply because you indicate that you want it that way or even because it is "right"; they will be moved if they are aware that it is either in their short-range or long-range interest to do so. And it is part of your job as a communicator to ensure that awareness.

Reference Groups

Another consistent finding of research on human behavior is that what people believe and do tends to be consistent with what is believed and done by their *reference groups,* that is, by other persons with whom they have pleasant contacts or with whom they would like to have pleasant contacts, or by individuals or groups with whom they are motivated to gain or maintain acceptance. We judge our own behavior and beliefs with reference to those individuals or groups from which we seek reinforcement, hence, the term. There can be negative reference groups as well as positive ones. For example, the fraternities on a campus may be a positive reference group for some students, but a negative reference group for others. Hence, when the interfraternity council endorses a position, it will tend to increase the probability of acceptance by those for whom fraternities are a positive reference group and decrease the probability of acceptance by those for whom they comprise a negative reference group. It is difficult for any of us to be convinced to agree with something with which those with whom we associate disagree, especially those whom we regard as authoritative or closely related to the issue. Consciously or not, we feel guilt or uncertainty concerning any action which runs counter to the expectations of our reference groups.

The fact that each of us has many reference groups complicates this matter and makes things more difficult for the communicator. Often some of our reference groups have conflicting expectations of our beliefs and behavior. You have probably experienced this conflict at times. Perhaps your family and your close friends had different expectations of your behavior in some situation; perhaps you have encountered conflict between the demands of your church whose norm is complete honesty and your employer and fellow employees whose norm is maximum sales; perhaps you have encountered conflict because one group of your friends has one belief about American foreign policy and another group has an opposing belief. Generally, at any given point in time, for any given action, one of our reference groups is more dominant; we tend to respond more strongly to its press. A communicator can have some influence here by reminding an audience of its reference group whose norms are most consistent with the point of view he is advocating.

Knowledge of reference groups is not only important to you as a communicator so that you can maximize the influence of those groups whose press is consistent with yours and minimize those whose press is inconsistent; it can also help you to predict the beliefs and patterns of behavior which your audience members bring to the communication situation.

Roles

Closely related to the notion of reference groups is the idea of *roles*. Just as an actor on the stage behaves differently when he is playing different types of roles, so all people act differently when they are playing their different roles—student, boyfriend, son, club president, etc. A knowledge of the expected behaviors for people in their various roles can help you to understand and to better predict their behaviors in communication situations. Careful observation of a variety of individuals in typical roles will help you to predict the ways in which people play the role of students in a college class and the ways in which they play the role of college sport at a football game; it will help you to understand and predict how a person's behavior will vary when he is at a political precinct caucus and when he is discussing politics at a party. To put all of this another way, our reference groups not only have accepted behaviors or norms for its members, but also somewhat different behaviors which they accept from those who are playing different roles.

Consistency

One of the most recent theoretical ideas in the behavioral sciences is that of the press within individuals toward consistency.[1] The theory, based on evidence from many studies, indicates the existence of strong pressure within individuals to make the various things they know, the various things they believe, and the various things they do all consistent within themselves

---

[1] Behavioral scientists use various terms for their descriptions of this penomenon—dissonance theory, balance theory, the congruity hypothesis, congruence theory—but the basic principle remains the same. For a concise description of some of the research on each, see Chester A. Insko, *Theories of Attitude Change*, Appleton-Century-Crofts, New York, 1967.

and with each other. Thus, if you believe that college professors do not care about students and you observe a professor going out of his way to help his students, you will feel pressure within you to either (1) change your belief about professors, (2) perceive the professor's act as in some way not really helpful but perhaps only self-serving, or (3) combine the two, i.e., become somewhat more favorable toward professors and yet still not perceive the professor's action quite as positively as a student with an initially positive attitude toward the faculty. In a speaking situation, if you mention that the governor of the state favors an increase in tuition at the state colleges and universities, the response of an audience member will depend upon his initial attitudes toward the governor and toward the proposed tuition increase. If he is more favorable to the governor than unfavorable to the increase, he will tend to improve his attitude toward the increase. On the other hand, if he is only slightly favorable toward the governor but very much against the increase, it probably will not affect the latter at all and make his attitude toward the governor more unfavorable.

Consistency theory provides further evidence for the importance of knowing what it is that your audience knows and believes, because this knowledge will enable you to predict how that audience will perceive and respond to various messages which you might prepare for them. As our description of consistency theory indicated, each member of your audience will tend to perceive and integrate the messages that he gets from you with what he already knows and believes in such a way to form a meaningful, integrated whole—in a way that is reasonable *for him.* If his initial knowledge and attitudes are quite different from yours, the way that he perceives and integrates your message will be quite different from the way that you would perceive and integrate it. Thus, *it is more important that you create your messages with the background and purposes of the audience in mind, than with your background and purposes completely dominating what you do.*

Perception and "Reality"

Most of us go through life firmly convinced that we perceive the world around us as it "really is." When we perceive a house, we *know* a house is really there; when we perceive someone displaying prejudice, we *know* prejudice is really there; when we perceive someone listening, we *know* that he is really listening. Anyone who doubts the reality of these things must be "blind" or "deaf" or "stupid." We become upset if this reality is questioned. We fail to realize that statements about what we perceive are statements of *belief,* rather than statements of *fact*—they are in large part statements about ourselves, rather than statements about the world. Walter

Lippmann in his famous book, *Public Opinion,* was one of the early scholars of communication to talk about the ways in which people respond not to the "world out there," but to the "pictures in their heads."

To be an able communicator, or to understand the processes of communication, it is very important to understand the difference between your perceptions and the world out there; it is also important that you recognize that this same phenomenon occurs among all of those with whom you communicate. The world in each of their heads is different, and all are different from the world in your head. Each of us gives a slightly different form and meaning to the stimuli from the world out there because each of us has had different past experiences which are relevant to a perception. In any given instance, our needs or purposes at that instant and our expectations or beliefs about the world affect what we perceive. From the infinite number of stimuli in our environment we selectively receive those which are consistent with our needs and beliefs, our purposes and expectations. This behavior, though it creates communication and other problems at times, is not stupid; it is necessary for survival in a complex world.

Each new experience further shapes our expectations about the world. We know "for sure" those things with which we have had many consistent experiences. Thus, we are able to make decisions; we are able to act.

Audience Analysis

The communication problem that these factors in perception create is that, too often, we make false assumptions about the perceptions of those with whom we are communicating; we assume greater homogeneity of past experience and, hence, greater homogeneity of perceptions and meaning than in fact exist. This is not to say that there is no similarity in the past experiences of most people. Clearly there is similarity, or there could be no communication at all. The commonality of our experiences makes it possible for us to communicate adequately for many purposes. We get into trouble when we assume that our successes at communicating about the price of eggs, the size of shoes, the color of a house, or the score of a basketball game, assure equivalent successes at communicating about beauty, love, foreign policy, and the economy. For topics of these sorts—and many others—it is essential to adequate communication that each of us consider more the experiences, expectations, and purposes of those with whom we are communicating. In some situations, where those involved are very heterogeneous or are unavailable for direct questioning or observation, other methods must be found. Some situations may even require formal interviewing or large-scale surveys.

Once you know something about the experiences, expectations, and purposes of those with whom you are communicating, you can use your knowledge to help you select examples, illustrations, arguments, and evidence. It can even help you to select the very language in which you couch these examples, etc.

Among the clearest examples of the way in which these various factors affect perception is the effect of prior attitudes on perception. There is clear evidence, for example, that audience members whose position is relatively close to the one you advocate will tend to perceive your position as even closer to theirs than it really is. Conversely, those whose opinions are very much different from the position you advocate in a speech will tend to perceive your speech as even further from their position than it really is. As a matter of fact, people with positions extremely different from the one you advocate may completely misperceive your speech. One study found that persons who were extremely prejudiced against minority groups tended not to get the point of a series of simple cartoons ridiculing bigots.[2]

On first observing such phenomena, you might conclude that these differences in perception are due to the fact that those who are prejudiced toward minority groups or those who disagree strongly with a position you advocate simply do not have as much prior knowledge about the topic. Evidence indicates, however, that those who tend to be most knowledgeable about an issue are not only those who are most favorable toward it, but also those who are most opposed to it. Those who know least tend to be the "neutrals."[3] Thus, if you graphed a curve of knowledge about Puerto Ricans against attitude toward Puerto Ricans, it would probably look something like this:

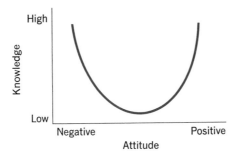

This means that simply "giving the facts" is not very persuasive; even more, it means that knowledge of the facts which an audience possesses is not the major kind of information that you need to know to move that audience or help it move itself.

---

[2]P. Kendall and K. M. Wolfe, "The Analysis of Deviant Cases in Communications Research," in *Communications Research, 1948–49,* ed. P. F. Lazarsfeld and F. N. Stanton, Harpers, New York, 1949, pp. 152–179.
[3]G. W. Allport, *The Nature of Prejudice,* Doubleday, Garden City, N.Y., 1958, p. 220; Bradley Greenberg, "On Relating Attitude Change and Information Gain," *Journal of Communication,* 14: 157–171, 1964.

Perception seems to be most clearly explained by the consistency theory which we described earlier. Many of the findings on perception indicate that individuals structure sensory impulses in such a way as to make their perception most consistent with what they already know, what they already believe, and the way in which they already behave. The problem for you, as for any communicator, is to find ways to overcome those forces which lead to a misperception of your message or to use that pressure for consistency in such a way that it increases, rather than decreases, the probability of your message being perceived correctly.

Using the Results of Audience Analysis

Knowledge of these theoretical notions about human behavior and sensitivity to what the audience knows and believes can help you not only to determine what to say, but also to organize what you say. For example, if you are convinced of your audience's need for some particular bit of knowledge or their need to take some action, but you know that the audience is unaware of its need, you ought to begin your speech by establishing that need. On the other hand, if the audience is already aware of the need, it would be better to go directly to the information or ideas that will help them to satisfy their need.

Sensitivity to the audience *and* the situation will also help ensure that the language you use is appropriate to both. We do not need to tell you that what is appropriate among your friends may be quite inappropriate among your fellow workers, and vice versa. For many of us, the language that is appropriate among our friends is inappropriate in school. Some studies in the ghettos, for example, have shown wide variances between so-called "home talk" and "school talk." Knowledge of this difference has led some people to conclude that we ought to educate the ghetto resident to use "school talk" all of the time—"to talk right." This, of course, is nonsense. There is no one "right" way to talk. There are many "right" ways, each right in a different situation. If a ghetto child attempted to use school talk consistently among his friends, he would not be a very effective communicator. In fact, he would soon have no friends. This is an extreme example of what can happen to you in your speaking. You will sharply reduce your effectiveness as a communicator if you fail to adapt your language to the audience and the situation. This is not to say that you must be a "phony" and try to impress a sophisticated audience or talk down to an unsophisticated one. It is to say that you must be sensitive to the appropriate language to use for a given group in a given situation.

Sometimes, in order to discover the knowledge, ideas, and needs of your audience, you must do some systematic research on the audience as well as on the topic. When you are speaking with people whom you know quite well, the need for such research is minimal—though careful observation of even this audience is important, both before, during, and after your interaction with them, to be sure that you have assessed the situation accurately. When you are going to speak with people whom you do not know very well, there is clearly the need for more systematic study of them. This does not usually mean a formal survey, though it may in rare instances. It may simply mean a few inquiries directed at people who are more familiar with them than you are. It may mean attempting to discover what they have said or written on the topic. One of our students, who was going to be interviewed for a job, went to the library and found some articles which had been written by some of the men who would be interviewing him. The knowledge thus gained was invaluable to him in that important communication situation.

One ought not only analyze and adapt to his audience, he must also *select* his audience. For many kinds of changes which you may be interested in bringing about in your organization or community or, even, in the state or nation, the audience that can make the difference is not the total population; the audience is often a rather select group of people who can make the decision and bring the change about. Thus, in the late 1950s, when a few leaders in Houston, Texas, decided that the time had come for the schools in the city to be integrated, they did not begin a citywide communication campaign to convince the general public of the rightness of their goals. They selected the small group of men in the community whom they believed were in a position to make a decision and take the rest of the community with them. In that particular case, the choice was roughly one hundred of the owners, presidents, or board chairmen of the largest businesses and industries in the community. These men were selected because they had the power to bring such a change about—and they did. During the early years following the Supreme Court decision of 1954 on integration of the schools, Houston became a model for smooth and trouble-free school integration.

Feedback

Audience adaptation of the sort that we have been talking about does not function solely to help in the *planning* of your speech. It is something that goes on *while* you are speaking and during all of your communicative interaction with others. In most communication situations you will find yourself in, there will be a give and take; you will be listening at least as much as you are talking. You will need to adjust what you say—and even how you listen or what you listen for—to what you hear and see. While you are speaking, even if it is a formal speech, you should be receiving messages from your audience to which you should adapt. These messages may be in the form of frowns, laughter, quizzical looks, heads nodding in agreement or shaking in disagreement, or perhaps people falling asleep. These messages coming to you from your audience should serve as a check on how you are doing; they should provide cues to what to do more of or less of or differently.

An extremely important part of the communicator's job is this sort of constant evaluation of his effect. Just as a good teacher constantly assesses what a class is learning so that he can adjust his teaching accordingly—repeating a unit when necessary, speeding up, trying to teach the unit in a different way, etc.—so a speaker must constantly assess the responses of his audience to see whether to adjust his communication plan. Does the audience seem interested? Do they seem to be "getting" the point? Are they responding to the point as you hoped they would? You cannot assume that the meaning of the nonverbal messages that you get from the audience will always be immediately clear. You must learn to "read" them.

Messages coming back to a communicator, whether the facial expressions of the audience, or grunts, or groans, or movement, or even verbal statements, are often called "feedback." This is a useful way to think about them. However, it may be even more useful to think not of yourself as a speaker, sending messages to an audience which sends feedback to which you can adjust. It may be better to think of yourself and everyone else involved in any communication situation as both sending and receiving messages all of the time. Thus, even when you are giving a formal speech, you are as much an "audience" as the people who are sitting and listening to you, and they are "speaking" to you loudly and clearly even though they may utter no sound. Just as they must learn to understand your verbal messages, you must learn to understand their messages, both verbal and nonverbal. Clearly, the same is true when there are only you and one other person involved in the communication situation.

Another major implication of the interdependence of sender, receiver, and situation is the effect which these interactions have upon you. Have you ever thought about the extent to which you lose control of your own behavior because of the feedback from a receiver of your message? For example, how is your behavior affected when you address someone by name and he growls, "Yeah, what do you want?" To what extent does your reaction affect the probability of your communication goals being achieved? You must become aware of the fact that you are often affected by feedback without even knowing it. Learn to be sensitive to feedback but, at the same time, learn to control your responses to it.

To improve your ability to speak, it is often helpful to talk about those matters with which you are most familiar, and you will sometimes get assignments in this course which suggest such topics. This makes it possible for you to focus upon other aspects of some communication process, without worrying too much about what you are going to say. It is also important, though, to get some practice communicating about matters other than those with which you are most familiar or which are most interesting to you. In a large proportion of the communication situations in which you will be involved in future years, especially where you are beginning with the needs of the audience rather than your own needs or convenience, you will not be able to talk simply about things with which you are quite familiar. Sometimes you will need to study a topic very intensively in order to learn enough to help those with whom you communicate. Sometimes, where you perceive a need to affect your environment—to get a particular city councilman or school board member elected, say, or an urban renewal plan adopted or a civil rights ordinance passed—you must do a good deal of research and thinking about the existing situation and possible alternatives and the arguments for each, before you can have much effect. Sometimes you will speak about ideas on which you are not completely convinced in order to test your knowledge or ideas through discussion and argument with others.

Steps in Audience Analysis: A Summary

Since we are interested in audiences here because we want to understand and improve communication, our audience analyses ought to focus on the ways in which what we observe or know about a particular audience and what we know about human behavior in general will affect the *communication processes* which we want to occur. There are five aspects of an audience which you should keep in mind when you are planning a speech or any other form of communication. These are: their knowledge, their interests, their beliefs or attitudes, their prior behaviors, and the number of persons who will be in the group.

- *Knowledge* is almost never an all-or-none matter. People differ widely in the amount of knowledge they possess and so they certainly will differ in what they know or understand about your subject. If you wish to extend their knowledge you will need to make some educated guesses about how much they know. And of course you will need to relate the new and unknown to the known. You will want most of all to save time and maintain interest by not dwelling at length upon those aspects of your subject already well known to your audience.

  You may well ask: What experience has my audience had with this subject? Will they be alert to new information? How can I select material that will extend their range of understanding?

- The major purpose for adapting to audience *interests* is to enable you to get the listeners' attention. People attend to what interests them. Unless we can get attention, not just for the sake of attention, but attention to some important aspect of our message, the communication doesn't get to first base.

  The interests of people in general and of any one person from time to time vary greatly, yet many people maintain fairly stable interests over long periods of time. We are all interested in meeting our biological needs, yet we also possess strong interests in meeting these needs in conformity with the provisions, mores, and conventions of our culture. When we participate in any kind of on-going activity we are interested in carrying this activity through to completion or closure. We are interested in conserving energy, retaining the status quo, or maintaining a pace and order which we enjoy. But if we do not approve of the status quo, if we experience dissonance or anxiety or intense motivation, we are interested in carrying on some activity which will reduce this unpleasant state of affairs. Because we can be forward-looking creatures, we are interested in ideas that facilitate our plans for the future and in counteracting any influence which might frustrate or disturb those plans. We are interested in exercising those habits which bring us satisfaction. We are interested in our own rights and privileges in our society, but we are also interested in gaining social acceptance and social approval. Such interests as these are common. Any communication in which we engage should be shaped in light of such interests in the audience.

■   What are the *attitudes or beliefs* of the listeners toward your subject? What political, religious, economic, aesthetic, and other prejudices are they likely to have? Their group affiliations, needs, and desires will determine their prejudices.

Often audiences may be classified in relation to your subject in one of the following ways: (a) They may be interested in knowing more about it and, if the topic is controversial, they may welcome your additional support to their convictions; (b) they may be indifferent to the subject or neutral if the proposal calls for their decision; (c) they may be opposed to your subject if it is objectionable or contrary to their beliefs.

These attitudes can be measured. For example, in the classroom, before you plan your talk, you could place your topic or proposition on the blackboard and invite each student to record on paper his reaction to it, as favorable, neutral, or opposed. Then, in planning a speech which will influence the attitudes of these listeners, you should consider why their preliminary attitudes are as they are. Have they read widely and discussed this subject? Have they had firsthand experience with it? Are they following the lead of someone or some group they admire?

As you are giving your talk, observe whether your listeners are attentive and responsive. If they are not, are there illustrations and other elements of good communication which you can use to make them so? Your job is harder if the listeners are visibly bored. You will attempt to begin with ideas and details that may shake them out of their lethargy and create curiosity and expectation.

What if most of them at the start are opposed to your topic? You will need to unfold your ideas by beginning with ideas they will accept and lead them on by successive steps from preliminaries to the final and more critical conclusions.

Since you will sometimes speak to persuade people to action, you need

- to know something about *the way they have behaved or are able to behave* about your subject. Have they performed similar acts in the past? Do they have the resources, including knowledge and skill, to do what you are asking? Do you know of any reservations or doubts which must be dispelled before you can get the desired response? Can you give them adequate reasons for action? Can you dwell upon these motives to create and release the energies necessary for action?

- The *size of the audience* is an important dimension because the magnitude of the response will depend in some ways on the number of people involved. The significance of this concept in advertising should be self-evident. It explains why consumer research organizations are so concerned with the measurement of the size of the audience. Your class may be of a fixed size, but you may at times want to address your comments to only a part of the class—perhaps only to the women.

There are many other dimensions of audience behavior you may need to consider at times. For example, can we recognize different levels in their social and cultural orientation? What do they expect of you in the occasion and situation? What are their capacities and talent? They have certain organizational roles, identities, physical characteristics, and attainments. In general these features will result in differences in their interests, information, attitudes, and other behaviors which we have suggested earlier.

Projects and Problems

PROJECT 1:   Select a controversial topic which particularly interests you and upon which you and your family or you and your friends disagree. Analyze the reasons for their beliefs and the factors that cause them to maintain these beliefs. Report the results of your analysis to the class, along with your plan for changing those beliefs through communication. Be prepared to defend your plan using the material from this chapter.

PROJECT 2:   Read chapter one of Walter Lippmann's *Public Opinion*. Report to the class on instances in which you have observed that "the world outside" and certain people's "pictures in their heads" differ. Discuss also the implications of these observations for communication.

PROJECT 3:   Read the introduction to Erving Goffman's *The Presentation of Self in Everyday Life*. Speak to the class on the relevance of Goffman's major points to communication or on your experiences that confirm or contradict his major points.

PROJECT 4:   Discuss the ethical problems of adapting your communication—especially the kinds of arguments you use—to your audience. Are there dangers here? If so, what are they and how might they be avoided or minimized? If you see no ethical problem or danger, present a convincing case to the class for this point of view.

PROJECT 5:   Read the article on "Research Findings in Broadcasting and Civil Rights" mentioned in the bibliography of this chapter. Describe to the class the way in which you could apply these ideas about changing attitudes to a speech on an issue other than racial prejudice.

References

Becker, Samuel, "Research Findings in Broadcasting and Civil Rights," *Television Quarterly,* 5:72–82, 1966.

Cantril, Hadley, *The Invasion from Mars.* New York: Harper Torchbooks, 1940.

Clevenger, Theodore, Jr., *Audience Analysis.* Indianapolis: Bobbs-Merrill, 1966.

Ellingsworth, Huber W., and Theodore Clevenger, Jr., *Speech and Social Action.* Englewood Cliffs, N.J.: Prentice-Hall, 1967. Chapter 5.

Gergen, Kenneth J., *The Psychology of Behavior Exchange.* Reading, Mass.: Addison-Wesley, 1969.

Goffman, Erving, *The Presentation of Self in Everyday Life.* Garden City, N.Y.: Doubleday, 1959. Introduction.

Holtzman, Paul D., *The Psychology of Speakers' Audiences.* Glenview, Ill.: Scott-Foresman, 1969.

Kiesler, Charles A., and Sara B. Kiesler, *Conformity.* Reading, Mass.: Addison-Wesley, 1969.

Larson, Carl E., and Frank E. X. Dance (eds.), *Perspectives on Communication.* Milwaukee: University of Wisconsin Speech Communication Center, 1968. See especially Samuel L. Becker, "New Approaches to Audience Analysis," pp. 61–77.

Lippmann, Walter, *Public Opinion.* New York: Macmillan, 1960. There are many reprintings of this classic which was first published in 1922. There is much wisdom here for someone attempting to understand audiences.

McLeod, Jack M., "The Contribution of Psychology to Human Communication Theory," in *Human Communication Theory,* ed. Frank E. X. Dance. New York: Holt, Rinehart and Winston, 1967. Pp. 202–235.

Oliver, Robert T., Harold P. Zelko, and Paul D. Holtzman, *Communicative Speaking and Listening.* New York: Holt, Rinehart and Winston, 1968.

Riesman, David, *The Lonely Crowd.* New Haven: Yale University Press, 1950.

Scheidel, Thomas M., *Persuasive Speaking.* Glenview, Ill.: Scott-Foresman, 1967. See especially Chapter 2, "Antecedents to Persuasive Speaking."

Smith, Henry Clay, *Sensitivity to People.* New York: McGraw-Hill Book Company, 1966.

Tagiuri, Renato, and Luigi Petrullo, *Person Perception and Interpersonal Behavior.* Stanford, Calif.: Stanford University Press, 1958.

Sam Falk, New York Times.

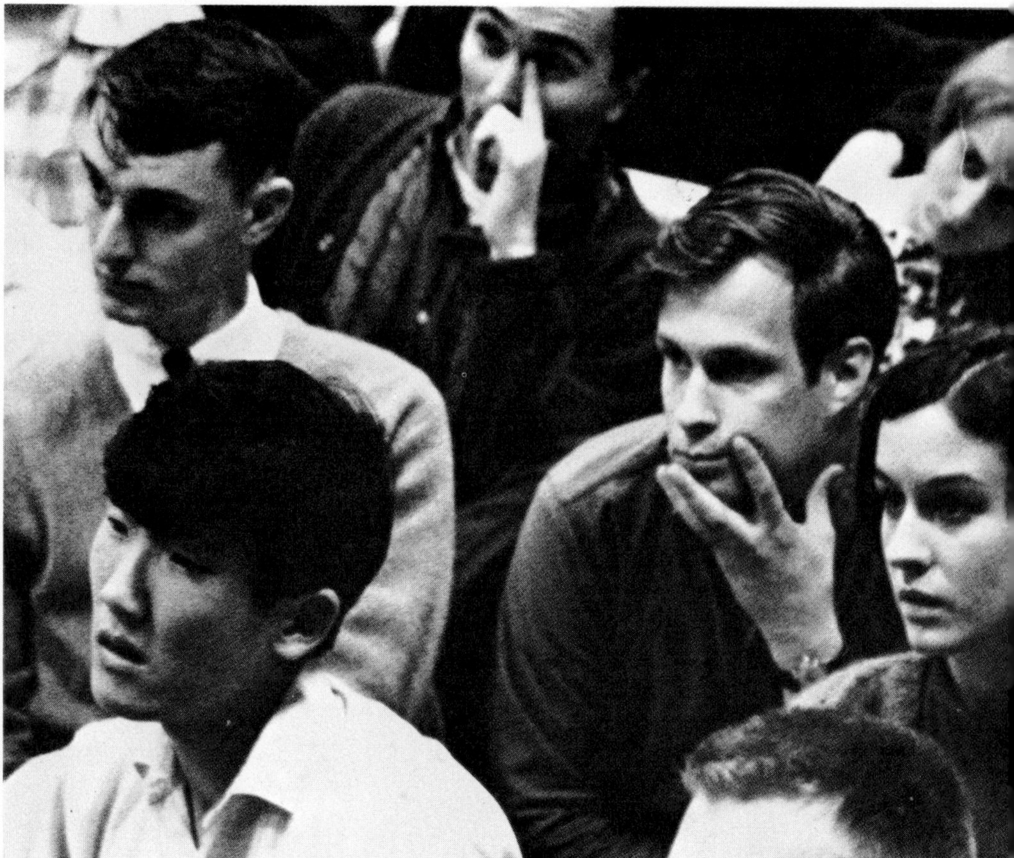

the communicator as a receiver: listening

We mentioned in Chapter One that whenever you are involved in a communication situation you are both a sender and a receiver virtually all of the time, even though one of these roles may dominate at any given moment. In this chapter, we want to talk about you as a receiver—the way in which you take in information and ideas and facilitate the work of those from whom you are getting messages. We will be talking primarily about listening—the reception of aural messages—though most of what we say about listening applies equally to reading or any other intake of information and

ideas. Keep in mind that we are talking about not only listening to formal speeches or lectures, but also listening during a discussion or conversation, as well as clear "reading" of feedback from others when you are speaking.

Listening is not only one of the best ways of learning new information and ideas, it is also one of the best ways of learning about people—those to whom you listen. As any sound book on how to win friends and influence people will tell you, more friends are won and people influenced by those who listen well than by those who speak well. People appreciate others who care enough about them and their ideas to listen carefully to what they say. Nothing can create more trouble among friends or in a family or business than people who just do not bother to listen to anyone else.

Listening is extremely important in almost all aspects of our lives: as members of a family, as participants in social and business interaction, as students. The majority of people report that they get most of their information about politics and national and world events from radio and television or from other people. Hence, good listening is essential for reliable information. Any effective business executive spends a good part of his time listening to his employees for ideas on how to operate the business better. For some of us—students, physicians, journalists, clinical psychologists, judges, social workers—listening is one of the major parts of our job. A recent study showed that the average adult spends better than a third of his waking hours listening.[1]

Listening is more than hearing; it is an active process of receiving and processing messages. Hearing is primarily a matter of sensory capacity; listening has to do with perception, comprehension, and other mental reactions. It is not merely a matter of placing yourself within earshot. It is not merely waiting until you can get in your word. Many, if not most, persons listen with the attitude that it is the responsibility of the speaker alone to put across the idea. Profitable listening requires much more of you than your presence. You must understand the ideas presented, evaluate and organize them, discover implications they may have, and select those you find worth remembering. If you make listening a thoughtful, critical process, you control your own thinking; if you do not listen critically, you are little more than a sponge, and often not a very good one.

Listening, as we use the term in this book, means not only attending to aural stimuli, but close attention to visual and other cues as well. Also, listening is not a single or simple mental process; it is an entire series of mental and even physical processes.

Causes of Ineffective Listening

Despite—or perhaps *because of*—the inordinate amount of time that we spend listening to parents, teachers, fellow students, and all sorts of

---

[1]Larry A. Samovar, Robert D. Brooks, and Richard E. Porter, "A Survey of Adult Communication Activities," *The Journal of Communication,* 19:301–307, 1969.

other speakers on radio and television and in face-to-face situations, most of us are very ineffective listeners. For evidence of our failure, replicate one of the "rumor" studies some time. Tell a detailed story to one person, especially one that is contrary to the attitudes and expectations of most people. Have him tell it to another person who did not hear it before, have him tell it to another, etc. By the time the story or "rumor" has gone through five or six persons, it is often almost unrecognizable. Much of the distortion which occurs in rumor transmissions is due to the fact that most of us are overly influenced by the habits or set we bring to the communication situation and the attitudes or expectations created by the situation. All of these phenomena affect our perceptions of the speaker and his message, especially when the message contains ideas which are new or with which we disagree. They then tend to disrupt our comprehension and retention of the message. We find it too easy to tell ourselves that the room is too hot or the seats too hard, or that the speaker is not worth listening to, that he is hard to hear or understand, that his delivery is bad, or that he is obnoxious or unsure of himself. Too often we are thinking about what we will say next, rather than listening first to what others are saying. We fail to become sufficiently involved with other persons and what they are trying to do or say. We are too easily distracted by other things going on and we rationalize by saying that the speaker is not interesting enough.

Be aware that when you are tired, tense, in a state of conflict, irritated, anxious, disappointed, or unhappy, that your ability to listen critically probably goes down. It then takes a special effort to be a good listener.

Though there is ample evidence of the pervasive force of all of these elements which interfere with listening, there is also evidence that you can overcome these disruptions by knowledge of them, knowledge of the important facts in effective listening, and conscious practice at listening to various kinds and levels of difficulty of materials. Study of the material in this chapter and practice of the sort suggested here should enable you to improve considerably your comprehension and retention of discourse.

Listening to Aid the Speaker

Listening is a cooperative activity, not a competitive one. Optimum communication can only go on when both or all parties involved work at it and try to help each other as well as themselves. An attentive listener is an aid to those who are speaking. Perceiving that you are listening will serve as positive reinforcement for them. It will help speakers to say what they want to say. Nothing "throws" a speaker more than the perception that no one is listening. Thus, when you look at a speaker and act alert and attentive, an essential message is communicated to him, the message that you are considerate and respect him and what he has to say. It tells him that you care enough to be attentive. It gives him confidence in you, and almost any speaker is most communicative with those in whom he has confidence.

Thus, through your *listening behavior,* without ever uttering a word, you can control many speakers to a very great extent. Not only can you give the speaker confidence and facilitate his speaking but, with other sorts of visual cues, you can cause him to slow down, repeat, rephrase, or become more lively. You can give either positive or negative reinforcement to a speaker with nonvocal cues. With simple vocal cues, of course, you can do even more. Research has shown, for example, that even in telephone interviews, when the interviewer mumbles "uh-huh" or "yes" after certain kinds of responses, he can soon have most respondents repeating those kinds of responses much more often than they would otherwise.[2]

Another key element in listening is the expectations that the speaker and others involved in the communication situation have of you. You must adjust your behavior to some extent to these expectations if you want the communication to proceed smoothly. We are not saying, of course, that there may not be times when it is important to do something which is contrary to expectations, when it is important to act or react in a way different from the norm of the group. When you do, though, you should be cognizant of the effect it will have and be certain that this is the effect you want. Even when your goal is to change the behavior or the norm of another person or group of persons, the way to maximize the probability of your achieving that goal may be for you to exemplify that different behavior.

It will also help the speaker and you if you keep your mind open to new ideas until, at least, you hear him out. You might take a cue from physicist Robert Oppenheimer, who talked about the fact that, in the contemporary world, we cannot sanction ignorance, insensitivity, or indifference:

When a friend tells us of a new discovery we may not understand, we may not be able to listen without jeopardizing the work that is ours and closer to us; but we cannot find in a book or canon—and we should not seek— ground for hallowing our ignorance. If a man tells us that he sees differently than we, or that he finds beautiful what we find ugly, we may have to leave the room from fatigue or trouble; but that is our weakness and our default. If we must live with a perpetual sense that the world and the men in it are greater than we and too much for us, let it be the measure of our virtue that we know this and seek no comfort. Above all, let us not proclaim that the limits of our powers correspond to some special wisdom in our choice of life, of learning, or of beauty.[3]

To put Oppenheimer's point in another way, learn to put yourself in the shoes of the speaker to get a sense of what he is trying to say and why he's trying to say it.

---

[2]See, for example, D. C. Hildrum and R. W. Brown, "Verbal Reinforcement," *Journal of Abnormal and Social Psychology,* 53:108–11, 1956.
[3]Robert Oppenheimer, "The Open Mind," Fund for Adult Education's *News Digest,* February 1, 1960, p. 1.

In short, for the communication process to work well takes effort, as well as skill, on the part of everyone who is involved in the interaction; all must be working for effective and efficient transmission and reception of signals from each.

Listening with a Purpose

There is no single "right" way to listen. You must adapt your listening behavior to the purpose of the moment, whether that purpose is enjoyment, inspiration, the acquisition of information, understanding attitudes and feelings of other people, or evaluating critically your own ideas and the ideas and communication of others. (We will discuss the foci for critical or evaluative listening in more detail in Chapter Seventeen "Measures of Effectiveness.") If you are listening to Walter Cronkite on television in order to get ideas on how to speak well, you will attend to different things than if you are listening to get information for a report on world affairs. If you are listening to someone reading Keats or Allen Ginsberg, you will listen

■ in still other ways. Therefore, *be conscious* of what you are listening for and adjust your mental and physical set accordingly. However, do not fall into the habit of hearing only what you want to hear, whether it has been said or not. Wishful listening is as harmful a psychological habit as wishful thinking.

■ In addition to being aware of your purpose or purposes, learn to *recognize each speaker's purpose and central ideas.* With a knowledge of his purpose and yours, you have a basis for assessing what he says and does in terms of relevance to these purposes, usefulness for these purposes, adequacy, and bias.

Effective listening is always a creative, as well as a recreative, activity. It is never more so, though, than when listening for enjoyment. Not only is the empathy that we mentioned before important at such times, but also imagination. In viewing a play or listening to a poem, for example, the creative act is incomplete until the receiver does his part by "filling in" and interpreting the work in terms of his experiences and understandings. Again, you will gain the most from such listening if you are receptive to new experiences and fresh modes of expression. At times, some theorists of art have said, you must be willing to suspend disbelief and accept the "reality" of a work of art. Do not be like the righteous viewer standing before a large work of art which was labeled "Mary;" "That doesn't look like a woman to me," she exclaimed. "No, my dear," said the artist, who unbeknownst to her was standing just behind her, "you are a woman; *that* is a painting."

■ When you are listening for information and ideas, *structure your listening.* Try to detect the major purpose of what is being said, the central theme, the main ideas, and the important relationships among the ideas and between the ideas and the theme. In addition to assessing the speaker's purpose, judge his expertness and good will. Discriminate between facts and opinions.

■   As you listen, *evaluate ideas* just as you evaluate material in planning a speech. Examine each idea for clarity, accuracy, logic, and relevance to the theme and to your purpose. Take cognizance of the source of the ideas.

■   *Weigh the evidence* carefully as you hear it. See whether the facts or exposition truly support the ideas. Consider whether parts of the speech are appealing to your motives or attitudes in a way which is irrelevant to the issue. A knowledge of the common logical fallacies and "tricks" of the dishonest persuader will help you in these judgments. Hasty generalizations, false analogies, arguing from questionable premises, and the *post hoc* argument—the assumption that because one event follows another it must have been caused by it—are some of the logical fallacies which the listener should guard against.

Propaganda

In recent years, the term "propaganda" has fallen into disrepute with many communication scholars. However, we believe that it is a label for an important idea for which we have found no other suitable label. By propaganda, we do not mean any persuasive message with which we or you disagree, which is the way the word has been used too often. By propaganda, we mean, rather, any persuasive message which is *deceptive* either because its origins or sources are veiled, the interests or purposes of the sources are hidden, the persuasive methods are misleading, or the effects which will occur if the message is successful are intentionally concealed. Deception or concealment is the key element in propaganda and, if this element is present, the message is propaganda whether it is a message which a foreign government is sending to us or one which we are sending to them, whether it is advertising or education, whether it is a call for a return to fundamental capitalism or a call for revolution. Any message is propaganda if it attempts to misdirect the thinking of its audience.

If you are to be a good listener, you must learn to recognize propaganda and to counteract its influence on your thinking. This recognition will be aided if you keep in mind the two paths that a propagandist tends to follow.

He may, in the first place, concentrate on exploiting all the pitfalls that human reasoning is susceptible to—building up generalizations on inadequate or misperceived data; applying the wrong generalization to a specific instance, and reaching a false conclusion; misinterpreting the sequence of two events or their coexistence in terms of a cause and effect relationship; or transferring an estimate of an event one is familiar with to a new, apparently similar one. . . . He may, on the other hand, follow the other path. Instead of attempting to misdirect a person's thought, he may try to obstruct it, to neutralize it. This he can do by flooding the mind with such an uncontrollable flow of emotion that the individual's thinking mechanism bogs down.[4]

Some years ago, the Institute for Propaganda Analysis identified a number of devices as propaganda techniques.[5] These labels oversimplify the processes of propaganda, but we believe that they may help you to remember some of the major techniques so that you can recognize and counteract them when you encounter them in a message. One such ■ device is *name calling,* which can cause you to perceive a person or object unfavorably. This is done by associating his or its name with some objectionable name or classification, such as "Communist," "right-winger," ■ "radical," "the establishment," and "traitor." The *glittering generality* is a device for gaining acceptability for propositions by labeling them with approved terms such as "freedom," "democracy," "progress," "liberal," and "a balanced budget." The technique of using sources of authority, prestige, respect, and reverence to create a favorable attitude toward a proposal is ■ called *transfer.* For example, most people will respond more favorably to the idea of the Peace Corps if you ask what they think of the late *President Kennedy's idea* of a Peace Corps. The church, the home, educational institutions, the Rock of Gibraltar, and the red cross of mercy are some of the sources of emotional approval for most people. Two communication scholars, Charles Osgood and Percy Tannenbaum, have demonstrated that one can predict with a high degree of reliability the way in which we can affect attitudes toward an idea by the source with which we associate that idea. For example, if you measure a group's attitude toward an idea and toward a well-known figure, you can predict the ways in which attitudes toward both the idea and the person will change when you inform the group that that person favors the idea. Attitudes toward source and person will tend to come together, and whichever the group feels most strongly about will have the greatest effect.

■ The *plain-folks* device is the expressing of an idea or proposal in terms of the simple, everyday experiences and personalities with which all of us are familiar. Politicians delight in using this technique for showing that, after all, they are like one of our neighbors and are therefore worthy of ■ our trust in public office. *Card stacking* is a scheme used to deceive by carefully selecting only favorable evidence. Half-truths are used as a smoke ■ screen to prevent the listener from really facing the facts. The *bandwagon* technique creates an impression of universal approval of an idea; an attempt is made to cause the individual to consider himself an outsider if he does

---

[4]Michael Choukas, *Propaganda Comes of Age,* Public Affairs Press, Washington, 1965, pp. 123, 125.
[5]Violet Edwards, *Group Leader's Guide to Propaganda Analysis,* Institute for Propaganda Analysis, Inc., New York, 1935.

not approve: "Two million people can't be wrong." "I nominate the next President of the United States." "Students for . . ."

Other questionable tricks of persuasion include appeals of fear, hate, anger, frustration, or discontent growing out of misfortune or lack of opportunity; the creation of scapegoats on whom to place blame; threats of trouble, wishful thinking, rationalization, rumor, distrust, flattery, and repetition; and identification with the great, the beautiful, and the good; and prophecies. The propagandist may be a head of state, or the person with whom you eat lunch. The use of such techniques does not, of course, imply that the proposal is inherently unworthy. You must decide for yourself whether the conclusions fit the facts. Just do not let yourself be blinded to the facts by these techniques.

■   It will help your purposeful listening if you *interpret what you hear in terms of your own experience,* as well as your purposes and the purposes of the speaker. The important way to test what you hear is to relate it to what you already know: Ask mental questions, make applications, provide examples, and reorganize what you hear into the most useful shape for your purposes. This use of your prior knowledge will help you to decide which ideas are relevant and useful, as well as whether they are true.

Effects of Attitude on Listening

When we are involved in communication, we are generally conscious of and concerned with the effects of what we perceive upon our attitudes. We should be equally conscious of and concerned with the converse—the effects of our attitudes upon what we perceive—for these attitudes can easily interfere with and bias our critical or accurate listening. Listening expert Ralph Nichols calls them "emotional filters" and warns us against letting our attitudes about a topic or our opinions of a speaker or his appearance filter out what the speaker is saying. Not only do negative attitudes affect what we perceive, positive attitudes do also. Consider, as a trivial example, the parent who "hears" nothing but pearls of wisdom from the lips of her child. We have a great number of studies that show that people have a tendency to misperceive information with which they disagree, or, if they perceive it correctly, to forget it quickly. Studies also show that when someone people like says something with which they strongly disagree, they will tend to interpret it differently than when they hear someone they dislike say it. These phenomena are often termed "selective perception" and "selection retention."[6]

As a listener, be aware of these factors which can cause you to be influenced in a communication situation without your complete awareness.

---

[6]See, for example, Joseph T. Klapper, *The Effects of Mass Communication,* The Free Press, New York, 1960, pp. 19–26.

All of the things that we have said about the press for consistency, the effect of reference groups and reinforcement, etc., apply to you. An awareness of the way in which these phenomena affect people will help to inoculate you against being overly persuasible. This awareness will operate similarly to the awareness that comes from hearing a persuasive speech in which the speaker reminds the audience that they will be hearing arguments on the other side or even tells them what some of those arguments are. This type of inoculation helps the members of the audience to build their defenses against these counterarguments. Just so, an awareness of psychological factors in persuasion will help you to build your defenses against these factors so that you are in more conscious control of your own decision making.

This is not to say that you should never change your attitudes or other behaviors in order to reduce your own inconsistency, or that you should never change your brand of shampoo or deodorant in order to improve your chances of finding love. This is to say that you should be conscious of such appeals and their probable effect upon you so that you are in control of that effect, rather than being in the control of others more sophisticated in the processes of communication.

We have talked a good bit about guarding against undesirable influence. On the other hand, do not become overly suspicious of everyone with whom you communicate. Recognize that most people are of good will. As we indicated earlier, optimum communication takes place when there is mutual trust and cooperation among those who are communicating with each other. In other words, meet the speaker at least half-way. If two or more people are to communicate effectively they must be able to respond in corresponding ways to words and other objects and ideas. Social psychologist Theodore Newcomb calls that "co-orientation"—the maintenance of similar orientations by those involved in a communication situation among themselves and toward the matters about which they are communicating. This is not to say that there must be total agreement or the same attitudes toward everything. However, there must be sufficient commonality for communication to occur.

Attention: The Base for Effective Listening

Effective listening is work. If you think of the word "attention," it will help you to remember the two key parts of good listening: "at" or focus—what you attend to—and "tension"—the energy which you put into that focusing. Listening is not a passive skill. Not only must you maintain a level of tension and focus on the relevant cues in the message, you must sift and organize them and then store what you find useful. All this requires effort.

Just as a speaker can speak or write a speech more easily if he has an outline of what he wants to say, so you as a listener can grasp and store what a speaker says if you have some fair notion beforehand of what he is likely to say and how he will say it. Clearly, you must be careful not to let your preconceptions mislead you. As we indicated earlier, there is a real danger of hearing what you expect to hear. On the other hand, intelligent expectations can aid listening and learning. Your expectations will generally be most accurate if you know as much about the speaker as possible, have a fairly clear notion of how he perceives you and others in the audience, and understand his purpose in speaking.

With reasonable expectations, you will not be forced into attempting the impossible task of trying to focus on *everything,* or trying to outline everything, or, the extreme, trying to copy down everything that the speaker says. With reasonable expectations, you can avoid the error of focusing on the wrong thing for your purposes, e.g., focusing on facts when what is relevant to you are the premises.

When you are involved in a communication situation, you can choose the main focus of your attention, your side-involvements, and the intensity of your involvements. Make these choices wisely, for not only will they affect what you get from the encounter, but also how others respond to you. Think, for example, of the times that you have been talking with someone at a party while his eyes constantly roamed the room to see who else was coming in. You quickly realized that he did not care about you at all, that he was paying no attention to you. If he had any hope of your being his friend or ally, after that experience his hope was probably a vain one. Any speaker will respond as you did if you attend to him—or fail to attend to him—in this way, if you fail to show that you care about what he has to say. So when you are involved in a conversation or discussion or some other communication situation, keep in mind that you have an obligation to maintain a certain level of involvement and to show that involvement. Be careful of any sort of external preoccupation or mind-wandering, self-consciousness or more concern with yourself than with others, other-consciousness or being distracted from the speaker and topic by someone else in the group, and interaction-consciousness or concern with the communication process itself rather than with the topic of the communication.[7]

In trying to develop your focus and span of attention, and to improve your listening ability, work on these *techniques of listening:*

1. Practice keeping a level of tension which will help your concentration.
2. Practice predicting the following things about a speaker:
   a. Where is he going in the message?
   b. What does he want me to know or understand or believe?
   If you predict correctly, in effect you get the point twice. If you predict

---

[7] See Erving Goffman, "Alienation from Interaction," in *Communication and Culture,* ed. Alfred G. Smith, Holt, Rinehart & Winston, New York, 1966, pp. 103–118, for an interesting discussion of some of these matters.

incorrectly, you can compare what the speaker did with what you predicted, which will give you a good start toward the analysis of his speech.

3. Listen for main ideas and for those parts of the message which cue your attention: sentences which predict, show development, show a relationship, indicate a transition, or summarize.

4. Listen "between the lines." Ask yourself what the speaker has *not* said that is relevant.

5. Learn not to lose focus because of distractions:
   a. unusual aspects of the situation
   b. unexpected dress or behavior of the speaker
   c. irrelevant behavior of others in the audience
   d. unusual or foul language
   e. unexpected topics that arise
   f. ideas that arouse your emotions

6. Learn to adjust to various listening situations so that they do not interfere with appropriate focus.

7. Learn to adjust to different speaking rates or different rates at which ideas are thrown at you.

8. Learn to focus upon the nonverbal as well as verbal cues. They can tell you something about the speaker's confidence. They often indicate something also about the speaker's attitudes toward what he is saying. Be careful not to mistake nervousness or inexperience, though, for insincerity or something else. It is important that you know the speaker well, if possible, so that you know the nonverbal cues to expect under normal conditions. In some cases, the inflections, pauses, and physical movements of the speaker are as relevant to focus on as what he says.

9. Develop your sensitivity to people as well as messages. Just as you must be a good people-reader when you speak; so you must be sensitive to people as you listen. Not only should you be sensitive to the speaker, but to other listeners as well. We indicated earlier that you must learn not to lose focus because of the irrelevant behaviors of others in a group or audience, but the responses which others make are often relevant to your purposes. In those instances, you must be able to read these responses accurately while, at the same time, focusing upon the relevant aspects of what the speaker is saying and doing.

10. Acquire the habit of reviewing what you have heard and seen.

Projects and Problems

PROJECT 1:   Try making a record of your listening time during one day. Keep a record of the different types of listening you do by making notes occasionally. Did any of it fail? Evaluate your success in this behavior. Report to the class on your listening.

PROJECT 2:   Observe the listening of others during a two-day period. What was listened to? What was the apparent purpose of the listening? How successful do you think the listening was?

PROJECT 3:   Hold a class discussion on discriminating factual reporting from promotion or propaganda. How does one tell the difference? What cues in what is said and how it is said suggest different purposes in communication?

PROJECT 4:   Discuss listening as a learning process. Compare and contrast learning from first-order experience and vicarious learning. What are the advantages and disadvantages of each?

PROJECT 5:   Read one of the references for this chapter and report to the class on what you learned about people as listeners. What can you suggest which might lead to improvement of one or more of the elements involved in receiving communication?

References

Barbara, Dominick A., *The Art of Listening.* Springfield, Ill.: Charles C Thomas, 1958.

Berelson, Bernard, and Morris Janowitz (eds.), *Reader in Public Opinion and Communication,* 2nd ed. New York: The Free Press, 1966.

Choukas, Michael, *Propaganda Comes of Age.* Washington, D.C.: Public Affairs Press, 1965.

Dichter, Ernest, *The Strategy of Desire.* Garden City, N.Y.: Doubleday, 1960.

Doob, Leonard W., *Public Opinion and Propaganda,* 2nd ed. Hamden, Conn.: Archon Books, 1966.

Dovring, Karin, *Road of Propaganda: the Semantics of Biased Communication.* New York: Philosophical Library, 1959.

Duker, Sam, *Listening Readings.* New York: The Scarecrow Press, 1966.

Edwards, Violet, *Group Leader's Guide to Propaganda Analysis.* New York: Institute for Propaganda Analysis, 1935.

Hanson, Donald A., and J. Herschel Parsons, *Mass Communication: A Research Bibliography.* Santa Barbara: The Glendessary Press, 1968, pp. 55ff.

Hunter, Edward, *Brainwashing.* New York: Pyramid Books, 1956.

Huseman, Richard C., Cal M. Logue, and Dwight Freshley, *Readings in Interpersonal and Organizational Communication.* Boston: Holbrook Press, 1969.

Johnson, Wendell, *Your Most Enchanted Listener.* New York: Harper, 1956.

Katz, Daniel, et al, *Public Opinion and Propaganda.* New York: Holt, Rinehart & Winston, 1965.

Klapper, Joseph T., *The Effects of Mass Communication.* New York: The Free Press, 1960.

Lindzey, Gardner, and Elliot Aronson (eds.), *The Handbook of Social Psychology,* 2nd ed. Reading, Mass.: Addison-Wesley, 1969. Vol. 3, Chapters 22, 23, 24; Vol. 4, Chapter 35.

Nichols, Ralph G., and Leonard A. Stevens, *Are You Listening?* New York: McGraw-Hill Book Company, 1957.

Payne, Donald E. (ed.), *The Obstinate Audience.* Ann Arbor, Mich.: Foundation for Research on Human Behavior, 1965.

Richardson, Lee, *Dimensions of Communication.* New York: Appleton-Century-Crofts, 1969. Chapters 16, 19.

Sargent, William, *Battle for the Mind.* Baltimore: Penguin Books, 1961.

Smith, Alfred G. (ed.), *Communication and Culture.* New York: Holt, Rinehart & Winston, 1966. See pp. 103–118.

Smith, Henry Clay, *Sensitivity to People.* New York: McGraw-Hill Book Company, 1966.

Toch, Hans, and Henry Clay Smith, *Social Perception.* Princeton: D. Van Nostrand, 1968.

Whyte, William H., Jr., *Is Anybody Listening?* New York: Simon & Schuster, 1952.

PART FOUR

The Message

Malcolm X indicted racist America.
The visual aid shows the aftermath of a Los Angeles Riot.
UPI.

the message

"What shall I talk about?" This is the ancient problem for successive classes of speech students and for many others who may be caught up in a speaking program before few or many observer-hearers. Your goal, at college or university, is to say something that you or others have not already said repeatedly, something that will not put your audience to sleep. Your problem is more than carefully developing a topic, once you have selected it, for example on "how and why to study." Your problem is more than scanning a list of suggested subjects, each of which is guaranteed to interest everybody.

In our discussion of this problem of speech topics, we will find it helpful to think of the message as the source and essence of the entire communicative occasion.

The Message: Its Purpose

A message rises out of the experiences and purposes of a human being to establish and maintain contact with one or more fellows. A person may succumb to fright and utter sounds that aim at his own and his mates' survival. Or he may be vocally stirred by signs of his victories, or by prospects of his physical, social, or material improvement.[1]

These purposes overlap. Most of them seem to imply formal speaking, preparation, and adequate audience adjustment to unfold something worthwhile. Much of our communication, however, is informal, broken, interspersed with motives and methods that produce a mosaic of varied message types. The drift of your thinking and oral participation may include the giving and receiving of knowledge; the give and take of controversial inquiry; the utterances of admonition, approval, eulogy; or just purposeless chatter.

Sources of Messages

Where do the ideas and their details come from? What are the sources of impulses that produce substance in the message? We look to the sensory stimuli that initiate the total processes of communication. Hundreds of

---

[1] See Chapters One and Two on goals.

stimuli activate the cortical centers of the brain at a given time. Smell, taste, sound, sight, and touch comprise your reaction to your environment at a given instant. These sensings at either the conscious or subconscious level, in turn, result in perceptive reactions of the brain and somehow lead to the thought-language–symbolization process.

These reflections on your message are addressed entirely to yourself. No eavesdroppers listen to your private "go go" with yourself as speaker, audience, occasion, speech, and method of transference. Formal grammar and syntax are absent. Even the ideas may loom and recede as your mind almost instantaneously confronts experiences suggested by immediate and more latent connections.

Within each person are the pulsations of cognitive and affective reactions. We have no sure feedback or method by which to check or analyze this internal movement. Only through the models and guides that analyze this movement as reflective thought can we follow through the procedure to understand and describe the message with its details.

You As a Source of the Message

Note that the content and direction of your message are colored by your personality and experience as you relate to your world. Obviously, your physical, psychological, logical, and social being is strongly marked by your inheritance and your environment. These factors determine the essence and detail of your discourse.

Your purposes in communication, your intellectual qualities and trends, your social intelligence, your emotional thinking, and your general emotionality all become the foundations of your thinking and expression.

Note these connections between you and your message:

■ *Personal experiences.* You will constantly draw on your own experiences and observations. For example, if you have lived in Yarmouth, Maine, you are familiar with clam digging and lobster fishing, the use of kelp as fertilizer, and down-East speech. If you have lived in the middle of Chicago, you are familiar with pollution, substandard housing, urban traffic, and people of varied backgrounds living close together.

■ *Reading and reflection.* Autobiographical or semifictional narratives are not the entire source of your messages. Your audiences—especially, though not exclusively, your peers—will be interested in your thinking and reading. If you read the sports page, you have a source of ideas to suit the season. The trends of the competitive sports world appeal even to the unathletic. If you follow the fashions, you can comment on the latest skirt length. National and international problems are inexhaustible. The news about inflation, strikes, political campaigns, taxes, and black power will suggest many messages. Make an inventory of your beliefs. Everyone has definite convictions on many issues; you have only to realize what these convictions are to capitalize upon them in your speeches. Possibly you have ideas about what should be done in the field of airplane manufacture (military or nonmilitary) in the next decade; about taxes on cigarettes; about English or communications as a required subject; about farm problems or the cost of living; about law, advertising, or personnel work as a profession; about further desegregation in the public schools. Stage, motion picture, and television plays furnish abundant messages. Your role as critic is important.

- *Hobbies and special skills.* Hobbies are good subjects for speeches because they have a special advantage of being personal and at the same time informational. What is your special interest, apart from or as part of your school, work, or job? Mechanical drawing? Meteors and other celestial phenomena? Cryptography?

- *Lectures, radio and television talks, conversations.* You have many opportunities to hear well-developed talks. Listen to a lecture and base a speech of your own on one of the ideas. A history professor, for example, stated that most students are grossly ignorant of American history and that our national security depends to a large degree upon a better grounding in that subject. Your re-creation of lectures will obviously be related to your independent thinking and your own investigations.

- *Courses of study.* Many students think of their courses as distinct and widely separated units of subject matter. Consequently they fail to profit from the merging of these bodies of knowledge. You can make use of your current studies in economic geography, history, science, English, and other courses.

Audience Interests As Sources of Messages

Ask yourself, "What does my audience want to hear about? What are my listeners' needs? What controversial issues confront them?" If they are concerned only with such matters as dating and tomorrow night's basketball game, how can you enlist and hold their attention when you introduce topics representing wider concerns?

In choosing topics and messages, most students of oral and written communication are self-centered rather than audience-centered. It is harder to answer the question "What are others interested in?" than the question "What means much to me?" You should be continually alert to the activities, opinions, and the vocations and avocations of your audience. Your mental and emotional projection into the minds and personalities of your listeners will provide you with subjects that appeal.

You may begin by passing imaginatively from the role of prospective speechmaker to that of prospective listener. Are the others in the group like you? Put yourself in their places. Ask yourself some questions about them: What are their ages, their weekly earnings, their attitudes toward government, their feelings about meeting strangers, and whom do they admire? Each group has character of its own. Marines, actresses, Wall Streeters, clergymen, Ivy Leaguers, hippies, and sorority sisters have distinctive characteristics.

Contemporary Scene and Immediate Occasions As Sources of Messages

The scene and occasion of your talk will, in many cases, suggest your message. You may have a good fortune to engage in an informal radio discussion with other students on the subject of "the negative income tax." If you are a college debater, your message and issue may be selected by your campus committee of the Speech Communication Association. Again, you may talk in a college campaign to raise funds for the Red Cross or for the community budget. In any case, you will be sensitive to the requirements of the hour—the nature of the occasion, the time of day, the audience, the specific aim of the group, and other details.

When you have thus analyzed sources of messages, check through the categories and decide both what you are interested in and what may appeal to your hearers.

General Characteristics of the Message

The message may be vocal or nonvocal. It may be audible sound or merely signs.

The message may be long or short. It may be a four-hour speech before the United States Senate or a one-minute classroom contribution. It may be an answer to some inquiry, an unbroken treatment of a theme, or a course interspersed with interruptions and cross-examination. It may be the mutual exchange of a panel, or an informal dialogue in class, in your dormitory, or over the local radio. Your message may be a series encompassing a considerable time span, with essentially the same purposes and message throughout. It may be Senator Fulbright's repeated criticisms since 1966 of the United States military-political program in South Vietnam. The message may originate with one individual; or it may have joint authorship or be the production of a group.

These messages, common in certain fundamentals, may vary widely in their close or wide adherence to the central idea. Some excellent speeches, as we know, have been discursive and even rambling. This textual tightness or looseness may have little relation to the length of the discourse or series of related discourses. Some communicators, feeling their way into the mood of the listeners, may adjust their materials and sequences to achieve more complete attention and persuasiveness. Woodrow Wilson, Franklin Roosevelt, Harry Truman, John Kennedy, and Lyndon Johnson in their political addresses were not always compact in thematic unity.

The message, again, may express robust logic and intellectual thoroughness but at the expense of emotional imaginativeness. Other messages may

Many public figures become so closely associated with their causes that man—or woman—and message seem to fuse. Such was the case with Malcolm X. Here, William F. Buckley, Jr., soars to heights of Conservative rhetoric.

Bernard Gottfryd.

Shirley Chisholm, above,
speaks for black rights,
women's rights, and her
Brooklyn constituency.
Antiwar leader Sam
Brown, above right,
helped mobilize youth
against the Vietnam war.
Margaret Chase Smith,
right, almost embodies her
sensible, centrist political
message.

To many, Cesar Chavez, left, has become synonymous with the causes of migrant labor and Chicano rights. Author of the best-selling study, *Sexual Politics,* Kate Millett, below, champions women's liberation.

Mary Ellen Mark.

be so charged with emotionality as to obscure and even dissipate the thematic aims.

The message, too, may be a model of oral discourse, with language suited to the subject and occasion. Or it may violate the standard assumptions required of forensic, deliberative, epideictic or other type of the traditional forms of expression. It may be the language of Franklin Roosevelt, Dwight Eisenhower, John Kennedy, and Richard Nixon at their best, when they delivered their inauguration addresses. Or, it may be that of Malcolm X deliberately adjusting his vocabulary and ideas to defy establishment norms.

Effects of the Message

The message or messages may or may not produce tangible results. Though we stress influence as the measure of communication, some messages because of their topics or their treatment have no observable outcomes.[2]

Short- and Long-Range Results

The measures of influence may sometimes be the immediate audience behavior. If the message secures votes, signatures to petitions, sales, or other tangible responses, we usually judge the speech as effective. But immediate audience response may be misleading (as when a considerable percentage of an audience derisively applauds a speaker). You must learn to "read" audience behavior accurately.

Students of speech also should attempt to gauge the influence of a message or messages through wider results. Historians, logicians, and rhetoricians are united in questioning immediate or short-range, cause-and-effect evidence and inference as proof (or lack of proof) of the effectiveness of communication.

Causes and effects, for example, are so numerous that it is almost impossible in some cases to describe relations in terms of a single cause and single effect. The speaker's message may be affected by contemporary events and distinctions which seem to be unrelated to the communicative event. Sudden threats of wars, turns in wars being waged, unexpected business fluctuations, revolutionary uprisings all complicate causal elements. We are really dealing with systems of events, with each system part of a larger one, the whole making up a wide pattern. Our problem is to single out a unit (in this case a message) as a cause; or to single out one outcome as the effect. Concentrating on consequences is necessary and practical, but we need to test carefully these relationships before we draw hard and fast conclusions.[3]

---

[2]See Chapter Seventeen on effectiveness.
[3]See Chapter Twenty-one for further discussion of testing "causal reasoning."

Some commentators have stressed that the major aim of communication is "perfection of performance" rather than the resulting audience behavior. James McBurney and Ernest J. Wrage state, for example, "Rather than measuring a speech by its results, and thus falling into the trap, which has deluded many speakers, critics, and educators with such unfortunate outcomes, the critic who applies the Artistic Theory judges a speech by the principles of the Art."[4]

We suggest that evaluating consequences inevitably leads to explanations of why the audience behaves as it does. The measure of effect must involve a review of the entire communicative process—focusing on the communicator's personality, the ideas of the discourse, its structure and language, adaptation to situation and audience, the symbols used, and all else that may explain the outcome.

Testing the Message

To help evaluate the results of your message, you should ask yourself several questions:

■ 1. *Have I properly limited my subject and message?* Most messages are unduly long and broad. In general, the message should be specific, focusing on a concrete aspect of a general idea. The time allotted for the message obviously restricts its scope and content. In a four-minute speech you cannot cover all the representative arguments for and against a permanent volunteer army in the United States and explain your choice of military policy.

■ 2. *Is the message adjusted to the interests, knowledge, attitudes, and needs of the audience?* The character of the audience determines the direction, scope, and other factors of the message.

■ 3. *Is the message adapted to the needs of the immediate occasion?* Sometimes the situation necessitates a broad approach and message; at others, the scope of your message and its content need to be sharply curtailed.

■ 4. *Does the message have structural validity?* Although the materials and appeals are largely governed by the needs and interests of those who listen, the structure of your discourse should usually reflect audience preferences for unity, for order that can be readily followed, for means that will help them to vivify the most important aspects of the theme. The audiences for the courtroom, radio, television, political campaign, and other special forms of speech each call for special types of organization.

■ 5. *Do the logical supports of the speech effectively help to enforce the message?* Cumbersome logic may impede the proper audience reaction. Conversely, absence of thought sequences may dissipate the effectiveness of the message.

---

[4]James McBurney and Ernest J. Wrage, *Art of Good Speech,* Prentice-Hall, Inc., Englewood Cliffs, N.J., 1953, pp. 29–30.

■ 6. *Do the motivational qualities of the discourse aid in the persuasiveness of the message?* Is it reasonably restrained? Excessive emotionality may destroy the message appeal.

■ 7. *Does the language facilitate the development of the message?* Over-richness of vocabulary may hinder the power of the ideas presented. On the other hand, language must help to interest the audience and make clear the ideas.

■ 8. *Does the message fulfill your controlling purpose?* If your aim is knowledge, for example, do your theme and its details contribute to this purpose? Similarly your message is to be judged by its support of your purpose to analyze a problem, change beliefs and attitudes, stimulate to action, impress, entertain, or solve a problem.

■ 9. *Does the message grow out of your experiences, interests, observations?*
These questions, we hope, will help you in the selection and development of your message: What subject and message shall I select? How shall I limit it? What speaking aim shall I attempt to fulfill? What specific adaptation shall I make in my message and purpose to obtain maximum response from my listener-observers? In the next chapter, we shall discuss the sources of supporting materials for messages.

Projects and Problems

PROJECT 1:   Using as a guide the criteria for "testing the message" suggested in this chapter, test the message used in one of the talks you made last week in class or elsewhere.

PROJECT 2:   Select seven message topics properly limited to illustrate each of the following controlling purposes: (1) to inform, (2) to analyze a problem, (3) to change or strengthen beliefs, (4) to stimulate to action, (5) to impress, (6) to entertain, (7) to solve a problem. Frame each as a purpose sentence. Arrange your exercise as follows: (a) subject, (b) controlling purpose of the message, (c) purpose sentence.

PROJECT 3:   Listen to a speaker, preferably in a situation in which you are one of the visible audience. Note the subject and title of his talk; judge his specific purpose. Present to the class a brief written report of your findings.

References

Berlo, David K., *The Process of Communication*. New York: Holt, Rinehart & Winston, Inc., 1960.

Bettinghaus, Erwin P., *Message Preparation*. Indianapolis: The Bobbs-Merrill Company, Inc., 1966.

Budd, Richard W., Robert K. Thorp, and Lewis Donohew, *Content Analysis of Communications*. New York: The Macmillan Company, 1967.

Cherry, Colin, *On Human Communication*. New York: Science Editions, Inc., 1961.

Ellingsworth, Huber W., and Theodore Clevenger, *Speech and Social Action*. Englewood Cliffs, N.J.: Prentice-Hall, Inc., 1967.

Gerbner, George, et al (eds.), *The Analysis of Communication Content*. New York: John Wiley & Sons, Inc., 1969.

McBurney, James H., and Ernest J. Wrage, *The Art of Good Speech*. New York: Prentice-Hall, Inc., 1953.

McCroskey, James C., *An Introduction to Rhetorical Communication*. Englewood Cliffs, N.J.: Prentice-Hall, Inc., 1968.

Miller, Gerald R., *Speech Communication*. Indianapolis: The Bobbs-Merrill Company, Inc., 1966.

Miller, George A., *Language and Communication*. New York, McGraw-Hill Book Company, 1951.

Mills, Glen E., *Message Preparation*. Indianapolis: The Bobbs-Merrill Company, Inc., 1966.

Nilsen, Thomas R., *Ethics of Speech Communication*. Indianapolis: The Bobbs-Merrill Company, Inc., 1966.

North, Robert C., et al., *Content Analysis*. Evanston, Ill.: Northwestern University Press, 1963.

Pool, Ithiel de Sola, *Trends in Content Analysis*. Urbana, Ill.: University of Illinois Press, 1959.

Wiseman, Gordon, and Larry Barker, *Speech—Interpersonal Communication*. San Francisco: Chandler Publishing Company, 1967.

sources of message materials

You have tentatively chosen a subject for your next talk. How will you develop your message? Some topics seem to develop themselves; personal experiences and observations provide you with an abundance of relevant materials. Other topics are more difficult to develop because it is not easy to find concrete and original support for them.

What materials do you need for your message, and how can you go about assembling them? You obviously need an idea or series of ideas as the framework. Your audience adjustment and activity determine to a large degree your topic and its development. This problem looms large as you begin to develop an outline. The supporting materials are the information that amplifies these ideas of your message. Such materials consist of examples, facts and figures, circumstantial details, illustrations, analogies, and comparisons. Included also may be the testimony of those who have reported on related situations or events and the opinions of authorities.

Message materials, in short, are the complex phenomena of our educational, political, social, physical, scientific, philosophical, and religious worlds, which we use for our individual purposes. Your problem is to bring to light, select, sift, and fashion the ideas into a direct talk that holds attention and invites reciprocal communication.

Techniques for Securing Materials

How can you delve into this vast storehouse and select materials that are appropriate and interesting?

When you have selected your purpose and topic, you have automatically determined the main idea or ideas of your communication. Your next task is to find materials which will expand or explain these ideas. Five principal techniques or skills will help you in finding these materials: thinking, personal experiences and observation, listening, talking (including interviewing), and reading (including note taking).

Thinking

Size up your topic mentally as you begin and complete development. Students often distrust their own ideas; in the presence of faculty experts, the inexperienced student may minimize the value of his own judgments. **101**

Speech improvement, like other forms of learning, depends partly on the exercise of independent thinking.

Thinking, as we stressed in the previous chapter, becomes the heart of your productive communication. Creative thinking of the highest degree is, we admit, that of the rare geniuses. But this reflective reaction to experiences and realities is the common property of all human beings and is not to be dismissed as limited to the chosen intellectuals.

Your individual reflection may be the most important element of your communication. Although your informational talk will contain facts from history, for example, or from science, it will be different from any other on the same subject. The difference will lie in your individual approach, your personal thinking. In order to improve the quality of your individual contribution to your talk you should adopt methods of thought which will maximize your acquisition of concepts and ideas.

■ 1. *Ask yourself about the importance of your subject to your audience.* Ask yourself such questions as: Is this subject timely, interesting, worth talking about? Do I know much about it? What do the listeners know about it and to what extent will they follow and accept my ideas? Such inquiries arouse your systematic, reflective reaction.

■ 2. *Ask yourself what does the subject mean?* Consider the clarification of terms and ideas apart from the specific dictionary definitions. An entire talk is often developed from an explanation of "what is a withholding tax?" or "what is time-and-motion study?" Your questioning of definitions and your search for reliable interpretations again stimulate your mental alertness.

■ 3. *Subdivide the subject matter and classify the subdivisions.* Cataloging ideas and data is by no means easy. It invites questions about economic, social, political, physical, and other relationships. It calls for judgment concerning such groupings. Marshalling ideas into categories will sharpen your awareness of methodical division and will stimulate you to further mental exploration.

As you complete a list of questions, you will group them into related units, reshuffle your groupings, and achieve a more detailed view of the subject. Experience in analysis and organization will provide a genuinely thoughtful basis for your speech. Talks that explain how to do something or how something works—the expository and informative type of speech—are developed by this method.

■ 4. *View your materials, for example, in a time order and consider causal relationships.* Your topic may be chronological. You, for example, may be giving to a forensics group on your campus a brief oral report of the experiences and records of the debating team during the college year. Undoubtedly, you will follow through some sort of time sequence. But the chronological or historical approach usually calls for more than a recitation of date after date. You must ask, "Why is this event important?" "What were the results?" This cause-and-effect method will throw light upon the strength and weakness of your university debating team in its platform and tournament records.

■   5. *Decide what problem is involved and what probable causes and results accompany it.* This approach is somewhat like that of the chronological method, but it is more typical of the "problem-and-solution" procedure of persuasive and discussional speaking. You raise questions concerning the sufficiency of alleged causes and ask yourself what course or courses of action will best deal with the problem.

If, for example, your subject concerns riots, medical aid for the aged, highway traffic control, water pollution, civil disobedience and the law, or public ownership of the local bus line, you will attempt to answer such questions as:

I.   Problem
1.   What evidence do you have of the existence of this problem?
2.   What are the apparent workings and results of the present event or situation?
3.   What are apparent causes of the problem?

II.   Solution
1.   What solutions are proposed by those who have looked into this problem?
2.   What is your own idea of what might be done?
3.   What more specific program or method would you offer for corrective action?
4.   How practicable, to you at any rate, do your proposals seem to be?

The subject of logical and productive thinking as opposed to random thinking is too complicated to be discussed at length in this chapter. However, we have discussed these processes in Chapter Twenty-one and other sections of this book. We include discussions of logical thinking as it is related to speaking. For the present, you will find it beneficial to explore your subject by means of the five modes of reflection suggested above. And you should apply these methods of inquiry in all phases of your subsequent preparation, observation, listening, discussion, interviewing, and reading. Your thinking should pervade your preparation from start to finish.

Experience and Observation

Our reactions to the outside world obviously furnish basic materials for many of our messages. First-hand reports of our jobs, travels, and other experiences, systematic reports based on our direct observation of how a machine or agency works or what other experiments signify usually give authenticity to our treatment of materials. Eric Sevareid, speaking out of London in August, 1969, gave distinction to his social-political commentaries by his reflections on London life—on the whole, a most optimistic one to Londoners.

Keenness of perception, ability to discriminate between what is casually seen and what is acutely observed, ability to synthesize details into a significant pattern—all give validity to our experience and observation as sources of message materials.

Listening

Stimulating ideas and facts are borne in upon you by speakers all through your waking hours. Consider these oral communicative situations that you experience constantly—lectures (in classrooms or elsewhere on campus), student colloquies or organized panels, committee meetings, give-and-take exchanges with others as you come and go, radio and television broadcasts, business conferences, sermons, political campaign speeches, and all sorts of other talks.

A few suggestions below may help you to utilize materials from your listening for your own speech.

- 1. *Adopt a receptive attitude toward other speakers,* whether they are on television or directly before you face to face. Note each speaker's voice, his repetitions, and if he is visible to you, his physical activity such as fumbling with his notes. Whether the speaker is a candidate for public office, your professor of zoology, one of your classmates, or the President of the United States, his ideas deserve respectful consideration, although you may later reject them.

- 2. *Concentrate.* Ignore extraneous noises. Make mental notes on what you hear, and jot things on paper if the situation permits. Be sure that you get the main ideas, even if you will not be able, as the young Lincoln was, to repeat later almost everything the preacher or politician has said.

- 3. *If you are attending a lecture, give yourself every possible physical advantage to hear well.* Sit near the center and at the front of the room.

- 4. *Get the communicator's point of view.* This will necessitate keeping an open mind and controlling your biases and enthusiasms.

- 5. *Help the communicator to establish a feedback response from you.* As he talks, you will silently carry on your part of the dialogue. You will silently raise questions and agree or disagree as if you were indeed speaking in the gaps created by his pauses. The speaker will respond to your close attention and to feedback cues he gets from you, and thus rapport will be established.

- 6. *Analyze what the speaker is saying and raise questions in your own mind.* Note the way the speaker begins. Why does he use this method? Does he announce his topic? Does he make his terms clear? What is his division of the subject? Do his ideas follow in logical sequence? Is his speech unified? Are his ideas valid? Do his reasoning and his factual materials carry out his evident purpose of giving you information or of impressing you or of persuading you? Answering such questions as these will stimulate you mentally and enable you to listen creatively and evaluate what you hear.[1]

Conversation and Discussion

If attentive and thoughtful listening informs and stimulates you, then you will benefit from conversation and informal discussions.

By means of such opportunities for discussion, Charles James Fox, who has been called the world's greatest debater, equipped himself for the stormy combats in the House of Commons in the late eighteenth century. Fox gained many of the arguments in his speeches by discussing political questions with friends and colleagues.[2] Franklin D. Roosevelt often revised his speeches after discussion with his colleagues, as did Winston Churchill "after hours of discussion." John Kennedy, Adlai Stevenson, and Richard Nixon did the same.

You can test your thinking and the effectiveness of your presentation in discussion with others. When a speaker has finished his remarks and calls for questions or statements from the floor, you have a valuable opportunity to participate. Discuss, then, with others what you propose to give in a classroom or other speaking situation.

Interviewing

For sources of your talks, you will become an inquiring reporter. Such a role will be worth your while in proportion to your preparation for it and your orderly management of what you are after.

1. Determine before the interview the purpose of your speech and the information and opinions you seek.
2. Know as much as you can about your subject before you attempt to interview.
3. Seek out an expert in the field of your proposed report.
4. Organize your procedure and frame your questions clearly.
5. Eliminate bias in your framing of your queries and throughout the interview.
6. Let your respondent do practically all of the talking.
7. Listen carefully, usually avoid note taking.
8. Note any sources mentioned in the interview.
9. Make the interview brief—do not bore your respondent.

---

[1] Additional suggestions for listening have been given in Chapter Seven.
[2] Loren Reid, *Charles James Fox, A Man for the People,* University of Missouri Press, Columbia, Missouri, 1969, pp. 336 ff.

Reading

If we have had a New Deal in speech making and listening since the advent of radio and television, we have also had a golden age of miscellaneous reading since the invention of the linotype machine and since elementary education has become universal. Lincoln, in his Indiana and Illinois boyhood and youth, had comparatively few books. He studied the *Kentucky Preceptor, Murray's English Reader, Weem's Life of George Washington, Indiana Statutes,* Scott's *Lessons on Elocution,* and a few great classics, including the Bible. We today have access to the ageless volumes, but in addition we can pick and choose from an endless variety of more recent printed matter. Most of us can visit libraries which contain scores and scores of books that bear directly upon the subjects that interest us.

Efficiency in Reading

When you have compiled a bibliography of relevant books and articles, the next problem is to assimilate the knowledge contained in them. What are the most efficient methods of reading? Teachers of speech are especially critical of talks based on undigested ideas. Too often, students echo the language of their sources and demonstrate little comprehension of the ideas, with the result that the content of the speech seems foreign to the speaker. How can you read both efficiently and creatively?

- *Approach every idea or source with an open mind.* At the outset, be objective. Do not pass by an article because it appears to contain ideas that you object to or facts that you question. Check your mental approach to guarantee fairness.
- *Read with a purpose.* Keep clearly in mind what your proposed topic is and what you already think about it. By remembering the overall purpose of your talk, you will be able to see in perspective the details you are accumulating.
- *Read first for general ideas.* When you are determining or arranging the general ideas of your subject, read your material to get the chief lines of argument and the conclusions reached in each book or article. In order to discover general principles quickly, read the introductory and summarizing passages and the topic sentences and note the organization and purpose of each paragraph.
- *Then read for details.* When your purpose is to find specific facts and when you already have in mind the general framework of the subject with which you are dealing, read closely in order to accumulate specific facts and details. As you read, ask yourself how these facts fit into your general outline.
- *Read for definitions and meanings.* Give particular attention to the differences in meanings attached to specific words by different authors; this

is especially important if you are reading in a field with which you are unfamiliar. In this way you will quickly become familiar with the concepts in the new field.

■   *Assert your own judgment as you read.* Constantly relate the arguments and ideas you encounter in your reading to your own experience and basic concepts. Check the source in the light of your own attitudes. This is what Emerson described as "creative reading." "When the mind is braced by labor and invention, the pages of whatever book we read become luminous with manifold allusion. Every sentence is doubly significant, and the sense of our author is as broad as the world."

Using the Library

In preparing your talks, learn how to find your way about the library. Know the most important books of reference, and how to find and make use of the appropriate magazines and newspapers. Have some idea of how to get at the immense fund of information in government documents; be alert to the possibility of using the many pamphlets issued by nongovernmental organizations; know where to find bibliographies; how to make convenient lists of references; how to read efficiently, and how to take notes.

The starting point, as you no doubt know, is to get a chart of the library—with its compartments for browsing, its general reading room, its government sections, its card files, its central desk where you will always get full cooperation and help.

With patience you will presently find yourself at home. Often the book you are interested in will be at the bindery or out on call or even lost. But your patience will help you to find substitutes. In using the card file, you will note whether the library uses the Dewey decimal system or the Library of Congress system, and you will consult a chart to spot the library location of the different categories. If possible you will saunter through the book stacks and browse among the books of your subject area.

The general steps described below constitute the procedure you should follow in getting library results for your proposed talk.[3]

■   *Consult standard references.* In the reference section of the library are encyclopedias, handbooks, and similar books of general and special information. These reference works are on the open shelves and are usually not to be taken from the library. They will provide an excellent starting point for research on almost any subject. In order to acquaint yourself with the wide variety of useful reference works, study Constance Winchell's *Guide to Reference Books.* This is the most complete guide to reference works available. Between editions, it is kept reasonably up to date with supplements.

---

[3]See Appendix B, "Sources of Information and Opinion."

Here are some of the reference works which you will probably be using most often:

1. *Encyclopedias.* First use the standard encyclopedias. Students sometimes search vainly for elementary material on a specific theme, forgetting that there is often ample information. Often it is not up to date. Information is readily available in encyclopedias such as the *Encyclopedia Britannica,* or *Encyclopedia Americana.*

2. *Special encyclopedias.* Special encyclopedias provide information in various fields. You may obtain helpful information from Seligman's *Encyclopedia of the Social Sciences* (fifteen volumes). For religious or philosophical material, you may refer to the *Catholic Encyclopedia,* the *Encyclopedia of Religion and Ethics,* the *Jewish Encyclopedia,* and the *Encyclopedia of Educational Research.*

3. *Yearbooks.* You will also find on the open shelves a collection of yearbooks which will supply up-to-date information on your subject. *The Americana Annual,* for example, gives a dependable survey of current events and biographical items for each year. Similarly useful are the *Britannica Book of the Year* (since 1917), the *New International Yearbook* (since 1907), and the *World Book Encyclopedia Annual* (since 1931). The *World Almanac* (since 1868) also has an astonishingly varied fund of information and an excellent index at the front. The *Statesman's Yearbook* (since 1864) and the *American Yearbook* (1910–1919, and since 1925) are likewise fruitful sources.

4. *Directories and biographical dictionaries.* You will frequently want to identify the authorities in the field in which you are working. Or perhaps you are planning to interview a member of your college faculty. Often you will find such people listed in *Who's Who in America, Who's Who in American Education, Leaders in American Education, American Men of Science,* or the *Directory of American Scholars.* For prominent Americans of other years see *Who Was Who in America* or the excellent general biographical source, the *Dictionary of American Biography* (1928–1937, twenty volumes), edited by John Allen and Dumas Malone, or the *National Cyclopedia of American Biography* (twenty-six volumes, publication begun in 1892). *Current Biography* gives biographies of people featured in the current press. See also *Webster's Biographical Dictionary* and *Biography Index; A Quarterly Index to Biographical Material in Books and Magazines.*

5. *Special references on current problems.* An important source for materials on current problems is the *Reference Shelf Series,* in which about ten issues appear each year. Included in this series is *Representative American Speeches,* an annual collection.

6. *Bibliographies of bibliographies.* Often, one of the most efficient means for locating the basic writings on a topic is to use one of the reference works which lists bibliographies. The most comprehensive bibliography of bibliographies published in English is Theodore Besterman's *A World*

Bibliography of Bibliographies. Another excellent one for recent topics because it is published semiannually is *Bibliographic Index: A Cumulative Bibliography of Bibliographies.*

■ *Consult Magazines.* Periodical literature on every subject is available in quantity. Familiar to most college students are the semiliterary news and "opinion" magazines, such as *Time, Newsweek, The Atlantic Monthly, Fortune, Harper's Magazine, The Nation, National Geographic Magazine, New Republic, Saturday Review,* and *United States News.*

A large crop of magazines, largely publishing condensed material from other publications, grew up in the United States in the 1930s. One of the most widely read of this group is *The Reader's Digest.* Others are *Science Digest, Religious Digest, Current Digest,* and *Magazine Digest.*

A magazine unique in its function is *Vital Speeches of the Day,* a fortnightly that publishes without comment recent American speeches.

In the field of education the *Speech Teacher, American Scholar, School and Society, English Journal,* and many others will prove helpful. In economics and business, the *American Economic Review, Barron's Weekly Financial World, Monthly Labor Review, Nation's Business,* to mention a few examples, are in most libraries. In sociology, *Survey Graphic, American Journal of Sociology,* and many others are available. In the fields of government, law, and current history there are such magazines as the *American Political Science Review, Annals of the American Academy of Political and Social Science, Current History, Current Events and Foreign Affairs.*

■ *Consult newspapers.* Although a considerable number of mediocre newspapers exist in America, there are many papers of high merit and good reputation. Some of these you will consult both for recent news and for background information, which are often contained in feature articles. *The New York Times,* for example, contains a great deal of information, as its index shows. Other important papers are *Christian Science Monitor, Washington* (D.C.) *Post, St. Louis Post-Dispatch, Louisville Courier-Journal, Des Moines Register, New Orleans Picayune, Minneapolis Star, Omaha Bee, Denver Post, San Francisco Chronicle,* and *Los Angeles Times.*

■ *Consult government documents.* Either through your library or, in some cases, by direct correspondence with the Superintendent of Documents in Washington, you can obtain various kinds of government reports and speeches providing accurate and authoritative materials. For example, the Statistical Abstract of the United States, published annually by the U.S. Bureau of Foreign and Domestic Commerce, is a "summary of authoritative statistics showing trends in trade and industry, as well as social progress." It presents figures on area, population, education, finances, wages, and a wide range of other subjects. The *Commerce Yearbook* gives detailed information about business conditions in the United States. *Commerce Reports* and the *Monthly Labor Review* are useful monthly surveys. There are many kinds of congressional documents, including reports of congressional committee hearings, which are useful for many political and current-affairs subjects. You may need the help of your librarian in finding such reports in your library or in ordering them, but the *Monthly Catalog of United States Government Publications* with a cumulative index published each ten years should be helpful.

The most important government document for speech students is without question the *Congressional Record,* which presents the proceedings of the House and Senate. It is issued daily, with fortnightly indexes.

■   *Consult private organizations.* More than 25,000 organizations in the United States publish proceedings, reports, journals, yearbooks, bulletins, monographs, and pamphlets of great value to students. Much of this material can be secured free or at a nominal cost by writing to the organization that publishes it. Much of it can be found in libraries. (See the latest issue of the *World Almanac* for the addresses of several hundred "Associations and Societies in the United States.") Typical of these organizations are the following:

American Federation of Labor and Congress of Industrial Organizations, Washington, D.C.
American Farm Bureau Federation, Chicago, Illinois.
American Medical Association, Chicago, Illinois.
National Association of Manufacturers, New York, New York.

The reading room, Library and Museum of Performing Arts, Lincoln Center, New York.
Alison Ames, New York Public Library.

■   *Obtain copies of radio and television broadcasts.* Many interviews, talks, and discussions are presented over radio and television. Some are printed and may be obtained at a nominal cost. Your own tape recordings of radio and television talks can be helpful.

■   *Prepare a Bibliography or List of References.* If you intend to spend several hours reading in preparation for a speech of ten or fewer minutes, make use of bibliographical sources, including indexes, in order to avoid hours of partially wasteful rambling through stray books and articles. Using these sources, prepare a working list of references of your own. Your list will not be an elaborate bibliography, but it should be selective, accurately recorded, and thorough within the limits of your subject. Your list should include (1) important bibliographies of the subject, (2) books, (3) magazines, (4) pamphlets and reports, and (5) newspapers.

1.   *Start with bibliographies.* Ask your reference librarian for the cumulative *Bibliographic Index,* each cumulative yearly edition of which includes more than four thousand bibliographies on numerous subjects. One or more of the items on your list should be the bibliography or bibliographies already available. Your own list will be more recent and better adapted to your immediate topic.

2.   *Use the Cumulative Book Index* (successor to the United States Catalog), which contains a record of almost every book published in the United States. A quick survey of recent numbers will at once suggest pertinent titles. *The Book Review Digest,* with its condensed review of recent books, also offers a convenient source of worthwhile book publications.

3.   *Consult the library card files for additional book sources.*

4.   *Refer to periodicals.* The special indexes will help you. *The Readers' Guide to Periodical Literature* is well known (or should be) to every college student. Refer also to special indexes, such as *Social Sciences and Humanities Index, Business Periodicals Index, Agricultural Index, Art Index, Education Index, Index to Legal Periodicals, Index Medicus,* and *Public Affairs Information Service.* These indexes are sometimes in the appropriate departmental library rather than in the general reference room. Also of value to college students is the Vertical File Service, an index of pamphlets and other ephemeral material.

5.   *Consult government documents.* Examine the indexes to the *Congressional Record* and perhaps the *Catalogue of Public Documents.* You will probably need the help of the librarian in locating these indexes.

6.   *List a few references from recent newspapers.* (*The New York Times Index* will help.)

7.   *List your bibliographic references systematically.* Use cards or slips of paper so that you can sort your items systematically, placing only one item on each card or slip. Classify the list into sections, such as (a) books, (b) magazines, (c) newspapers, and (d) pamphlets. For books and pamphlets,

include the author's last name, his first name or initials, the exact title of the book, the volume number or edition number if there has been more than one, the name of the publisher, and the place and date of publication. For example:

Anderson, Dorothy, and Waldo W. Braden, editors, *Lectures Read to the Seniors in Harvard College by Edward T. Channing.* Southern Illinois University Press, Carbondale, 1968.

For periodicals and newspapers, list (usually in this order) author's name, the title of the article, the title of the periodical, the volume and pages, the date:

Riesman, David, "The Search for Alternative Models in Education," *The American Scholar,* 38:377–388, Summer 1969.

Note the following sample of bibliographical items on the subject, "Should the colleges and universities outlaw student protests involving violence?"

Boffey, P. M., "Campus Unrest: Riots Bring Danger of Punitive Backlash," *Science,* 164:161–165, April 11, 1969.
Mitchell, J. N., "Colleges Must Outlaw Terror; Excerpts from Address, May 1, 1969," *U.S. News,* 66:75, May 12, 1969.
"Hesburgh's Law: The Problems of Campus Secular or Catholic," *Commonweal,* 89:719–720, March 14, 1969; "Reply," W. J. Wilson, 90:151, April 18, 1969.
"Joint Commission on University Life," *School & Society,* 97:204, April 1969.
"Rebels, Amnesty and Property," *Christian Century,* 86:807, March 5, 1969; "Discussion," 86:600, April 23, 1969.
"Nixon, R. M., "To Stop Campus Violence; Excerpts from Remarks," April 29, 1969, *U.S. News,* 66:74, May 12, 1969.
"Universities: A New Balance of Power; Change at Harvard," *Time,* 93:42, April 25, 1969.
Miles, M., "Whose University?" *New Republic,* 160:17–19, April 12, 1969; "Reply with Rejoinder," D. Bell, 160:30–31, May 3, 1969.
Brustein, R., "Whose University? The Case of Professionalism," *New Republic,* 160:16, April 26, 1969.

Taking Notes

Your final step in collecting ideas and details for your speech is to take notes on what you read. Students are often tempted to eschew the whole mechanical process of note taking as a bore and a waste of time; others are ultraconscientious copyists who put down almost everything. Reliance on your memory is unwise if you wish to accumulate and classify many details. Indiscriminate reproduction is also unfortunate because it hinders your grasp of general principles. A sensible procedure is somewhat as follows:

1. Use cards or papers of a uniform size. Notebooks are inconvenient if you intend to shuffle the items into any order.
2. Aim to get the gist of an idea or an article.
3. Place one fact on a card.
4. Tag each card at the top with the topic or division under which the statement or fact falls.
5. Cite at the bottom of the card the exact source. Be accurate and complete in the citation. You will later appreciate your meticulousness here.
6. Quote accurately, but avoid long quotations.

Specimen Note Card

Communication and
Persuasion Research

Communication and persuasion research is still in an embryonic stage . . . But interest will be reflected in progress toward the laws that link communication variables with the persuasion process.

Gerald R. Miller, "Communication and Persuasion Research: Current Problems and Prospects," Quarterly Journal of Speech, 54: 269–276, October 1968.

---

7. In the main, note facts rather than general opinions.
8. Establish a general scheme for your reading and for the classification of your notes. Begin with a plan which you can modify later.
9. Write legibly.

The purpose of this chapter is to provide you with guides to finding suitable materials for your talks. Only when you have something of significance to tell your audiences can you justly lay claim to their time and attention. Your preparation for purposeful and worthwhile speech making will include reflective thinking, reading, and discussion of your topic.

Projects and Problems

PROJECT 1:   At your next classroom or other campus lecture, take notes and concentrate closely on the speaker, according to the suggestions in this chapter. Be prepared to repeat as accurately as you can in a four-minute talk the essentials of that lecture. (You may substitute any public lecture given on the campus.)

PROJECT 2:   Interview a faculty member on a special topic chosen by you. Make a five-minute classroom talk in which you give the essence of that interview. Follow the suggestions for interviewing given in this chapter.

PROJECT 3:   Read an entire book or an extended article in a recent magazine. Present to the class a brief summary and interpretation of the book or article. In your reading, follow the suggestions in this chapter.

PROJECT 4:   Prepare a list of references in cooperation with three of your colleagues. Select a controversial subject that calls for recent references. Include at least one reference from a printed bibliography, at least five from recent books, at least five from representative magazines, at least two or three from a representative daily newspaper, at least five from documents. The entire list should comprise some twenty or thirty references and should be prepared according to the suggestions in this chapter. Submit your list to your instructor for criticism and then have it mimeographed for use by the entire class.

PROJECT 5:   Select a subject which requires library reading but which is limited in scope. Get your instructor's approval of your topic. You may decide to use the subject of the bibliography you prepared for project 4 above. Take at least twenty systematic notes from several sources, according to the suggestions in this chapter. Be prepared to submit your notes for criticism and inspection by your instructor and by two or three of your classmates appointed for this purpose.

Retain your references and notes: they may be supplemented and used later in your more extended talks.

References

Adler, Mortimer, *How to Read a Book.* New York: Simon & Schuster, Inc., 1940.

Aldrich, Ella V., *Using Books and Libraries,* rev. ed. Englewood Cliffs, N.J.: Prentice-Hall, Inc., 1946.

Barzun, Jacques, and Henry Graff, *The Modern Researcher.* New York: Harcourt, Brace & World, Inc., 1957. Chapter 1.

Brigance, W. Norwood, *Speech.* New York: Appleton-Century-Crofts, 1952. Chapter 10.

Bryant, Donald C., and Karl R. Wallace, *The Fundamentals of Public Speaking,* 3rd ed. New York: Appleton-Century-Crofts, 1960. Chapter 6.

Crowell, Laura, *Discussion: Method of Democracy.* Chicago: Scott, Foresman and Co., 1963, Chapter 4.

Ehninger, Douglas, and Wayne Brockriede, *Decision by Debate.* New York: Dodd, Mead and Co., 1963. Chapters 4 to 6.

Nichols, Ralph G., and Thomas R. Lewis, *Listening and Speaking.* Dubuque, Iowa: William C. Brown, 1954. Chapters 1 and 3.

Nichols, Ralph G., and Leonard A. Stevens, *Are You Listening?* New York: McGraw-Hill Book Company, Inc., 1957.

"The material furnished by the sense is constantly wrought into symbols." Suzanne Langer.

thought in speech communication

Function of Thought in Speech

Speech and its message are primarily concerned with ideas. Although we do not dismiss the affective or emotional-imaginative qualities that are always present in informative-persuasive oral exchange, we assume that thought is the key to all worthwhile communication. As Norwood Brigance, a contemporary authority in speech, stated:

Reason's basic use, then, is to show men how to fulfill their needs and how to solve tough problems. If Reason be man's newest and weakest intellectual achievement, it is also the extremely important one by which he climbed slowly, painfully, and with many backslidings, from slavery to civilization. Let there be no misunderstanding of its importance. Without the effective use of Reason, at least by a creative and dominant minority, no free society can maintain itself.[1]

The individual, we agree, is a "bundle of emotions" and the purist's concept of "man as a thinker" is misleading. Reaction is the product of complicated cognitive, affective, and motor activity. Some tendencies are primarily intellectual and logical; others are largely emotional. The assumption of most contemporary scholars of speech, nevertheless, is that communication is primarily a logical process; that haphazard behavior is minimal and is explained by man's prior experiences and his present needs.

His behavior is often the result of the interaction of his present perceptions (perhaps including the perception of your message) with those present needs and prior learning.

The Referent

The basis of all good communication lies in the experiences of the communicator with events, situations, "felt difficulties," and his reactions to "things." First is the speaking situation, the source of stimulation external to the sensory organs of the speakers or writers.

This stimulation continues within the organism. Once a sensory receptor has been stimulated, nerve currents follow along the spinal cord and

---

[1] William Norwood Brigance, *Speech: Its Techniques and Disciplines in a Free Society*, Appleton-Century-Crofts, New York, 1952, p. 147.

normally up through the base of the brain to the higher reaches of the cortex, out again along efferent tracts to muscles and glands.[2]

These contractions and secretions, further sensory stimulation reverberating to the cord and brain, effect further changes. This sensory reaction thus may come from immediate contact with "the thing itself" (the so-called "external object") or from earlier experiences that through recall are again vivified and made active.

Recall or memory is not only remarkable for this recording of sensory experiences, but also for using these traces to develop and produce original "abstract ideas."

In fact, how we make anything of our memory traces is one of the great mysteries of brain research. From the millions upon millions of mosaic patterns of traces tucked away in your head, you can at a moment's notice reassemble that particular set of traces which forms a particular scene. Years later you can reconstruct an image of the smashed car in your mind's eye. Apparently, you can play with the pieces of memory's mosaics. They seem to be universal apart, atoms of experience that can be put together in an enormous number of ways to form *new images* and *new ideas*.[3]

What are these facts that are the recordings directly or indirectly of stimuli, internal or external? They are the concrete or abstract materials out of which we try to interpret relationships or from which we try to draw conclusions. "They have to do with the existence of things, the occurrence of events, and the character of phenomena." They are the laboratory material assembled for experimental hypotheses. For the historians they are the record of careers and of local and national movements to be verified by every research means. Therefore, educators, psychologists, political scientists, microbiologists, and all others try to relate their thinking and utterances to facts.[4]

The modern world, increasingly pervaded by science, looks more and more to "facts" as the foundation of all exploration and scientific advance.

Thought and Reference

To "positivist" philosophers, semanticists, and many speech teachers and researchers, *fact* is that which deals with the thought-word-thing relationship.

The referent (*Ding an sich*), however we describe or assume it, is the source of stimulation. Through sensory reactions, including sound, sight,

---

[2] See Chapter Eight, "The Message."
[3] John Pfeiffer, *The Human Brain*, Pyramid Publications, New York, 1962, p. 95.
[4] See John Dewey, *How We Think*, D. C. Heath and Company, Boston, 1933, pp. 71–78, 91–101.

and temperature, we become aware of the original thing represented by the sign or symbol. According to Susanne Langer, the fact is "that which we conceive to be the source and context of the signs to which we react successfully."[5]

Between thought (or meaning) or ideas and the referent exists a relationship—direct or indirect. The connection between the sensory experience and the "ideas" may be direct, as when we react to a color, smell, or sound. Or the connection may be indirect, as when we refer to Franklin D. Roosevelt through a chain of situations, that is, between the word, the statements of the historians, the supplementary contemporary accounts, the testimony of those who saw and heard Roosevelt, and finally Roosevelt himself.[6]

We agree with Langer's interpretation of the evolution of thinking and ideas as being more than an echo of sense impressions. "Any attempt to formulate such principles as association by contiguity, or similarity soon runs into sheer unintelligible complication and artifice. Ideation proceeds by a more potent principle. . . . The material furnished by the sense is constantly wrought into symbols, which are elementary ideas."[7]

Thought, Language, and Symbolization

From initial sensory activity to communication are the channels that emerge as symbolization and language. As Langer puts it, "The basic need which certainly is obvious only in man, is the need of symbolization." Alfred Korzybski concludes: "Man's achievements rest upon the use of symbols."

Language is the most highly developed of the multitudinous forms of symbolism. Human beings seem to have the unique ability to make anything stand for other things. Language, by centuries of agreement, composed by lung, throat, teeth, lips and resonance channels, has become identified with specific needs, experiences, attitudes, and ways of living.[8]

These symbols, to be distinguished from the mental processes from which they spring, are, we hope, reflective of the "thinking" and "ideas" that they are supposed to represent. These terms, which theoretically hark back to "facts," may be only relative; they may or may not represent reality. The "facts" are no more certain than the testimony of those who vouch for them. The alleged information of today may become the myths of tomorrow. A new set of "truths" is to be created out of these symbols.

Every symbol, as is obvious, contains both intensional and extensional meaning. Language proclamations hardly work. "Not only does the literal

---

[5]Susanne Langer, *Philosophy in a New Key*, Mentor Books, New American Library of World Literature, Inc., New York, 1948–1962, p. 225.

[6]C. K. Ogden and T. A. Richards, *The Meaning of Meaning*, Routledge & Kegan Paul, London, 1953, p. 11.

[7]Langer, *op. cit.*, p. 46.

[8]See Chapter Twelve, "Verbal Systems of Communication."

word or term soon bulge with synonyms, metaphorical meanings, but specific designation becomes overcoated with suggestiveness."[9]

Thought and the Reflective Process in Communication

Inference is the ability to describe the activity between personal experiences, data, facts, region of the referent, and related phenomena. The process is the reflection or thinking region of the reference. The process of describing and evaluating the relationship between facts or the concepts in the region of the reference is that of reflection (cognitive reaction).

This movement from fact to fact or event to wider associations is often explained psychologically and logically as the experience of every human being in his attempt to adjust to his environment or to establish and maintain equilibrium in his world of ceaseless change. This perceptive quickening, early in the infant's development, is the inception and growth of reactions that are more than merely physiological activities of an animal organism. The incubation of mental discernment is early under way, labeled by psychologists and others as cognitive structure. It is the domain of the myriad recordings of information, experience, with mental discrimination that seems to accompany our life from the womb. The individual is thus adding experience and reactions. Man's primary concern is to fit the random and uncoordinated elements of his experience into patterns that are meaningfully consistent and predictable. This is the cognitive structure of the speaker and the frame of reference out of which he must operate.[10]

Representative Modes of Inference

Focusing on the broader relationships of these instances, particulars, testimony of witnesses, and incidents is the inferential activity of all who sooner or later have the urge and necessity to communicate.

The impelling motive may be curiosity, fear, or other primary reaction. John Dewey has described this process as "thinking." The reflection is grounded in perplexity and conflict. With no perplexities, Dewey would say, man is thoughtless. "Men do not, in their natural state, think when they have no troubles to deal with, no difficulties to overcome." This concept of thinking has led in modern psychology to consonance and cognitive dissonance learning and attitude change theories. Just as change brought about by personal problem solving has its beginning in a state of doubt, uneasiness, and conflict to be resolved, the communication intended to

---

[9]A. Craig Baird, *Rhetoric: A Philosophical Inquiry,* The Ronald Press Company, New York, 1965, p. 148.

[10]Cf. Hubert W. Ellingsworth and Theodore Clevenger, Jr., *Speech and Social Action,* Prentice Hall, Inc., Englewood Cliffs, N.J., 1968, p. 22. See also Chapter Twenty-one, "Persuasion: Cognitive Domain."

produce change must give attention to that dissonance in the listener's thinking which is perhaps necessary to get him to give any attention to your argument. The mental grappling with the problem and the more systematic examination of the way out are the design of thinking and the inferential procedure. The thinker's internal and external drives and the motivative activity thus quickened produce a chain reaction of reflective materials. The more specific reaction to phenomena is supplemented by an attempt to decipher the relatively unknown. This movement from the known to the unknown, the leap in the dark, is reflective inference. The representative modes of reasoning or inferring are: (1) specific instances and details leading to generalization, (2) analogy, (3) causal relations, (4) authority, and (5) other types.[11]

This relationship of referent, reference, and symbol (an expansion of the Ogden-Richards diagram) may be indicated somewhat as follows (note that each category overlaps the others and that the process is unitary):

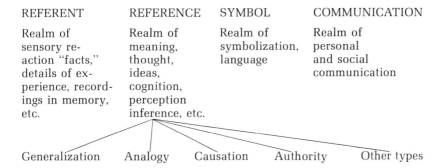

REFERENT	REFERENCE	SYMBOL	COMMUNICATION
Realm of sensory re-action "facts," details of ex-perience, record-ings in memory, etc.	Realm of meaning, thought, ideas, cognition, perception inference, etc.	Realm of symbolization, language	Realm of personal and social communication

Generalization   Analogy   Causation   Authority   Other types

Thought and Analysis in Communication

Inception and systematic development of thought in communication can be helped by preliminary analysis of the field or area to be presented. Aristotle in his treatment of rhetorical thought stressed invention of argument by the method of *topoi,* "lines of argument." Some of these inquiries had to do with the analysis of audiences, attributes, and attitudes such as love, hatred, justice, happiness, fear, and benevolence. Other topics or inquiries concentrated on the more specific subject matter of the speech itself, as economic, social, historical, or scientific content.[12]

Though the Aristotelian applications of *topoi* are artificial and limited, the principles of systematic analysis are helpful in any analysis of communicative subject matter. Typical of these questions for analysis are those concerning the chronological, spatial, definitional, logical, problem-solution,

---

[11]For details of logical methods, see Chapter Twenty-one.
[12]*The Rhetoric of Aristotle,* trans. Lane Cooper, Appleton-Century-Crofts, New York, 1932, Book 2.

and psychological approaches. The problem-solution method, for example, has been that of "stock issues," often applied by debaters, discussants, and other students of controversial speaking and writing.

For a detailed treatment of analysis and thought in communication, see Chapter Twenty-one, especially the section, "Analysis of the Specific Problem."

Conclusion

In conclusion, each of the methods of inference may be used with equal effectiveness in each of the distinct types of speeches that inform, convince, move to action, and entertain. Obviously, the devices used in exposition are mainly definition, particulars, and instances. In argumentative and persuasive speeches, instances, statistics, analogies, cause-and-effect sequences, and testimony are frequently used. Speeches in which entertainment is an important purpose make use of concrete details, short narratives, anecdotes, quotations, and references to the speaker, the audience, and the occasion. But no particular type monopolizes any of these modes of treatment. The various forms of development outlined in this chapter by no means exhaust the list. You may add others, or you may suggest a somewhat different grouping of these elements. The methods here stressed are those which effective communicators have long used. If your talk is to be comparatively free from unsupported assertions, from vague thinking, and from dull, uninteresting treatment, you will develop your ideas by these concrete, particular, factual, and analogical and causative techniques.

Projects and Problems

PROJECT 1: The development of a talk by the use of specific facts and figures.

Purposes of this assignment: To study and apply the use of facts and figures as the main material in the development of a speech.

Procedure: You will concentrate on figures and specific facts as the backbone of your three-, four-, or five-minute talk. Cite on the margin of your outline the exact source of your figures. For statistical examples, consult the bulletins of learned societies (e.g., *Speech Monographs*, for facts concerning experimental data in speech studies), the *Congressional Record*, speeches as reported in *Vital Speeches of the Day*, or elsewhere.

Subjects for this speech:

1. The trend in the stock market will probably be upward (or downward).
2. We are in for a period of inflation (or deflation).
3. College student enrollment has been steadily increasing and will continue to do so.
4. The Medicare program assures improvement in American health.

PROJECT 2:   The development of a speech by the use of comparison and contrast.

Purposes of this assignment: To study and apply the use of comparison (including analogies) and contrast as the main material for your speech.

Procedure: Proceed as in Project 1. Stress analogies and contrasts.

PROJECT 3:   The development of a speech through incidents and authorities.

Purpose of this assignment: To study and apply the use of incidents and testimony by authorities in the development of your speech.

Procedure: Proceed as in the projects above. Incorporate as the main elements of this speech either incidents, anecdotes, questions, authorities, or some combination of these methods. Be sure to limit the subject.

Subjects for this speech (any other subject to be chosen):

1.   The argument for ending the ghettos.
2.   Franklin D. Roosevelt was a "great speaker."
3.   We are heavily influenced by environment.
4.   The spirit of intolerance is rising in the United States.
5.   My experience in Alaska.
6.   English as a universal language.
7.   American cities 100 years from now.
8.   If I were a Communist.
9.   If I were a labor leader.
10. Is the American university obsolete?
11. Americans are succumbing to the "mass mind."
12. National advertising methods should be condemned.
13. Is black power to be supported?
14. Are Americans unduly conservative?
15. Has the church a future?

References

Brigance, William Norwood, *Speech: Its Techniques and Disciplines in a Free Society.* New York: Appleton-Century-Crofts, Inc., 1952. Chapter 9.

Burtt, Edwin Arthur, *Right Thinking.* New York: Harper and Brothers, 1946. Pages 3–16, 17–30, 289–315.

Columbia Associates in Problems of Philosophy: An Introduction to Reflective Thinking. New York and Boston: Houghton Mifflin Company, 1923.

Creelman, Marjorie B., *The Experimental Investigation of Meaning.* New York: Springer Publishing Company, 1966.

Kallen, Horace M., *The Philosophy of William James.* New York: Modern Library, 1925. Chapter 4, "How We Know."

Langer, Susanne, *Philosophy in a New Key.* New York: Mentor Books, 1962.

Larrabee, Harold A., *Reliable Knowledge,* rev. ed. Boston: Houghton Mifflin Company, 1964.

Mill, John Stuart, *System of Logic.* New York: Longmans Green, 1872. Book III, Chapter 9.

Ogden, C. K., and T. A. Richards, *The Meaning of Meaning.* London: Routledge and Kegan Paul, 1923. Chapters 1 to 3.

Robinson, J. H., *The Mind in the Making.* New York: Harper and Brothers, 1921. Pages 40ff.

Thonssen, Lester, A. Craig Baird, and Waldo W. Braden, *Speech Criticism,* 2nd ed. New York: Ronald Press, 1970. Chapter 12, "Integrity of Ideas."

ΔΗΜΟΣΘΕΝΗΣ

Mburg sculp

Demosthenes. Athenian orator. BC 385–322.

organization and outlining

The organization of ideas in the speech message serves several basic functions. First, patterns of organization enable you to shape your materials for their better adjustment to your audience. Second, such structural design will help your listeners to understand and better appreciate your message.

The major function of organization is that it offers the best preparation for any discourse. Much of the meaning we would communicate, as well as the meaning others derive from our communication, involves the process of categorizing our thoughts.[1] One sequence of main ideas sometimes conveys a different meaning from another.

Your categories of ideas must represent the essence of your subject. You arrange material to achieve a particular emphasis. Your organization provides an opportunity to pretest your logic, for it can help you to see the relationship of the details you select to your purpose. It can also help you to control the relative amount of time devoted to each part of your speech. Organizing gives you a chance to consider psychological implications and to select points and lines of development in light of probable audience interpretation. It is also a time to make decisions about the style of your speech. The style to be used may determine your organization.

A clear framework will aid you in recalling your ideas and will increase your fluency. It may also enhance your credibility as a speaker. Audiences respond more completely to speeches that are organized. The well-structured speech holds attention and helps listeners to comprehend more easily.[2]

A reader of the previous edition of this book reminds us that the less motivated the audience, the more important is organization. According to this reader and the communication research which has been done on organization, "For an audience that has little motivation, arousing their

---

[1] See Jerome S. Bruner, Jacqueline J. Goodnow, and George A. Gustin, *Study of Thinking,* John Wiley and Sons, Inc., New York, 1966; R. G. Smith, "Effects of Speech Organization upon Attitudes of College Students," *Speech Monographs,* 18:292–301, 1951.

[2] The testimony that audience reaction is more favorable to well-structured materials than to the unorganized ones is overwhelming. See, for example, E. Thompson, "An Experimental Investigation of the Relative Effectiveness of Organizational Structure in Oral Communication," *Southern Speech Journal,* 26:59–69, 1960; and F. H. Knower, "Studies in the Organization of Speech Material," *Journal of Educational Research,* 39:220–230, 1945. Cf. Raymond H. Wheeler and Francis T. Perkins, *Principles of Mental Development,* T. Y. Crowell, New York, 1932, pp. 292–296.

interest and their felt need for the information that you have to present must be done immediately. For most audiences, especially one which is well educated or which disagrees with your position, a two-sided message is more effective than a one-sided one. Two-sided messages have the additional advantage of 'inoculating' the audience against counterpersuasion."

So important did the classical rhetoricians regard organization that they stressed it as one of the five major components of oral communication: *inventio, dispositio, elocutio, memoria,* and *pronunciatio.*

Aristotle conceived *dispositio* as principally planned adaptation to the audience and the speech. To him the essential "parts" of the speech were thesis and proof. He treated briefly poem, statement, epilogue, but stressed chiefly the principles of adaptation. He advised the selection, the order, and adaptation of materials of the speech be made in view of the audience, subject, speaker, and opponent.[3]

To Cicero, *dispositio* was the adapting of the product of *inventio* to a particular situation. He discussed the grouping of ideas in the natural order but stressed that the construction of each speech should be determined by the specific audience problems involved.[4]

Dispositio involves the selection of materials, their arrangement, and their proportion. These are governed by matters of the speech situation and by the variable conditions involved.

Concept of Organization

What is the concept behind this second part of ancient rhetoric? Organization comes closest to a satisfactory translation and modern interpretation, but the connotation also implies commitment to plan or outline.

According to Russell Wagner, *dispositio* means "the functional selection of and use of materials for a particular purpose." For him as well as the classical rhetoricians in general, *dispositio* is "planned adaptation." The audience-adjustment factor determines (1) the selection of materials with the communicative ends in view and (2) their adaptation applied in the relevancy of materials, the order of their unfolding, and the massing of the points for impressiveness.[5]

Systematic steps in organization will guide you to an effective pattern of your ideas:

1. Decide upon the objective of your speech—the audience reaction you hope for.

---

[3]See Charles Baldwin, *Ancient Rhetoric and Poetic,* Macmillan, New York, 1924, p. 67.

[4]See Cicero, *De oratore,* trans. E. W. Sutton and H. Rackam, Heineman, London, 1942, vol. 1, pp. 436ff.

[5]See Russell H. Wagner, "The Meaning of Dispositio," in Herbert A. Wichelns (ed.), *Studies in Speech and Drama in Honor of Alexander Drummond,* Cornell University Press, Ithaca, N.Y., 1944, pp. 285–294.

2. Express your purpose in a topic or thesis sentence.
3. Divide your subject into a few main points.
4. Organize your material so as to ensure audience adaptation, unity, and the massing or emphasis of the points.
5. Organize the introduction to ensure orientation of your subject and the interest and attention of your audience.
6. Organize the main body so that you move forward from one aspect of your subject to another in a way that will be logical to your audience.
7. Organize the conclusion so that it reinforces your initial speaking purpose.

Selection

Selection, the process of choosing the ideas and their supports for the message, is the most difficult of the steps effecting satisfactory division or organization. The starting point here, as in dealing with other aspects of communication, is that of *audience analysis.* Your identification with your audience and the occasion becomes a major determinant of what should be included and what excluded or expanded.

Selection is also aided by a clear-cut *thesis* or statement that embodies both your overall idea and your more specific aim of informing or persuading. Your thesis should be sufficiently definite to guide properly every step in preparation.

The discovery and selection of materials to illuminate and enforce certain speaking purposes constitute analysis or division of the discourse.

After audience analysis and the framing of a clear-cut thesis, the next step is the focusing on essential questions (or topics framed as sentences) to which the general thesis relates.

The final step is the selection for actual communication from this deposit of relevant ideas. Only questions of major concern are to be included.[6]

This process of selection based on analysis involves close scrutiny of each argument or idea to be treated. A prediction of audience reaction at every turn of the ideas and the determination of what is important and what is relatively irrelevant are essential.

Proportion

The aim of proportion is to set out the most important ideas and parts so that the listener or reader can properly appreciate their relative importance and react, presumably favorably, to the communicator's purposes. The rhetorical aim is to secure impressiveness and stronger retention.

Proportion, as a principle of disposition (structure), is partly a matter of ■ *position.* What is presented at the beginning or end is generally more easily remembered than what is here and there included. The trained speaker will

---

[6]See Chapters Ten and Twenty-one on thought.

place at the beginning ideas or information of major importance to the success of his theme. These preliminaries may comprise a somewhat formal explanation of the plan of treatment, a fairly complete statement of the purpose of the speech or article. Proportion calls for an impressive beginning. The end should also be couched impressively. Summaries and restatements add to a satisfactory proportion. However, the tendency of some speakers or writers to overexpand the final section may cancel the maximum effect of such endings.

■   The other half of proportion is *space*. We tend to be most impressed by what a good speaker talks chiefly about. What is held before the attention longest should penetrate further than that which is briefly revealed. Thus repetition of ideas through explanation, illustration, logical detail, comparison, contrast, and other methods will help these important concepts to be relatively impressive.

Obviously, as we have said, selection and proportion are interacting and overlapping processes. What is important enough to be included and which of the included ideas need the most space and position are problems that concern adjustment to the needs and behavior of the audience.

Order or Arrangement

The problem of arrangement is one of handling the discourse in general and that of proper ordering of the various parts of the message. What is the best order for a speech in general to follow?

Classical Approaches

Speeches, as teachers often have reminded us, should have at least three well-defined divisions or parts: an introduction, a main body, and a conclusion. Plato, in the fourth century B.C., stated that a speech should have a beginning, middle, and end. It should be put together like "a living creature." Aristotle, also of the fourth century B.C., stated that ideally a speech should have only two parts: (1) statement of the case and (2) proof of it. Usually, however, as he explained, a speech should contain (1) an introduction, (2) statement of the case, (3) central idea, (4) partition of main points, (5) proof or refutation, and (6) peroration or conclusion. This elaborate division applied to courtroom pleas. Modern rhetoricians have reverted to the simple structure suggested here, with recognition of subdivisions that somewhat echo the classical Roman approach.[7]

---

[7] See Lester Thonssen, A. Craig Baird, and Waldo W. Braden, *Speech Criticism,* 2nd ed., The Ronald Press Company, New York, 1970, Chap. 15, "The Structure of Oral Discourse"; Donald K. Darnell, "The Relation between Sentence Order and Comprehension," *Speech Monographs,* 30:97–100, 1963; Halbert E. Gulley and David Berlo, "Effect of Intercellular and Intracellular Speech Structure on Attitude Change and Learning," *Speech Monographs,* 23:288–298, 1956.

The simple distinction of parts here recommended parallels the steps you as speaker take. First you will introduce yourself and your ideas to the group; gain attention; establish need; provide an eleboration on your ideas so that they are established and emphasized; finally, climax the whole with a summary or appeal. The creation of goodwill for the speaker and his thinking is the aim of the introduction. The successive marshaling of the ideas to be implanted is the work of the main body. The effort to consolidate these impressions makes up the conclusion.

Rhetorica ad Herrenium, published about A.D. 86 by an unknown author, provided a pattern of speech during the days of Cicero. According to this source, invention was developed in six divisions of the speech: *exordium, narratio, divisio, confirmatio, confutatio,* and *conclusio.*[8]

Other writers have proposed as many as nine parts. Whatever the number used, as we have suggested, would be strongly related to the type of discourse and the occasion.

Modern Approaches

■ John Dewey proposed the *problem-solution* approach to organization. To him, the pattern included in successive steps: attention getting, statement of the problem, possible solutions, the best solution, and action to implement the solution.[9] This formula is helpful both in preparing for persuasive communication, and with some modifications for almost every other type of speech communication.

■ Alan Monroe, another contemporary, has developed a plan of organization, the *motivated sequence,* which has been widely applied by students of communication. It is based on five parts: gaining attention, showing the need, presenting the solution, visualizing the results, and requesting action or approval. This approach strongly resembles the Dewey proposal. It also reflects the salesmanship method, often suggested in manuals on selling, in which the need step is enforced by the fulfillment or satisfaction and the "closing of the sale."

What is the relation of the Dewey and Monroe structures to the conventional introduction, body, and conclusion divisions? The standard introduction includes the attention step; the main body develops need, solution, and visualization of results; and the conclusion is the action step.

■ Another general format for a discourse begins with *specific examples or cases* which are *contrasted with generalizations or principles* of the message. Often a speech is more interesting and less likely to arouse negative attitudes if the concrete elements are first presented and the more contro-

---

[8] Cf. Augustus S. Wilkins, *M. Tulli Ciceronis "De oratore,"* 3rd ed., Clarendon Press, Oxford, 1890–93, vol. 1, pp. 56–64. Cf. Baird, *Rhetoric,* op. cit., pp. 176ff.
[9] See John Dewey, *How We Think,* pp. 71–78, 91–101.

versial sections or the persuasive ends are unfolded later.[10] This is especially important with an audience that is initially unfamiliar with or opposed to your proposals.

In such cases, the listeners and observers are more likely to listen and absorb the specific illustrations, with the later implications gradually deduced. Thomas Huxley began a lecture on "a piece of chalk," by dwelling on the composition of chalk and its origin in the sea bottom off the cliffs of South England. Huxley moved from this concrete informational approach to his final position, that of the evolution of the universe.

Less antagonism is aroused if this method of unfolding is followed. Its limitations are that this movement from the familiar and concrete stage to that of the more controversial conclusions often takes time. You cannot effectively present the conclusions until the negative or neutral listeners accept and understand your illustrations.

■ Still another format is that of following a *climax order,* beginning with the least important arguments and following through with the most important. Research indicates that the climax order is more effective when the issue is familiar to the audience and one about which they have great concern. The anticlimax order is more effective where the topic is unfamiliar and the audiences are uninterested.[11]

Specific Methods of Arrangement

Organization should stem from a careful analysis of the audience and your topic. Knowing how you will organize your speech will be especially helpful in the selection, classification, and proportioning of materials as you assemble them into an orderly whole. The organizational patterns presented below reflect this analytical approach. The use of any one of them depends much on the purpose of the speech, the character of the audience, the occasion, and to a considerable degree the type of content normally assembled in view of these rhetorical purposes and conditions. The patterns are not independent, of course, and you may find it valuable at times to use a combination of patterns in a single speech.

■ *Time Order.* In the time-order pattern, the message items are arranged in chronological sequence—past to present or present to future, or in some case a reverse time order may be appropriate.

---

[10] See Jane Allyn and Leon Festinger, "The Effectiveness of Unanticipated Persuasive Communications," *Journal of Abnormal and Social Psychology,* 62:36–40, 1961; Judson Mills and Elliott Gronson, "Opinion Change as a Function of the Communicator's Attractiveness and Desire to Influence," *Journal of Personality and Social Psychology,* 1:173–177, 1965; Judson Mills and Elliott Aronson, "Desire to Influence and Liking for the Audience," *Journal of Experimental Social Psychology,* 2:152–159, 1966.
[11] See H. A. Sponberg, "A Study of the Relative Effectiveness of Climax and Anti-Climax Order in an Argumentative Speech," *Speech Monographs,* 13:25–44, 1946.

- *Topographical or Space Order.* Topographical or space order means that the materials are arranged according to some pattern of space—from near to far, local to national, bottom to top, front to rear, inside to outside, and so on. This method is more often used in descriptive narrative than in argument or exposition. During the flight to the moon of Apollo XI in July, 1969, the daily accounts were largely those of successive distances traversed to and from the earth, each step including the lapses.

- *Classification Order.* The classificational or topical pattern calls for grouping under economic, literary, scientific, religious, political, social, educational, or other categories. For example, speech is highly important in contemporary American life. It promotes political cohesion and progress. It facilitates social intercourse and experiences. It stimulates economic activities. Thus, a speech about speech could be organized on the basis of these topics, with a section devoted to expanding upon each of these reasons that oral discourse is important.

- *Causal Sequence.* The causal order or development traces causes and/or results to a given agent, situation, or condition. Chapter Twenty-one gives detailed treatment of such logical methods. Most argumentative talks use some variation of the causal sequence. The Dewey analysis, mentioned above, focuses on the conditions calling for a change (the bad situation and the possible disastrous results if unchecked, and the beneficial results if a given solution is presented). The following argument, for example, employs a causal sequence: Violence in Chicago at the time of the Democratic National Convention there in 1968 adversely affected national support for that party in the November, 1968 election. The alleged causes of that violence lay in unemployment, popular opposition to the continuing Vietnam war, social, economic, and political discrimination against minority races, and resentment of the power of the political establishment of that city. The alleged results of the violence, if uncurbed, would have been the deterioration of interracial forbearance and progress. The immediate results were deterioration of interracial cooperation, further defiance of police power, and further abandonment of loyalty to the Democratic party.

- *Problem Solution.* The problem-solution pattern is practically identical with the causal. It simply puts more emphasis on the comparison of possible solutions and the advocacy of one. In addition, it may develop conditions that threaten sound solutions.

- *The Psychological Method.* Here the organization is governed mainly by the speaker's analysis of the motivations of the hearers. All discourse, as we have stated repeatedly, should be guided by the nature and needs of the audience. The psychological treatment, however, is more obviously adjusted directly to the fears, hopes, self-interests, and other drives and attitudes of those who listen. The unity and organization to be found in the speech are determined chiefly by this attention to dominant motivations. Woodrow Wilson, on his western tour in 1919, with his twenty-odd speeches in support of the League of Nations, used loose sequence of ideas and appeals, but a structure obviously linked with drives.

■   *Refutatory Method.* One other method of the speech development is that of almost pure refutation. The seasoned debater, for example, will make mental or other notes during an extended speech to be replied to. Though these points, as previously argued, may have full logical sequence, the rebuttalist will restate only those sections that to him are especially vulnerable.

Charles James Fox gained his reputation as "the world's greatest debater," in the British parliament of the late eighteenth century, by being a refutational speaker; his greatness lay in his skill at delivering immediate and extemporaneous denunciations of his opponents' positions. A more recent example occurred on September 6, 1969, when Senator Gale McGee of Wyoming in a television program replied to the arguments given a week before on the same program by former Senator Wayne Morse. McGee's arguments, a strong defense of America's involvement in South Vietnam, were delivered without much concern for the logical sequence of his speech as a whole.

The Introduction, Main Body, and Conclusion

How long or short should be the introduction? As we have indicated, such questions can be answered only by a careful analysis of the given audience, the immediate situation, including time limits, and the character and purpose of the discourse. For a brief talk (3 to 5 minutes) or one in which you extemporaneously find yourself part of a dialogue or panel, you will obviously hope to (1) establish good will between your auditors and yourself, (2) explain what your subject is or involves, and (3) make clear your theme and purpose. Your subject and purpose may on occasion need to be inductively and tactfully unfolded to audiences hostile to your proposed conclusions.

Enlisting Attention and Goodwill

Your initial job, as in all communicative situations, is to enlist the cooperation and response of the audience. This need applies equally to a face-to-face group and a radio or television audience. At the start your listeners may be preoccupied with other thoughts or activities, or they momentarily may be curious about you as an unknown talker; they may be bored with or indifferent to your topic, or they may be prejudiced against you because you are, say, a North Irish protestant or a sophomore recently jailed for participating in an illegal New Left demonstration. Cicero's advice to the young men of Rome was to "render auditors well-disposed, attentive, teachable." Whatever else these words may mean, they do demand that you somehow evoke directly from the group some response—hopefully a favorable one.

■ 1. *You may begin with a personal reference.* Note the personal start, mingled with humor, and statement of his subject by Fletcher Byrom, president of the Kopper Company, when he delivered his talk "Hang Loose" at the International Marketing Congress, American Marketing Association, Atlanta, Georgia, June 16, 1969:

> *My name, in case you missed it, is Fletcher Byrom. I am 50 years old and I am the chief executive officer of one of America's 200 largest corporations. So far as I know, I am in full possession of all my faculties. My doctor and my insurance counselor tell me I am in good physical condition. I think I can outhustle, out-talk and outwork any man in this room.*
>
> *Despite this, today I am thinking about the man who will be my successor. Not because anyone is pushing—not because I am getting any urgent internal alarms—but because I believe every chief executive, from the minute he moves into the big upstairs office, ought to be thinking about the fellow who will some day take his place. And that is the meat of what I want to discuss with you this afternoon.*
>
> *I won't pretend I don't know who the next boss at Koppers might be. But life is full of surprises. The man who succeeds me might be one of almost 1,400 people in our Pittsburgh headquarters. He might come from one of our 174 other locations. We have even been known to go outside our own organization, and the next chief at Koppers could conceivably be someone in this room. So please listen carefully, whoever you are out there.*[12]

■ 2. *You may begin by announcing the topic.* Robert S. Small, President of the Board of Trade and the Dan River Mills, opened his address before the New York Board on "Tell It Like It Is," on June 19, 1969, as follows:

> *I had two reasons for choosing as my topic: "Tell It Like It Is." One, it's the "in" thing to do, and if you don't believe me, visit any college campus (providing you have proper escort, of course), or ask your teenage child. Second, when you have the facts as the foundation for your story, why not "Tell It Like It Is?"*[13]

■ 3. *You may begin by referring to the importance of the occasion.* Chief Justice Earl Warren in the rotunda of the Capitol at Washington, D.C., on November 24, 1963, opened his address on the assassination of President John F. Kennedy two days previously, as follows:

> *There are few events in our national life that unite Americans and so touch the heart of all of us as the passing of a President of the United States. There is nothing that adds shock to our sadness as the assassination of*

---

[12]*Vital Speeches of the Day,* 30:604, July 15, 1969.
[13]*Vital Speeches of the Day,* 30:655, August 15, 1969.

*our leader, chosen as he is to embody the ideals of our people, the faith
we have in our institutions and our belief in the fatherhood of God and
the brotherhood of man.*

We are saddened; we are stunned; we are perplexed.[14]

Senator Edmund Muskie opened his address on "The Astronauts at the
Moon," at Jeffersonville, Indiana, on July 25, 1969, as follows:

*During most of the past two weeks, our people have been unified in a
way that only great moments of triumph or tragedy seem to produce.*

*In the affluent suburbs; in the steaming inner cities; in our troubled
universities, and in neighborhoods where the schools are inadequate and
overcrowded; in mountain and seashore resorts, and in homes where
families cannot afford a summer vacation; beside clear lakes, and on the
shores of polluted rivers; whether we were white or black, rich or poor,
young or old, supporters or critics of the war in Vietnam, Democrats or
Republicans, New Left or Old Right—the magnificent adventure of Apollo
XI gripped us all.*[15]

■ 4. *You may begin with a direct defense of your ideas and self.* Richard
M. Nixon began his nationwide radio and television apologia, "the Checker
speech," September 23, 1952, as follows:

*My fellow Americans: I come before you tonight as a candidate for
the vice-presidency and as a man whose honesty and integrity has been
questioned.*

*Now, the usual political thing to do when charges are made against you
is to either ignore them or to deny them without giving details. I believe
we have had enough of that in the United States, particularly with the
present Administration in Washington, D.C.*

*To me, the office of the vice-presidency of the United States is a great
office, and I feel that the people have got to have confidence in the integrity
of the men who run for that office and who might attain it.*

*I have a theory, too, that the best and only answer to a smear or to an
honest misunderstanding of the facts is to tell the truth. And this is why
I am here tonight. I want to tell you my side of the case.*[16]

■ 5. *You may begin with a humorous or mock-heroic reference.* Note the
opening of Governor Mark Hatfield's address at Philadelphia, May 27, 1964.

*A recent theater production carried the title, "Stop the World, I Want
to Get Off." From what I read about the national debates on foreign policy,
there are quite a number of Americans who wish it were possible.*

---

[14]*Congressional Record,* 109:21592, Nov. 25, 1963.
[15]*Congressional Record,* July 31, 1969, Appendix E 6515.
[16]A. Craig Baird, *Representative American Speeches,* H. W. Wilson Company, New
York, 1952–53, pp. 74–82.

> *For them, the title of a TV play of some years ago may provide the proper answer: "You Say Goodby But It Doesn't Go Away."*[17]

■ 6. *You may begin by citing a striking fact or giving a condensed narrative.* President Franklin D. Roosevelt on December 8, 1941, began his appeal to Congress for a declaration of war against Japan thus:

> *Yesterday, December 7, 1941—a date that will live in infamy—the United States of America was suddenly and deliberately attacked by the naval and air forces of the Empire of Japan.*[18]

Organization of the Body

If the introduction has been well designed and if the division of the subject, based upon the specific purpose, has been clearly done, the problem of organizing the main body of the speech is mostly taken care of. Your job is to state clearly the essential ideas or propositions that make up your subject division and to relate them to each other in the best order. First and last, you will continue to select and arrange these divisions with an eye to their acceptability to your listeners. Here too, selection, audience adaptations, order of development, and proposition of ideas are applied in detail as they were in the introduction.

■ *Selection of ideas.* You may wonder, in view of the audience and the limited time at your disposal, what two or three main points of your topic you should stress. It may be wisest to talk mostly about one point and to only illustrate others.

In the body of your talk you will continue to make clear your specific purpose. You will see that the statements or ideas representing your division of the subject are clearly enunciated throughout. You will not make the customary mistake of trying to cover everything in three minutes. Furthermore, you will insert enough repetitive, transitional, summarizing, and topic-introductory sentences to make the listener see the relevancy of the materials and the significance of your structure.

■ *Order.* Arrange your material and subject ideas in the order most appropriate for securing both logical sequence and audience acceptance. Refer again to your plans of analysis or division. You may use the chronological, topographical, definitional, logical, problem-solution, psychological, or other procedure.

The treatment thus may be that of the historian or biographer. Or the material may be developed according to space relations from the near to remote (report on the Apollo moon flight) the definitional method (what

---

[17] *Vital Speeches of the Day,* 30:533, June 15, 1964. By permission.
[18] A. Craig Baird (ed.), *American Public Addresses: 1740–1952,* McGraw-Hill Book Company, New York, 1956, p. 266.

is jazz? moonlighting?); classificational or topical (rhetoric draws on various areas of learning for its method and substance: 1. logic, 2. psychology, 3. language, 4. ethics, 5. literature); cause-and-effect method (urbanization of our society is steadily increasing: 1. the demand for industrial jobs is expanding; 2. mechanized farms and size of the agricultural units are increasing); the problem-solution method (the number of automobile deaths as a result of drinking drivers is increasing; the more rigid policy of can- celling driving licenses is necessary). Any one of these or any combination of methods may be used.

Induction, as we have said, seeks support for general hypotheses or assumptions. Deduction, though it uses premises as evidence, takes for granted that these, too, are checked and verified by inductive testing.

Will you proceed from the limited to the more general? It all depends. Often you gain your point by moving from several concrete items to a wider statement of principles until the logical goal is accepted. On the other hand, when you want your audience to accept a belief about a particular case, when your time is limited, and when your audience requires the most rigid logic, your treatment may well begin with the generalization.

The problem of selecting the order for presentation of topics constantly arises, and the relative importance and appeal of topics must be considered. Should the strongest proposition be placed first, last, or in a middle position? What of the climax and the anticlimax order?

In their investigation of speech structure in relation to attitude change, Gulley and Berlo concluded: "The best advice the rhetorician can give the speaker is that the climactic order seems slightly preferable. Yet, this advice must be qualified inasmuch as one can not 'guarantee' more effective results."[19]

It is impossible to answer the question of most effective order without an understanding of each audience and the specific requirements of the meeting.[20]

Organization of the Conclusion

The conclusion, like the beginning, may have a function other than that of adding to the listener's knowledge of the topic. The final sentence, or perhaps paragraph, should summarize what has been said, especially if your remarks have been rather complicated. If your subject matter is in special need of repetition, a somewhat longer summary may be in order—perhaps

[19]Gulley and Berlo, op. cit., p. 297.
[20]See Ray Ehrensberger, "An Experimental Study of the Relative Effectiveness of Certain Forms of Emphasis in Public Speaking," Speech Monographs, 21:94–111, 1945; L. W. Doob, "Effects of Initial Serial Position and Attitude upon Recall under Condi- tions of Low Motivation," Journal of Abnormal and Social Psychology, 48:199–205, 1953; Harold Sponberg, "The Relative Effectiveness of Climax and Anti-climax Order in an Argumentative Speech," Speech Monographs, 13:35–44, 1946.

a recapitulation in slightly different language. In general, good advice is for any speaker to stop when he is done.[21]

The function of the conclusion, however, is often more than making clear what has been said. You must also impress your speaking or listening colleagues and inspire them to action. Your conclusion may end with a challenge, an applicable quotation, a summary, a prophecy, an appeal, a series of questions, or other material and techniques to enforce your purpose. Examples of some of these types of conclusions follow:

■ 1. *Summary.* Note how Charles W. Eliot concluded his address on "Five American Contributions to Civilization":

> These five contributions to civilization—peace-keeping, religious toleration, the development of manhood suffrage, the welcoming of newcomers, and the diffusion of well being—I hold to have been eminently characteristic of our country, and so important, that, in spite of the qualifications and deductions which every candid citizen would admit with regard to everyone of them, they will ever be held in the grateful remembrance of mankind. They are reasonable grounds for a steady glowing patriotism. They have much to do, both with causes and as effects, with the material prosperity of the United States; but they are all five essentially moral contributions, being triumphs of reason, enterprise, courage, faith and justice, over passion, selfishness, inertness, timidity, and distrust. Beneath each one of these developments there lies a strong ethical sentiment, a strenuous moral and social purpose. It is for such work that multitudinous democracies are fit.[22]

■ 2. Prophecy. Martin Luther King, Jr., delivered this address at the Lincoln Memorial in Washington on August 8, 1963, before over 200,000 people who had come to the Capital in support of civil rights legislation. The conclusion:

> So let freedom ring—from the prodigious hilltops of New Hampshire, let freedom ring; from the mighty mountains of New York, let freedom ring—from the heightening Alleghenies of Pennsylvania!
> Let freedom ring from the snowcapped Rockies of Colorado!
> Let freedom ring from the curvaceous slopes of California!
> But not only that; let freedom ring from Stone Mountain of Georgia!
> Let freedom ring from Lookout Mountain of Tennessee!
> Let freedom ring from every hill and mole hill of Mississippi. From every mountainside, let freedom ring, and when this happens . . .
> When we allow freedom to ring, when we let it ring from every village and every hamlet, from every state and every city, we will be able to speed up that day when all of God's children, black men and white men, Jews and Gentiles, Protestants and Catholics, will be able to join hands and sing

---

[21]Cf. Frederick H. Turner, Jr., "The Effect of Speech Summaries on Audience Comprehension," *The Central States Speech Journal*, 21:24–29, 1970.

[22]Charles W. Eliot, *American Contributions to Civilization*, The Century Company, New York, 1897, pp. 34–35.

in the words of the old Negro spiritual, "Free at last! free at last! thank God almighty, we are free at last!"[23]

■ 3. *Quotation.* Robert T. Oliver, at South Dakota University, July 17, 1969, on "Sacred Cows" concluded as follows:

> *The distance between East and West is considerable—physically, psychologically, and culturally. For these two parts of the human race to understand one another sympathetically and to work together effectively will require effort guided by both intelligence and character on both sides. The gulf that lies between us will not be bridged unless or until, somehow, we and they alike manage to attain the vast tolerance and insight represented by Edwin Markham, when he wrote:*
> *"He drew a circle to keep me out,*
> *Heretic, rebel, a thing to flout;*
> *But love and I had the wit to win—*
> *We drew a circle that took him in."*[24]

■ 4. *Personal appeal.* Woodrow Wilson concluded his first inaugural address, March 4, 1913, with a personal appeal for support of his national program:

> *This is not a day of triumph; it is a day of dedication. Here muster, not the forces of party, but the forces of humanity. Men's hearts wait upon us; men's lives hang in the balance; men's hopes call upon us to say what we will do. Who shall live up to the great trust? Who dares fail to try? I summon all honest men, all patriotic, all forward-looking men, to my side. God helping counsel and sustain me!*

■ 5. *Personal vindication and eulogy.* Note Al Capp's conclusion of his address, "Is This Your University?" at the Franklin Pierce College, Ridnige, New Hampshire, April 27, 1969, in which he castigated many colleges for their handling of the student protest movement:

> *And that's why I can say that colleges like yours, as yet too unproven to have become arrogant, and too determined to prove yourself to be anything but courageous, are the hope of the future. Because I believe that America has a future.*
> *It has become unfashionable to say this; it may be embarrassing to hear it; but I believe that Americans are the kindest and most generous of all people.*
> *I believe there are no underprivileged Americans; that even the humblest of us are born with a privilege that places us ahead of anyone else, anywhere else; the privilege of living and working in America, of repairing and renewing America; and one more privilege that no one seems to get much fun out of lately—the privilege of loving America.*[25]

[23]Robert T. Oliver and Eugene E. White, *Selected Speeches from American History,* Allyn and Bacon, Boston, 1966, pp. 289–294.
[24]*Vital Speeches of the Day,* 35:668–672, August 15, 1969.
[25]*Vital Speeches of the Day,* 35:634–636, August 1, 1969.

The Outline

An outline enables you to survey your case as a unit, to note digressions, to size up the major and minor divisions of your analysis, to evaluate the order of your topics, to gauge more carefully the length of your speech, to take a second look at your definitions, and to inspect your illustrations and other facts all of which should be inserted in your outline. This blueprint will aid you in assimilating more easily the talk itself. In short, the outline, if properly used, should make you a better speaker. But you must never feel compelled to follow it slavishly.

Principles and Rules for Outlining

For your convenience in constructing the outline, we suggest that you apply standard principles and rules. Your instructor may have decided views about methods of outlining; his advice concerning these mechanics will be important. The suggestions given below can be modified or interpreted to suit your needs. Most of these rules are those which speakers have consistently followed and they are based upon the experience of many speechmakers.

■ 1. *Prefix to the outline a clear statement of your subject.* Use as few general terms as possible. Knock out the ambiguous words. Be sure that the statement represents a careful limiting of the general field you have chosen for your talk. Be sure that your subject statement (topic sentence) reveals clearly and concisely the content and direction of your discourse.

■ 2. *Generally organize your outline into introduction, discussion, and conclusion.*

■ 3. *Use complete sentences throughout.*

■ 4. *See to it that your statements of main ideas say exactly what you mean.* Be sure that they are the main ideas, that they do not overlap, and that they are arranged in the sequence which facilitates their understanding or support for your purpose.

■ 5. *Use suitable symbols and indentations.* The customary system of numbering, lettering, and indenting is as follows:

I. _____
   A. _____
      1. _____
         a. _____
           (1) _____
             (a) _____

■ 6. *Where logic is an issue give each division at least two heads.* Where one subpoint is adequate for support or illustration, a single subdivision may suffice. Have few main headings in your outline. Otherwise your division may represent no division at all. Keep the wording short.

■ 7. *See that each subtopic is logically subordinate to the topic under which it is placed.* See that the entire framework, both in its large elements and in its minor statements, is a logical unit. If you have placed ideas together with care, each subhead will support a more general proposition.

■ 8. *Include in your introduction those steps necessary to secure a proper unfolding of your subject.* Usually include some of the following: (a) reason for the speech or other data that identify you and your topic with the audience and the occasion, (b) explanation of terms, (c) the purpose sentence (often in the form of a question), and (d) a statement of the topics you propose to develop.

■ 9. *In your conclusion include a summary or any other material necessary to reinforce or apply the ideas previously developed.*

■ 10. *On the margin or in the body of the outline, insert at the appropriate point the exact source of any material quoted or cited from printed sources.*

■ 11. *Include the concrete materials composing your speech, motivative as well as logical, but in the outline avoid much personal comment (make an outline, not an essay).*

Types of Outlines

Speech outlines are here suggested with some differences in outlining indicated, determined by whether the speech is to inform, entertain, or persuade.

■ *Outline for an informational speech.* Outlines for the short informative, or expositional, speech are comparatively simple. The subtopics provide further details about the main topics rather than, as in the case of the typical argumentative outline, give reasons for the support of propositions.

■ *Outline for an argumentative or persuasive speech.* The outline for a persuasive speech is more elaborate. Although much exposition is included, the framework of the outline consists of a series of reasons. "For" or an equivalent word is used in such an outline to link main and subideas to demonstrate the reasoning process. Thus:

I. Wider support of educational television is needed, for
    A. The claim that the educational needs should be handled exclusively by commercial stations is not justified, for
        1. Few commercial stations can afford to devote much of their daytime service and best evening hours to nonprofit educational shows, for
            a. (Further subtopics)

A full outline of this argumentative type is a *brief*.

- *Outline for a panel discussion.* The discussion outline varies somewhat from the expositional or argumentative form. Its pattern usually includes (1) cause for discussion, (2) definitions, (3) goals to be considered in any solution of the problem, (4) a diagnosis or analysis of the problem corresponding to the step, in the argumentative brief, that examines the need for the proposed change, (5) examination of representative solutions, and (6) arguments to support the solution that is chosen by the group.

  This individual outline, converted from a series of declarative statements to one made up of impartial questions, then becomes a *group outline* for use by the members of the panel, who set out to answer these questions.

- *Outline and the speaker's notes.* Once you have assembled a satisfactory outline, ask what is to be done with it. Should you carry it with you and speak directly from it? Certainly not; it will cramp your speaking style. Should you memorize it as it stands? This would probably not be too helpful. Should you write a full speech from it and recite the results verbatim? You may write the speech, but you will not have time to memorize it nor should you do so. The more practicable procedure is to draft a few *speaker's notes* from your material—catch phrases that will guide you in the speech itself, if you feel you must have such support. These notes are for you alone. Your aim in such preparation is to develop skill as an extempore speaker. You will make both an outline and speaker's notes; the latter will be much more abbreviated, informal, and private than the former. And you may easily disregard any such "props" in your short speech.

Projects and Problems

PROJECT 1: To identify and word main ideas in a speech you are assigned, read one of the speeches in Appendix C of this text which has been assigned by the instructor. Select and word the speaker's main ideas. Bring these to class in written form and compare your analysis with the analyses of other members of the class.

PROJECT 2: To apply the principles of developing a subject by time sequence, prepare and present a five-minute speech in which the two or three main divisions of the topic are in chronological order. Subjects for this speech (to be further limited):

1. the development of communism in Russia
2. the black civil rights struggle
3. the development of professional football in America
4. production of a printed book
5. the process of a bill through the state legislature (or Congress)
6. the Telstar operation
7. Early Bird

8. the early life and speech education of John F. Kennedy (or any other important speaker)
9. the United Nations during the past year
10. America's latest space flight
11. the Soviet Union's latest space flight
12. pacifism

PROJECT 3: To apply the principles of developing a subject by classification, prepare and present a five-minute speech in which the two or three main headings will be classificational or topical. Subjects for this speech (to be limited further):

1. the qualifications of a good speaker
2. the qualifications of a good listener
3. factors in highway safety
4. production of a play
5. the advantages of living in New England (or any other section of the United States)
6. characteristics of a satisfactory television talk
7. labor-management relations
8. the Alliance for Progress

PROJECT 4: To apply the principles of developing a subject by logical order, prepare and present a five-minute speech in which the two or three main headings are in logical or cause-and-effect order. Subjects for this speech (to be limited further):

1. the economic threat from the European Common Market.
2. smoking and lung cancer
3. national scholarships for students in colleges and universities
4. our antiquated county government system
5. railroad economic woes and proposed consolidations
6. jet-plane landing strips
7. channels for commercial and military flight in the United States
8. educational television
9. prohibition of nuclear explosions in space
10. automation and employment
11. racial equality and desegregation in housing
12. student power
13. Black Africa and the threat to whites there
14. the ecumenical movement
15. birth control
16. American foreign aid without military elements

PROJECT 5: To study and apply methods of systematic outlining, prepare and deliver a short speech based upon one of the topics and methods of dividing the subject as suggested in projects 1, 2, and 3 above. Accompany your talk with a full-sentence outline, to be handed to the instructor before the delivery of the speech. At the following class period the outlines will be returned, with comments on methods of outlining. At the discretion of the instructor all subsequent classroom speeches will be accompanied by satisfactory outlines.

For the instructor: Assign the questions under "Organization and Outlining" in the *Teacher's Manual.*

References

Baird, A. Craig, *Rhetoric.* New York: Ronald Press, 1965. Chapter 9.

Bruner, Jerome S., Jacqueline J. Goodnow, and George A. Austen, *A Study in Thinking.* New York: John Wiley & Sons, Inc., 1966.

Cronkhite, Gary, *Persuasion.* Indianapolis: The Bobbs-Merrill Company, 1969. Chapter 8.

Deese, James, *The Structure of Associations in Language and Thought.* Baltimore: The Johns Hopkins Press, 1965.

Ellingsworth, Huber, and Theodore Clevenger, Jr., *Speech and Social Action.* Englewood Cliffs, N.J.: Prentice-Hall, Inc., 1967. Chapter 4.

Hovland, Carl, Irving Janis, and Harold Kelley, *Communication and Persuasion.* New Haven: Yale University Press, 1963. Chapter 4.

Letterer, Joseph A., *Organizations: Structure and Behavior.* New York: John Wiley & Sons, Inc., 1964.

McCroskey, James, *An Introduction to Rhetorical Communication.* Englewood Cliffs, N.J.: Prentice-Hall, Inc., 1968. Chapter 11.

Mills, Glen E., *Message Preparation.* Indianapolis: The Bobbs-Merrill Company, 1966.

Thonssen, Lester, A. Craig Baird, and Waldo W. Braden, *Speech Criticism,* 2nd ed. New York: Ronald Press, 1970. Chapter 15.

Wiseman, Gordon, and Larry Barker, *Speech: Interpersonal Communication.* San Francisco: Chandler Publishing Company, 1967. Chapter 4.

Symbols Systems

verbal systems of communication

The story is told of the man who went into a large, modern drugstore and asked for a small tube of toothpaste. The clerk handed him one marked "Large." The customer returned it and repeated that he wanted the small size. The clerk replied, "That *is* the small size."

"What's the large size called?" asked the man.

"That's Giant."

"Is that the biggest?"

"Oh, no. Next is King, then Economy, and then the biggest of all—Family!"[1]

This story illustrates one of the many problems we have in understanding and using language well. You might condemn advertisers and others who use or abuse language in this way, but your condemnation will probably have little effect on the behavior of those who do it. If you are to be an effective communicator, it is far more important to try to understand than to condemn; it is far more important to try to understand the way in which language works, the variations which we find within the English tongue, and the variety of functions which language serves.

There are many symbolic systems, but natural languages are the most developed, the most subtle, and the most complicated of all. They are the product of abilities which are unique to man. Though we do not yet understand completely how man develops the ability to manipulate verbal symbols, we are fairly certain that it is related to the integration of some unknown characteristics of his central nervous system with his unique vocal and hearing systems. We are becoming increasingly convinced that our linguistic system is affected by our biological inheritance.[2] You have probably heard the term "language" used to describe the interaction that occurs among members of various animal species. For example, some zoologists speak of the "language of the bees." But, as linguist James Deese has pointed out, though many nonhuman species can interact, this interaction is not linguistic in any meaningful sense; it has no symbolic system that we can call a language. "Perhaps many animals . . . communicate with one another, but they do not do so by a concatenated, syntactic, rule-bearing sequence of symbols. In fact, the concept of symbol is probably grossly inappropriate as applied to animal communication."[3]

---

[1] Roul Tunley, "The Big Package Flap," *Saturday Review*, April 9, 1966, p. 64.
[2] See James Deese, *Psycholinguistics*, Allyn and Bacon, Boston, 1970, p. 115.
[3] *Ibid.*, p. 119.

What Is Language?

Before going further, we probably ought to indicate somewhat more clearly how we are using the term "language." Since it is difficult to communicate the many and complex facets of the term with a single definition, we will provide three definitions and then suggest some of their implications. These implications will be further amplified throughout the remainder of this chapter.

One linguist has defined language as "a socially institutionalized sign system . . . , the result of centuries of gradual development and change."[4] Another says language is "a system of arbitrary symbols by which thought is conveyed from one human being to another."[5] A key element of language for contemporary scholars is stressed in the definition of language as a set of symbols with rules of grammar which may be either explicit or implicit. Note the key terms in these definitions. They will help you to understand what language is and how it works. Most important, these understandings should help you to be a more effective user of language—a more effective communicator.

The Elements of Language

The two basic elements of a language, as these definitions indicate, are a set of symbols and a structure, or a vocabulary and a syntax or grammar.

■ The first element is the *vocabulary or set of symbols*. By a symbol, we mean anything which, by common agreement, stands for something else. Symbols are arbitrary; there is no necessary logical connection between the symbol and the thing symbolized. A cross is the symbol of the Christian church, but it may also be simply two sticks nailed together to hold up a tomato plant. Not all symbols are part of a language, of course, and not all are verbal symbols. The cross, a flag, a road sign are nonverbal symbols. These will be considered more fully in the next chapter. Whether verbal or nonverbal, the most useful symbols are definite, consistent, and universal. They need to be definite or specific so that the intended users know to what each refers. Each needs to be reasonably consistent—its referent must not shift too rapidly—or users of the symbol will confuse each other. It needs to be sufficiently universal for most members of the language community to agree to its referent or referents.

It takes more than meaningful words to make a meaningful sentence, of course. And different arrangements of the same words can result in different meanings. The important element which shapes the meaning of groups of
■ words is the *structure or syntax or grammar*. Thus any language must have

---

[4] John B. Carroll, *Language and Thought,* Prentice-Hall, Inc., Englewood Cliffs, N.J., 1964, p. 8.
[5] John P. Hughes, *The Sciences of Language,* Random House, New York, 1964, p. 6.

grammatical rules. This does not mean that every speaker to communicate well must follow precisely the same rules or that speakers must follow the rules set down in the so-called grammar books.

Despite what many of us may have learned at one time, rules of grammar are not important primarily because they provide a basis for distinguishing between the educated and uneducated, or between the careful and the careless. In itself, grammar is unimportant. It is only important because it makes it possible for us to express an infinite variety of meanings through an infinite variety of sentences. It is a powerful means for converting ideas into communicable form. It makes communication and organized, abstract thinking possible.

There is a third element which is important in our definitions of language and crucial to our understanding of the way in which language works. Not only is language unique to man, as we noted earlier; it also exists in the human social context and is shaped by that context. A language shifts with the life styles and needs of its users. In a very real sense, whenever someone utters something—anything at all—he is talking about himself. When he says, "That is a large tree," or, "He is dull," or, "She is a radical," he is saying something about his perceptions, the meanings that he has accepted for those terms, and about his conception of tree sizes, what he finds interesting in men, or his own political orientations. To understand such messages, we must understand the speaker.

Language and Thought

Obviously, man not only affects language but is affected by language. He learns and is persuaded by words that he hears and reads. Less obviously, as semanticist Samuel Hayakawa noted in one of the early works on general semantics, he is also affected by his unconscious assumptions about language.

These unconscious assumptions determine the way he takes words—which in turn determines the way he acts, whether wisely or foolishly. Words and the way he takes them determine his beliefs, his prejudices, his ideals, his aspirations—they constitute the moral and intellectual atmosphere in which he lives, in short, his semantic environment.[6]

You remember as a youngster accepting the "fact" that certain words were "bad," certain words were "fighting words." If anyone called you one of those, the only thing that you could do was to fight him. Looking back on such thoughts now, they seem silly. Yet, even as adults, we continue to make signal or habitual responses to many words. For many of us some of these

---

[6]S. I. Hayakawa, *Language in Action*, Harcourt, Brace & Co., New York, 1941, pp. xi–xii.

words are "radical," "protest," "demonstration," and even "peace." For others of us, some of these words are "conservative," "the establishment," "Americanism," and even "the American flag." Too often, we respond to these terms or labels without thinking, without recognizing for example that protest$_1$ is not protest$_2$, and protest$_2$ is not protest$_3$, just as conservative$_1$ is not conservative$_2$, and conservative$_2$ is not conservative$_3$. It was these kinds of responses that undoubtedly contributed to the senseless persecution of German-Americans during World War I and Japanese-Americans during World War II in the United States, to the mass slaughter of Jews in Nazi Germany in the 1930s, and to the ill-treatment of nonwhites through most of our country's history.

These phenomena are somewhat related to another hypothesis about the way in which we are affected by our language. This is the linguistic-relativity or Whorf-Sapir hypothesis (after its major advocates). The basic tenet of this hypothesis is that the structure and vocabulary of our language affect the way in which we perceive our environment. As Benjamin Whorf put it, "We cut up and organize the spread and flow of events as we do largely because, through our mother tongue, we are parties to an agreement to do so, not because nature itself is segmented in exactly that way for all to see."[7] This hypothesis was developed from the observation that languages differ in more ways than simply the fact that different sounds are used to denote the same object. Many of the concepts and constructions of one language have no exact counterparts in other languages. From this observation, some scholars have inferred that the thought processes of the speakers of one language differ from those of speakers of other languages. For example, if your language categorizes different species together (such as trees and flowers), you will tend to think of them in the same way and will see more similarities between them than if your language categorizes them in quite different ways.[8] This is an interesting hypothesis, and one which is fruitful to consider as we work at improving our communication. However, you should recognize that the linguistic-relativity hypothesis has never been proved. There has never been a truly adequate test of it, and in recent years, as interest in other linguistic theories—most notably generative theory—has grown, there has been relatively less interest in linguistic relativity. It has not been disproved, but it is open to serious question. Given our present knowledge about language, one can make a stronger case for influence in the other direction—not that language influences culture, but that culture or environment influences language. In cultures with a more rigid class system, for example, there are more variations in the form of personal address, such as the German *du* and *Sie*.

---

[7]B. L. Whorf, *Language, Thought, and Reality,* ed. J. B. Carroll, M.I.T.-Wiley, Cambridge, Mass., and New York, 1956, p. 240.
[8]*Ibid.,* pp. 212–213.

An organization such as the United Nations, which operates primarily through verbal communication, has demonstrated many times that language can function as the moral equivalent of war or peace.

The UN hears individual as well as official views. At left, Arthur Ashe speaks against the policy of *apartheid* in sports. At right, a representative of the United Methodist Church addresses the same hearing. Below, delegates exchange views in the lounge outside the General Assembly Hall.

All pictures, United Nations photos.

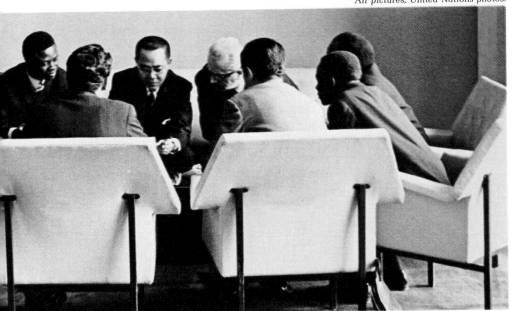

Language Learning

There are many things that we do not yet know about the ways in which we acquire and use language, or the process by which any one of us gets from an idea to the statement of that idea. Existing theories of learning can explain the way in which we learn parts of our language through imitation. For example, a child imitates a sound made by one of his parents and is rewarded if the imitation is reasonably accurate. Learning theory can also explain the way in which we acquire part of our language through a reinforcement-shaping procedure. This generally occurs at an early age when a child makes some sort of random sound which again is sufficiently close to what his parent considers a word for the parent to reinforce it. As the child grows older, the parent reinforces only those sounds which closely approximate the word or sound that the parent wants. Such learning, however, can account for only a minute portion of the language skill which the average person acquires. It fails to account for the large amount of creativity we display in using language.

An extremely large percentage of the sentences that we speak and understand are sentences that we have not encountered before. Yet, each "new" sentence we utter follows the system or rules of our language. Psychologist George Miller suggests that we acquire skill at using language in much the same way that we acquire skill at walking. We obviously have some command of the "rules," but most of us couldn't possibly describe them.[9] This is not an adequate explanation for those of us who want to achieve maximum understanding of language so that we can better understand and improve our communication. Whatever theories we develop in the future need to be precise and take into account the infinite uses to which we are able to put the finite materials available in our language.[10]

■ The theory to date which best explains our linguistic behavior is the *generative theory*.[11] At this stage in your study of communication, there is probably no need for a detailed knowledge of generative theory; however, you should know its major premises. The first of these is that each of us learns a *finite* set of rules (a grammar or syntax) which he can use to generate an *infinite* set of statements. The second major premise is that there is an innate biological representation of the abstract structure of language built into the human nervous system which facilitates or makes possible the acquisition of the set of rules. To put this somewhat differently and perhaps more accurately, the organization of the human nervous system

---

[9]See George A. Miller, "Psycholinguistics," in Gardner Lindzey and Elliot Aronson (eds.), *The Handbook of Social Psychology*, 2nd ed., Addison-Wesley, Reading, Mass., 1969, Vol. 3, pp. 666–794.

[10]Deese, *op. cit.*, p. 34.

[11]Roderick A. Jacobs and Peter S. Rosenbaum, *English Transformational Grammar*, Blaisdell Publishing Co., Waltham, Mass., 1968, pp. 17–21, 279–282; Noam Chomsky, "Current Issues in Linguistic Theory," in Jerry A. Fodor and Jerrold J. Katz (eds.), *The Structure of Language*, Prentice-Hall, Inc., Englewood Cliffs, N.J., 1964, pp. 51–52.

makes it impossible to learn a set of rules which differs in any important way from the sets learned by all other human beings. Third, generative theory conceives of two types of structure in language which are essential for getting from meaning to sound and from sound to meaning; these are *surface structure* and *deep structure*. The form of a sentence is given by its surface structure; the meaning of a sentence is conveyed by its deep structure. The processes by which one gets from meaning to a phonetically interpretable sentence are called *transformations*. Two sentences could have the same surface structure and yet mean quite different things, i.e., have different deep structures. Take for example, "What hurt the boy was being examined by the doctor." This could mean that the process of being examined was painful to the boy or that the doctor was trying to discover the source of the pain. Conversely, two sentences could have different surface structures and yet have the same deep structure. For example, "This brown book belongs to Mary" and "Mary owns this brown book." If you continue to study communication, as we hope you will, you should hear much more of generative theory in the future. We believe that in the years ahead linguistic research growing out of this theory will add much to our understanding of how we acquire and use language. This knowledge should help us to teach English or other languages more effectively and to be more effective communicators.

The Meanings of Meaning

One of the most important concepts for you in understanding language and communication is the concept of *meaning*. Most of us have a very much oversimplified notion of what meaning is and, because of this, we often fail as communicators. "Look *that* up in your Funk and Wagnalls" may be a good line for a running gag on television, it is not good advice for anyone seeking a relatively complete understanding of the things people say to him. Dictionaries provide only a small portion of the meanings in our language and fail to reflect accurately the wide range of meanings for many terms within various groups in our population.

A writer of dictionaries is primarily a historian; his job is to tell us the various ways in which a word has been used in the past. He does not attempt to tell us what each word "really" means (as many users of dictionaries assume) or what it "ought" to mean; he records rather what it has been used to mean by communicators up to that point. Thus, a dictionary is a useful *guide;* it is not an infallible rulebook. New situations create new meanings. As Hayakawa has noted, looking under a "hood," we should ordinarily have found, 500 years ago, a monk; today, we find an automobile engine.[12] Another scholar of language has illustrated the way in which dictionary definitions can be misleading in his story of

---

[12]Hayakawa, *op. cit.,* p. 58.

a New England horse-trader who sold a farmer a nag under the guarantee that she was "sound of wind and limb, and without fault." When, on the way home, the farmer's new purchase walked bang into a stone wall, he turned back and remonstrated furiously that the horse, despite the warranty, was blind. "Ah, sir," replied the dealer, "blindness is not her fault; it's her misfortune."[13]

As the author of this story noted, it is difficult to know why people tell lies when the truth can be just as misleading.

There are many meanings of meaning, or types of meaning, all of them relevant to an understanding of the processes of communication.

- The first and most generally recognized type of meaning is *denotation*. It is for this type of meaning that dictionaries are most useful (though not infallible). Denotation is like pointing to the thing named or the referent. It is like a label. If it is not obvious to you that denotation is not synonomous with meaning, consider the terms "George Washington" and "the first President of the United States." These have the same referent, but different meanings. If they had the same meaning, "George Washington was first President of the United States" would mean the same as "George Washington was George Washington."[14] This example shows not only that meaning is not identical with the denoted object, but that we can denote the same object with more than one sign of a different meaning. For example, the man lounging on your sofa can be denoted by the words "Joe," "him," "my friend," "that guy," etc. Conversely, since meaning is not identical with the denoted reality, different objects can be denoted by the same sign, e.g., the "foot" of a mountain and the "foot" of a table.[15]

The second and somewhat less generally recognized type of meaning is
- *connotation*. This is the type of meaning Hayakawa was talking about when he noted that some words snarl and some words purr. It is largely connotation which causes us to respond differently to the words "sweat" and "perspiration," even though they have the same denotation. In short, connotation refers to the attitudes, feelings, emotions, and values which we associate with a symbol. Connotative meanings, in large part, develop from the prior experiences an individual has had with a term—whether those experiences were pleasurable or unpleasant, or whether the context in which the term was usually encountered was positive or negative. These factors, which affect the connotative meaning of a term quite often, vary systematically among individuals so that there is much more heterogeneity

---

[13]Louis B. Salomon, *Semantics and Common Sense,* Holt, Rinehart and Winston, New York, 1966, pp. 84–85.

[14]Example suggested by G. A. Miller, "Some Preliminaries to Psycholinguistics," in R. C. Oldfield and J. C. Marshall (eds.), *Language,* Penguin Books, Baltimore, 1968, p. 204.

[15]This distinction between meaning and the part of reality denoted has been discussed extensively by Laszlo Antal. See especially his *Questions of Meaning,* P. Mouton & Co., The Hague, 1963, pp. 30–31, in which the last two examples were suggested.

among people in the connotative meanings that they have for many terms than in the denotative meanings that they have for the same terms. Some scholars divide connotative meaning into *expressive* and *evocative* meaning. By expressive they mean those utterances which are the emotional responses of a speaker or a writer to some stimulus; by evocative they mean those utterances which are designed to evoke an emotional response from the hearer or reader. In trying to understand communication and in trying to improve your ability to communicate, this may be a useful distinction.

■ A third important kind of meaning is *structural* meaning. This is the meaning which is dependent upon the ways in which words are used in relation to each other. The pattern in which the words are used or encountered communicates a particular meaning. To demonstrate the influence of structure, you can cast some sounds which have no denotative or connotative meaning in the usual sense into a sentencelike structure and you will discover that the statement evokes certain meanings in those who hear it. For example, "The pflugit has pligims."

■ A fourth important type of meaning is the *contextual* meaning. We seldom use words in isolation. In communication, their meaning is affected not only by the structure of which they are a part but also by the words that surround them—in phrases, sentences, paragraphs, and even at times in longer units of discourse. This fact is recognized, consciously or subconsciously, when a public figure complains of being quoted "out of context." There is the realization that taking a word or phrase or sentence out of the total communication context in which it was uttered changes the meaning which it evokes in the listener. There are two quite different types of factors which affect contextual meaning, one linguistic and the other nonlinguistic. Among the linguistic factors which affect the meaning of a term, as we noted before, are the other words with which it is surrounded. Among the nonlinguistic factors are the situation in which the term is used and the facial expressions and gestures which one uses when he says the word. Some terms are ambiguous until we are given a context. The word "nut" is an example. It would have a different meaning in the context of a speech about plumbing and a speech about strange people—just as it would have a different meaning if the speaker held up a hard, dry seed or if he pointed to you as he said the word. Context is important for other kinds of words because their noncontextual meaning is relative. For example, the word "hot" when applied to the weather denotes quite a different temperature than when applied to soup or molten steel. The context adds precision to the term.

Changes in Meaning

Whatever type of meaning we consider, it is extremely important to recognize that meanings are dynamic. Hayakawa made this point in the most extreme form possible when he stated that "no word ever has exactly the same meaning twice."[16] Though extreme, this is a useful way to think of language. It helps to remind us that meaning is not static. Word meanings change as an individual develops and grows in experience. Word meanings change with context—and no two contexts are totally the same. A Russian semanticist, Lev Vygotsky, believes that meanings also change with the changes in the way we think.

The relation of thought to word is not a thing but a process, a continual movement back and forth from thought to word and from word to thought. In that process the relation of thought to word undergoes changes which themselves may be regarded as development in the functional sense. Thought is not merely expressed in words; it comes into existence through them.[17]

In short, meaning, like communication itself, is a process. No single theory of linguistic change is adequate to explain the changes that we see going on. We only know that change moves in many directions and for many reasons. Though most meanings change slowly—or else communication would be rendered virtually impossible—they do change. If all of the parties to an act of communication are aware of this fact and are sensitive to the sorts of changes which are occurring, there can be a greater sharing of meaning and, hence, more effective communication.

One of the clear indications of the way in which language is constantly changing is the changing verbal taboos and the related fact that verbal taboos vary among groups in our population. Words related to physiological and sexual matters in our culture appear to encounter the most taboos. These are changing but, among most groups, words referring to the act of sexual intercourse, for example, are still taboo. However, words referring to most parts of the body are more easily accepted today than they were not too many years ago when people would say "limb" rather than "leg." Hayakawa claims that the reason we refer to parts of a chicken as "white meat" and "dark meat" is that ladies of the nineteenth century were indisposed to say "breast" or "leg."[18] Even today, we often talk of going to the "washroom," the "restroom," or the "john," rather than the "toilet." It is important for you to be aware of the taboos of the individuals or groups with whom you communicate—as well as your own. As a receiver, do not let your taboos interfere with your reliable reception of messages. As a speaker or writer, do not violate the taboos of your audience unless you are aware of what you are doing and want the effect that such violation tends to bring. Be aware that, for many individuals with whom you communicate, taboo terms can drown out the rest of your message.

---

[16]Hayakawa, *op. cit.*, p. 65.
[17]Lev Semenovich Vygotsky, *Thought and Language*, trans. Eugenia Hanfmann and Gertrude Vakar, The M.I.T. Press, Cambridge, Mass., 1962, p. 125.
[18]Hayakawa, *op. cit.*, p. 95.

Another sign of our constantly changing language is the fact that no language is ever "perfect," no individual is ever completely consistent in his performance. At any given point in time there is a certain amount of fluctuation in the speech of any person or any speech community in the frequency of use of alternative words, alternative constructions, alternative pronunciations, etc. These fluctuations probably account for what appear to be undue arbitrariness in much of any language; e.g., the fact that "campfire" and "campground" are spelled as one word, while "camp chair" is spelled as two words. They probably also account for the fact that some words in certain contexts appear to have no meaning at all because we can substitute their opposites or even delete them without changing the meaning of the utterance. For example, when you enter data on a questionnaire, you are "filling it in" or "filling it out." When you reduce your car's speed you are "slowing *up*," "slowing *down*," or "slowing."[19]

"Good" English

Our reference groups—those groups or individuals to whom we look for norms or with whom we compare ourselves—have a great influence on our linguistic habits. You should be aware of these influences on yourself and on those with whom you communicate. You should be aware of the fact that your concept of "proper English" and the concept that others have of "proper English" probably result from reference-group influence. You should be aware of the fact that there is no absolute criterion of "correctness," just as there is no absolute criterion of the "beauty" or "aesthetic merit" of language. Our attitudes on these matters are conditioned by our culture and vary widely among groups. Robert Hall lists eight types of norms, each of which could lead to a different concept of "correctness."

1. The literary norm in which the usage of "the best authors" serves as a model.
2. The historical norm in which the criterion is the usage of an earlier time.
3. Popular speech, set up more or less in opposition to literary usage or to the language of the upper classes. One manifestation is the deliberate use of forms such as "ain't" or "he don't" to show one's independence.
4. The norm of efficiency in which that language which serves its function with the least ambiguity and expenditure of effort is the model.
5. The norm may be set by an authority, from a "schoolmarm" to a dictionary.
6. The presumed "logic" inherent in the grammatical structure of some particular language sometimes sets the norm. However, no language perfectly follows any logic. In Sapir's terms, "all grammars leak."

---

[19]These examples are from Salomon, *op. cit.*, pp. 6, 9.

7. Geographical norm or regional standards. You will find different norms of correctness in different parts of the United States, or even in different parts of some cities.
8. Although the myth of an aesthetic absolute is dying, the linguistic norm of some groups is still influenced by the idea of beauty or aesthetics.[20]

Adapting Language to Your Audience

For optimum communication, the language choices which you make must be affected by those with whom you are communicating. We are not concerned here with understanding language in the abstract; we are concerned rather with the optimum use of language for communicative purposes. Our criterion of language use, therefore, cannot be some abstract notion of "correctness"; it must be rather the situational notion of "appropriateness." There are situations in which it is appropriate to say "yeah" and there are situations in which it is not. There are situations in which it is appropriate to use "head" to refer to a drug user and there are situations in which it is not. Fred Williams, who has studied the linguistic habits of children from economically depressed areas, describes what he labels "home talk" and "school talk." He notes that these children clearly distinguish between what is appropriate talk for school and what is appropriate talk within the neighborhood gang.[21] At one time, educators, employing the traditional absolute standard of "correctness," would have labeled the "home talk" inferior. As we have become more conscious of the primacy of the communicative function of language, however, we have realized the untenability of that position. Not only would school talk be less effective than home talk with one's fellow gang members, it could result in a punch in the nose or even getting thrown out of the gang, just as home talk in the school could result in a trip to the principal's office and possibly being thrown out of school. Though these are extreme examples, they have their counterparts in all of the communicative situations in which we become involved. Accepting this position clearly does not mean that you accept the position that "anything goes"—quite the contrary. It does not mean that you need to follow no rules; it simply means that you must find your rules in the audience, rather than in the traditional grammar book or dictionary alone. "Correctness," in other words, should be defined in terms of acceptability and what is understood by your particular audience rather than in terms of some arbitrary canons of good usage.

Some scholars have tested this sort of agreement between source and receiver with what is known as the Cloze procedure. In this procedure, every

---

[20]Robert A. Hall, *An Essay on Language,* Chilton Books, Philadelphia, 1968, pp. 39–43.
[21]Fred Williams and Barbara Sundene Wood, "Negro Children's Speech: Some Social Class Differences in Word Predictability," *Language and Speech* (in press).

fifth or so word is deleted from a passage and subjects must fill in the blanks. It has been found that people can generally fill in these blanks with amazing accuracy. In other words, there is a high degree of agreement and, hence, high predictability on what word was in the blank space.[22]

One scholar, Donald K. Darnell, using these principles and Cloze procedure, and recognizing that different professions have specialized languages, developed a special method for testing the English language proficiency of students from other countries who want to study in America. As most contemporary linguists do, he assumed that it was more important for foreign students to conform to the language norms of the group in which they wanted to be a part—successful engineering students, successful humanities students, etc.—than for them to have memorized rules of "good usage." Therefore, he developed tests by taking standard prose passages from each field of study and deleting every tenth word from each. He then had successful students in each field fill in the blanks. The test of language proficiency for the foreign students was filling in the blanks for material from their field of study to see whether their word choices approximated those of the American students in their field. Darnell believes that this sort of test, which takes into account the kind of material a student needs to use and the kinds of people with whom he needs to communicate, is much more predictive of one's ability to get along—to communicate well—than the traditional test that measures awareness of linguistic rules or ability to answer questions about the language.[23]

Darnell's assumptions and procedures are consistent with our position that adherence to some formal set of rules about language use is not as important for effective communication as adherence to the norms and expectations of the group with which you want to communicate. This does not mean that you need never be concerned with what we have traditionally considered to be good grammar, for there will almost certainly be times when you want to communicate with others for whom rule-book grammar is the norm and who expect other educated people to adhere to it.

Though it is not a necessary adjunct to the above, we also believe that you should have a personal style which is superimposed upon the rules which you derive from each audience; you should have your particular or distinctive variations in language. Some scholars believe that you have a personal style of this sort whether you are conscious of it or not, that it is a reflection of your personality. These stylistic idiosyncracies have even been used to settle disagreements about the authorship of certain materials.

---

[22] For a more complete description of the Cloze procedure, See W. L. Taylor, " 'Cloze Procedure': A New Tool for Measuring Readability," *Journalism Quarterly,* 30:415–433. 1953.

[23] See Donald K. Darnell, "CLOZENTROPY: A Procedure for Testing English Language Proficiency of Foreign Students," *Speech Monographs,* 37:36–46, March 1970.

Effects of Language Variation

Research on communication gives abundant evidence that some language variables can affect the comprehension and retention of information. The variables which appear quite consistently in these studies are complexity or unfamiliarity of the words in the message and length of sentences. Some researchers have used these basic findings in further research to develop formulas for determining the "readability" or "listenability" of messages. Rudolph Flesch, for example, has developed various formulas for "reading ease." The most useful is probably RE (reading ease) = 206.835 − .846wl − 1.015sl (where wl is the average number of syllables per 100 words and sl is the average sentence length in words.[24] This index and variations of it have been found to correlate to a high degree with comprehensibility of both spoken and written materials. Edgar Dale and Jean Chall developed an index of reading ease on a somewhat different basis than Flesch's, but it works similarly and seems to predict comprehensibility about as well. The equation is Reading Grade Score = .1579x_1 + .0496x_2 + 3.6365, where x_1 is the percent of words not in the "Dale List of 3000 Familiar Words" (a copy of which can be found in the Dale and Chall publication) and x_2 is the average sentence length in words.[25]

Some people find this reduction of style to formulas abhorrent. We are not advocating that you test everything you want to say with one of these formulas before you say it. We are not even advocating that you necessarily ever formally test a message with one of them. We are advocating that you be aware of the effect of language complexity and sentence length on comprehension. Though the use of unfamiliar or complex words and long and complex sentences may impress some listeners, they reduce the amount which these listeners will understand and retain from your message.

The effect of language variables on comprehension and retention is far clearer than the effect on persuasion. At this point, there seem to be few useful generalizations that we can make about the latter. It is not even certain, for example, that the clarity of a message affects its persuasiveness. It does seem certain, though, that the language which you use will affect your audience's perceptions both of you and your message. Using language which is very much at variance with the norms and expectations of your audience will have a very different effect than language which is consistent with those norms and expectations. It may be an effect that you want; you may want to shock the audience or cause them to think that you are quite different than they are. In general, though, we suspect that if you vary much

---

[24] See Rudolf Flesch, "A New Readability Yardstick," *Journal of Applied Psychology,* 32:221–233, June 1948.
[25] See Edgar Dale and Jean S. Chall, "A Formula for Predicting Readability," *Educational Research Bulletin,* 27:11–20, 37–54, 1948.

from the norms and expectations of your audience you will hinder, rather than aid, effective communication.

We noted earlier the hypothesis about the effect of our native language on the way in which we perceive the world—the linguistic-relativity hypothesis. A related issue is the degree to which our common use of polar opposites in English—hot–cold, war–peace, true–false, good–bad, loyalty–treason—blinds us to the infinite number of points between. Some semanticists believe that this "two-valued orientation" reduces our ability to resolve controversies. Failure to free ourselves from the habit of arguing in terms of polar opposites gets us into interminable and static debates about being a "hawk" or a "dove" on the question of the conflict in Southeast Asia, eliminating ROTC from our campuses or retaining ROTC on our campuses, etc.[26] Be aware of these problems and try to minimize the negative effects of the two-valued orientation on your own communication habits and thinking.

Projects and Problems

PROJECT 1: To review the principles of effective use of language in speech. Purposes of this assignment: To review the language principles involved in one of the suggested topics. Use illustrations. Draw on the suggestions of this chapter and the references cited at the end of the chapter. Subjects for this speech:

1. What is the evidence to support the conclusion that "oral language is essentially different from the written form"? Cite any sources.
2. "Your thinking is just as wide as your vocabulary." Discuss.
3. Discuss: "The word is not the thing."
4. Explain: "Two-valued orientation." See S. I. Hayakawa, *Language in Thought and Action,* or any other book on semantics.
5. Slang of college students.
6. Describe some of the changes in language which have occurred in recent years.
7. Explain and discuss contextual meaning.
8. Explain and justify your criteria for "good English."

PROJECT 2: Some communication scholars have asserted that meanings are in people, not in words. Do you agree or disagree? Why?

PROJECT 3: Observe and describe a sample of the language behavior used by some of the students in your college in informal conversation. How do you suppose this behavior differs from the language behavior of these same students while giving an oral report in a college class?

---

[26]Both Salomon, *op. cit.,* pp. 41–46, and Hayakawa, *op. cit.,* pp. 179–180, have discussed the two-valued orientation in some detail.

PROJECT 4:   Read one of the following sections from these works which are listed in the bibliography for this section and report to the class as indicated following each reference below:

Wendell Johnson, "The World of Words," in *People in Quandaries,* pp. 112–142. Discuss Johnson's ideas on verbal levels of abstracting.

Wendell Johnson, "Practical Devices and Techniques," in *People in Quandaries,* pp. 205–239. Discuss the practicability of Johnson's ideas for today's communicator.

Thomas Wolfe, "The Language That I Seek," in Kottler and Light, *The World of Words,* pp. 47–53. For someone concerned with communicating about important issues—to inform or persuade—rather than to write novels to entertain, what useful ideas can be gleaned from Wolfe?

Carl Sandburg, "Kid Talk—Folk Talk," in Kottler and Light, pp. 23–29. What inferences do you draw from this paper about "good English"? Are Sandburg's descriptions dated?

Harrison E. Salisbury, "The Gang," in Kottler and Light, pp. 168–179. Same as for Sandburg paper.

Clifton Fadiman, "On the Utility of U-Talk," in Kottler and Light, pp. 179–187. What is Fadiman's point? Do you agree or disagree? Why?

George Orwell, "The Principles of Newspeak," in Kottler and Light, pp. 347–356. What is Newspeak? Is it a good thing? Why?

F. A. Philbrick, "Bias Words," in Anderson and Stageberg, *Introductory Readings in Language,* pp. 176–184. Discuss biased words, using examples other than those in this paper by Philbrick.

I. A. Richards, "The Command of Metaphor," in Anderson and Stageberg, pp. 228–240. Discuss the use of metaphor in informative or persuasive discourse.

PROJECT 5:   Make a linguistic survey among a group of your friends or other adults who come from different parts of the country or whose parents were raised in different parts of the country. You can use the following questionnaire for this purpose. Analyze the results and report back to the class on the kinds of terms which appear to distinguish people from one part of the country from people from another, or that distinguish urban from rural residents.

LINGUISTIC QUESTIONNAIRE

Name _____ Birthplace _____

Town and state in which you lived for most of your first twenty years
_____

Size of town in which you lived (circle):   Farm.   Under 1,000.   1,000–5,000.
5,000–25,000.   Over 25,000.

Parent's birthplace: Father _____
Mother _____

For many ordinary things, different people use different words. We are trying to find out whether some of these differences are associated with the part of the country from which one comes. On this questionnaire are recorded some of the differences which we know occur. We hope you will help us by recording your usual usage.

1. Please put a circle around the word in each group which you ordinarily use.
2. If you use two words in one group equally often, circle both of them.
3. Do *not* put circles around any other words, even though many of them will be quite familiar to you. We are interested only in those words which *you* tend to use.
4. If the word you do ordinarily use is not listed in the group, please write it at the end of the group and circle it.
5. Words printed in capital letters are there only for explanatory purposes.

Example: SHELF OVER FIREPLACE: mantlepiece, (mantle,) tussock, clock-shelf, fire-board, shelf.

1. duck bumps, goose bumps, goose pimples, goose flesh.
2. HOLES IN ROADS: chuck holes, chug holes, pot holes, holes.
3. griddle cakes, pancakes, batter cakes, hot cakes, flannel cakes, flapjacks, slapjacks, fritters, flitters.
4. sitting room, parlor, front room, living room, best room.
5. baby buggy, baby carriage, baby coach, baby wagon, baby cab.
6. skip class, skip school, play hookey, play truant, run out of school, slip off from school, cook Jack, bolt.
7. catch a cold, catch cold, get a cold, take cold.
8. OBSTINATE: set, sot, pig-headed, bull-headed, headstrong, ornery, contrary, stubborn, owly, otsny.
9. resembles, takes after, favors, features, looks like (HIS FATHER).
10. relatives, people, folks, kin, kinfolks, home-folks, relation, family, relations.
11. raised, brought up, reared, fetched up (REFERS TO CHILDREN).
12. FAMILIAR TERM FOR MOTHER: ma, maw, mom, momma, mommer, mammy, mother.
13. FAMILIAR TERM FOR FATHER: pa, paw, pop, popper, papa, pappy, pap, dad, daddy, father.
14. ROAD PAVED WITH CONCRETE: cement road, hard road, surface road, slab, pike, pavement.
15. WEB OUTDOORS: spider web, spider's web, cobweb, spidernest, dew-web.
16. lightning bug, firefly, firebug, candlefly.
17. toadstool, frogstool.
18. spring onions, young onions, green onions, shallot, scallion, rareripes, multipliers, live-forevers, potato onions.
19. seed, stone, pit (OF A CHERRY).
20. faucet, tap, spigot (OVER A SINK).
21. lima beans, butter beans (LARGE, FLAT, YELLOWISH: *NOT* PODS).
22. FOOD TAKEN BETWEEN MEALS: a bite, a snack, a piece, lunch.
23. warm over, warm up, heat up (FOOD).

24. bedspread, coverlet, coverlid, counterpane.
25. (BURLAP CONTAINER) burlap sack, gunney sack, burlap bag.
26. (PAPER CONTAINER) paper sack, paper bag, poke, sack, bag.
27. LARGE, OPEN TIN VESSEL FOR WATER, MILK, ETC.:   pail, bucket.
28. IRON UTENSIL FOR FRYING: skillet, frying pan, spider.
29. IRON UTENSIL WITH LARGE OPEN TOP FOR BOILING POTA-
     TOES, MEAT, ETC.:   pot, kettle.
30. CHANNEL FOR RAINWATER AT EDGE OF ROOF: gutters, eaves-
     troughs, eavetroughs.
31. LARGE PORCH WITH ROOF: porch, veranda, stoop, portico.
32. UNFINISHED ROOM AT TOP OF HOUSE: garret, attic, loft, cock-
     loft, sky-parlor.
33. ON ROLLERS: window shades, roller shades, blinds, curtains, shades.
34. thunderstorm, thunder shower, tempest, storm, electric storm.
35. sunrise, sun-up.

(This questionnaire is adapted from one used by Harold Allen in compiling
his *Linguistic Atlas of the Upper Midwest*.)

References

Alexander, Hubert G., *Language and Thinking: A Philosophical Introduction*. Princeton: D. Van Nostrand Co., 1967.

Anderson, Wallace L., and Norman C. Stageberg (eds.), *Introductory Readings on Language*, rev. ed. New York: Holt, Rinehart & Winston, 1966.

Antal, Laszlo, *Questions of Meaning*. The Hague: Mouton & Co., 1963.

Benjamin, Robert L., *Semantics and Language Analysis*. Indianapolis:
Bobbs-Merrill, 1970.

Brown, Roger, *Words and Things*. Glencoe, Ill.: The Free Press, 1958.

Carroll, John B., *Language and Thought*. Englewood Cliffs, N.J.: Prentice-
Hall Inc., 1964.

Chase, Stuart, *The Power of Words*. New York: Harcourt, Brace & Co., 1954.

Dean, Leonard F., and Kenneth G. Wilson (eds.), *Essays on Language and
Usage,* 2nd ed. New York: Oxford University Press, 1963.

Deese, James, *Psycholinguistics*. Boston: Allyn & Bacon, 1970.

Flesch, Rudolph, *The Art of Readable Writing*. New York: Harper, 1949.

Hall, Robert A., *An Essay on Language*. Philadelphia: Chilton Books, 1968.

Hayakawa, S. I., *Language in Thought and Action*, 2nd ed. New York:
Harcourt, Brace & Co., 1964.

Hughes, John P., *The Sciences of Language*. New York: Random House, 1964.

Jacobovits, Leon A., and Murray S. Miron (eds.), *Readings in the Psychology
of Language*. Englewood Cliffs, N.J.: Prentice-Hall Inc., 1967.

Jacobs, Roderick A., and Peter S. Rosenbaum, *English Transformational
Grammar*. Waltham, Mass.: Blaisdell Publishing Co., 1968.

Johnson, Wendell, *People in Quandaries*. New York: Harper, 1946.

Kottler, Barnet, and Martin Light (eds.), *The World of Words: A Language
Reader*. Boston: Houghton-Mifflin, 1969.

Miller, George A., "Psycholinguistics," in Gardner Lindzey and Elliot Aronson (eds.), *The Handbook of Social Psychology,* 2nd ed. Reading, Mass.: Addison-Wesley, 1969. III, 666–794.

Oldfield, R. C., and J. C. Marshall (eds.), *Language.* Baltimore: Penguin Books, 1968.

Pei, Mario, *The Many Hues of English.* New York: Knopf, 1967.

Salomon, Louis B., *Semantics and Common Sense.* New York: Holt, Rinehart and Winston, 1966.

Ullman, S., *Semantics, an Introduction to the Science of Meaning.* New York: Barnes & Noble, 1962.

Vetter, Harold J., *Language Behavior and Communication.* Itasca, Ill.: F. E. Peacock Publishers, 1969.

Vygotsky, Lev Semenovich, *Thought and Language,* trans. Eugenia Hanfmann and Gertrude Vakar. Cambridge, Mass.: The M.I.T. Press, 1962.

Whorf, B. L., *Language, Thought, and Reality,* ed. J. B. Carroll. Cambridge, Mass., and New York: M.I.T.-Wiley, 1956.

Wilson, Graham, *A Linguistics Reader.* New York: Harper and Row, 1967.

Class or concert speaking.

John Epy Lovell, The Young Speaker, *Cincinnati, 1852.*

nonverbal symbol systems

Contemporary man, when faced with the need to communicate something to someone, tends to think of *words*—either in spoken or written form. Despite Marshall McLuhan and Marcel Marceau, we still think of our society as largely verbal; we have been conditioned to think of communication in terms of words and using them is still a "natural" tendency. However, reliance on words alone, or words as the dominant element, can result in inefficient or ineffective communication. Consider, for example, explaining to someone how to drive a car without nonverbal aids, or describing the

appearance of a person, or teaching someone how to pluck and dress a chicken, or instructing a class in swimming. This consideration should make it obvious that much communication, to be effective, cannot rely solely upon words. In fact, if you become sensitive to the varieties of communication going on about you, you will discover that there is a great deal of nonverbal communication in our society, even though much of it is unintentional.

This is not to say, of course, that nonverbal communication is always or necessarily more effective than verbal communication. The over-generalization of the cliché that "one picture is worth a thousand words" can be made immediately obvious by considering what picture will explain the way to make out a federal income tax form. The important thing is to develop an understanding of nonverbal forms of communication so that you will be sensitive to the kinds of purposes and situations for which they will be useful.

Acquiring this understanding is not easy, for there is surprisingly little research on nonverbal communication. We have no knowledge of it comparable to that we have for verbal communication. Consider, for example, the complexity of messages. We have ample evidence from research to help us predict the kinds of verbal materials which are more difficult for audiences to comprehend. We know that the length of sentences and the use of words with prefixes and suffixes affect the understandability of prose messages. We have no comparable data for visual or other nonverbal "passages." We have little reliable data on the factors which make one visual aid, for example, simpler or more complex than another, or that make one gesture more communicative than another, or that contribute to the association value of a nonverbal symbol. This chapter, therefore, will largely be raising questions for you to consider and, at the same time, attempt to present to you the little that is known about the nonverbal aspect of communication.

The gestures of the gentlemen at the right indicate sacred ascription ("Thou art clothed with LIGHT as with a garment") or sacred deprecation ("Ye gods, RESTRAIN your wrath").

Communicator's action	Studied by	Resultant skill or art	Communication system		
uttering	linguistics	speech-tonal	verbal		
scratching	glyptics	writing			
	pictics	drawing	visual	audio-visual	
molding	plastics	sculpture			
building	tectonics	architecture			
moving	kinesics	dance			
producing sound	melodics	music			nonverbal
touching	haptics	fondling			
producing odor	aromatics	perfumery			
producing taste	edetics	cooking			
space separation	proxemics	cultural adaptation			

Nonverbal Systems

First of all, it is important to be aware of the wide variety of systems of symbols that exists beyond the oral and written verbal systems described in the preceding chapter. The accompanying table shows the way in which different types of actions result in different types of codes.[1]

Though nonverbal symbols can be any of the wide variety of types noted in the table, our discussion will center largely on two or three types. Most of the principles which you develop about these should be applicable to codes of all types.

The first thing to note about nonverbal symbols is that none has a "basic" or "real" or "universal" meaning—all are neutral. As someone has noted, a symbol is like flypaper, something to which meanings get stuck. Consider,

---

[1]This table is adapted from material in Randall Harrison, "Communication Theory," in Raymond V. Wiman and Wesley C. Meierhenry (eds.), *Educational Media: Theory Into Practice,* Charles E. Merrill Publishing Co., Columbus, Ohio, 1969, pp. 59–92. The material chart is adapted from is on pp. 71–72.

The gestures at the left suggest removal, repulsion, and/or aversion in varying intensities.

A Manual of Gesture, *Chicago, 1875.*

for example, the meanings which have become "stuck" to the cross, which is merely two crossed sticks. The fact that the cross does not have the same meanings for all men helps to call our attention to the fact that the locus of the "sticking" is not at the point of the object, but within the mind of the individual person. Thus to utilize nonverbal symbols effectively, one must understand his audience. One must also understand that many nonverbal symbols may have an even less stable set of meanings than verbal symbols do. We saw the belief in stable visual symbols carried to its extreme in nineteenth-century public speaking books, as the figures on pages 172–173 illustrate.

The idea that these gestures have these clear and stable meanings seems foolish to us today. One cannot help but wonder about the assumptions which you and we make about the meanings of other nonverbal symbols. How often do you assume that a symbol must be clear to others because its meaning is perfectly clear to you? It might be interesting for some of our assumptions to be put to the test, as they often are for other communicators. One author, for example, who has suggested the need for an international symbol for "fragile," tells the story of a crate of glassware being unloaded from a ship in India. On top of the crate was a symbol often used to indicate that the contents of a box are fragile—a broken wineglass. The Indian dock

worker saw the symbol and thought it very strange. He could not understand why anyone would want to buy a box of broken glass. He shrugged, picked up the crate, and threw it onto the back of the truck.[2]

Mark Twain, in *The Innocents Abroad,* suggested the nonuniversality of nonverbal symbols in quite another way. He told about Matthews, the actor, who once was lauding the ability of the human face to express the passions and emotions hidden in the breast. Matthews asserted that the countenance could disclose what was passing in the heart plainer than the tongue could.

"Now," he said, "observe my face—what does it express?"
"Despair!"

[2]Dick Shea, "Toward a Universal Non-Language," *New York Times Magazine,* November 22, 1964, p. 66.

"Bah, it expressed peaceful resignation! What does this express?"

"Rage!"

"Stuff! It means terror! *This!*"

"Imbecility!"

"Fool! It is smothered ferocity! Now *this!*"

"Joy!"

"Oh, perdition! Any ass can see it means insanity!"

Mark Twain's insight was the forerunner of much research which has showed precisely the same thing. Facial expression alone is not always the valid medium of communication that many of us expect. Nonverbal symbols are like language in that the message received is not always the message sent. People differ in their abilities both to represent and to interpret message systems.

We will be able to make our nonverbal communication more reliable—will be able to understand and predict the responses such stimuli will evoke and will be able to create more effective nonverbal messages—if we first try to understand the audience more thoroughly. The prior knowledge, attitudes, and experiences of the receiver will have a tendency to shape the meaning of nonverbal stimuli to which he is exposed, just as they tend to shape the meaning of the verbal stimuli.

Varied Meaning

In planning any sort of nonverbal message, or the nonverbal part of a message, you must consider whether the intended receiver has learned your meanings for the stimuli or whether, in the course of the communication encounter, you can insure his learning them. Has he learned to associate bar graphs or pie charts with such concepts as the cost of living or the disposition of the tax dollar? If not, can you provide cues in the context which will help him to understand such associations? You might take a cue here from the Russian film theorist, Pudovkin, and from more recent communication scholars in this country, who demonstrated the way in which the meaning that the audience "sees" in a facial expression can be altered by the visual stimuli which precede it. In one series of experiments, these scholars used a basic motion picture scene showing a man approaching and turning to look at something. This was followed by a closeup of his face which, when viewed alone, appeared relatively emotionless. However, when shots of a baby, an attractive girl, an accident, and a man on a burning tankcar were alternately edited into the film, each preceding the closeup of the man's face, members of the audience (each of whom saw only one version) reported seeing different emotions expressed on the man's face. One recent study has even showed the way in which completely unrelated stimuli are organized and interpreted by an audience to make sense, a sense which is consistent with their prior attitudes and their understandings of the situation. In this study,[3] three groups of fraternity men were each shown a videotape. The sound on all videotapes was the same—a speech against fraternities. The visual portion, however, was different for each group: one was the speaker delivering the speech, one was a pleasant film of a locomotive journey across the French countryside, and another was an unpleasant film of garbage, burning refuse polluting the air, and dumped materials contaminating streams. These variations in the visual portion of the message sharply affected the discussion which took place among the fraternity men afterward. Those who saw the speaker spent most of their time discussing the points made in the speech. Those who saw either the train or garbage (pleasant or unpleasant) version spent most of their time discussing the implications of the combination of visual and aural. As the researchers said of the viewers:

They came to some decisions about the reasons for the content of the film that had never been intended by the experimenters. They decided, for example, that the reason for showing a film of a steam engine was that fraternities—like steam engines—were antiquated. In fact, they determined that every scene was in some way subliminal support for the message. The "unpleasant" section . . . decided that the idea behind showing scenes of garbage was that fraternities accept only the social elite and discard—like garbage—everyone else.

Thus, though the researchers purposefully used films in the second two versions that they believed to be unrelated to the speech, the audience, being exposed to speech and films together, made sense out of the juxtaposition—gave meanings to the films which they would not have in a different context.

The implication of these findings for you as a communicator should be clear; you must be conscious of the need for an audience member to organize his environment in a way that makes sense to him. In doing so, he is likely to give meaning to elements of your message that you did not intend and, so, to misperceive your intent. Sometimes, these elements are so minor that you might not even think of their existence or, if you do, might not realize that they will be noticed by an audience. In any message, there are many elements which are irrelevant to the sender's purpose, except insofar as they are needed to carry the basic elements. As an obvious example, if a communicator's goal is to help a viewer understand what a sphere is, the color of the sphere is probably irrelevant to the communicator, but it must be some color in order to carry the spherical quality. When a speaker is involved in a discussion of campus regulations, his posture, the clothing

---

[3] William G. Freeman and Daniel J. Perkins, "Persuasion in Situations of Pleasant and Unpleasant Distraction," unpublished paper, Communication Research Laboratory, Department of Speech and Dramatic Art, University of Iowa, January, 1969.

that he wears, the fact that he does or does not have a beard may be irrelevant, yet they may affect the perceived meaning of the verbal message. One of the problems of a communicator is knowing how to minimize irrelevant or distracting cues, how best to help the receiver realize what is most important and relevant, and what is least important and relevant. There are many examples which could be cited in which the communication failed because the audience attended to an irrelevant aspect of the message or gave unintended meaning to it.

Overlapping Sense Modalities

A somewhat different phenomenon which we need to consider if we are to understand nonverbal communication is *synesthesia*. We know that an individual often abstracts some common quality from quite different stimuli which he sees or hears and thus tends to perceive two objects as similar even when the differences are far greater than the similarities. For example, he may abstract the quality of greenness or roundness. It now appears that he can also abstract some common quality from stimuli received via quite different sense modalities and thus see these stimuli as similar, even though one may be a visual stimulus and one other an auditory stimulus. This phenomenon, termed "synesthesia," could explain why a rapidly ascending series of musical tones is often perceived as similar to the act of running up a flight of stairs. Synesthesia seems to explain the generality and the effectiveness of much of our use of nonverbal symbols in communication. However, though it is always reassuring to have an explanation that makes our environment easier to understand, it is not sufficient cause for hasty acceptance of the explanation. Though synesthesia probably has some basis in reality, the question remains of whether one *learns* to generalize across sensory modalities or whether such stimulus generalization is *natural* and the learning is in the other direction, learning to discriminate among these similar stimuli. Or is it a combination of both? These are basic questions for anyone interested in understanding nonverbal communication.

Besides the question of how individuals acquire these various meanings for symbols, there is the question of which meanings they have and have not acquired. One can cite many examples (in addition to Mark Twain's actor) of assumptions made by communicators about the meanings which people have for stimuli which, upon investigation, turn out not to be valid. Beliefs about film and television transitions are a prime illustration. Film and television directors and textbook writers tell us of the distinct meaning of each type of transitional device: a slow fade has the psychological effect of a descending curtain in the theater, saying "This is the end"; the combination of a fade-out and fade-in may be used to denote a lapse of time between two scenes taking place in the same set, and so on. Yet, research shows that these transitional devices do *not* have a common meaning for film-makers. Many of us have similar beliefs about the meaning evoked in audiences by various musical devices, by certain vocal qualities, certain movements of the body, or certain graphic devices. To what extent are these beliefs justified? Under what conditions? For what types of audiences? Under what conditions are they not so? The truth of the matter is, we do not know. These are basic communication questions which you must attempt to answer through observation and study.

Verbal and Nonverbal Systems

In planning your messages or trying to understand a communication situation or process, it is a good idea to consider some of the similarities and differences between verbal and nonverbal messages or message elements. Certainly one of the major ones is *structure*. Verbal messages tend to be linear; we are able to transmit or receive only one word at a time; we must listen to or read a string of words before we can grasp the total idea. A nonverbal message, on the other hand, is often global or all-at-once, e.g., a chart or a photograph, or it too may have continuity and syntax.

Unfortunately, we do not yet know very much about the grammar or syntax of nonverbal "languages," how different structures or organizations of a nonverbal message affect what we see or how we respond. We do know, however, that nonverbal symbols with continuity such as motion pictures, are interpreted differently than nonverbal symbols without continuity, such as still pictures. We do not know the precise ways in which nonverbal grammars are analogous to verbal grammars. We do not know the effect of the global or all-at-once structure of some nonverbal messages, as opposed to the linear structure of most verbal messages.

Another difference between nonverbal and verbal messages is that many nonverbal elements can have an infinite number of values, while verbal elements tend to have a somewhat more restricted number of values. As one trivial example, there are an infinite number of variations in size which an object may have and still be carried in one's hand; yet, there are an extremely limited number of words to describe these sizes. Similarly, consider the possible variations in intensity of the color red one can make verbally. Again, it is unclear whether this difference between verbal and nonverbal messages makes a difference. There is some evidence that the complete independence of the visual from the verbal may be an illusion. It is obvious that there can be many variations of size or intensity which no individual can discriminate. In addition, and more important, there is some evidence from cross-cultural studies that people whose language has *names* for a greater variety of values or intensities can discriminate among more differences than people whose language has fewer such names. Thus, the nonverbal communicator may be quite dependent upon the verbal habits of his audience. This is not to say that one cannot learn responses

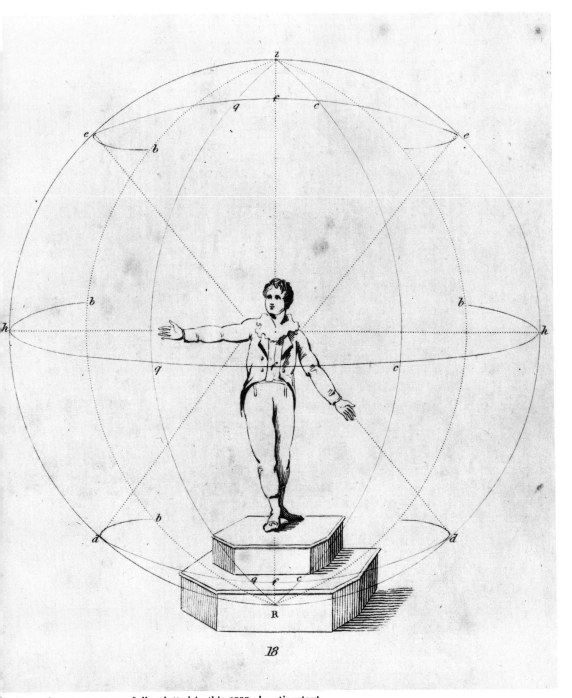

he lines of gesture are carefully plotted in this 1806 elocution text.

Chironomia, or a Treatise on Rhetorical Delivery, *Rev. Gilbert Austin, London, 1806.*

Each gesture within the plotted globe conveys a different message.

Chironomia, or a Treatise on Rhetorical Delivery, *Rev. Gilbert Austin, London, 18*

This collection of illustrated texts for schoolboys admonishes that much credit is due the neat and graceful bow. "There should be no parade or affectation, but all marked by the manliness of a noble boy, who thinks more of propriety and excellence than he does of mere show."

"This posture not unfrequently becomes necessary in the exercises of school exhibitions; . . . the pupil has but to recollect that he should kneel upon the knee *farthest from* the party addressed. Young children and rustics generally fall upon *both* knees.

This attitude of "*aversion* mingled with *fear*" accompanies these lines after the word brain:

Take—*take* it from my loathing lip,
Ere madness fires my brain:

Bless thee! oh bless thee, wandering air!
  Thrice blessed my heavenly guide!
Soon will my weary feet be where
  My heart long since has died.

"The *course* begins immediately after the word *air;* the hands come together upon the word *thrice,* making the *stroke,* and are kept in this position till the speaker pronounces the word **soon,** when they part in an *outward curve,* and fall to *rest* on the word *feet.*"

John Epy Lovell, The Young Speaker, *Cincinnati, 1852.*

to a visual or auditory stimulus or some other type of sensory symbol without having a name for it. This would obviously not be true. But it is true that, for some reason, those whose language does not provide for such responses or discriminations apparently tend not to learn them.

The nonverbal stimuli with which you, as a communicator, must be most concerned are those which any speaker creates, consciously or not, whether he tries to control them or not. These are the stimuli created by his person as an instrument of communication:

1. Facial expression
2. Eye contact
3. Posture
4. Gesture
5. Other movements of the body
6. Clothing
7. Vocal quality
8. Inflection
9. Rate

All of these elements "say" something to an audience. Some of the things they say are obvious and predictable; others are not. Clearly, if you speak very rapidly, in a monotone, with a minimum of bodily movement, and an expressionless face, most members of the audience will infer that you are not very interested in what you are talking about. If the audience is generally well dressed and you are unkempt, they will probably infer that you do not care what they think about you and that you do not think much of them; hence, your credibility will be reduced. On the other hand, if you are interviewing or speaking with a group of poor persons in a ghetto, "dressing up" or dressing very fashionably can also reduce your credibility. In many cases—perhaps in most—the meanings which these nonverbal cues evoke from an audience have nothing to do with the intent or state of the person being observed. For example, he may avoid eye contact with the audience because he is nervous, but the audience is very likely to infer that he is "shifty-eyed," hence not to be trusted. Interestingly, many studies of audience perceptions of emotions communicated by facial and vocal expressions show a fair degree of reliability among receivers in their judgments, even though the emotion that they perceive is not the one felt by the person being observed. In other words, the meaning evoked fairly consistently from the audience is not necessarily the "true" meaning—the meaning intended by the source. From these findings and those from some of the cross-cultural studies, it is clear that we learn to respond to the cues of facial and vocal expression; hence, it should be possible to improve our skill at both sending and accurately perceiving such cues. It also seems clear from the cross-cultural studies that there are differences among cultures in their nonverbal as well as their verbal languages.

Certain ways of expressing a specific emotion as appropriate for a situation are learned in the process of living in a culture. The learning operates not only for the expressor but also for the individual who must judge the emotional expression. It is by such learning of larger contexts that the happy Chinese girl is seen as "happy" by her fellow villagers and as "shy" or "bland" by Western Europeans.[4]

In comparing facial expression and vocal quality and inflection as modes of communicating emotions, Dusenbury and Knower concluded that "although the visible means of communication seem on the whole to be better than the oral, the extent to which this is true depends upon the performer, the receptors of stimulation and the mood to be communicated."[5]

The most striking examples of high agreement among perceivers, with questionable relationship to accuracy, are the studies which have found that listeners agree quite well on the personality traits of speakers whom they do not know but whose voices they hear; but these judgments have little relationship to the personality traits which standard tests show the speakers to have.

Thus, if you are to use your voice and face and body for optimum communication—for communicating what you want to communicate—it is essential that you become sensitive to the particular kinds of persons with whom you will be communicating and attempt to adjust your behaviors to them.

Visual Aids

The types of nonverbal stimuli which are second in importance only to one's voice and body are the so-called visual aids. These vary from quite simple, quickly produced aids to exceedingly complex, carefully planned objects. Among the widely used visual aids are the following:

■   1. *Blackboard.* This classroom standby can often be used effectively. However, as you know from the experiences you have had in many classes, it can also be used ineffectively. The use of the blackboard must be as carefully planned as the use of any other visual device or the rest of one's message. Avoid the haphazard, professorial scribble.

■   2. *Large paper pad on portable easel.* Material can be sketched on the pages beforehand and the pages simply flipped during the presentation. An alternative is to lightly pencil outlines or reminders on each page which you can use as cues to what you will write or sketch, but which the audience cannot see.

---

[4] Jerome S. Bruner and Renato Tagiuri, "The Perception of People," in Gardner Lindzey (ed.), *Handbook of Social Psychology,* Addison-Wesley, Reading, Mass., 1954, Vol. 2, p. 637.
[5] Delwin Dusenbury and Franklin H. Knower, "Experimental Studies in the Symbolism of Action and Voice," *Quarterly Journal of Speech,* 25:73–75, 1939.

■ 3. *Flip cards.* These are similar to the paper pad on which material has been sketched beforehand, except that these are generally more carefully prepared.

■ 4. *Enlarged photographs.*

■ 5. *Flannel or felt board.* This consists simply of a piece of flannel or felt, pulled taut and fastened on a flat board, which serves as a base for cutouts. Light cutouts of paper or cardboard with a piece of sandpaper glued rough side out to their backs can be stuck to the flannel board simply by pressing them to the board. The rough sandpaper catches and sticks on the flannel or felt. Small pieces of flannel or felt are sometimes used in place of the sandpaper, but they do not stick as well. Two other precautions should be taken to reduce the possibility of your cutouts falling. One is to tilt the top of the flannel board back slightly, rather than having it perfectly vertical, and the other is to press each cutout firmly to the flannel board when you place it on. Obviously, you should use sharply contrasting colors for the flannel or felt and the cutouts which will be used.

■ 6. *Magnetic board.* This is similar to the flannel board in function and use but consists of a metal board rather than one covered with flannel. The cutouts have strips of magnetized metal on their backs. A magnetic board is somewhat more dependable than a flannel board and can support heavier cutouts. You even can throw a cutout at a magnetic board and it will stick.

■ 7. *The object or objects about which you are talking.* Any experienced communicator will show and demonstrate an object, when feasible, rather than simply trying to describe it.

■ 8. *Models.* These are extremely useful when the object about which you are talking is too small to be seen well by the audience (e.g., a light meter) or too large to bring along (e.g., an airplane). They are also useful when the actual object is too complicated visually or constructed in such a way that the audience cannot see easily what you want them to see. This would be the case with certain parts of a computer or with an automobile engine. Models can also be useful sometimes to visualize an abstract idea, as biologists have done with the concept of inherited traits.

Your problem, as a communicator, is selecting from this vast storehouse of nonverbal stimuli the ones that will be most effective *for your particular purposes, for your particular audience,* and *for your particular audience situation.* For example, you would probably use a different type of visual to gain attention than you would use for teaching recognition of an object. In teaching recognition, you would use a different visual with an audience that had some knowledge of the object than one which did not, and a different *size* of visual at least for an audience of fifty than an audience of one or two.

Nonverbal Functions

Though any nonverbal stimulus may be used for a variety of purposes, you should generally have a primary purpose in mind for each, and develop it in such a way that it will best serve that purpose. Among the many purposes that nonverbal stimuli serve are the following:

■   1.   *To catch and hold the attention of your audience.* Here, the unusual quality of the stimulus and its contrast with the environment are important. The eye patch on the man in the shirt ads is a good example of a nonverbal stimulus used to gain and hold attention. An example of the importance of an attention-demanding stimulus which contrasts with its environment is found in a communication study done for the Air Force. The problem attacked by the researchers was to find a stimulus which could be used to warn a pilot of danger and which would be certain to attract his attention when he was busily attending to many other messages and tasks. The researchers found that the recorded voice of a woman was most effective in this situation. The nonverbal quality of "femaleness" contrasts with the normal sounds a pilot is hearing and, thus, instantly attracts attention. The careful use of this finding may save many lives.

■   2.   *To orient the listener or reader to the attitudinal intent of the communicator.* Here, nonverbal stimuli function the way feedback does to orient a speaker to his listeners. Thus the posture, actions, and tones of voice suggest whether the verbal message arises from such contexts as mirth, fear, surprise, anger, or approval.

■   3.   *To evoke a favorable impression of credibility and personality.* A speaker's facial expression, vocal quality, gesture, dress, and other actions affect the audience's perceptions of the speaker's credibility and whether he thinks what he is talking about is important. Keep in mind that relatively simple nonverbal cues can sharply alter the audience's perceptions of you or the ideas about which you are talking. Advertising agencies often use this phenomenon consciously to change the "image" of a product. For example, dyeing one's hair was once thought to be something only evil women did. Then an advertiser began showing women with dyed hair and a child—indicating that these women were good mothers, hence "ladies," and hence, there was nothing wrong with dyeing one's hair.

■   4.   *To emphasize meaning.* A great deal of evidence shows that the use of visualization increases retention of information and, in many cases, increases the probability of audience acceptance. For example, when agricultural extension workers wanted to persuade farmers in this country and abroad to adopt hybrid seed corn, they planted a field of hybrid corn beside a field of regular corn. As the corn in the two fields grew, the "message" was obvious to everyone and, hence, quite persuasive. Nonverbal stimuli can help an audience learn to recognize an object (e.g., to recognize a tufted titmouse from its appearance or sound), to make needed associations (e.g., to associate the picture of a bird with the Spanish word for bird), and to reconstruct an object (e.g., to be able to draw a tufted titmouse or imitate its sound).

■   5.   *To suggest an intangible idea.* We mentioned the use of models for this purpose earlier. Advertisers have attempted to suggest the taste of a cigarette (whether successfully or not we do not know) with the photograph of an attractive girl on the seacoast with wind blowing in her hair.

The qualities which a good nonverbal message has are analogous to the qualities of a good verbal message: clarity, simplicity, a bit of redundancy, and adaptation to the audience. If you plan the nonverbal aspects of your message with clear purposes in mind, and you understand your audience and the communication situation, clarity should be no problem. Clarity is enhanced when the nonverbal messages are kept as simple as possible, stripped of nonessentials. Never try to say too much with a single visual aid, for example; avoid clutter; and definitely keep the amount of verbal material on a visual to a minimum. In addition, keep the size of the intended audience in mind or, more specifically, the maximum distance of any audience member from you. Adjust size and loudness of your nonverbal stimuli accordingly. The best sort of redundancy for insuring comprehension and retention is "saying" the same or similar things through different modes of communication. Thus, the attention of the audience will probably be held better and they will retain more of the material if an idea is communicated both verbally and visually, rather than simply being repeated in the verbal mode.

Above all, in planning your nonverbal stimuli, use your imagination! Take a cue from the designer who thinks less of *symbols,* and more of the *symbolic value of things.* If he were attempting to communicate the essence of the modern age, especially the intangible notion of man's control over the universe, such a designer would probably select the pushbutton as the most relevant symbol—it can start a vehicle toward the moon or turn on a vacuum cleaner.

Projects and Problems

PROJECT 1:   Hold a class discussion on just what may be included in nonverbal symbolism. Remember that symbols are economical substitutes for more direct representation of mental states and processes. You must recognize that while symbols may arouse meaning, not all stimuli that arouse meaning are symbolic. Consider whether the suggestions in the chart adapted from Harrison (p. 173) are all symbolic.

PROJECT 2:   Observe two or more people in interpersonal communication in a relatively free unrestricted situation. Report on what their voices told you of their messages. What was the significance of the postures, movement, and voices? What, if any, nonverbal symbols other than voice, postures, and movement were communicated to you, and what was your interpretation of each?

PROJECT 3:   What nonverbal symbol systems can you identify that have been formalized and institutionalized? Was elocution one of them? Make and report on a list of your reactions to what you consider nonverbal symbols. Relate them to verbal communication.

PROJECT 4: Discuss the comparative synesthesia across the lines of the sensory modalities. How do you account for differences of verbal and nonverbal systems in the same person?

PROJECT 5: Hold a series of class reports on references suggested in this chapter. Make a list of ideas for the use of nonverbal symbols you might like to work into your communication practice.

References

Birdwhistle, Ray L., *Introduction to Kinesics. An Annotation System for Analysis of Bodily Motion and Gesture.* Washington, U.S. Department of State, Foreign Service Institute, 1952.

Campbell, James H., and Hal W. Hepler, *Dimensions in Communication, Readings.* Belmont, Calif.: Wadsworth Publishing Company, Inc., 1965. Section Three, Randall Harrison, "Non-Verbal Communication: Explorations in Time, Space, Action, and Object," pp. 158–173.

Crystal, David, *Prosodic Systems and Intonation in English.* London: Cambridge University Press, 1969.

Davitz, Joel E., *The Communication of Emotional Meaning.* New York: McGraw-Hill Book Company, 1964.

———, *The Language of Emotion.* New York: Academic Press, 1968.

Efron, David, *Gesture and Environment.* Morningside Heights, N.Y.: King's Crown Press, 1941.

Hall, Edward T., *The Hidden Dimension.* Garden City, N.Y.: Doubleday & Company, Inc., 1969.

———, *The Silent Language.* Garden City, N.Y.: Doubleday & Company, Inc., 1959.

Knapp, Peter H., *Expression of the Emotions in Man.* New York: International Universities Press, Inc., 1963.

Lindzey, Gardner, and Elliot Aronson (eds.), *The Handbook of Social Psychology,* 2nd ed. Reading, Mass.: Addison-Wesley Publishing Co., 1969. See Renato Tagiuri, "Person Perception," Vol. 3, Chapter 23.

Ore, Oystein, *Graphs and Their Uses.* New York: Random House, 1963.

Ruesch, Jurgen, and Weldon Kees, *Non-Verbal Communication.* Berkeley, Calif.: University of California Press, 1956.

Smith, Henry Clay, *Sensitivity to People.* New York: McGraw-Hill Book Company, 1966.

Wiman, Raymond V., and Wesley C. Meierhenry, *Educational Media Theory into Practice.* Columbus, Ohio: Charles E. Merrill Publishing Company, 1969. See Randall Harrison, "Communication Theory," pp. 59–92.

PART SIX

Channels of Communication

Gluyas Williams, from Hear! Hear!, Simon and Shuster, 1941. Cartoon courtesy of W. J. Dent, London.

principles and processes

We have come a long way since the days when information and man moved at the same rate. In early times, the range for immediate communication was the range of the human voice and ear or the range of the human eye; the speed of information flow across a greater range was limited by the ability of man to run. Man has increased his speeds greatly in recent times, with the assistance of the horse, the combustion engine, and now the jet, and will undoubtedly increase them even more; it has been predicted that he will someday be able to move at 30 to 40 percent of the speed of light. However, the movement of information has been equal to the speed of light for a number of years—since the advent of broadcasting. The result is that today one can literally talk to millions of people simultaneously. Because of this and the fact that such a large proportion of the attention of most people is focused upon the media, one scholar of human behavior has asserted that one cannot even be heard today if his message is not transmitted by the media—if it is not given the "amplification" of the mass media. For some purposes, such as trying to get a political candidate elected or trying to market a product on a nationwide basis, this is undoubtedly true. On the other hand, for other purposes, such as teaching a class or influencing the operation of a club or normal-sized business establishment, it is clearly not true. In this chapter we will suggest some of the factors that should influence your choice of channels of communication and which will help you to understand and use them more intelligently.

Channels and the Senses

The channels of communication can be looked at in two quite different, though equally important, ways. They can be considered in terms of the five human senses (sight, hearing, touch, taste, and smell) or as the various media of communication (face to face, telephone, print, film, radio, and television). Within each category system, a sophisticated communicator will differentiate among subcategories. For example, as indicated in the last chapter, one must understand the differences in the possible uses and effects of various messages designed to be perceived through the sense of sight. It is naive to attempt to generalize too quickly across graphs, photographs, gestures, facial expressions, print, and colored light. Similarly, within any one of the gross categories of media, one must discriminate among carriers. **191**

There are important differences within the print medium, for example, between communicating via the mimeographed throwaways used by some groups on college campuses, or through the student newspaper, *Playboy* magazine, *Harpers*, the *New York Times,* or the *Village Voice.* Each is most useful for some purposes with some audiences. Just as with the various sorts of visual stimuli, it would be naive to assume that because all of these are print media, all of the same generalizations about communication can be applied to each.

It is fruitful to think of the five senses as five major pathways through which your message can get "inside" the members of your intended audience. For any stimulus to affect an audience member, he must first sense it through one or more of these pathways—he must hear it, see it, touch it, taste it, or feel it. It is probable that, in most instances, your message will be most effective if you utilize more than one of these channels—not only because one channel may reinforce the other or because different aspects of the message are better suited to different channels, but also because it enables the source to *control* these channels and keep out distractions or what communication theorists call "noise." For example, when you are speaking, the members of your audience will be seeing something. Whether that "something" distracts from or reinforces your aural message is probably dependent upon whether you create something relevant for him to see. This may be a set of gestures and facial expressions which can help to evoke some of the responses that you seek, or it may be a set of pictures or graphs or even a demonstration. In other words, the more you control the total communication environment—assuming that you do it intelligently—the greater the chances that you will be able to achieve the purposes for which you are speaking.

Channels, Purposes, and Content

Since we usually depend upon one primary channel for any particular message, many communicators and communication scholars have asked which channel is superior to the others for communication. Analysis of the studies that have been done shows clearly that this is not a meaningful question. More meaningful, because it may be answerable, is the question of which particular channel is superior to the others *for a particular audience, under particular conditions, and for a particular purpose.* Thus, before deciding on a channel, you ought to have clearly in mind the audience which you hope to reach, the sorts of communication skills and habits the audience members have, what each receiver is to do with the data he receives, and the situation in which the communication is to occur. Of these considerations, most important is what the receiver is to do with the information that he receives. Clearly, for some goals, a number of channels or media are interchangeable; one will be as effective as another. (Thus, it should have been no surprise that when studies were done comparing the retention by college students of lecture material they heard from a "live" teacher with retention from a teacher on television with retention from the same material which they read, differences were negligible.) On the other hand, for other sorts of things which you might hope your message will do for your audience, there are sound theoretical reasons and some evidence indicating that different channels will not be equally effective. For example, if your goal is to have receivers be able to recognize some part of your message when they encounter it again, the optimum channel for the message is that in which they will encounter it in the future. So if you want receivers to be able to recognize the message when they *hear* it in the future, you probably ought to use an audio mode in the original message. On the other hand, if you want them to recognize it when they run across it in future reading, you probably ought to use the visual mode for the original message. In other words, the more closely a communication situation approximates the situation in which learned responses are to be made, the more successful the communication will be.[1]

Usually, of course, as a communicator in your business or family or organization, you will not be concerned solely with a single message but, rather, with a set of messages—a campaign or a continuous series of communication encounters to keep the organization running and to help the individuals and the groups to achieve their and your goals. Whether at any given moment you are considering such a series or a single message, you ought to think through the probable relationships between your purposes and the available channels. Though you would do so only on very rare occasions, you could diagram these relationships thus:

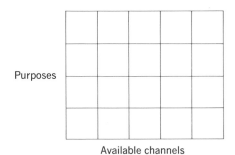

Purposes

Available channels

If you then began to add the kinds of content which must be used with these channels to achieve your purposes, you would have a three dimensional diagram such as that on page 194.

[1] See S. S. Stevens (ed.), *Handbook of Experimental Psychology,* John Wiley, New York, 1951, pp. 663–666, 676.

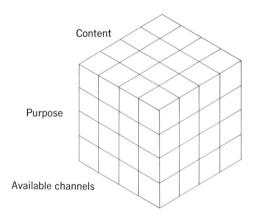

Within this diagram or matrix you could indicate the cells where a particular bit of content could be transmitted via a particular channel to achieve a particular purpose. You could see which kinds of content could not be transmitted by available channels or which could not serve any of the purposes. You could see which purposes could not be served by the channels available or the content which you have in mind. You could see which bits of content should serve more than one purpose and where a purpose is to be pursued with more than one bit of content or through more than one channel. You would then be in a position to predict the additional content that needs to be added and the content that can be deleted because it is unnecessarily redundant or because it serves no purpose.

Multichannel Messages

Though you will only rarely do this sort of formal analysis of your messages, you should go through something of this sort of thought process in planning most of your important messages or communication campaigns.

In a large proportion of the communication in which we engage, we use more than one channel. This is obviously so in a film or a television program, or when a speaker uses visual aids. However, even in an ordinary speech, discussion, or conversation, we employ both speech and visual cues, for we gesture or display some sort of facial expression, while we talk and listen. In planning such multiple-channel communication, or in trying to understand the situations in which it goes on, it is important to discriminate at least four types of multiple channel messages:

1. Those in which the content in one channel is basically unrelated to that in the other channels.
2. Those in which the content in the two channels is related, though not the same.

3. Those in which essentially the same content is presented via both channels.
4. Those in which contradictory content is presented via the two channels.

In general, when essentially the same information is presented simultaneously via two channels (print and audio have been tested most), the evidence is clear that receivers tend to retain more than when it is presented via only one channel. This seems to be especially true where there is interference with the message. For example, in one study poems were presented to different audiences orally, in print form, and in a combination of the two when there was a good bit of extraneous sound and where the visual message was partly obliterated by black dots (a type of visual "noise"). Audience members understood and retained best when they were exposed to the combination of aural and visual versions of the message, rather than to either one alone.[2]

It also appears that when *related* content is presented on the two channels, receivers tend to retain more than they do from information presented via a single channel. However, the evidence is less clear here than it is for more purely redundant information in two channels.

If one carefully examines the studies on multiple-channel learning, the most reasonable explanation for the usual superiority of the multiple channels is that using more than one channel provides additional cues or stimuli which the receiver can learn responses to. However, these additional cues are only useful if they are present in the situation where the learning is to be used. In cases where they are not—where cues from only one channel are present—the original message is just as effective, perhaps even more effective, if it is presented solely in that one channel. The cues from the second or third channel are irrelevant.

As one would expect, when unrelated information is presented simultaneously on two channels, comprehension and retention are reduced. The loss increases with the increasing difficulty of the messages, and when the messages in the two channels are of unequal difficulty the less difficult messages suffer most.[3]

In general, it appears that brief auditory stimuli are more "attention demanding" than brief visual stimuli are. However, you must always consider the particular demands of the situation—the situation in which communication is to take place. A housewife listening to the radio while cleaning house probably attends to what she hears less than someone alone in his car listening. Similarly, if someone is alone in his car, he probably

---

[2]Hower J. Hsia, "Output, Error, Equivocation, and Recalled Information in Auditory, Visual, and Audiovisual Information Processing with Constraint and Noise," *The Journal of Communication,* 18:325–345, 1968.
[3]A more detailed analysis of multiple channel communication can be found in a paper by Frank R. Hartman, "Single and Multiple Channel Communication: A Review of Research and a Proposed Model," *Audio-Visual Communication Review,* 9:235–262, 1961.

attends more to what is on the radio than someone driving with others in the car. Most people in their homes probably attend to television programs more than they do to radio programs because they are more likely to be doing other things which compete for attention while listening to the radio.

Channels and Impact

Where there is distraction, and it is the same for an aural and a visual message (which it seldom is outside the classroom situation or the communication research laboratory), voice messages are usually comprehended and retained better than print messages.

The results of many studies show that receivers retain more information from messages they hear than from messages they read. On the other hand, an almost equal number of studies show the receivers retain more from messages they read. A careful analysis of these studies indicates that the discrepant results can be accounted for in terms of differences in the quality of the speaker, the difficulty of the messages, and the ability level of the receivers. In general, it appears that for complex messages and well-educated receivers, the print medium tends to be superior; for simple messages and children or relatively uneducated adults, the auditory medium is superior. There is also a limited amount of evidence indicating that pictorial messages are superior to either visual or aural verbal messages. However, further studies, utilizing a variety of visual and verbal stimuli and a variety of learning criteria, are needed before we place too much confidence in this last generalization.

There is some evidence that those who hear a verbal message recall different aspects of the message from those who read it. In addition, there are consistent differences between the messages produced by people asked to speak about a topic and those produced by people asked to write about the same topic.

In one study,[4] half of the subjects heard a message twice with only a brief period in between and the other half were asked to read it twice. Immediately afterward, half of each group was asked to write all that they could remember of the message and the other half was asked to speak all that they could remember. Those who reproduced the message orally produced a large body of material, but with a relatively smaller vocabulary. There is no significant difference between the modes of expression in the number of different ideas reproduced, but there was more redundancy of ideas in the spoken mode. The differences in recall associated with the

---

[4]Milton W. Horowitz and Alan Berkowitz, "Listening and Reading, Speaking and Writing: An Experimental Investigation of Differential Acquisition and Reproduction of Memory," Queens College of the City University of New York. (Mimeographed, no date.)

different channels for receiving the message were more pronounced. Subjects who heard the message were able to reproduce a larger portion of it, with more ideas, fewer omissions of important units, and a stylistically superior reproduction. However, they also produced more distortions of the message than subjects did who read it.

Most studies which have tested the difference in effects on attitude change between aural and printed messages have failed to find any significant difference.[5] However, there is some evidence that attitudes toward a speaker can be affected by the medium of communication through which one is exposed to him. For example, in one study done some years ago of three potential presidential candidates who appeared on the "Meet the Press" television program, it was found that college students who saw the television program with Senator Robert Taft became less favorable toward him, but those who read the transcript of the program instead of seeing it became more favorable toward him. The attitudes of those who simply heard the sound track remained unchanged. For Governor Thomas Dewey, the findings were reversed: Those who saw his television appearance became more favorable, those who read the transcript became less favorable, and again those who heard the sound track remained essentially the same. On the other hand, attitudes toward Senator Richard Russell became more favorable no matter through which medium of communication the students were exposed to him.[6]

In an independent study utilizing two "Meet the Press" programs, one with Governor Dewey and one with Governor Adlai Stevenson, which tested the retention of information from hearing the sound tracks against retention of information from both hearing and seeing the programs, no significant difference was found.[7] Though one must be careful of generalizing from only one or two studies, it appears that the medium may make more of a difference on credibility of a speaker than on retention of or attitude toward what he says.

Not only are audience members often affected differently by messages they receive through different channels, communicators also tend to create somewhat different messages when they are using different channels. In general, if one is writing and speaking under similar conditions on the same topic, he will tend to use shorter words and sentences when speaking than when writing. As a result, the speeches are easier to comprehend according to the various tests of message difficulty such as the Flesch Reading-Ease

---

[5] See, for example, Don Richardson, "Shift-of-Opinion and Retention of Material as a Function of Reading and/or Hearing," *The Southern Speech Journal*, 32:41–48, 1966.
[6] Samuel L. Becker, "The Impact of the Mass Media of Society," in Raymond V. Wiman and Wesley C. Meierhenry (eds.), *Educational Media: Theory into Practice*, Charles E. Merrill, Columbus, Ohio, 1969, pp. 27–54.
[7] Harold E. Nelson, "Two Methods of Presentation of 'Meet the Press' Compared," *Journal of Broadcasting*, 1:274–277, 1957.

formula. Speeches also tend to have more such personalized words as "I," "me," "you," "us," and "we." On the other hand, the written messages tend to have a more varied vocabulary.[8] Evidence also indicates that most of us use more nouns and adjectives when we write than when we speak, but use more verbs and adverbs when we speak.[9]

Findings such as these raise interesting questions about the relative effects of messages via these different channels. Most of the research has compared written and spoken forms of the *same* verbal message. However, the question of relative effectiveness of written messages *as they generally tend to be constructed* and spoken messages *as they generally tend to be constructed* has yet to be answered. From what we have so far discovered about such constructions, we would predict that comprehension and retention of such "natural" messages will tend to be relatively greater for the spoken form than the laboratory studies, which controlled factors such as vocabulary and sentence length, have shown.

When one turns from differences among the effects of single messages which are sensed in different ways to differences among the effects of the mass media, the problem changes in both quantitative and qualitative ways. Not only are some of the differences which we noted before magnified, but some completely different questions arise about the effects and, hence, optimum uses of the various media. Some variations in effect and, hence, optimum uses, are related to the differences in the situations in which a member of the audience is ordinarily exposed to the medium. As we have mentioned, one seldom gives undivided attention to the radio—one listens while driving, while working around the house, while studying or reading, and so on. One tends to view television with one or more other members of the family and, again, while intermittently talking or reading or doing other things. Even though movie attendance is even more of a social activity in one sense—since one generally attends with family members or friends (movies have an important mating function in our society) and views the film surrounded by a relatively large group of persons—because the movie house is darkened there is less distraction from one's close attention to this medium than there is from others. Reading, of course, is generally the most individual and independent sort of media consumption.

Another difference among the media is in the usual timing of exposure. If you examine your media habits, you will discover that there are generally particular parts of the day when you read the newspaper, listen to the radio, view television, attend a motion picture, or read books. With radio or television especially, one can predict the kinds of people in the audience fairly well by the time of day that a broadcast occurs.

---

[8]An example of the studies which have examined these relationships is James W. Gibson et al., "A Quantitative Examination of Differences and Similarities in Written and Spoken Messages," *Speech Monographs*, 33:444–451, 1966.
[9]See Joseph A. DeVito, "A Linguistic Analysis of Spoken and Written Language," *Central States Speech Journal*, 18:81–85, 1967.

There are also differences in the attitude of receivers toward each medium of communication and their expectations of it. The major difference in effect here, though, is probably between one of the mass media and face-to-face communication. The simple fact that one's message is carried by a mass medium increases its credibility. Two communication scholars, Paul Lazarsfeld and Robert Merton, have termed this the status-conferral function of the mass media.[10] The fact that one is on television or on radio or is writing in the daily newspaper gives him and his message a status which they would not have if, instead, he simply knocked on a receiver's door and gave him the same message.

Channels and Message Structure

The last of what we believe to be the major differences among media is in the way each medium structures messages and, at times, affects content. We will return to this point in a moment.

It is unlikely that you will ever give a formal speech on radio or television or publish an essay in a commercial newspaper or magazine. However, it is *not* unlikely that you will want to use the media to communicate messages to one or more publics. Unless you become President of the United States or hold other high office or become a broadcast commentator or newspaper columnist, your message will need to take forms other than the formal speech or essay to get into the media. Even Presidential candidates seldom rely on broadcast speeches to any great extent. In the 1968 campaign, for example, Richard Nixon used a "Meet the Press" format in which various panel members asked him questions and he responded in a relatively extemporaneous way. You may want to buy or, if yours is other than a commercial purpose, talk the management into giving you space for a newspaper advertisement or time for a twenty-to-thirty-second radio or television spot. You may try to get your message into a newscast or the pages of the newspaper as a news story. Some British politicians, for example, have become quite skillful at developing two or three extremely short sections in their speeches which make their major points and stand out as interesting and isolatable segments and can therefore be easily spotted and picked out by a newsman for quotation on radio or television or for recording or filming for newscasts. These politicians develop these sections carefully so that they will be short enough to fit as items on such newscasts. Other political candidates in Britain, as in this and other countries, ensure use of the newspaper and broadcasting stations for the amplification of their messages by the distribution of press releases or complete copies of their speeches to reporters. This is generally done in ample time

---

[10] Paul F. Lazarsfeld and Robert K. Merton, "Mass Communication, Popular Taste and Organized Social Action," in Wilbur Schramm (ed.), *Mass Communications*, University of Illinois Press, Urbana, Ill., 1960, pp. 497–499.

before the speech is given so that the reporters can write their stories and have them ready to go immediately after the speech is delivered. You can use these same techniques for any messages that you want widely circulated—whether you are campaigning against air pollution, raising funds for a rehabilitation center, or starting a movement against urban renewal.

If you are to gain access to the media in these ways, you must understand the needs and practices of the particular station or newspaper or magazine in which you want your message. You must know deadlines for particular newscasts or issues, kinds of materials which they are likely to use, and the form in which they are likely to use it. Establishing good working relationships with program directors of stations and with newsmen can increase the probability of your message being disseminated via the mass media and their help can insure it getting out in the best way. Those who work professionally in the media know its requirements and know its audiences. They will help to keep you aware that most members of the radio or television audience did not tune in just to get your message, nor did many readers buy a paper in order to read your story. People come into the mass media audience for a great variety of reasons—the most usual of which is to be entertained. They are generally not committed to what you are committed to; they will not view or listen or read your message just because you think it is important. They are ready to turn away from you the moment they are bored or believe that your message is irrelevant to their interests. It is your job, with the help of the professionals who work in the media, to be certain that your message is not boring to, nor perceived as irrelevant by, this audience.

To this point, we have been talking about the media largely in terms of your using them to distribute your messages through time and through space. For the sorts of communication which you will probably be doing most of the time, the media will be even more important to you in quite a different way. Not only must you think of them as means of reaching audiences, you must understand them as fully as possible as sources of information for you, because those with whom you communicate have gotten, are getting, and will continue to get information from the media which affect their responses to your messages. Therefore, you must be aware of the effects of the media on information diffusion and on the shape of that information which is diffused.

Until relatively recent years, virtually the sole source of information that one had about events beyond the scope of one's immediate experiences was interpersonal communication. For the small core of elites, there was also the book—primarily the novel. Today, most adults obtain most of their information from the popular press, the film, and the electronic media. The result is that the information available to all men varies less—there is greater commonality in the picture of the world in their heads to which they respond. Former Republican National Chairman Leonard Hall recognized this fact in his story about Maine, traditionally a Republican state. People were born Republicans, so they went to the polls and voted Republican. Then suddenly, they voted for some Democrats. Hall says that he asked an elderly Maine resident about what had happened. "Well," was the response, "we can't do anything with this television. Our children were brought up to think that Democrats had horns. Now they see them on television and realize some of them don't have horns a-tall." [11]

This is not to say that this picture of the world in the heads of man is now an accurate one—that the media transmit events without distortion. There is bias in the selection of events to be covered and distortion of those events which are selected. Most readers, listeners, and viewers never question the cliché that the media cover the events that they do because these events are news. "All the News That's Fit to Print" reads the masthead of the *New York Times*. Audience members fail to realize that such assertions are tautological, for the events covered are "news" solely *because* they are printed in newspapers or broadcast on radio or television. Thus, because the media equate news with conflict or, at times, with entertainment, people tend to get a lopsided image of reality. We usually only learn of the interaction among nations when they are in conflict, of relationships among the races when there is trouble, and of student-faculty-administration matters on college campuses when these groups are in disagreement.

Not only does the public get a distorted picture of reality because of the selectivity of the media in covering events, but also because the requirements of each medium result in a "shaping" of each event that is covered. Rare is the newspaper story organized in an accurate time sequence. Newspaper stories rather tend to be organized like a pyramid, with the most spectacular part of the story first and the details on which the story is based last, where many readers never see them. In broadcasting, every event, no matter what its nature, must be constantly interesting so that the attention of the audience will be held. The result, to cite a trivial example, is that there never has been a dull baseball game on radio. A content analysis of presidential campaign telecasts in 1960 and 1964 demonstrated the way in which not only the medium of television, but the program format within this medium affects the content of messages.[12] When candidates appeared on interview programs, they were "far more apt to justify their positions on reasoned grounds and also more inclined to critically assess their stands vis-a-vis the opposition." On the other hand, in their straight speeches, they tended more to "concentrate instead on attacking rival policy positions and give little attention to the business of defending their views against opposing

[11]Leonard W. Hall, "How Politics Is Changing," in James M. Cannon (ed.), *Politics U.S.A.*, Doubleday, Garden City, N.Y., 1960, p. 109.
[12]C. David Mortensen, "The Influence of Role Structure on Message Content in Political Telecast Campaigns," *Central States Speech Journal*, 19:279-285, 1968.

criticism." They also tended to depend more on unsupported assertions in rallies than in interviews.

Not only do the media and the program formats used "shape" the messages which they transmit, they are sometimes responsible for changing the event itself. Radio and television, for example, are credited with changing our national political conventions because the parties wanted to make them more continually interesting to the broadcast audience and to eliminate anything that might show the parties in a poor light. The mass media are responsible for the development of the presidential press conference, and as each new medium of communication has spread across the country, the conference has been adjusted to fit its demands. Election campaigns are now planned largely with the opportunities afforded by the mass media in mind.

As a communicator, it is essential that you study the media and the ways in which they are used by those with whom you communicate if you are to be successful in working in the contemporary context.

Projects and Problems

PROJECT 1: Consider and report to the class on your sources of information and ideas. For what kinds of information do you turn to television? Radio? Newspapers? Magazines? Other people? What differences do you usually find among these various sources when they deal with the same general topic?

PROJECT 2: Keep a diary for a day on all of the sources from which you get and the people to whom you give information or ideas about one issue of current concern to many people, such as the women's liberation movement, student power, racial prejudice, or reform of the college or university. Report to the class on your findings and the implications of these findings for anyone wanting to persuade others on the issue.

PROJECT 3: Read "Media Managers, Critics, and Audiences," by Gilbert Seldes in the White and Averson book noted in the references for this chapter. Consider the following dichotomies which Seldes sets up on page 41:

"Demand precedes supply—Supply creates demand."
"The public gets what it wants—Audiences take what is offered."
" 'Ratings' prove popularity—'Ratings' indicate preference between simultaneous offerings."
"The audience is always right—The managers' concept of the audience is often wrong."

Select one of these pairs and report to the class on which position you believe is more correct and why. Then discuss the implications of this position for the kinds of communication in which you are interested.

PROJECT 4: It has been claimed by some scholars that the world pictured by our entertainment media—radio, television, film, the novel—must be taken into consideration if we are to understand the effect of one of our speeches or the way in which any of our discourse functions. In a speech to your class, indicate whether you agree or disagree and present a persuasive case for your position. You may find relevant material in the Warshow book noted in the set of references at the end of this chapter.

PROJECT 5: Read "Contemporary Functions of the Mass Media," by Jack Lyle on pages 187–216 of the government report, *Mass Media and Violence*, noted in this chapter's list of references. Discuss the implications of the ideas in this paper for someone like you who is interested in improving communication.

References

Chester, Edward W., *Radio, Television and American Politics*. New York: Sheed and Ward, 1969.

Greenberg, Bradley S., and Edwin S. Parkers (eds.), *The Kennedy Assassination and the American Public*. Stanford, Calif.: Stanford University Press, 1965.

Katz, Elihu, and Paul F. Lazarsfeld, *Personal Influence, the Part Played by People in the Flow of Mass Communication*. Glencoe, Ill.: The Free Press, 1955.

Klapper, Joseph T., *The Effects of Mass Communication*. New York: The Free Press, 1960.

Lange, David L., Robert K. Baker, and Sandra J. Ball, "Mass Media and Violence," in *Report to the National Commission on the Causes and Prevention of Violence*, Vol. XI. Washington: U. S. Government Printing Office, 1969.

Rosenberg, Bernard, and David Manning White (eds.), *Mass Culture*. Glencoe, Ill.: The Free Press, 1957. See especially Paul F. Lazarsfeld and Robert K. Merton, "Mass Communication, Popular Taste, and Organized Social Action," pages 466–468.

Schramm, Wilber, *Mass Communications*, 2nd ed. Urbana, Ill.: University of Illinois Press, 1960.

———, *The Process and Effects of Mass Communication*. Urbana, Ill.: University of Illinois Press, 1954.

Waples, Douglas (ed.), *Print, Radio, and Film in a Democracy*. Chicago: University of Chicago Press, 1952.

Warshow, Robert, *The Immediate Experience*. New York: Atheneum, 1970.

White, David Manning, and Richard Averson (eds.), *Sight, Sound, and Society*. Boston: Beacon Press, 1968.

Extremely shy and with a high-pitched voice, Mrs. Eleanor Roosevelt took voice lessons from the lady at left, Mrs. Elizabeth von Hesse.

voice

Communicating effectively calls for a firm control of speaking voice as well as other aspects of speech. There are people who get by sometimes with almost any kind of voice, but we should not be satisfied with "getting by sometimes." We want to do the job of communication creditably and with all the skill we can command, because the times we do *not* get by may be the most important times in our lives.

You in Your Voice

Besides speech, the voice serves several supplementary functions. For your friends, your voice is your name in the dark or over the telephone. Friends and strangers alike infer many things from your voice: your emotional state at the moment, something of the attitude and purpose with which you speak—an important part of context—and some characteristics of your personality. Are you lazy, careless, insensitive to delicate situations or even typical social expectations? Rightly or wrongly, people will detect in your voice indications of such tendencies. You become so accustomed to your own voice that you are not aware of what it tells others about you.

The chief purpose of voice study is to help you achieve competence in its use. By competence we do not mean necessarily "golden tones" or the sepulchral voice of the opera announcer on the radio; we mean rather adequate *flexibility* and *control* for your purposes. For some purposes—those of the teacher, preacher, broadcaster, actor, personnel worker, airport traffic-control operator, salesman—a great deal of flexibility and control is essential.

The voice, like writing and the telegraph, is a medium of communication. By means of articulated sounds, it transmits language and other symbols. Because it fails to transmit an individual word successfully, poor voice production can cause the loss of the meaning of a whole sentence. Speech is a multisymbolic activity and some of the symbol systems or codes are carried by the voice. The voice carries meaning not only through the sounds of words, but also by means of quality, loudness, pitch, and time patterns which reveal the attitudes, moods, and personality of the speaker.[1] Such commonplace statements as "I didn't like his tone" and "It wasn't what

---

[1] See Delwin Dusenbury and Franklin H. Knower, "Experimental Studies of the Symbolism of Action and Voice, I," *Quarterly Journal of Speech,* 24:424–436, 1938, II, 25:67–75, 1939; Franklin H. Knower, "Analysis of Some Experimental Variations of Simulated Expressions of the Emotions," *Journal of Social Psychology,* 14:369–372, 1941.

he said, it was the way he said it" remind us forcefully that meaning in speech is evoked by many aspects of the voice. It has been shown that skill in the use of the voice is correlated with ratings of general effectiveness in speech.[2] Although voice control alone cannot assure effective speech, in certain situations speech may fail hopelessly without it.

How Effective Is Your Voice?

In a study of air traffic-control operators carried out for the Federal Aviation Agency a critical incident analysis was made of malfunction and inefficiency caused by voice characteristics.[3] The following faults are cited in order of their frequency of occurrence in this investigation:

Too fast	Anger or irritation in the voice
Weak	Poor voice quality
Hesitant	Too slow
Too loud	Trailing off
Poor phrasing	Monotone
Pitch too high	Vocalized pauses

Many of the people in this study were not aware of their faults, even though they interfered with job performance. Similar results could be found within many occupational groups.

Many beginners in speech have weak, indistinct voices. Others artificially declaim or "orate." Many are unable to project and seem to ignore their audience. Some are too breathy, speak too fast, or have a monotonous delivery. A few have organic difficulties, such as cleft palate, poor teeth, and vocal paralysis. No attempt is made in this book to analyze or discuss treatment for the organic defects, but many of them are remediable. The student who finds that he needs to correct a defect of this type should consult a speech pathologist for guidance in overcoming his problem.

Some speech deficiencies are caused by nervousness, irritability, and lack of confidence. Inadequate preparation also causes poor voice control, uncertainty, and lack of confidence. Quite apart, then, from organic handicaps, many speech students need to give more attention to the way in which they control voice production in conversation, in more formal speaking, or in both.

What Constitutes a Good Voice?

■ *Audibility.* When you speak, you must be heard without strain upon yourself or upon your listeners. Many persons who are accustomed only to the

---

[2] See Franklin H. Knower, "The Use of Behavioral and Tonal Symbols as Tests of Speaking Achievement," *Journal of Applied Psychology,* 29:229–235, 1945.
[3] Henry M. Moser, *A Voice Training Manual,* Federal Aviation Agency, Washington, 1962.

soft and moderate tones of informal speech do not make themselves clearly heard even in a small room. On the other hand, a voice which is too loud for the situation is also objectionable, for it not only hammers the eardrums but also shocks the social sensitivities. More beginners in speech have weak voices than loud. The degree of loudness you need depends, of course, upon the size of the group, the acoustics of the room, and the amount of noise.

- *Fluency.* A second standard of a good voice is fluency. The ideas of your speech should be presented as rapidly as the audience can grasp them. This obviously does not mean that you should always talk as rapidly as possible. Your rate should vary with the type of material you present, your mood and personality, the audience, and other factors in the speech situation. Most beginners tend to speak too rapidly. If you use many vocalized pauses, such as "ah," "er," or "uh," the rate is slowed down and the listener is distracted.
- *Pleasantness.* Your voice must not only be clearly audible, but it must also be reasonably pleasant for most situations. Of course, voices which are so loud that they irritate or so weak that the listeners must strain to hear are unpleasant. Unpleasantness is more commonly associated with vocal resonance than with loudness. Voices that are harsh, guttural, or raspy; metallic, shrill, or nasal; wheezy or breathy—all are unpleasant for listeners. Abnormally high pitch and tempo that is too fast or too slow are also unpleasant. If your voice can be clearly heard, if you speak at a rate that is easy to follow, if your tone is resonant and flexible enough to be used meaningfully, then your voice will achieve an acceptable standard of pleasantness.
- *Meaningfulness.* We have suggested earlier that the voice carries many meanings other than those suggested by the words. Your inflections, pauses, rate, loudness, and voice quality should help to convey not only the meanings of your words and sentences but also your attitudes toward the audience and toward the ideas your words and sentences are expressing. Consider, for example, the many *different* meanings that your voice can give to the simple words "You are a soldier."
- *Flexibility.* The opposite of flexibility is monotony or lack of variety. Ordinarily, effective speech is conversational in pattern. Ideas are expressed in a variety of tones and at a variety of rates; these vocal variations do not occur in a regular stereotyped pattern, as in the chant or in singsong speech; they are not arbitrary and mechanical variations, but depend upon your thought and should reflect your attempt to adjust to your particular listeners.

Improving Your Voice and Voice Control

At least four steps are involved in voice improvement: (1) a clear understanding of breathing, phonation or the production of sound, and resonance, and the related attributes of loudness, rate, pitch, and quality; (2) a clear understanding of your own vocal skills and limitations; (3) systematic

practice in voice improvement; and (4) systematic evaluation of your progress. In this chapter we shall analyze these four steps and set forth principles
to guide you in your program for a better voice.

It is common for students hearing the playback of the first record of their
voices to exclaim, "Do I sound like that?" We do not hear ourselves as others
hear us. Our associates, too, become accustomed to our voices and frequently overlook qualities that would be distracting to someone meeting
us for the first time.

■ An important factor in voice improvement is the ability to *hear your own
voice.* This sounds simple, but it is not. Learning to hear your own voice
is best begun by learning to hear the voices of others, to distinguish among
slight variations in loudness, rate, pitch, and quality. Then you must learn
to make these discriminations in your own voice.

■ *Listening* carefully *to recordings of effective speakers* is a good way of
becoming acquainted with desirable vocal characteristics. Recording your
own speech will be helpful in comparing your habitual voice with these
standards. Get the feeling or sensations involved in producing standard
tones. A competent critic who can listen and advise and point out differences will be a great help in guiding you to the development of new voice
standards.

When you have clearly distinguished between old vocal habits and those
■ you must work to develop, the next step is *systematic and persistent
practice.* Practice at first on material planned to make the new forms of
expression easy. Drill materials are commonly of this type. (See, for example, the projects at the end of this chapter.) As soon as possible, you should
practice with material and in the situations in which the new habits are
expected to function. You cannot expect the speech-laboratory voice drills
alone to be sufficient to fix the new habits in daily speech.

■ Practice in *oral reading* and in *rehearsing extempore speeches* is helpful
in voice improvement. These procedures are open to you: (1) You may work
mechanically to produce the voice changes you seek in the new habit; (2)
you may focus your attention on the variation of meaning to be conveyed;
or (3) you may combine the "mechanical" and the "naturalistic" methods
of improving your vocal habits. Although mechanically formed habits may
at first seem artificial, they should function quite naturally when the skill
is thoroughly developed. Just guard against becoming like the old-time radio
announcers who would cup their hands around their ears to enable them
better to hear their "well-rounded" tones. When one finished a performance,
he knew how he had sounded but had not the slightest notion of what he
had said. Most of the listeners were much impressed by the voice but
retained few of the ideas. Communication had broken down. Always keep
in mind that the purpose of developing control of your voice is not display,
but is rather to facilitate the communication of ideas through the ability
to state and shade these ideas accurately.

Gauge your progress, reminding yourself that improvement in almost any direction does not take place overnight, but comes only through successive stages of development that are sometimes not very clearly marked. Even in driving an automobile, real skill comes only after repeated trips through traffic and over highways.

1. Cultivate Proper Breathing

Adequate use of the power mechanism is the first requirement in developing a good voice. Fortunately, for most of us this is no problem except when we are nervous. Proper breathing in speech depends upon three factors. First, the lungs must retain enough air to make it unnecessary to pause within a phrase to breathe. Second, the muscles which regulate expiration must be sufficiently controlled to exert strong and steady pressure upon the breath stream. And third, this pressure must be exerted without causing undue tension in other muscles involved in voice production, particularly in the muscles of the larynx. The chest (or thoracic) cavity may be expanded in three directions—upward, outward, and downward. Breathing patterns involving upward expansion of the chest are *clavicular;* those involving outward expansion are *thoracic* or *medial;* and those involving downward expansion are *diaphragmatic.* Individual patterns of breathing often involve combinations of these elementary types. The clavicular pattern is least likely to produce effective speech because it provides the least expansion of the lungs, it is the most difficult to control, and it is more commonly associated with laryngeal tensions. Diaphragmatic breathing provides the greatest lung expansion; it is the most easily controlled pattern of breathing, and it is least likely to cause undesirable tension in the vocal musculature.

Normal breathing is rhythmical; that is, the time taken for inspiration equals the time taken for expiration. During speech, the time taken for the expiration greatly exceeds the time taken for inspiration. Although most persons acquire their breathing habits quite accidentally, the extent of control can be improved with conscious effort. The development of good breathing habits for speech is a process of modifying reflexive and accidentally acquired habit patterns of muscular action so as to achieve the necessary supply of controlled air pressure with the least exertion and superfluous tension.

2. Cultivate Proper Phonation

The second process of voice production is phonation. When the vocal folds of your larynx (vocal bands) are brought closely together and set in vibration by the force of the breath stream, a vocal tone is initiated. The pitch and some other characteristics of your tone are the result of the nature and operation of the vocal folds and other muscles of the larynx. Whispered speech and unvoiced or voiceless sounds, as we shall see later, are produced without the vibration of the vocal folds. The fundamental pitch of the voice is determined by the rate of vibration of the vocal folds as a whole. The overtones are produced by the segmented vibration of the folds, and the rate at which the folds vibrate is dependent upon their length, thickness, and tension. The quality of your voice is influenced by the capacity of the folds to set up vibrations of the frequency that can best be reinforced by your vocal resonators (air chambers in the head and throat).

3.   Cultivate a Pleasing and Responsive Voice Quality

"Quality" is that characteristic which makes one voice different from another in harshness, hoarseness, stridency, thinness, breathiness, and nasality. Quality is one of the most complex of the physical attributes of the speaking voice. It is influenced by and influences each of the other elements. Because communication can be facilitated or hindered by the quality of your voice and because listeners tend to judge your personality and state of mind in part from your voice quality, you should work for voice control to insure that that quality reflects you as a person and the meaning you wish to communicate.

Voice quality is determined primarily by resonance or lack of resonance. The main vocal resonators are the pharynx, the mouth, and the nasal cavities. Hanley and Thurman have described the problems which result in the major undesirable vocal qualities:

> *Nasal* quality is characterized by strong modification of the vocal cord tone by resonance from the nasal cavities during the production of sounds normally essentially nonnasal.
> *Breathy* quality results when the vocal cords are not brought closely enough together during the production of tone, and air rushing through the glottis produces friction heard as a whisperlike noise in addition to the vocal cord tone.
> *Thin* quality is essentially lacking in resonance. It is flat and colorless, and it gives the impression of "smallness."

These spectrograms demonstrate how easily confused the sounds of "five" and "nine" can be. Thus telephone companies train their operators to pronounce "niyan."   *Bell Telephone Laboratories, Inc.*

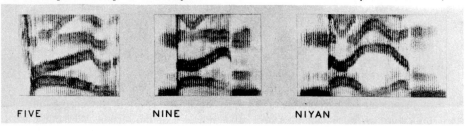

FIVE   NINE   NIYAN

Strident quality sounds hard and piercing; it is apparently caused by strain and tenseness in the resonators during voice production.

Harsh quality is unpleasant and rough; it is caused, apparently, by strain and great effort in the larynx.

Hoarse quality is characterized by a rasping, grating, sometimes husky sound as is often heard in persons with laryngitis. It may also be a result of misuse, such as too much shouting at a sports event.[4]

Improvement in voice quality requires analysis of personal problems and practice in the new pattern of resonance until it becomes a skill. Work to sharpen your ear for the changes in quality of voice. Free your neck, throat, and mouth muscles of interfering tensions. This is not to say that total relaxation is the ideal. Alertness, as opposed to tension or complete relaxation, is generally conducive to the best voice quality. Also, if you speak too fast, slow down by giving duration to speech sounds. Practice to develop a wide vocabulary of tones. Concentrating on the thoughts to be expressed will help you overcome your inhibitions about responding to ideas and feelings that you and your audience can share.

For exercises in cultivating a pleasing voice, see Project 4 at the end of this chapter.

4.   Articulate Properly

Articulation, the fourth of the physiological processes of voice, will be discussed in greater detail in Chapter Sixteen. We shall content ourselves here with the statement that the major articulators include the lips, tongue, jaw, and the soft and hard palates.

5.   Cultivate Control of Loudness

What constitutes adequate vocal intensity? The voice should be sufficiently loud to be heard easily. Listeners who must strain to hear are likely to stop listening. Variation in vocal intensity, however, is necessary to emphasize and subordinate ideas, to give words acceptable pronunciation by stressing certain syllables, and to make speech interesting. Listeners tire easily of uniform loudness. So it is not surprising that the quality that distinguishes effective from ineffective speakers is not the ability to be loud, but rather the ability to control and adapt one's loudness to the situation and to one's intended meaning.

You need not shout to achieve force in speaking. But your voice must be firm, vigorous, and well controlled. You must learn to consciously control your loudness to adapt to the situation in which you are speaking. No one,

---

[4]Theodore D. Hanley and Wayne L. Thurman, *Developing Vocal Skills,* Holt, Rinehart and Winston, New York, 1962, p. 166.

for example, likes to converse with someone who shouts at him as though he is giving an oration in the school auditorium. Obviously, you will need more force to be heard by a large group of listeners than by a small group. Speaking outdoors or in the presence of competing noises and other distractions requires more force than speaking indoors or in places where there are no distractions. Forceful ideas uttered in an indifferent manner lose some of their vigor. A speaker who cannot suit the vigor of his voice to the vigor of his ideas seems insincere.

Achieving better control of loudness may simply require a new attitude toward the value of intensity in speaking. Some victims of stage fright rationalize weak voices by claiming that they do not want to be loud. Such reasoning sometimes represents the avoidance of responsibility. However, using a vigorous tone for useful purposes will result in satisfaction rather than embarrassment.

A vigorous voice is dependent upon breath control and, often, simply opening one's mouth more. Loudness can also be increased by raising the pitch of your voice. Experiment with modification of vocal intensity by variation of pitch, oral activity, and breath pressure. Find the best pattern of resonance for giving your tone body and volume. A cramped throat and mouth, with muscles tensed, may make the voice more piercing but ordinarily do not make the voice more pleasantly vigorous. Avoid letting your voice trail off at the end of a sentence. Practice intensity control in exercises and everyday speaking activities until it becomes a habit. (See Project 1 at the end of this chapter for exercises in loudness control.)

6.   Control Your Speech Rate

Your speech should be fluent but neither too hesitant nor too gushy. Say your words slowly enough to be understood and fast enough to sustain the audience's interest. In speaking, this is ordinarily between 130 and 150 words per minute, and in oral reading it is between 150 and 175 words per minute. The discussion of light subjects and the presentation of simple narrative material and exciting ideas can be carried on at a faster rate than the presentation of complicated instructional material in unfamiliar subject-matter areas. When a number of listeners are included in the discussion (other things being equal), the rate should be slower than when there are only one or two persons. Situations involving distraction require a slower rate than situations which are free from distraction.

Rate variation is an effective way of suggesting the nature of the thought being expressed and the relative emphasis to be given to it. The timing of the punch line, for example, is very important. Practice to determine your most effective rate in speaking and oral reading. Your speaking rate should vary with relative importance of the ideas, and it should never be so fast that your phrasing or emphasis suffers.

Speech that is too fast is characterized by the shortening of vowel sounds and pauses. Nervous speakers frequently give the impression of trying to express what they have to say before they forget. Mumbling sometimes gives the erroneous impression of a rapid rate, whereas drawling of continuant sounds, long pauses, vocal stumbling, repetition of words, and intrusion of "ah," "uh," and "and ah" result in a slowed rate. Rates that are too fast or too slow do not permit normal variation in speeding up or slowing down for expression. The absence of variation in rate produces monotony; an arbitrary pattern of rate variation that does not accurately suggest or reflect the ideas discussed confuses listeners.

Monotone is influenced by all the attributes of voice, but rate is certainly one of the more frequent types of monotone. Gestures with the hands and other appropriate bodily movements may help you to overcome monotone. It is almost impossible to be active and monotonous at the same time.

A speaker who knows too little about his subject may speak more slowly than one who is thoroughly familiar with it. Fatigue, characteristic reserve, or a depressing mood also slow down speech. The hyperkinetic or excitable person, on the contrary, is too fluent and needs to slow down his rate to the mood and speed of comprehension of his listeners. The task of controlling speech rate appears to be relatively simple, but it may require considerable practice. Mechanical practice in developing rate control should be considered only a step in habit formation. Always remember that your main purpose is to improve communication.

If you are overly dependent on such vocalizations as "er" and "ah," have a friend listen to your speech and signal you whenever you use one of these sounds. This will be distracting at first, but it will help you break your dependence on this habit.

For exercises in rate control, see Project 2 at the end of this chapter.

7. Develop Satisfactory Pitch Control

The pitch of your voice is an important signal of your intentions. It communicates to the listener as much as rate and loudness do, and it should suggest the mood of what you want to say.

The best pitch level for your normal speech is determined by the structure of your larynx, or voice box, and your resonators. It is probably the pitch which you have developed by habit. If you believe that your habitual pitch level is *not* your optimum one, do not try to change it without the advice and guidance of an expert. In general, your pitch should be high enough to permit lowering and low enough to permit raising for contrast. Inflectional slides, steps, and patterns are useful in communication. Remember, however, that regular pitch changes that disregard meaning and produce singsong effects are confusing and distracting.

In order to develop effective control over pitch you should learn to hear pitch patterns. Become aware of pitch in ordinary communication, and practice exercises such as those suggested in Project 3 at the end of this chapter.

The skills you acquire by drill or in isolated projects must be exercised in the pattern of speech activity as a whole if they are to be of much value to you. Only perpetual attention to voice development in the normal social uses of speech over a long period of time will produce lasting results. If you develop vocal skills in isolated situations, however, you may with effort transfer these skills to your everyday speech.

Projects and Problems

PROJECT 1: Do the following exercises as directed:

   a. Simulate a yawn by standing erect, taking a deep breath, throwing your arms up, and stretching. Then relax and expel the air from your lungs as vigorously as possible. Note the feeling of vigorous contractive action of the waist muscles in this process.

   b. Stand erect in a place where you can push against a wall with one hand. Count to ten in a normal voice, taking a separate breath for each count. Then repeat the exercise while pushing vigorously against the wall with one hand, allowing the waist muscles to contract vigorously on each count. Can you get a stronger tone by exerting pressure as you push?

   c. Read the following sentences, using a single breath for each sentence. Do not lower vocal intensity at the end of the longer sentences.

I don't want to go.
The engineer cautioned us to drive slowly.
*Deep, well-controlled breathing is required to read a long sentence on one
    expiration.*
Scarlett O'Hara, the heroine in Gone with the Wind, *was a Southern beauty
    of great personal pride, ambition, and will power, who would make any
    ordinary sacrifice to achieve her ends.*

   d. Try to read the first part of the following sentences normally, and the last part forcefully, without raising the pitch.

You must not come in here; please move along.
If we win that victory, what a celebration we shall have.
*I believe in a program for the preservation of peace, but certainly not peace
    at any price.*

   e. Read the sentences in Exercise *d* again, and this time raise the pitch of the last phrase to increase intensity of the voice.

   f. Note that the following passages are separated by broken lines. Read the first part in a confidential undertone, the second part in a normal voice for a small room, the third part with the intensity necessary for a small auditorium, and the fourth part with the intensity necessary for a large auditorium.

Some few weeks ago a Professor Robert Paul Wolf in a New York Times Sunday Book Review wrote in review of a book called The Making of a CounterCulture: *"American society is ugly, repressive, destructive and subversive of much that is truly human." This view of American society "is now acknowledged to be true by virtually every sensible man and woman." Now most Americans and indeed most sensible Americans don't share that view.*

Yet many commentators in our press and television do say that our society is sick and the gap between "Middle America" and "Media America" grows. In a recent Newsweek *article Stewart Alsop noted this national masochism among political writers and called it the "New Snobbism." James Reston perceived it in students and called it "New Pessimism." Daniel Boorstin discerned in academic circles and called it "spiritual appeasement"—this lack of faith in our own ideals and institutions. And in the artistic world Archibald MacLeish describes it as the "new flatness"—this increasing tendency for poets and artists to want to indict instead of inspire—to tell life like it is, instead of what it should be. A recent spate of Broadway plays like* Matter of Robert Oppenheimer *and* The Great White Hope *peddle guilt and apology.*

Just as man without aspirations is not a whole man, so a nation without a vision and faith of what it might be is desolate and sterile. Because there is a lack of fulfillment in our ideals, there is a lack of faith. But just because America is not acting up to all the ideals of the Declaration of Independence and the Constitution doesn't mean we should hang our heads in shame or beat our breasts in self-flagellation. No society would be worth the price of admission if it did not proclaim ideals which were beyond its present realization. If ever American society fulfills all its ideals it would be because the ideals were outrageously low. Sure our country has not lived up to all its ideals but then no country ever had higher ideals to live up to.

Many centuries ago another society which was losing faith in itself heard a stern lecture. The society was the Jewish colony in Rome. In the epistle to the Hebrews the writer exhorts them not to be apologetic about their heritage. He urges them to remember Abraham, Jacob, Joseph, and Moses, and their dreams to establish a promised land. He says that their failure to realize their hopes did not diminish the greatness of that dream. It just meant that the unfinished task became the mission of their sons and sons' sons. Finally he tells them "Don't throw away your heritage . . . Don't cringe but live proud in your faith."

So must we not reject the heritage of Washington, Jefferson, Lincoln and Wilson. Instead of cursing the gap between our ideals and reality, let us try to close it. Instead of faulting the promise of America, let us try to fulfill it.*

---

*From James C. Humes, "Dissent and Involvement: The Need for Catalysts," *Vital Speeches of the Day*, 36:183, 1970.

g.   Read the following paragraphs in a forceful voice and at a rapid rate. Then read them slowly. Listen to the difference in general effectiveness and intensity at the two rates of speed.

No one man can speak for the South. No one man can—by himself alone— define the beliefs of the people of this great region. But all of us and each of us must assume and exercise some degree of responsibility for persuading this nation to heed what we have to say.

We must make clear what we believe.

We must set the record straight.

We must, finally, stand together in unity and pursue with determination a course to victory.

That is our outline of duty.

At the outset, let us establish one fact firmly.

Gathered here tonight, we are Texans, we are Louisianans, we are Southerners. Of these allegiances we are proud. We are honored by the heritage with which we are endowed.

But, in our hearts, we are—first and last—Americans. When we speak of duty, we speak of duty to our country. We acknowledge no loyalty greater than our loyalty to America. By that standard, we regard no principle as worthy, and we accept no cause as just unless it will contribute to the lasting strength of America, our America. It is our love for our country—not our pride in our region—which impels us to undertake this fight for principle.*

h.   Read the following paragraphs with different degrees of variation of force. Read the first part with monoforce—without variation in the amount of force—the second part with a moderate degree of conversational variation of force, and the third part with a wide variation of vocal force.

Ladies and Gentlemen: Just ten days ago the Space Task Group submitted to President Nixon its recommendations for future space activities. The document details for the President's consideration the different paths he may elect to follow in implementing a national space program.

"Our opportunities are great," the committee said, "and we have a broad spectrum of choices available to us."

I'm as aware as any man of the need for solutions to growing ecological and social problems here on earth.

We must tackle those problems and solve them. But we also need to exploit our achievements in space.

I am convinced we can do both. In fact, my main point here today is that the two are directly related.

This nation needs a balanced space program, a well planned series of steps that will carry us into the next century. I will outline some of the steps that should be taken during the coming decade.

---

*From Alan Shivers, "The South Must Be Admitted to Full Partnership," *Vital Speeches of the Day,* 21:972, 1955.

I contend that those steps, in the long-term, will make this earth a better place in which to live. In that sense, space activities are not competing with programs of ecological improvement or social betterment. They are actually complementing them.*

PROJECT 2: Practice the following exercises in rate control.

a. Read the following sentences rapidly or slowly as the meaning suggests:

Watch out! It's hot.
Please let me do it.
They trudged wearily up the trail.
Come as quickly as you can.
The fried pheasant is delicious.
What a beautiful view you have from this window.

b. Read the following selections rapidly or slowly as the meaning suggests:

Bowed by the weight of centuries,
He leans upon his hoe.—Markham

The day is cold, and dark, and dreary.—Longfellow

And slowly answered Arthur from the barge,
The old order changeth, yielding place to new.—Tennyson

And next comes the soldier,
Sudden and quick in quarrel.—Shakespeare

c. Read the following selection as rapidly as you can without mumbling or falling into a staccato pattern of articulation.

Speak the speech I pray you, as I pronounced it to you,—trippingly on the tongue; but if you mouth it, as many of our players do, I had as lief the towncrier spake my lines. Nor do not saw the air too much with your hand thus, but use all gently, for in the very torrent, tempest, and as I may say, whirlwind of your passion, you must acquire and begat a temperance, that may give it smoothness. Oh! It offends me to the soul to hear a robustious periwig-pated fellow tear a passion to tatters,—to very rags,—to split the ears of the groundlings; who, for the most part, are capable of nothing but inexplicable dumb show and noise. I would have such a fellow shipped for o'erdoing Termagant; it out-Herods Herod. Pray you, avoid it.—Shakespeare

d. Read the following paragraph as slowly as you can without drawling.

---

*From Robert Anderson, "Future Space Flights: The Search for Knowledge," *Vital Speeches of the Day*, 36:175, 1970.

*During the whole of a dull, dark, and soundless day in the autumn of
the year, when the clouds hung oppressively low in the heavens, I had been
passing alone on horseback, through a singularly dreary tract of country,
and at length found myself, as the shades of the evening drew on, within
view of the melancholy House of Usher. I know not how it was,—but, with
the first glimpse of the building, a sense of insufferable gloom pervaded
my spirit. I say insufferable; for the feeling was unrelieved by any of that
half-pleasurable, because poetic, sentiment with which the mind usually
receives even the sternest natural images of the desolate or terrible. I looked
upon the scene before me—upon the mere house, and the simple landscape
features of the domain—upon the bleak walls—upon the vacant eyelike
windows—upon a few rank hedges—and upon a few white trunks of
decayed trees—with an utter depression of soul which I can compare to
no earthly sensation more properly than to the after-dream of the reveller
upon opium—the bitter lapse into everyday life—the hideous dropping off
of the veil.**

e.   Try reading the selection in Exercise c slowly, and the one in Exercise
d very rapidly. Report on the differences in effect of rate of reading on the
moods of these selections.

f.   Read the following sentences using a short pause at the places marked
with a single dash, a moderate pause at the places marked with two dashes,
and a long pause at the places marked with three dashes.

*I beg your pardon.—That was a mistake.——I was wrong.———I beg your
pardon.—But you have tried me very sorely.——You have intruded upon
a private trouble—that you ought to know must be very painful to
me.———But I believe you meant well.——I know you to be a gentleman,—and I am willing to think you acted on impulse,—and that you will
see tomorrow what a mistake you have made.——It is not a thing I talk
about;——I do not speak of it to my friends,—and they are far too considerate to speak of it to me.—But you have put me on the defensive:——you
have made me out more or less of a brute,——and I don't intend to be so
far misunderstood.———There are two sides to every story,——and there
is something to be said about this,—even for me.——When I married,—I
did so against the wishes of my people—and the advice of all my
friends.——You know all about that.——God help us! who doesn't?———It
was very rich, rare reading for you,—and for every one else who saw the
daily papers,——and we gave them all they wanted of it.———I took her
out of that life——and married her—because I believed she was as good
a woman—as any of those who had never had to work for their living,——and I was bound that my friends—and your friends—should recognize her—and respect her—as my wife had a right to be respected;——
and I took her abroad—that I might give all you sensitive, fine people—a
chance to get used to the idea of being polite to a woman who had once*

---

*Edgar Allan Poe, "The Fall of the House of Usher," *The Works of Edgar Allan Poe,*
P. F. Collier & Son Corporation, New York, 1903, vol. II, p. 145.

been a burlesque actress.——It began over there in Paris.——She had every chance when she married me—that a woman ever had————all that a man's whole thought and love and money could bring to her.——And you know what she did.—And after the divorce——and she was free to go where she pleased,—and to live as she pleased,—and with whom she pleased,————I swore to my God that I would never see her nor her child again.—I loved the mother, and she deceived me,—and disgraced me—and broke my heart—and I only wish she had killed me.*

    g.   Read the following selection, using duration of vowel sounds to slow down the rate.

This brave and tender man in every storm of life was oak and rock, but in the sunshine he was vine and flower. He was the friend of all heroic souls. He climbed the heights and left all superstitions far below, while on his forehead fell the golden dawning of the grander day.

He loved the beautiful, and was with color, form, and music touched to tears. He sided with the weak, and with a willing hand gave alms; with loyal heart and with purest hands he faithfully discharged all public trusts.

He was a worshipper of liberty, a friend of the oppressed. A thousand times I have heard him quote these words: "For justice all places a temple, and all seasons summer." He believed that happiness was the only good, reason the only torch, justice the only worship, humanity the only religion, and love the only priest. He added to the sum of human joy; and were every one to whom he did some loving service to bring a blossom to his grave, he would sleep tonight beneath a wilderness of flowers.

Life is a narrow vale between the cold and barren peaks of two eternities. We strive in vain to look beyond the heights. We cry aloud, and the only answer is the echo of our wailing cry. From the voiceless lips of the un-replying dead there comes no word; but in the night of death hope sees a star, and listening love can hear the rustle of a wing.†

    h.   Time yourself in reading the following passage. A good reading rate is 150 to 175 words per minute. Does your rate approximate this speed?

No thoughtful person can doubt that freedom of speech, freedom of press and freedom of assembly are vital to democracy itself—they are part of its very blood stream.

Only by free public discussion and free public criticism can the people be steadily sure that the will of the majority still prevails. Anyone who is inclined to feel that in times of national danger criticism of the govern-ment must be ruthlessly suppressed, should remember that two years ago it was the rising wave of popular criticism in Great Britain which over-whelmed the shuffling and indecisive leadership of Neville Chamberlain,

---

*Richard Harding Davis, *Van Bibber and Others*, Harper & Brothers, New York, 1892, pp. 317–318.

†Robert Ingersoll, *The Works of Robert G. Ingersoll*, vol. XIII, pp. 389–391.

and placed Winston Churchill in power. But while our constitutional democracy thus protects and, to maintain its integrity must protect, the civil liberties of the people, we must keep in mind that these civil liberties, freedom of speech, press, and assembly are not absolute. They are limited by the rights of others and by the demands of national security. The rights of minorities do not rise above those of the majority. An outvoted minority may demand the right of orderly public criticism of public officers and public policy, but it enjoys no right of obstruction, no privilege of undermining the accepted policy of the government by conspiracy, sabotage, incitement to resistance or disobedience to law. Submission by the minority to majority decisions is as vital a part of the democratic process as is the protection accorded by the majority to the civil liberties of those who have been outvoted.

This delicate balance of majority and minority rights in a democratic nation calls for constant and thoughtful compromise and adjustment. In time of national danger it becomes increasingly difficult to maintain a decent respect for freedom of speech, freedom of press, and freedom of assembly. We face today, and we shall probably face in greater measure tomorrow, two serious dangers to these fundamental civil liberties. One of these dangers arises from the fact that the national security in a crisis like this makes necessary a curbing of freedom of speech, press, and assembly which would be indefensible in times of peace. The framing of these restrictions and the enforcement of them must be confided to our national public officials, and there is constant danger that they may go too far. The second danger is that popular hysteria will demand of the government unreasonable restrictions of civil liberty. There is much less danger that arrogant public officers will tyrannically override the liberties of a protesting people, than that an intolerant public opinion will not only permit but demand the complete suppression of minority rights.*

PROJECT 3:   Development of pitch control.

   a.   Read the first third of the following paragraph in a monopitch, the second part with moderate pitch variation, and the third part with marked pitch variation. Listen to the effect of the differences.

On Robert Burns

"I think Burns," said Robertson, the historian, "was one of the most extraordinary men I ever met with. His poetry surprised me very much; his prose surprised me still more; and his conversation surprised me more than both his poetry and prose." "His address," says Robert Riddle, "was pleasing; he was neither forward nor embarrassed in his manner; his spirits were generally high; and his conversation animated. His language was fluent, frequently fine; his enunciation always rapid; his ideas clear and vigorous, and he had the rare power of modulating his peculiarly fine voice, so as to harmonize with whatever subject he touched upon. I have heard

---

*Robert E. Cushman, "Civil Liberty in Time of National Defense," *Vital Speeches of the Day*, 8:142–143, 1941.

*him talk with astonishing rapidity, nor miss the articulation of a single
syllable; elevate and depress his voice as the topic seemed to require; and
sometimes, when the subject was pathetic, he would prolong the words
in the most impressive and affecting manner, indicative of the deep sensi-
bility which inspired him. He often lamented to me that fortune had not
placed him at the bar, or the senate; he had great ambition, and the feeling
that he could not gratify it, preyed on him severely.''—Anonymous**

b.   Read the following stanza from Wordsworth's "Daffodils" twice. Read
it once with marked emphasis on the mechanical rhythm of the verse. Read
it a second time with changes of inflection to bring out the meaning of the
verse, but with subordination of the pitch changes to the pattern of rhythm.

*I wandered lonely as a cloud
That floats on high o'er vales and hills
When all at once I saw a crowd,
A host of golden daffodils;
Beside the lake, beneath the trees,
Fluttering and dancing in the breeze.*

c.   Read the following sentences with an upward or downward step in
pitch as indicated.

*Come ↑ here.
How ↑ much?
It's ↓ nonsense.
Strike ↓ hard.
You may pick it up, ↑ but handle it with care.
I loved the excitement, ↓ but I am very tired.
The plan of the attack, ↓ because of the presence of mines, ↑ was changed
   at the last moment.
If any of you are doubtful, ↑ and I suspect some of you are, ↓ here is the
   proof.*

d.   Read the following sentences with an upward or downward slide as
indicated.

*Isn't that a beautiful sight? ↓
He doesn't know the meaning of ethics. ↓
I have tried everything. ↑
Is that what you mean? ↑
I've never doubted it for a moment. ↓
Now, what do you say to that? ↑
Now, what do you say to that? ↓*

---

*From James O'Neill and Andrew Weaver, *The Elements of Speech*, Longmans, Green
& Co., Inc., New York, 1933, p. 151.

How do you do this? ↑
How do you do this? ↓
Drive to the end of Summit. ↓
He won't believe it. ↑
I simply will not permit it. ↓

 e. Read the following sentences in a pitch pattern which conveys the suggested emotional meaning.

I am tired, and discouraged, and very blue.
I am so excited. It seems almost too good to be true.
You fiend! You'll suffer for this.
Watch out! There's a rattler.
Jim? Now, there's a good sport.
The poor little tyke seems to be in great pain.
Well! I never expected to see you here.
The sense of loss seems more than I can bear.
I wonder if I shouldn't go, after all.
I have never been so sure of anything in all my life.
The inspiration of the service in the cathedral was an experience I shall
    long remember.

 f. Bring to class a poem or piece of emotional prose of your own choosing, and demonstrate the use of pitch variation in communicating the meaning of the passage. Listen to the reading of others to develop an awareness of pitch changes.

PROJECT 4: Development of vocal quality.
 a. Loosen up any tension in the muscles interfering with effective resonance by the following exercises:

(1) Drop the head forward as if you had fallen asleep sitting up. Relax the neck muscles until the head seems to bounce. Try letting it drop backward in the same way.
(2) Let the jaw muscles relax and drop the jaw in a relaxed manner, opening the mouth as far as possible. Start slowly and then increase the rapidity with which you say the word "bob." Relax and let the air push the lips out from the teeth as far as possible.
(3) Relax the cheek muscles and blow out the cheeks as far as possible. Start slowly and then increase the rapidity with which you say the word "bob."
(4) Repeat the word "who" three times: (a) with high pharyngeal resonance as when you yawn and say "ho hum," (b) with relaxed pharyngeal resonance, (c) with a definite attempt to get resonance from the oral cavities.
(5) Repeat the sentence, "It's a very fine thing," twice: (a) tense the muscles of the soft palate; (b) relax the muscles of the soft palate.
(6) Sound the vowel in "ah" beginning with a whisper and gradually

phonating the tone until you get a full resonant tone; then gradually aspirate the tone until the sound is whispered.

(7) Push against the wall and practice relaxing the muscles of the neck and mouth until you can say with a clear tone, "I am working to control relaxation of my speech muscles."

b. Develop resonance in your vocal attack by use of the following exercises:

(1) Count to ten: (a) as if counting out pennies on a table; (b) as if giving telephone numbers to a receiver with difficult telephone connections; (c) as if counting with difficulty the number of persons in a party barely visible in the distance; (d) as if "counting off" in doing sitting-up exercises; (e) as if "counting out" a man in the ring.

(2) Utter each of the following statements in a fully resonated positive tone:

"We came, we saw, we conquered."
"We have met the enemy and they are ours."
"We have just begun to fight."
"Ship ahoy! Ship ahoy!"
"Open—'Tis I, the King."
"Stand, the ground's your own, my braves!"
"Roll on, Thou deep and dark blue ocean—roll!"

Read a passage of ordinary prose carrying the pattern of sharp vocal attack necessary for these sentences into ordinary reading.

c. Try saying the sentence, "How does this gadget work?" in the following ways: with a tense throaty whisper; with a nasalized whisper; with an open mouth resonance; with aspirated tone; with high metallic tones; with highly nasalized tones; with raspy, harsh, throaty tones; with relaxed muscles and open mouth.

d. Read the following paragraph twice, at first as rapidly as you can with intelligibility for a small group, then slowly, as you would if addressing a large audience. Note the greater ease with which tones can be resonated at a slower rate. Listen for quality differences in the reading of others.

It is for us, the living, rather, to be dedicated here to the unfinished work which they who fought here have thus far so nobly advanced. It is rather for us to be here dedicated to the great task remaining before us,—that from these honored dead we take increased devotion to that cause for which they gave the last full measure of devotion; that we here highly resolve that these dead shall not have died in vain; that this nation, under God, shall have a new birth of freedom; and that government of the people, by the people, for the people, shall not perish from the earth.—Abraham Lincoln

e. Work on the following exercises for the development of a tonal vocabulary.

(1)   Pronounce the word "well" to indicate the following meanings:

> *I never would have thought it possible!*
> *What do you want? I am very busy.*
> *That's a small matter.*
> *Now, let me think a minute.*
> *So you thought you could get away with it!*
> *I am very pleased to see you.*

(2)   Read the question "What are you doing?" as it would be expressed by the following characters: a burly policeman; an old man or woman; a half-frightened child; an ignorant, shiftless tramp; a fond young husband.

(3)   Read each of the following sentences twice, first in a monotone, and then with a tonal quality suggested by the emotional mood of the sentence.

> *It's a beautiful night.*
> *I wish I could remember where I have seen that face.*
> *Say that again, and smile when you say it.*
> *My! You think you're smart, don't you?*
> *I never thought you would sink low enough to do a trick like that.*
> *We'll have dinner at the Ritz, see a show, and dance all night.*
> *So sorry. There are no more tickets for tonight. Next! What can I do for*
>   *you?*
> *I never want to see your face again. Now get out.*
> *Isn't he a cute little thing! And he's only five.*
> *I have never known anyone who seemed to be such a thoroughly good*
> *man.*
> *There doesn't seem to be any use trying. I'm thoroughly beaten.*
> *Watch out! You'll hit that car!*
> *I am so full, I feel as if I'd bust; and it was all so good.*
> *We're so proud of Steve. He takes his honors like a man.*

f.   Select a poem that expresses a mood with which you sympathize and read it for the class in a vocal tone which expresses the mood. Listen critically to the vocal quality of your classmates.

References

Black, John W., and Wilbur E. Moore, *Speech: Code, Meaning, and Communication.* New York: McGraw-Hill Book Company, 1955. Chapters 2 and 3.

Bronstein, Arthur J., and Beatrice F. Jacoby, *Your Speech and Voice.* New York: Random House, 1967. Chapters 1 to 5, 15 to 18.

Eisenson, Jon, *The Improvement of Voice and Diction,* 2nd ed. New York: Macmillan, 1965.

Fairbanks, Grant, *Voice and Articulation Drillbook,* 2nd ed. New York: Harper & Row, 1960.

Fisher, Hilda B., *Improving Voice and Articulation.* Boston: Houghton-Mifflin, 1966.

Hahn, Elise, D. W. Lomas, Donald Hargis, and Daniel Vandraegen, *Basic Voice Training for Speech,* 2nd ed. New York: McGraw-Hill Book Company, 1957.

Hanley, Theodore D., and Wayne L. Thurman, *Developing Vocal Skills.* New York: Holt, Rinehart and Winston, 1962.

———, *Student Projects for Developing Vocal Skills.* New York: Holt, Rinehart and Winston, 1962.

Heinberg, Paul J., *Voice Training for Speaking and Reading Aloud.* New York: Ronald Press, 1964.

King, Robert G., and Eleanor M. DiMichael, *Improving Articulation and Voice.* New York: Macmillan, 1966.

Mayer, Lyle V., *Fundamentals of Voice and Diction,* 3rd ed. Dubuque, Iowa: Wm. C. Brown Co., 1968.

Van Riper, Charles, and John V. Irwin, *Voice and Articulation.* Englewood Cliffs, N.J.: Prentice-Hall, Inc., 1958.

Cornell Capa, Magnum.

articulation and pronunciation

Articulation and pronunciation both concern the formation of the sounds of spoken language. Articulation refers to the systematic modification of vocal tones to form the vowel and consonant sounds used in speech. A sound is misarticulated when it is formed in a way that is not acceptable to the auditors. Pronunciation, like articulation, refers to the acceptable utterance of language sounds—specifically to the production of the sounds contained in individual words without substitutions, additions, omissions, inversions, or misplaced accents. Since certain differences in procedure are appropriate for the study and improvement of articulation and pronunciation, we will return to pronunciation later in this chapter.

Why Study Articulation?

Obviously articulation is important to satisfactory communication. Even though your pitch, rate, loudness, and quality may be well controlled, your speech may be impossible to understand if you run words and syllables together; if you mangle your medial or final consonants; if you fail to distinguish between similar but different sounds, as in "tin" and "ten," "fife" and "five," "wet" and "whet," "fussy" and "fuzzy." Americans are described as "lip-lazy" because they tend to be poor articulators.

Two Criteria of Satisfactory Articulation

■ The most important criterion of satisfactory articulation is that *sound must be so articulated that speech is intelligible.* Many words in our language differ from others only in the articulation of a single sound; failure to articulate the distinguishing sound properly can cause confusion between two words. (Note the words compared above.) Although listeners may eventually discover the right word and thus the meaning from the context, poor articulation slows down communication and renders it inefficient.

■   A second criterion of satisfactory articulation is *social acceptability.* By this we do not mean acceptability by "high society"; we mean rather acceptability by whomever you are speaking with. There is no authority in our country to prescribe the exact manner in which sounds are to be made. A degree of exactness completely acceptable to some persons is considered crude and unpleasant or a sign of phoniness by others. Some **227** standards which are not questioned in most lively informal speech are wholly inappropriate for formal occasions. In other words, your standard must be determined in large part by the *expectations of your audience in the particular situation* in which you are talking. You should achieve the skill and the control of your articulation so that you can meet the demands of any situation and any audience.

Methods of Improving Articulation

■ 1. *Study the organs of articulation.* Acquiring a clear understanding of the function of the organs of articulation helps make sense out of the principles of articulation and accelerates the process of improvement. These organs are the jaw, lips, teeth, tongue, hard palate, soft palate, and breathing mechanisms. The muscles of the inner surfaces of the resonance cavities of the mouth and the pharynx also operate to determine the shape of the oral cavities, which modify tones to cause the distinctive quality of the vowel sounds. Chronic inflammation of these surfaces or deformities in them may seriously affect articulation. The muscles of the larynx, moreover, are responsible for distinctions between the voiced and the voiceless sounds. In a sense, the ear also serves as an organ of articulation. If we don't hear clearly the sounds we make, we may articulate poorly.

Our purpose here is not to study the structure and function of the articulatory organs in detail.[1] An explanation of the organic basis of articulation, however, will help us to understand classification of the sounds of English speech.

■ 2. *Study the sounds of English speech.* The sounds of speech vary considerably as different persons make them, and the purpose of the study of articulation is not to obtain perfect uniformity among all persons. Sounds exist in families called *phonemes* and you should learn to make each sound in such a way that it is clearly understood and acceptable as a member of the phoneme family to which it belongs.

Students usually associate sounds with the letters of the alphabet. It is helpful to think of the sounds themselves as the units of articulated speech: The sounds of the word "hurt," for example, are *h-r-t* rather than "aich-you-are-tee." Specialists in the study of language sounds have developed the science of phonetics, with a systematic set of phonetic symbols in which each sound family, or phoneme, has one symbol. These symbols are presented in Appendix A. A student who plans to become a professional in the field of communication should study these symbols and made them his own. The *diacritical marks* used in the dictionary, on the other hand, are an attempt to provide symbols for sounds by using marks over the letters

---

[1] If you wish to study articulatory processes in detail, you will find the works cited at the end of this chapter helpful.

of the alphabet. For the purposes of the average student, diacritical marks will be sufficient. The marks employed in the vowel classification presented in the next section are derived from Webster's *New International Dictionary.*

■   3. *Distinguish among vowels, diphthongs, and consonants.* The three main types of speech sounds are vowels, diphthongs, and consonants. *Vowels* consist of relatively unmodified voice (that is, voice in which there is little interference with the outgoing air), whereas *consonants* consist of voice modified by the same type of friction or stoppage which, in part, produces the sound. One or more of the organs of articulation (the vocal folds, tongue, soft palate, hard palate, lips, teeth, jaw) modify or interfere with the free exhalation of air to produce consonants. *Diphthongs* are combinations of vowel sounds produced as one sound, such as *i* in "ice," a combination of *a* and *i*.

The differentiation of vowel sounds is initiated by the vibrations of vocal cords and is influenced by the resonators. These areas may be located on a vowel parallelogram or triangle as it is sometimes called, as indicated by the accompanying chart. *Front vowels,* in which the highest part of the tongue is toward the top of the mouth and ranging downward, are the *e* of "be," the *i* of "bit," the *e* of "bet," and the *a* of "tan." The *u* of "but" is a *midvowel,* as is the *a* of "ask," with the highest part of the tongue drawn back somewhat in the mouth. *Back vowels* range upward from the *a* in "car" to the *oo* in "fool," with the highest part of the tongue toward the back of the mouth.

VOWEL PARALLELOGRAM

Front vowels		Back vowels
ē (i) be		o͞o (u) boot
ĭ (ɪ) bit		o͝o (ʊ) foot
ā (e) ape		ō (o) moat
ĕ (ɛ) bed	ȧ (ə) about	ô (ɔ) law
ă (θ) hat	u (ʌ) but	ä (ɑ) top

The principal diphthongs are the *u* of "use," the *o* of "hole," the *ou* of "ouch," the *a* of "day," the *i* of "light," the *e* of "feet," and the *oi* of "oil." Although some of these are considered single sounds, careful study will reveal them to be combinations of sounds.

Consonants, as we have seen, are produced by interference with the free expiration of breath. All consonants may be classified as either voiced or voiceless. *Voiced consonants* are accompanied by a vibration of the vocal cords (bands or folds). Many consonants are matched or paired; the muscular adjustments that produce voiced and voiceless "twins" are alike except that the cords are vibrated to produce the voiced sound. Examples are *g* and *k*, *d* and *t*, *b* and *p*, and *v* and *f*.

Nasal consonants are resonated chiefly through the nasal passages: *m, n,* and *ng.* The *stop plosives,* as the term implies, are formed by blocking the air stream and then releasing the sounds explosively. Voiced stop plosives are *b, d,* and *g.* Voiceless stop plosives are *p, t,* and *k.* Moser[2] has recently completed some studies which give us a number of interesting ideas about our speech sounds. The sounds most frequently confused are those which are immediately across from each other on the parallelogram or those immediately above or below each other. The back vowels tend to be more frequently confused than the front vowels.

Confusion among the consonants arises among those sounds articulated in the same manner. These include:

p t ch k
b d j g
m n ng
o r
f th s ch sh h wh
v th z j zh wh
w y wh

■ 4. *Identify the sounds with which you have difficulty.* Test yourself systematically to determine which sounds cause you difficulty. (Note the test in Project 1 at the end of this chapter.) You are not likely to be aware of your own shortcomings. When people tell you to slow down or to talk louder they may merely mean that you should articulate more clearly. Vowels that are frequently misarticulated are *a* as in "bad," *e* as in "get," *i* as in "fish," and *u* as in "just." The diphthong *ou* as in "out" is frequently perverted to an *au* sound. Consonants that commonly cause difficulty are the *aspirate* and *fricative* sounds, characterized by a rustling friction of the breath, such as *s, z, ch, dz, sh, zh, f, th, v,* and *wh.* The *n* sound is often substituted for *ng,* and *t* is often erroneously produced by a glottal stop rather than an explosion between the tongue and hard palate. The *t, d, p, b, k,* and *g* sounds are sometimes exploded when they should merely be stopped by the articulators. The *w* sound is sometimes substituted for *r,* in such words as "bright." These are some of the most common misarticulations. Make a systematic analysis of your articulatory habits in order to discover and correct your personal variations.

■ 5. *Apply sufficient breath pressure as you sound consonants.* Be sure you sound with sufficient accuracy and fullness such plosives as *p* in "pour," *b* in "ban," *d* in "dote," *g* in "gill," *t* in "talk," *k* in "cap," and *h* in "hill." Be sure to articulate fully medial and final consonants, such as the *l* in "asleep," the *t* in "cut," and the *s* sound in "trace."

---

[2] Henry M. Moser, *One Syllable Words,* Air Force Command and Control Development Division. Technical Note 60–58, Bedford Mass., 1960; see also Moser, *A Voice Training Manual,* Federal Aviation Agency, Washington, 1962.

■   6. *Analyze speech recordings for articulatory excellence.* For example, listen to the RCA Victor *Hamlet,* as read by Laurence Olivier. (Note especially Act III, scene ii.)

Methods of Improving Pronunciation

■   1. *Use the pronunciation which will be understood by and acceptable to your audience.* Though we often speak of the three major dialects within the United States—Standard American, Eastern, and Southern—there are many *subdialects* within each of these. The extent to which these subdialects should be considered *substandard* is a major issue among linguists and other educators today. Many linguists stress that there can be no one "correct" pronunciation, that language is dynamic, and that we must consider the community or part of the community in which communication is occurring. We believe these things to be true, but urge you not to use these facts as an excuse for careless speech. You must learn to *control* your pronunciation, just as you learn to control all other aspects of your communicative behavior. This means that you must be able to meet the pronunciation standards of the well-educated persons of the region in which you expect to spend your life, as well as the most acceptable standards of the well-educated persons of your particular community or neighborhood. Good pronunciation is that which will be clearly understood by those with whom you speak and which will not call attention to itself.

Foreign accents and dialects present a problem closely associated with regionalism in articulation and pronunciation. Some foreign languages do not employ all the sounds of English. Other languages contain sounds which differ considerably from similar English sounds. It is these sounds which cause the most difficulty in learning a new language. Differences in the inflectional patterns and intonations of languages also cause difficulty. Although it is no disgrace for your speech to reveal the country of your origin, dialectal characteristics are a source of distraction and confusion in communication. The use of dialect is especially to be deplored when the speaker trades upon it as a sort of affectation in speech to which he attaches false cultural values.

■   2. *Reproduce speech sounds accurately.* There are five common classes of pronunciation errors: substitution, addition, omission, inversion, and misplaced accent. Although it is not always possible to place a mispronounced word in one of these classes exclusively, the classification serves a practical purpose in understanding and improving pronunciation. Some examples of each class are listed below:

Substitutions:	agin for again
	fer for for
	bak for bag
	wuz for was

Additions: ca(l)m for calm
fore(h)ead for forehead
rem(i)nent for remnant
pang(g) for pang
across(t) for across

Omissions: col for cold
reconize for recognize
dimond for diamond
eights for eighths
battry for battery

Inversions: calvery for cavalry
interduce for introduce
pervide for provide

Misplaced Accent: adúlt for adúlt
résearch for reséarch
superflúous for supérfluous
impotent for ímpotent
futilé for fútile

What are the causes of these pronunciation errors? Words are mispronounced for a number of reasons. One is spelling. Words are not always pronounced as their spelling suggests; moreover, spelling provides no clue to accent. Some errors are caused by failure to note changes of pronunciation for words serving different linguistic functions. Words are sometimes mispronounced because they are confused with similar words. Other words are mispronounced because of misarticulation of sounds contained in them.

Probably most mispronunciations occur because the words were first heard mispronounced or because the first pronunciation was a bad guess which initiated the habit of mispronouncing.

■ 3. *Pronounce each word according to its proper syllabication.* Avoid altering or omitting syllables. Children say "A'rab" for "Ar-ab," and some people use "ho-mog'-o-nous" for "hom-o-ge'-ne-ous."

■ 4. *Let the requirements of the speaking situation govern your pronunciation.* When you are speaking in a large auditorium or when you are competing with noises, be a bit more precise in your pronunciation to ensure the listener's comprehension. Careful pronunciation is also a means of stressing important ideas.

■ 5. *Obtain a good dictionary and check your pronunciation constantly.* There is no substitute for the habit of checking pronunciations in a good up-to-date American dictionary. As we noted in Chapter Twelve, however, the dictionary is not infallible, for it is based on past usage, and language and our pronunciations of language are constantly changing. When most educated people begin to pronounce a word in a way other than that cited in existing dictionaries, this new pronunciation is almost certain to be accepted in a short time. Before long, it will even appear in new editions of dictionaries. In short, dictionaries follow rather than lead or dictate acceptable pronunciation. Also, and perhaps even more important, dictionaries generally fail to take into account the many dialects within any language and, hence, the different pronunciations which are acceptable—and, at times, even expected—within each group. For all of these reasons, use a dictionary as a guide, not as a bible.

Projects and Problems

PROJECT 1: A test of articulation.

The following exercise in speech sounds should help you to identify any sounds with which you have difficulty. The sound to be identified and tested is indicated after each number by means of the markings used in Webster's. The first word contains the sound in a prominent position. Some of the other words in the list contain the sound, and some do not. Pronounce the words aloud and underline those which contain the sound you are testing. Check the line to the left of the number for all sounds on which you need further work. Listen to the reading of others to note how they produce these sounds. For a short form of the test, do only the items marked by an asterisk.

_____	1.	ē	feet, fit, date, eat, me, egg, fill, seen
_____	*2.	ĭ	dill, deal, it, pit, peat, pet, duck, dick
_____	*3.	ĕ	get, git, dale, end, shall, yet, enter, out
_____	*4.	ă	pat, pet, as, den, leg, rock, rack, dad
_____	5.	å	ago, up, lute, policy, fallen, bath, tuba, toot
_____	*6.	ŭ	cud, cod, utter, just, shot, tuck, dude, put
_____	7.	ä	far, fur, on, want, had, luck, caught, ah
_____	8.	ô	caught, cut, doll, gun, tuck, owl, nod, coat
_____	9.	o͝o	took, tuck, tune, could, crux, group, drew, wolf
_____	10.	o͞o	spoon, spewn, ooze, whom, luck, shoe, beauty, put
_____	11.	ū	you, rue, hue, food, fuel, feel, pew, full, fool
_____	12.	ō	coal, cull, oboe, slow, mutton, brow, cod, opus
_____	*13.	ou	cowed, kayoed, bough, ton, gun, rot, crayola, out
_____	14.	ā	pain, pen, pun, eight, tell, flay, Iowa, hail
_____	15.	ī	like, lick, aisle, race, won, tiger, spy
_____	16.	oi	loin, line, bird, fine, toy, murder, voice, tall
_____	17.	m	mere, beer, ear, home, bill, robe, mop, summer
_____	18.	n	new, drew, under, dole, pew, pan, pants, singing
_____	*19.	ng	singing, sinning, rank, ran, rag, rang, ram, tinkle
_____	*20.	p	pour, more, whip, paper, cap, bees, robin, slap
_____	21.	b	ban, man, pan, robe, sober, baby, cob, rim
_____	*22.	t	Ted, dead, cad, madder, cut, feed, biting, three
_____	*23.	d	dote, tote, gad, mat, radio, fated, bat, tin
_____	24.	k	cap, gap, bagging, tackle, brig, kill, crew
_____	25.	g	gill, kill, rag, bucky, raking, core, fling, age
_____	*26.	r	roar, wore, hear, weep, deride, very, bar, weed

____	27.	l	lay, pray, wake, little, camel, seal, sole, asleep
____	28.	f	fly, ply, safe, differs, divers, have, thigh, wife
____	29.	v	vain, bane, fat, proof, leave, unveiling, wail, live
____	*30.	th	thank, tank, they, zinc, swath, sin, anything, bass
____	*31.	th	thy, vie, thigh, loathe, fat, sigh, mother, cloth
____	*32.	s	saw, thaw, miss, shaw, trace, recent, clash, graze
____	*33.	z	zoo, Sioux, boys, vice, lazy, noose, aphasia, place
____	*34.	sh	ship, sip, cheap, mash, explosion, suit, fishing, shoot
____	35.	zh	garage, garish, entourage, rajah, vision, mirage, ocean, cortege
____	*36.	wh	where, wear, vile, while, winter, wheat, witch, bewhisk-ered, white
____	*37.	h	hill, gill, hinge, unhang, hurrah, who, rehash, wheel
____	*38.	w	way, whey, swine, whet, chair, fight, wise, quiet
____	39.	y	yam, lamb, Jell-O, yellow, onion, jeer, set, young
____	*40.	ch	cherry, sherry, Jerry, etching, leech, lush, ridge, chum
____	41.	dz	gin, chin, just, badge, richer, soldier, magic, pitching

PROJECT 2: Articulating difficult sounds.

Find two to three pages of prose which develop an idea of interest to you. Go over the passage and underline all sounds with which you have difficulty. Practice reading until you can articulate all sounds clearly and acceptably. Read another similar passage to see if you can articulate all sounds effectively without further study of them. Listen to the typically difficult sounds as produced by others in doing this exercise.

PROJECT 3: Understanding the phonetic symbols.

Turn to Appendix A and study the phonetic symbols until you know them. Your speech will be criticized at times with phonetic symbols, and you should have a clear understanding of the sounds for which they stand.

References

Bronstein, Arthur J., *The Pronunciation of American English*. New York: Appleton-Century-Crofts, 1960.

———— and Beatrice F. Jacoby, *Your Speech and Voice*. New York: Random House, 1967. Chapters 6 to 14.

Holder, William, *Elements of Speech, 1669*. Menston, England: The Scholar Press Ltd., 1967. An enjoyable facsimile of a work on speech published in the seventeenth century, useful for comparing the conceptions of pronunciation and speech of a previous period and now.

Kantner, Claude E., and Robert West, *Phonetics*, rev. ed. New York: Harper & Row, 1960.

Partridge, Eric, *The Gentle Art of Lexicography*. New York: Macmillan, 1963.

Sledd, James, and Wilma R. Ebbitt (eds.), *Dictionaries and That Dictionary*. Fair Lawn, N.J.: Scott-Foresman, 1962. A collection of papers on diction-aries as history versus dictionaries as law and the controversy which followed the publication of Merriam-Webster's *Third New International Dictionary.*

Van Riper, Charles, and Dorothy Edna Smith, *An Introduction to General American Phonetics,* 2nd ed. New York: Harper & Row, 1962.

Wise, Claude M., *Introduction to Phonetics.* Englewood Cliffs, N.J.: Prentice-Hall, Inc., 1957.

——, *Applied Phonetics.* Englewood Cliffs, N.J.: Prentice-Hall, Inc., 1957.

—— and Lucia Morgan, *A Progressive Phonetic Workbook for Students in Speech,* 2nd ed. Dubuque, Iowa: Wm. C. Brown Co., 1967.

PART SEVEN

Bases for Evaluation

Eve Arnold, Magnum.

measures of effectiveness

Importance of Speech Evaluation

Speech communication is in large part the processes by which we achieve mutual understanding and action concerning issues that have to do with individual and community survival and progress. Free and competent speaking is the foundation of orderly political advancement, especially in the American political system of widespread voting, representative government, and strong influence of public opinion on legislation and policy making.

During the recent decades some students of public address have dismissed platform eloquence and other forms of oral communication as out of date, along with the other formalities of the eighteenth and early nineteenth centuries. Nevertheless, the cracker barrels, street corners, courtrooms, conference chambers, legislative halls, lecture rostrums, private homes, and college protest gatherings continue to have their effective and ineffective talkers. Indeed, the public address extensions of radio and television have multiplied the potential power of oral communication beyond anything envisioned by former orators and rhetoricians. These mass audiences, aided by the multiplicity of printing presses and newspapers, have extended in turn their own vocal give-and-take to their grass-roots neighbors. Thus we are more than ever a nation of talkers. Despite the irrelevance, triviality, and even futility of some of our vocal exchange, our national character, thought, and political and cultural conduct are directly the product and reflection of these communicative interactions among people.

This barrage of ideas and other information calls for your proper preparation to accept or reject what you receive. Your responsibility as an auditor, viewer, and in turn a contributor is not to accept or reject uncritically what you hear or read. Your audience role—which you usually accept whether you realize it or not—is to discriminate between the good and the bad and so to approve or reject. Thus can you support or reject the ideas that promote or block ongoing democracy.

Your problem, then, is how to separate valid from invalid talk, sound from crooked thinking, worthwhile utterance from blatant nonsense. Your practical concern is to formulate standards by which to deal wisely with ceaseless torrents of words. It is not enough for you to follow your hunches and so to conclude, "I like this speech," or "He is a lopsided square, and **239**

everything he says bores me to death." Before you vote at the polls, demonstrate for or against anything, decide as juryman, go on strike, buy the goods,
or join up with some speaker who sounds sensible to you, you should be
able to justify your reactions and reflect more than blind bias.

Principles of Speech Evaluation

How shall you analyze and evaluate speeches, long or short simple classroom assignments by others, broken dialogues and discussions with your
student peers? Do the same principles govern your instructor's answers to
your queries and pronouncements of great public leaders beamed to you
over television?

- Your starting point is to understand what is *oral communication.* Speech
as communication originates with a speaker who uses his voice and body
to gain and hold the attention of one or more within his range. He aims
to contribute something to their pleasure, knowledge, understanding, attitudes, and conduct.

- The next step is to understand *the communicator's audience* with its
current attitudes and tastes. The student audiences of the University of Iowa
in 1970, for example, were different from those of Harvard College in 1770.
Oral styles, voice mannerisms, bodily action, dress, platform conventions,
conversation conventions of speakers and their hearers have changed as
have all other fashions.

- A third component of the communicative situation is *the message* or
document itself—whatever is uttered, long or short, important or trivial.
Its language is an instrument for conveying ideas, for revealing details of
instances, facts, testimony, for amplifying materials (e.g., questions, definitions, rhythmical constructions), and for affecting the desired intellectual,
emotional, and imaginative stimulation and response.

- A fourth factor is the *occasion.* These constituents of speaker, audience,
and speech originate and develop in the speaking situation itself. Talkers
and their associated human beings communicate at a point in time and
place. The immediate and larger background establishes the atmosphere
in which the speech exists. What happens is colored not only by the physical
and other elements of the specific occasion but by the wider environment
that envelops the speaking event.

- A final factor is the *voice, bodily accompaniment and* other *transmission
agencies* (e.g., printed forms) that complete the communicating transaction.[1]

A given communicative act, then, is properly described as the interplay
of these five factors. If the speaker is handicapped by vocal or mental quirks
or confusions, if the speech is poorly phrased, if the auditors are hostile
or ignorant, unable to hear or to understand a strange tongue, or if the
speaking situation is blocked by natural disasters or a mob, communication

---

[1]See Chapters Two and Three.

obviously fails. When, on the other hand, the speaker, his ideas, and his organs of communication operate efficiently and are adapted properly to the audience, when the auditors have adequate intelligence and willingness to attend and respond, the results have a greater probability of being effective.

You are advised to strike a balance among these factors. Some speakers whom you listen to or otherwise evaluate may be strong in ideas and weak in other speech processes, or objectionable because they fail to demonstrate an understanding of the audience. You are to understand that various factors make up the criteria: thought, organization, supporting and amplifying details, language, audience adaptation, speaking personality, voice, articulation, bodily action. You can hardly give an exact numerical rating to each item and exclude or include it on such a basis. A weighing of these elements in relation to the total impression or influence will tend to determine your judgment in each case.

What of the scope and specific methodology of your rhetorical judgment? As a critic of speaking you are practicing an art or social science rather than a pure science. Your judgment is a qualitative one, based partly on the facts but partly on a more intangible reflective pattern. As an evaluator you collect the available data, formulate the materials into meaningful units, apply logical and psychological criteria to the measurement of this object of the study, and frame a conclusion derived from this methodical procedure.

Standards of Evaluation

What standards, if any, are you to apply to the evaluation of speeches? Also, what have been the inadequacies of the standards thus far applied? Should the critics, for example, adhere to Aristotle's *Rhetoric* and related writings, or should they modify or add to Aristotle the principles of Cicero and Quintilian? Or, should the entire system of older authoritative rhetoric be rejected as outdated?

Norwood Brigance, editor of the two-volume *History and Criticism of American Public Address,* stated in his preface:

the reader will find a wide diversity in patterns of treatment. To those who would prefer that one standardized pattern of rhetorical criticism be followed, we answer that it would have been neither possible, nor, in our opinion desirable. It would not have been desirable because the best scholars are not all adherent to the same philosophy of criticism. Some prefer the pure Aristotelian patterns. Some prefer their Aristotelianism diluted. Others adjure it all together. Among such vigorous dissenters no collation would have been possible.[2]

---

[2] N. W. Brigance (ed.), *History and Criticism of American Public Address,* New York, McGraw-Hill, 1943, 2 vols. Marie Hochmuth (ed.), *A History and Criticism of American Public Address,* Longmans Green, New York, 1954, vol. III.

A balanced view of contributions of rhetorical criticism would confirm Brigance's experience in testifying to the "variety of techniques and standards in the two volumes." The same variety exists in the Hochmuth collection cited in footnote 2 and in the occasional volumes that have assessed speakers and in various articles on speech criticism in the speech journals. Neoclassical or postclassical standards of rhetorical criticism would properly suggest the diversified approaches to these evaluations. Post-Aristotelian patterns, though heavily indebted to Aristotle, have reflected the concepts of Cicero, Quintilian, Bacon, Ramus, Campbell, Blair, Priestley, Whately, Bentham, Arnold, Woolbert, Winans, Burke, Richards, and various others of Medieval, Renaissance, and modern English and American schools. These writers and thinkers on oral and written communication have certainly had independent judgments. Their principles and methods of evaluating rhetorical theories and applications have much significance.

Each critic of communication has reacted to those forces of his age that facilitate effective communication. For example, the rise of modern science and the development of popular government have modified the criteria of appropriate or effective communication. Critics in the latter part of the twentieth century have been influenced by the new logic, semantics, mass society, psychology, sociology, aesthetics, space, and other sciences. These movements have profoundly affected the theories and applications of communication and the accompanying rhetorical criticism.

Despite these accretions, basic concepts of communication continue to contribute heavily to the shaping of mature critical judgments. If blind adherence to the formulas and precepts of ancient Greece and Rome throttles creative approaches, so equally does exclusive concentration on techniques and methods limited to the recent decades produce only poorly disciplined and superficial communicative standards and judgments. You are to use common sense in following those principles that govern your answer to the questions "What is a good speech?" and "What criteria do you apply to the given speech or speeches?"

Not only should you be familiar with the standards of criticism or evaluation of communication which have been developed over time by various scholars, you should also take into consideration two other factors before you decide upon the particular approach or particular criteria to be used for your evaluation. First, consider the *purposes* of those involved in the communicative situation—both the speaker and the members of the audience. An evaluation which disregards these risks being totally irrelevant to the phenomena being studied. Secondly, consider your *own* purposes in making the evaluation. Are you evaluating the speech in order to decide whether to accept it or to follow the speaker's proposals? Are you evaluating it in order to determine whether it is or will be effective with some particular audience? Are you evaluating it in order to help the communicator become more effective in moving people or more effective in making a favorable impression on certain kinds of auditors? Are you evaluating it in order to discover why it was or wasn't effective at fulfilling its purpose? Perhaps you are evaluating a group of effective speeches in order to develop or refine a set of principles about what makes various types of contemporary communication effective. Or you may be evaluating a speech or analyzing it in order to find out why the speaker said and did what he did. By deciding on your purpose or purposes, you will be able to select more intelligently from the various suggestions about evaluation below.

You should also consider the ways in which your criteria might differ when you evaluate a more or less formal speech, discussion, conversation, debate, or some other type of discourse.

Details of Evaluation

Consider in detail your evaluation of typical and representative aspects of communication and their combined character.

1. Size Up the Speaker As Best You Can

The speaker is, after all, a key factor in the communicative performance. If he is a classmate, a friend or an associate, you normally know something about him. If you are trying to judge a speech you have listened to on television, you will probably need to acquire more information about the speaker.

In any case, a speaker is the product of his total experience and background—home, school, associates, and earlier experiences and relationships that have molded his speaking personality and communicative methods. Speakers have many inherited tendencies as well as ones acquired directly from their surroundings. These formative influences account for much of a speaker's language, ideas, social adjustments before one person or more, hidden prejudices, and much else that comes to the surface—even in a brief four-minute talk.

Note the speaker's personality without becoming too critical of small items that may prejudice you. Does he say what he says with conviction and sincerity? Does he have self-confidence (or braggadocio), humor (none or too much), taste, tact, generosity, goodwill, modesty? If his communication indicates to you genuine possession of these traits, you can gauge him as especially strong in speaking personality.

■ *Note the speaker's control of his vocal mechanism.* Does he read his speech or give it from memory? Does he stumble in extemporization? What of his gestures and movements as he speaks? Is his pitch unduly high? Is his rate too slow or too fast? What of his loudness (too lively or sluggish communication)? Does he speak as a native of Indiana, Michigan, Mississippi, Maine? Is what he says free of bombast and declamation? Is he at ease?

■ *Ethos and credibility.* Important aspects of the personality of the speaker are his motives and specific intent in the speech.[3] Though these factors are often difficult to assess, the listener should do his best to analyze them. We often do know a great deal about a speaker's public reputation. A prior impression of the speaker's character is an extrinsic factor in the total impression we get of the speaker. The intrinsic factors are the message itself and what the speaker does during the act of communication.

How accurate is a speaker's public reputation? What are the standards by which it is estimated? The facts and the generalizations are hard to pinpoint, experimentally or otherwise. The general patterns by which a reputation is built are sometimes obscure, sometimes fairly clear.

According to Aristotle, a speaker's ethical quality has three dimensions: intelligence, character, and goodwill. The effectiveness of communicative appeals depends on "the moral character of the speaker, or on the production of a certain disposition in the audience, or on the speech itself by means of real or apparent demonstration."[4]

How does the audience gauge intelligence, character, and goodwill of the speaker? To Aristotle, these traits are evidenced by an analysis of what is "virtuous"; the audience must be convinced that the communicator is virtuous. He can create such a quality of virtue either for himself or for those who are associated with him. The elements of virtue include justice, courage, temperance, magnificence, magnanimity, liberality, gentleness, prudence, and wisdom.[5] The Aristotelian view of the intellectual, social, and moral qualities basic to ethical analysis continues to be validated by experimental and theoretical work in communication.

Carl Hovland, Irving Janis, and Harold Kelley, in their studies of source credibility, have identified expertness, trustworthiness, and intention as the chief ethical elements perceived by audiences.[6] J. C. McCroskey, in his factor analysis of the ethos of speakers, consistently found two factors: authoritativeness and character or trustworthiness. He noted they were equivalent to the two major factors in ethos emphasized by classical rhetoricians.[7]

■ *Intrinsic factors of a communicator's ethos.* Intrinsic ethos is that which is developed by the speaker or source during the act of communication. You, as speaker, develop your case by discussing the ideas and their logical supports. You also inject without artifice the motivational qualities that help to increase audience interest and to move them favorably. The ethical

---

[3] See Chapter Eighteen, "Ethics."
[4] J. C. W. Welldon, *The Rhetoric of Aristotle,* Macmillan, New York, 1886, p. 1336a.
[5] Lane Cooper, *The Rhetoric of Aristotle,* D. Appleton Co., New York, 1932, pp. 46–47.
[6] Carl Hovland, Irving Janis, and Harold Kelley, *Communication and Persuasion,* Yale University Press, New Haven, 1953, chap. 2.
[7] See J. C. McCroskey, "Scales for the Measurement of Ethos," *Speech Monographs,* 30:65–72, 1966.

qualities crop out not only in the ideas and their details, but in each part of the organization—in the exordium, the main body, and the conclusion. Your selection, order of unfolding, and methods of summary affect the audience's perceptions of your expertness and trustworthiness. Your language and delivery too can enhance or lessen your ethos. Ethical strength or weakness thus accompanies every phase of the discourse, beginning before you actually open your mouth and concluding sometime after the discourse is done.

These details of personality and process are not the be-all and end-all of your analysis of a speaker, but they furnish clues to his general communicative influence. The more you can know about the experiences of those you criticize, the better will be your insight into their thinking, language, and interpersonal communicative habits.

2. Evaluate the Social-political Background of the Talk

If the speech you are listening to is of the moment, try to relate it to economic and other events and problems that fill the headlines and flow over the air.

Just as the personality of the speaker is heavily affected by his total experiences prior to his audience appearance, so is the thought of the speaker dominated by the political, economic, and cultural climate of his day. As a student who is evaluating the speeches of others, you should immerse yourself in contemporary issues, such as the most recent economic currents. To deal with discourse on economic questions as you deal with these times in the 1970s, for example, you should understand the problems of inflation, recession, and unemployment; you should be familiar with monetary restraints, the cost-of-living index, the Dow Jones Averages, and the Federal Reserve Board.

Over the air, in congresses, in pulpits, in and around college classrooms, at business conferences, at dinners, on farms, in villages, in the great cities, these problems are grappled with sensibly and nonsensibly. To appreciate any speech of your time, you will identify every speaker with the world that, partly at least, molds him.

3. Analyze the Specific Audience

As every speech is of the times, so is it of the immediate audience. A very effective speech means that the differences between the speaker and the group melt. If you are the speaker, fusion occurs—but not your loss of leadership. If you are successful, you take "sovereign possession of the audience," but the audience also takes possession of you.

We have often reminded you that you are to know the occasion. Ask yourself, why this occasion? Is speech making the major concern? What is the size of your group? Try to understand something of its homogeneity, biases, mental habits and attitudes, race, politics, occupations, religion, traditions, economic level, sex, age, and other data. These factors furnish a profile for you as a judge after the speech.

In many cases it will be a specialized audience, about which you cannot find out too much (unless it happens to be an occasion on your own campus). In other instances, where the speaker is appealing by radio and television to a nationwide audience, your problem is to fathom as best you can, with the aid of the press and opinion polls, the probable attitudes of these national listeners.

As a critic of speeches, you will be somewhat of a historian. You will weigh first-hand documents, attempt objectively to classify and interpret facts and trends and mold them into consistent patterns, hesitate about inferring simple cause-and-effect phenomena. These are the procedures of a historian; they are also skills essential for good speech evaluation.

As a historian, you are both biographer and social chronicler. As a biographer, you will summon and test facts concerning your speaker's total career and your interpretation of your speaker's personal activity. As social historian, you will place every speaking event in its social milieu. You will make an adequate analysis of the economic, social, political, literary, educational, religious, and other factors involved, laying stress on those trends and forces bearing directly on the particular communication event. As a critic of speeches then, you are more than annalist, biographer, or social chronicler. Using your investigative competency, you relate the details of ideas, language, structure, delivery, occasion, audience, and speaker's background to the speaker's contribution—or lack of it.[8]

4.   Concentrate Chiefly on the Speech Message Itself

What is its purpose? Or rather, what is the purpose of whoever produces it? Does it try merely to give additional knowledge or is it an attempt to persuade the listeners to accept some controversial position? Is the speaker hoping to get the listeners to act in unison or is he merely trying to keep them awake and interested? Whatever the purpose, the critic should recognize it and decide whether the speaker has to a reasonable degree achieved it.

■   *a.   Weigh ideas and their supports.* Every important speech contains an idea or ideas. What are these ideas? How original are they? How consistent? How sensible? How are they related to the messages of other contemporary speakers? How clearly are they expressed? How acceptable are they to the

---

[8]See, for example, S. Judson Crandell, "The Beginning of a Methodology of Social Control Studies in Public Address," *Quarterly Journal of Speech,* 33:36–39, 1946; see also Anthony Hillbruner, *Critical Dimensions: The Art of Public Address Criticism,* Random House, New York, 1966, Part I, "Extrinsic Factors in the Criticism of Public Address" and Part II, "Intrinsic Factors in the Criticism of Public Address," pp. 9–173.

immediate audience? Most important, how well do they meet the *needs* of the audience? These basic ideas almost invariably relate to current economic, religious, social, and other problems and difficulties. What does the speaker you attempt to evaluate say about the Soviet Union, the control of nuclear weapons, further exploration of the moon, South Vietnam and peace, Israel versus the Arab world, Britain and the Conservative government, strikes, military draft legislation, inflation, civil rights, school integration, ghetto abolition, urbanization versus rural interests, reconstruction of college and university curricula and student participation in administration, ecumenical movements, birth control, minimum annual wages, or other problems? Your task is to set forth the lines of argument or the controversial positions and estimate their "worth."

What are the mental skills of a competent speaker? His ideas are more than commonplace; he provides more than usual insight into the issue he handles. He defends, interprets, and now and then modifies his assumptions and propositions in the light of his developing wisdom and the turn of events.

Reviewing of your thinker's ideas touches upon his ability to define and analyze a problem. Besides possessing a breadth of thinking and the ability to define and analyze, the effective speaker-thinker shows himself to be a kind of economic and social philosopher. He generalizes from specific instances, traces causes and results. At his best, he is a genuine philosopher.

Analyze the speaker's supporting ideas, evidence, and affective details. Even in a short speech, concrete items should be presented to support the central idea or ideas—hypothetical or actual cases, anecdotes, analogies, definitions, cause-to-effect illustrations, and similar material, one or more of which will embody the essential thought.

In your examination of content, you yourself will need to become something of a logician. You will apply tests of acceptable definitions, inference, alleged "fact," analogy, reasoning, generalization from cases, authority, refutation, and in general, sound thinking. A logical appraisal of any speech is difficult but necessary. You will need more than a hunch to decide whether the speech and speaker reflect straight thinking.[9]

The able communicator appeals to audience needs, drives, attitudes, sentiments, and habits. He appeals to motives of self-preservation, acquisition of goods and comforts, personal and social satisfactions, prospects of recognition, power, challenges to duty, justice, and self-sacrifice.

The details that enforce the speaker's ideas directly are "cognitive"; those that are primarily identified with emotional reactions are "affective." We note the unity of these factors in human reaction. No hard and fast line can be usefully drawn between logic and emotion, but for convenience we often treat these aspects of a speech separately.[10] We decide whether the

---

[9] See Chapter Eight, "The Message," and Chapter Ten, "Thought."
[10] See Chapter Twenty-one, "Persuasion: Cognitive Domain," and Chapter Twenty-two, "Persuasion: Affective Domain."

motivational features of a speech, e.g., appeals to loyalty, patriotism, pride of achievement, are justified as logical, "good psychology," or both. In addition, then, to being somewhat of a logician, you must also be a student of psychology. Note the items that deal with the speaker's personality and prestige: They are part of your analysis of motives, but are here stressed as important sources of the affective (as well as logical) results. Speakers add to their audience effectiveness if they reveal (and possess) intelligence, goodwill, and character, as noted by Aristotle and by many later rhetoricians.

■   *b. Evaluate the structure of the speech.* Organization is no mere mechanical detail of the speech pattern. The speaker's management of arrangement reflects his thinking. You will note the speaker's rhetorical purpose and his specific methods in unfolding his aims to his hearers. In some cases his outline is exact and tight—with a formal opening, seriatim treatment of related topics, and conventional appeals at the end. In other cases, equally effective, he may resort to "psychological" unity. As a critic you will note: which ideas and materials are included as well as those that are omitted—a problem of selection; the unity, logical or motivative; the clearness with which successive ideas are unfolded; the relationship of sequence to audience needs and interests; and the proportion of time and space allotted to an idea. These are problems in your evaluation of structure or organization.

■   *c. Evaluate the communicative language.* Communicative effectiveness depends much on language skill. Words and their combination give meaning to ideas and their imaginative-emotional associations. The speaker's invention is implemented by his language and enables him to secure maximum transmission of his "thought" or "meaning."[11] The effective speaker's words are generally keyed to the ear and to his voice. His compositions are accurate, clear, appropriate, and colorful. He avoids ambiguity, unnecessary vagueness, floridity, triteness, and general dullness. He will not have an extremely limited vocabulary and therefore will not resort to repetition. The occasion and audience will affect his language as well as his thinking. Depending on his audience and topic, he may be factual and scientific or idiomatic and informal. His language may be free from sophistic exaggeration, and he will be well-read enough and possess a sufficiently broad vocabulary for his style to be simple—in its restraint.

■   *d. Evaluate the use of channels.* The effectiveness of a speaking event depends in part on the character and completeness of the transmission agency. As we have noted before good channel process is a matter of the satisfactory use of voice, body, and various audio and visual aids.

Good speaking is a combination of all of these qualities of communication. The details of ideas, structure, language, and channels are not ends in

---

[11]See Chapter Ten, "Thought."

themselves. Each is important, but, relative to the total effect, any one element is secondary; the final judgment of the performance is of its totality.

5. Evaluate the Immediate and Long-range Influence of the Speech

The impression given by the speaker is to be measured not simply by the intrinsic value of the speech itself, i.e., as well as you can judge it by your presence or by reading it in print, but by its effect on immediate and later audiences. Making this long-range evaluation is an important part of your role as critic.

Every speaker hopes for immediate approval of his performance, whether his purpose is to add information or to change the attitudes and conduct of the hearers. He looks for some applause, at least nods of approval, or remarks that indicate audience endorsement. He looks for indications of support for him and his ideas, favorable comment in newspapers, and, if he is a politician, telegrams, laudable letters, and increased campaign contributions. If he is a student, he hopes that his instructor will give him some sign of merit.

One of your most difficult jobs as critic is to judge the effect of the speech from hidden and delayed audience responses as well as immediate and observable ones. Audience polls, for example, may reveal strong opposition to a speaker and his message before, and not much of a change immediately after the performance; but the later social results may show that this speaker's message over a period of months has made a more favorable impression than was immediately discernible. The problem here is to explore the wider currents of cause and effect and separate the influence of the speaker's activity in affecting social change from the plurality of other causes at work.

Your role as logician at this point is arduous. You are to separate as best you can the many complicated elements related to consequences and, by the aid of whatever facts and inferences you can muster, single out the prime influences of the special speech or speeches that you are trying to judge in their wider range.

Final Judgment in Speech Evaluation

Even after your logical estimates of the speech are complete, you are still confronted with a moral or ethical judgment correlative with your intellectual appraisal. In the next chapter we shall discuss in detail the responsibility of every speaker for his utterances.

What is the test of whether the speech is a "good one"? The immediate and later behavior of the hearers as a result of a specific speech or series of speeches is that test. As speech critics and students of communication, we often have the responsibility of judging the worth of a speech by its impact on social change. You as critic are thus more than a logician, psychologist, or rule-of-thumb communicator. You are to be aware of the societal results of a speaker's utterances. The assumption is that unless public speeches by a given speaker on specific issues influence an audience or audiences to make social progress, or at least work against social deterioration, then those speeches should never have been produced.

In this sense rhetoric means commitment, and the speaker and the critic have cast their lots on the side of social and ethical progress.

Speech Rating Forms

What should be the application by speech instructors and students of the forms available for evaluating speeches and speechmakers? Such forms, extensively used for learning purposes and to some extent for rating standings in speech classes and in competitive speaking events, have the usual limitations of such mechanical treatments.[12]

The purpose of most rating forms is to establish some standard for determining relatively excellent performance and to aid each performer to better understand his own and others' performances. The assumption is that speaking performance improves when one is aware of which aspects of his performance are good and which are poor.

A number of recent studies deal with the limitations of such measuring devices. The weaknesses lie both in the construction of the form and in the unreliability of the raters. Thompson listed as weaknesses in the rater's judgments, faulty reception of the speech being evaluated and different interpretations of the message as received.[13]

Those who devise rating forms may differ widely on what are the impor-

---

[12] Examples of research of problems relating to assessment of speaking skills and rating include: Keith Brooks, "Some Basic Considerations in Rating Scale Development: A Descriptive Bibliography," *Central States Speech Journal,* 9:27–31, Fall 1957; Samuel L. Becker, "The Rating of Speeches: Scale Independence," *Speech Monographs,* 29:38–44, March 1962; Samuel L. Becker and Carl A. Dallinger, "The Effect of Instructional Methods upon Achievement and Attitudes in Communication Skills," *Speech Monographs,* 27:70–76, March 1960; Theodore Clevenger, Jr., "Influence of Scale Complexity on the Reliability of Ratings of General Effectiveness in Public Speaking," *Speech Monographs,* 32:153–156, June 1964; Robert N. Bostrom, "Dogmatism, Rigidity, and Rating Behavior," *Speech Teacher,* 13:283–287, November 1954; Gerald R. Miller, "Agreement and the Grounds for It: Persistent Problems in Speech Rating," *Speech Teacher,* 13:257–261, November 1964; Larry L. Barker, Robert J. Kibler, and Rudolph W. Geter, "Two Investigations of the Relationship among Selected Ratings of Speech Effectiveness, and Comprehension," *Speech Monographs,* 35:400–408, August 1968; Wayne Thompson, "Is There a Yardstick for Measuring Public Speaking?" *Quarterly Journal of Speech,* 29:87–91, 1943: Wayne Thompson, "An Experimental Study of the Accuracy of Typical Speech Rating Techniques," *Speech Monographs,* 11:65–79, 1944; Franklin H. Knower, "What Is a Speech Test?" *Quarterly Journal of Speech,* 30:485–493, December 1944.

[13] See Wayne Thompson, *Speech Monographs, loc. cit.*

tant categories. One widely used form, for example, consists of eleven items (subject, analysis, materials, organization, language, adjustment to speaker, bodily action, voice articulation, fluency, general effectiveness); another form has only eight (speech attitudes and adjustment, voice and articulation, language, audience interest and adaptation, ideas, organization, general effectiveness); others vary even more.

Becker, after an extensive testing of speech rating, concluded:

Serious thought should be given either to revision of present rating forms, or better definitions of the individual scales. The goal should be to have each scale measure a relatively independent aspect of the performance. Perhaps the speech form should be reduced to three scales, a content-analysis scale, a delivery scale, and a language scale. Additional investigation of this problem, including the testing of various scales, should prove fruitful.[14]

Thompson concluded: "The yardstick for measuring speaking skill has not been found. The perfect yardstick will probably never be found.[15]

Even though a "perfect yardstick" is not available, we believe that you can learn much from using the existing yardsticks—the existing rating forms. You can improve your ability to evaluate speeches by rating the speeches of others with these forms, and you can improve your own speaking ability by considering the detailed ratings on such forms which your teacher and peers give to you.

Projects and Problems

PROJECT 1. "Justifiable criticism is free from subjective treatment." Comment.

PROJECT 2. Write a criticism of a speech recently given by an important national leader. What comments does your instructor have on your evaluation?

PROJECT 3. Prepare a paper in which you set forth the fundamental differences between oral and written composition.

PROJECT 4. To what extent should you as speech critic assume social usefulness as the aim of any speech? If, in determining the effect of a particular speech, you observe the unethical use of data or devices, how shall you deal with such a matter in your evaluation?

---

[14]Samuel L. Becker, "The Rating of Speeches: Scale Independence," *op. cit.*, p. 44.
[15]Wayne Thompson, "Is There a Yardstick for Measuring Speaking Skill?" *Quarterly Journal of Speech*, 29:87–91, 1943.

PROJECT 5.   Collect five specimens of speech criticism found in newspapers and periodicals. Try especially to secure a number of reports by editorial writers and columnists on speeches of major importance. Comment on each criticism.

PROJECT 6.   Comment on the possible relation between the criticism of speeches and the improvement in quality and the enlargement of influence of public addresses.

PROJECT 7.   What is the relation between speech criticism and such fields as ethics, psychology, and politics?

PROJECT 8.   To what extent should the literary considerations of permanence and beauty enter into your judgment of a speech?

PROJECT 9.   Differentiate between impressionistic and judicial speech criticism.

References

Baird, A. Craig, and Lester Thonssen, "Methodology in the Criticism of Public Address," *Quarterly Journal of Speech,* 33:134–138, 1947.

Blau, Joseph L., "Public Address As Intellectual Revelation," *Western Speech,* 21(2):77–83, Spring 1957.

Burke, Kenneth, *A Grammar of Motives.* New York: Prentice-Hall, Inc., 1952.

——, *A Rhetoric of Motives.* New York: Prentice-Hall, Inc., 1953.

Cathcart, Robert, *Post-Communication.* Indianapolis: Bobbs-Merrill, 1966.

Fotheringham, W. C., "A Technique for Measuring Speech Effectiveness in Public Speaking Classes," *Speech Monographs,* 23:31–37, 1956.

Hillbruner, Anthony, *Critical Dimensions.* New York: Random House, 1966.

——, "Creativity in Contemporary Criticism," *Western Speech,* 24(1):5–11, Winter 1960.

Knower, Franklin, "What Is a Speech Test?" *Quarterly Journal of Speech,* 30:485–493, 1944.

Nichols, Marie Hochmuth, *Rhetoric and Criticism.* Baton Rouge, La.: State University Press, 1963. Chapter V.

Robinson, Karl F., and E. J. Kerikas, *Teaching Speech—Methods and Materials.* New York: David McKay, Inc., 1963. Chapters XI and XII.

Thompson, Wayne, "Is There a Yardstick for Measuring Speaking Skill? " *Quarterly Journal of Speech,* 29:87–91, February 1943.

Thonssen, Lester, A. Craig Baird, and Waldo W. Braden, *Speech Criticism,* 2nd ed. New York: Ronald Press, 1970. Chapters 1 and 2.

Wiseman, Gordon, and Larry Barker, *Speech—Interpersonal Communication.* San Francisco: Chandler, 1967. Chapter 7.

ethics in speech communication

Importance of Ethics in Communication

Almost every communication, whether the source recognizes it or not, harms or helps in some way those who listen and react. Talk is hardly ever neutral. It consists prevailingly of fact or error, truth or falseness, useful or useless influences on behavior. Hence, there is an important dimension of ethical responsibility in every act of communication. If your communication is justified, you will produce results that are socially constructive, whatever

your specific message. Your ideas and their expression in language and voice will enforce patterns that are socially, politically, and logically desirable.

As Gerald Miller states it, "Every communicative act, of necessity, involves a value dimension; it stems from certain ethical and/or aesthetic premises. Not only do we seek to understand how speech communication motivates men, we also reflect upon the question of whether it is good for them to behave as they do."[1]

The history of public address as well as the theory of practical discourse attests to the power of ethical decisiveness in important situations. Ethical and unethical speaking helped to produce Socrates, Hitler, and a long list of other communicators whose roles in society, for good or ill, have been tremendously influential. Audiences have often succumbed to false doctrines and in turn have generated sinister propaganda. On the other hand, communicative saviors have repeatedly appeared in times of great crisis to provide the communicative leadership that explains much of what is best in our civilization.

Ethics as Value Judgments

Basic to the fruitful working of ideas, rational and emotional techniques, and the application of language, delivery and other aspects of communication is ethics.

Ethics to the Greeks meant the "customs of a race." (The Latin equivalent was "moral philosophy," from *mores,* customs.) More especially the term meant "the systematic study of the ultimate problems of human conduct ($\ddot{\eta}\theta os$), character, and ($\ddot{\epsilon}\theta os$) custom. The moral quality of ($\ddot{\eta}\theta os$) distinguishes it from $\ddot{\epsilon}\theta os$, 'behavioral neutrality.'"[2]

Ethics thus is concerned not so much with behavior as it exists but as it ought to be. The attempt of those who study communication in terms of ethics is not so much a search for facts as for underlying values. The search is for answers to such questions as: What is the ideal individual and the "good" society? What is the ultimate aim and end of human conduct? What is the highest good? How can communication help to realize it? How can communication help to realize well-being, the goal of human life?[3]

Concepts of Ethics

Ethics is the study of individual and social good.[4] It is "the systematic study of the nature of value concepts, 'good,' 'bad,' 'ought,' 'right,' 'wrong,' etc.,

---

[1]Gerald Miller, *Speech Communication,* Bobbs-Merrill Company, Inc., New York, 1966, p. 8.
[2]Ernest Barker, *The Politics of Aristotle,* Clarenden Press, Oxford, 1946, p. 356; Cf. Thomas E. Corts, "The Derivation of Ethics," *Speech Monographs,* 35:201–202, June 1968.
[3]W. D. Ross, *Aristotle,* Meridian Books, New York, 1959, p. 186.
[4]Cf. R. N. Beck, *Perspectives in Philosophy,* Holt, Rinehart and Winston, New York, 1961, p. 3.

and of general principles which justify us in applying them to anything."[5]
Ethics assumes that the individual (and group) has some understanding of
differences in values and takes responsibility for making decisions concerning these important judgments. The ethical component of communication is the set of values upon which the speech or interaction is based.

Ethics and Relativity

Where and how may truth, wisdom, the *summum bonum* of this world,
be found? Early philosophers viewed the universe as absolute, with all
issues firmly answered and centered. These deductive philosophers theo-
rized confidently about this unified world and logically and religiously
interpreted their theories. They thought they had penetrated to the heart
of this universe and revealed it through their speculations.

The rise of science undermined this absolutism. The nineteenth- and
twentieth-century scientific advances under Einstein and his contemporaries
called for more tangible methods of determining knowledge and truth.
Today's philosophical universe strongly reflects pragmatism and instru-
mentalism for describing and interpreting the world. Pragmatists, such as
William James and his school, determined truth by its works. Truth was
tested by its consequences. The idea was true if it was useful. This meant
that knowledge constantly changed; there were no certainties, no ultimate
and concrete superstructure, no final definitions, no permanent "facts." It
appears now that the pendulum may be swinging back the other way.
Questions are being raised increasingly about whether we have depended
too much on scientific thought alone, whether we need to consider more
humanistic values and humanistic "truths."

Even if you do not reject all scientific modes of thought, as we hope you
will not, scientific ways of examining human conduct and its outcomes need
not make you a nihilist or aimless existentialist. Though all important
questions are complex and every issue leads to many related complexities,
we are still committed in our thinking to the framing of hypotheses, the
rejection or retention of assumptions, and the examination of outlooks only
partly clear—all in a spirit that is committed to the notion of a "better
society."

Ethics as Measured by Social Consequences

Ethics, as measured by its results in individual and social conduct, is a
problem in "social utility." Will communication or a series of communications produce social gains for those involved? If we assume that we can
measure such results, how "useful" are they? Winston Brembeck and William

---

[5] Alfred Cyril Ewing, *Encyclopaedia Britannica*, University of Chicago, Encyclopaedia
Britannica, Inc., Chicago, London, Toronto, 1929–44, vol. 8, p. 757.

Howell advocate the social context theory of ethics and applications of it to persuasion. They have to a considerable degree adopted the position of Vilfredo Pareto in his *Mind and Society:* "Ultimately survival potential of the group is involved." [6]

What are the determinants of group survival and progress? Social utility, we agree, is an abstract and academic term. By attempting to understand the interests and needs of the group, gauging the influence of our thinking and utterances on these common social conditions, and estimating as best we can the positive or negative outcomes of our communication, we can begin to understand Pareto's concept of ethics and the "survival potential."

Ethics and Standards

What are we measuring when we measure ethics by social consequences? If we assume that what we have analyzed works out according to our reasoning and desires, what confidence can be placed in the selection of consequences that we tentatively posit and expect? Though no universal agreement concerning what is right in a given case can be dogmatically pronounced, within reasonable limits we have the benefits of cumulative experiences that suggest standards for our choices. All of the world's cultures have provided a social context for desirable behavior within the framework of that culture. Experiences and reactions to environment and cohesion to communal life become the customs, laws, cultural inheritance, traditions, and practices of a tribe or a race. The best of these concepts and administrations make up the literature and other written and spoken records of a people.

The standards and concepts of Western civilization developed similarly. The cultural sentiments of Aristotle and other classicists have been mingled with those of the later thinkers. These expositions and adjurations are strongly reinforced by Judeo-Christian morality and its guides for conduct. These we have inherited and most of us still follow them, though sometimes in modified form. The ethical standards that confront us are thus flexible and change with each new generation and its experiences. But, that they have a large degree of stability is shown by their social utility.

Assuming that we have dependable principles that are guiding our discourses, how can we measure the immediate and wider results? First of all, we need to analyze the wider results in many situations. Although logical analysis is difficult, we should proceed, using what wisdom we can muster,

---

[6] Vilfredo Pareto, *The Mind and Society,* edited by Arthur Livingston, Harcourt, Brace and Company, New York, 1935, quoted in Winston L. Brembeck and William S. Howell, *Persuasion: A Means of Social Control,* Prentice-Hall, Englewood Cliffs, N.J., 1952, p. 445.

to apply these principles of value that give our speech communication its ultimate justification.

Although we cannot find an ethical yardstick satisfactory to all, the principles of social behavior and the analysis of specific appeals in relation to audiences will more and more yield patterns of genuine ethical progress. You who communicate will be "good men and women skilled in speaking and writing." Your position may continue to be that of Socrates: "When you strive for noble ends, it is also noble to endure whatever pain the effort may involve." [7] There is still hope for our society if most of us continue to strive in this way.

The Speaker, the Message, and Ethics of Communication

Judgment concerning ethical results is further confirmed or questioned by an analysis of the ethical role of the speaker-agent and of the content of his discourse. An examination of the moral qualities of the agent and of his ideas, supports, audience adaptation, and language in the message itself should strengthen or weaken any conclusions concerning the social outcomes of the discourse. [8]

The major debates and most important questions in the United States during the early 1970s involved great ethical issues as well as political, philosophical, economic, military, social, or educational questions. Specifically, some of the questions were: Should a program of birth control be adopted by the federal government? Should state legislatures liberalize their abortion laws? Should the federal government enact legislation to prohibit cigarette smoking in the United States? Should sex education be taught in all public schools? Should state governments outlaw DDT? Should negotiation and settlement replace strikes in major American industries? Should the federal government establish a policy of price and wage controls? Should the United States withdraw all its armed forces from Southeast Asia within two years? Should college and university students who engage in "campus violence" be immediately expelled? Should marijuana be legalized? Should the Post Office be turned into a government-owned corporation? Should the military draft in the United States be discontinued?

Each of these questions, regardless of its immediate arguments, involves basic issues concerning the welfare of society and individual rights. These important national controversies call for strong, philosophical, and ethical discussions which should increase the probability of wise and just action.

Making ethical choices would be a simple matter if one could simply

---

[7] Plato, *Phaedrus, Ion, Gorgias, and Symposium,* tr. Lane Cooper, Oxford Press, New York, 1938, p. 64; quoted in A. Craig Baird, *Rhetoric,* Ronald Press, New York, 1965, p. 115.

[8] See Chapter Seventeen, "Measures of Effectiveness," for discussion evaluating the speaker and his ethical responsibilities.

choose between right and wrong, good and evil. Unfortunately, one must generally choose among relative goods or relative evils. For example, one cannot simply choose between what is good and bad for the individual; one must often choose between what is good for the individual and what is good for the society. It is certainly "good" to advocate every individual's right to associate or not associate with whomever he pleases, but it is also "good" to advocate that no one be excluded from a country club because of his race or religion or sex. We assume you believe that if someone owns a house he ought to be permitted to sell it to whomever he pleases. However, we assume you also believe that no one should be prevented from buying a house because of his race, religion, sex, or other feature. On such issues you cannot have it both ways. You must make a decision about the greater good, and this is not always an easy thing to do.

The question of whether one can be *too* patriotic is an ethical issue which currently bedevils many people in our country. Not very many years ago "My country, right or wrong," was considered by most Americans to be a highly ethical position. Nowadays many are beginning to question this position and are beginning to insist that we must weigh the national good against the world good or even the human good. They believe that an extremely high degree of nationalism may be as detrimental to mankind—or more so—than an absence of nationalism or patriotism. It is not a simple issue, but it is an ethical issue which you probably will need to face in some of your communication.

Another difficult ethical choice that a communicator often must make is among means to a good end. We must often face the issue of whether good ends justify unethical means. If you are certain that what you want others to do is "right" and "for their own good," are you justified in withholding information which might cause them not to do it? Are you justified in falsifying evidence? We believe that you are not. We believe that in a democratic society, the means by which decisions are made may well be as important in the long run as the decisions themselves. Democracy, like communication, is a process—not a product—and it is important that that process be an ethical one. Since the processes of communication are essential parts of the democratic process, they too must be ethical.

An often neglected ethical issue in communication has to do not with what you might say, but rather with what you might not say. Too often, when there are important issues to be determined, when people are needed to take a stand, we remain silent rather than speak out. Too often, for example, we see a wrong in our society, we see someone discriminated against or someone who needs help, and we fail to speak out because of timidity or fear of becoming involved or even harmed. We believe that such timidity, such failures to fulfill our responsibilities as citizens and as human beings are as unethical as anything that we might do.

Projects and Problems

PROJECT 1.   Each member of the class will answer one of the following questions in a brief presentation to the group:

   a. What is "high moral character" and how important is it in persuasion?

   b. May a communicator be neutral concerning ethical commitments and expression?

   c. What is the nature of personality and its relation to the ethics of the speaker?

   d. What is the "social content" theory of the ethics of oral communication?

   e. What is the problem and relationship of politics and ethics in oral communication?

   f. How can sincerity, honesty, and similar ethical traits be detected or measured?

PROJECT 2.   The class and instructor will arrange for a series of dialogues between members, based upon one of the issues listed under project 1 above, or on some similar problems related to ethics in oral communication.

References

Allport, G. W., *Personality*. New York: Holt, 1937.

Binkley, Luther J., *Contemporary Ethical Theories*. New York: Philosophical Library, 1961.

Brembeck, Winston, and W. S. Howell, *Persuasion*. Englewood Cliffs, N.J.: Prentice-Hall, Inc., 1952. Chapter 24.

Dewey, John, *Outlines of a Critical Theory of Ethics*. New York: Hillory House, 1957.

Ehninger, Douglas, "Decision by Debate: A Re-examination," *Quarterly Journal of Speech,* 45:282–287, 1959.

Eubank, Ralph, and Virgil L. Baker, "Toward an Axiology of Rhetoric," *Quarterly Journal of Speech,* 48:157–168, 1962.

Haiman, F. S., "An Experimental Study of the Effects of Ethos in Public Speaking," *Speech Monographs,* 16:190–202, 1949.

Haiman, F. S., "A Re-examination of the Ethics of Persuasion," *Central States Speech Journal,* 3:4–9, 1952.

Johannesen, Richard L. (ed.), *Ethics and Persuasion: Selected Readings*. New York: Random House, 1967.

Minnick, Wayne, *The Art of Persuasion*. Boston: Houghton Mifflin, 1957. Chapter 12.

Murphy, Richard, "Preface to an Ethic of Rhetoric," in D. C. Bryant (ed.), *The Rhetorical Idiom*. Ithaca, N.Y.: Cornell University Press, 1958.

Nilsen, Thomas, *Ethics of Speech Communication*. Indianapolis: Bobbs-Merrill Co., 1966. Chapters 1 to 3.

Oliver, Robert T., The *Psychology of Persuasive Speech,* 2nd ed. New York: David McKay, 1957. Chapters II, III, XVI.

Rivers, William L., and Wilbur Schramm, *Responsibility in Mass Communication.* New York: Harper and Row, 1969.

Ross, D., *Aristotle on Ethics.* New York: Meridian Books, 1959. Pp. 183–229.

Sattler, W. M., "Conceptions of Ethos in Ancient Rhetoric," *Speech Monographs,* 14:55–56, 1947.

Thonssen, Lester, A. Craig Baird, and W. Waldo Braden, *Speech Criticism,* 2nd ed. New York: Ronald Press, 1970. Chapter 14.

Weaver, Richard N., *The Ethics of Rhetoric.* Chicago: Henry Regnery Co., 1953.

Speech Types

discussional communication

As you probably know, college students spontaneously talk about or discuss the problems, trivial or major, that touch their experiences and immediate interests. Little resembling the silent generation of collegians twenty years ago, today's students react with vigor to such issues as college grading systems (pass-fail versus letter grades), student ratings of teachers and the "firing" of incompetent ones, the justification of student demonstrations, the virtues and vices of the reigning political party in Washington, space travel, the American commitment to the defense of Western Europe, international controls of atomic power, the United Nations, the military draft, and the best route to peace. In classrooms, corridors, student unions, and wherever one finds the ebb and flow of undergraduates and graduates, the talk goes on.

Discussion also plays an important role in business and industry. In the active management of a corporation, for example, executive sessions and conferences are held for the exchange of information and policy determination. The problems of competition, production, distribution, sales, advertising, public relations, and personnel are worked out cooperatively between various administrative units, governed somewhat by guidelines furnished by the board of directors. At each corporate level discussion is used for planning and for dealing with a ceaseless series of operational problems. Discussions are also important at sales promotion meetings, national and regional conferences, and conventions of trade associations with industry-wide problems.

America, perhaps more than any other nation, is organization-minded. Conferences of organizations—educational, industrial, legal, scientific, religious, social, literary—are innumerable. Youth congresses, conferences of college administrators or academic leaders, governors, mayors, church unions, promoters of mental health and art education, all these are examples.

Participants in community chest and other fund-raising drives meet to discuss the direction and methods of their campaigns. "Great Books" groups, other adult study clubs, community forums, interracial councils, labor union conferences, the League of Women Voters, the Young Republican and the Young Democratic Clubs constantly utilize discussion or quasi-discussion in their deliberations.

In education, both at elementary and higher levels, discussion is an **265** important part of the learning processes. Elementary school children give and take in their "sharing" sessions as well as in much of their other classroom work. More and more sophistication of the oral "sharing" process is being exhibited as older educational groups deal with economic, social, literary, and other subjects—up and into the graduate seminars. These discussions generally follow some form of the method of reflective inter-course.

Radio and television, too, have been agencies for establishing and ex-tending the popularity of panels, dialogues, round tables, and audience participation programs. "Face the Nation," "Directions," "Meet the Press," "Issues and Answers," "The Advocate," and other programs have stimulated listening millions to carry out their own off-the-air discussions.

Discussion is important mainly because, along with debate, it is the foundation of the democratic process. Our talking with each other is an essential tool of our democracy, the agent by which we analyze problems and frame public policies. As Macaulay put it, "Men are never so likely to settle a question rightly as when they discuss it freely." [1] The secret ballot by which our public officials are elected is based on free speech, free press, free assembly, and open discussion. According to John Stuart Mill, "Liberty, as a principle, has no application to any state of things anterior to the time when mankind have become capable of being improved by free and equal discussion." [2]

Even when the United States entered the Second World War, President Franklin D. Roosevelt stated, "I am convinced that it is more important than ever that the people be encouraged freely to assemble to discuss their common problems. Indeed as I have said before, this is one of the essential freedoms that we are determined to defend. I have in mind more particularly enlisting the efforts of the schools and colleges in sponsoring public discus-sion and study groups." [3]

What Is Discussion?

Discussion is not mere talking. Conversation serves a useful purpose in promoting good fellowship and exchange of ideas and attitudes, but it does not systematically focus on specific ideas or necessarily attempt to resolve differences.

Discussion, moreover, is not debate. The debater or arguer, even before he faces his audience, has already analyzed the subject, framed his argu-

---

[1] Thomas Babington Macaulay, *Southey Colloquies in Literary Essays: Edinburgh Review,* Oxford University Press, London, 1933, p. 32.
[2] John Stuart Mill, *On Liberty,* Ticknor and Fields, Boston, 1863, p. 8.
[3] *National Extempore-Discussion Contest on Inter-American Affairs,* Bulletin, Wash-ington, D.C., 1942, quoted in A. Craig Baird, *Argumentation, Discussion, and Debate,* McGraw-Hill Book Company, New York, 1950, p. 5.

ments, and presumably made up his mind. He sets out to influence others to accept his propositions.

Discussion, furthermore, is not persuasion—in the usual sense of that term. The highly skilled persuader, especially one who manipulates modern advertising media, bypasses the arguments or the bases for the positions of an audience and attempts to substitute other "standards of reference," that is, other drives or motives. Discussion, on the other hand, is an attempt to bring out all the arguments and all the possible bases for each position so that the best possible decision can be arrived at. *Discussion directly faces problems and attempts to resolve them through a mutual and rational exchange of information and ideas.*

Some audience members might attempt to escape the controversy by flight from the crowd. But the day of individual or collective isolation—such as existed before the Second World War, for example—is no longer possible. Our individual fortunes are cast, clearly, with the group, just as our national fortunes are cast with the world.

Another way of avoiding discussion is silent acquiescence to group decisions. The philosophy of acquiescence leads to one of two equally unacceptable positions: either we permit ourselves to be bandied about by those of dominant wills, or we put our faith in the ultimate survival of truth regardless of our speech or our silence. The assumption that events will shape a proper course will lead only to our frustration; if we linger while others take the helm, the day star for us may never come.

Still another evasive method is yielding to authority. If the authority decides fairly and constructively, all may be well. But reliance upon authority, as history has repeatedly provided, too often leads to disaster. Without free advocacy, untrammeled deliberation, and participation by many in the decision-making process, the result is very likely to be disastrous to the people involved. The Czechoslovakian protest against Soviet military control in 1968 well illustrates how decisions acceptable to a nation need to be made by the people themselves rather than by outside dictation imposed by military force. In most cases where discussion fails, it is due not to the guns of an authoritarian regime, but to our own failure to make the effort to participate.

Discussion, then, in contrast to debate, conversation, confrontation, silent acquiescence, withdrawal, compromise, or authoritarian submission, has the following distinctive characteristics: (1) its purpose is to analyze and resolve a problem; (2) its method is primarily that of group interaction; (3) it evokes reflective thinking rather than emotionally controlled reactions; (4) it is deliberative rather than advocative; and (5) it is usually oral communication.

■   1. *Discussion aims to analyze and resolve a problem.* This problem may be one of fact or of policy. The concern may be with any perplexing situation—whether immediate need for better information or for a long-range pattern of action. Some years ago scientists and others were asking for more information on the problem of whether flight to the moon was possible. This question covered a wide range of scientific materials, to be grappled with by experts in meteorological, astrophysical, geological, chemical, and other areas of knowledge, and was answered only after much discussion and experimentation by scientists. The conclusion of the scientists was confirmed by the astronauts who landed on the moon in July 1969. This question was then succeeded by other questions of knowledge concerning the establishment of manned bases on the moon and flights toward Mars and more distant planets.

Other questions of fact lead to endless discussion, often complicated by the semantic confusions of meanings. "What is automation?" "What is Africo-Americanism?" These kinds of questions have called forth a wide variety of definitions, and in some gatherings the disputes have led to little or no added knowledge.

Discussants, not content with added information but bent on some action step, have asked, "Shall we endorse a program for automation in American industry?" "Shall our university erect another building to alleviate our parking congestion?" "Shall our university add courses in Afro-American history?" "Shall a much larger number of Black students be admitted to the undergraduate colleges of our university?"

Each question obviously requires definitional-expositional answers prior to the attempt to get group consensus on the action to take or the steps to be used in implementing that action.

More specifically a question of policy requires a procedure that will help the group to determine and define the difficulty or problematic situation; it requires analysis of the proposed methods of dealing with it, the weighing of each proposal judicially, concentration on the course that the group prefers, and determination of a specific course of action which reflects the group's conclusions.

Whether the aim of a group is to add knowledge or proceed further to action, that aim is practical.

■ 2. *Discussion is a group activity.* Discussion requires the association of several minds in thinking and acting. The assumption here is that group judgments are generally superior to those of one individual, because these judgments are evaluated and refined by the composite judgments of those involved. The personality of each individual is thus emphasized rather than submerged, as individual judgments are inspected and diagnosed objectively. This assumption about group judgments has been verified by experimental studies that suggest that groups of individuals discussing tend to accomplish more in creative thinking than individuals isolated in their creative experience.[4] The outcome of a discussion is thus the result of

[4] See Bernard Bass, "Group Effectiveness," in Robert S. Cathcart and Larry A. Samovar (eds.), *Small Group Communication: A Reader,* Wm. C. Brown, Dubuque, Iowa, 1970, pp. 7–18.

redundant behavior and performance of the participating individuals. What these associates accomplish as a unit rather than what one brilliant individual contributes should be the measure of the success (we refer here chiefly to problems of policy).

We believe that the probability of wise decisions by a group is increased if there is maximum interaction within the group. As a member of a group, therefore, you should participate actively and react to each of the other members, just as each of them should react to everyone. If you were to chart the communicative exchanges of a group which is working well, you would find that you had drawn lines between all members of the group, rather than merely between each member and the chairman.

In other words, if we had three round tables with six discussants in each and were to find that our chart of the interactions looked like those on this page, we would predict that the best decisions were made by the group on the right. The participants on the left largely ignore the chairman and the other discussants. Each goes his own way; genuine discussion is absent.

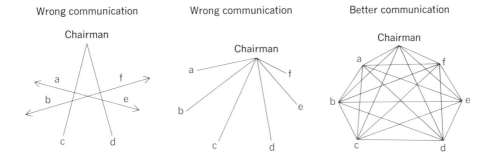

What is happening in the middle is more nearly discussion—but centers on the chairman and largely ignores the other contributors. On the right better communication is taking place in that each member integrates fully with the utterances of each other member. The chairman is not ignored, but the group is not too dependent upon him.

The discussion climate must be one of freedom for each participant. Not only must there be group interaction, but also a common interdependence and respect for the interests of each member. Group decision making should not be a case of "majority rule" but rather of consensus. Although the group is made of individuals, each with his own needs and attitudes, societal objectives must inhere in the judgments. The decisiveness of a few individuals must not dominate the scene and govern the outcome. Implied in satisfactory group orientation is mutual respect, understanding of the ideas and attitudes of the other members, commitment to a principle of equilibrium between individual and group interests, and the resulting consensus.

■   3.   *Fruitful discussion evokes reflective thinking in contrast to undirected emotional responses.* The atmosphere of a good discussion encourages intellectual activity; it rules out disorganized and aimless talk. The purposeful reflective thinker distinguishes assumptions from facts, studies contexts and backgrounds, notes causes and effects, tests authorities and testimony, generalizes in view of the facts, and checks his own tendency and that of others to mistake assertions for proof and to substitute biases and prejudices for well-reasoned conclusions. Reflective thinking is characterized by a disciplined attitude and an orderly testing of evidence and argument.

■ 4. *Fruitful discussion inquires rather than advocates.* In a mood of inquiry, problems are explored for the purpose of gaining information and deciding upon subsequent action. The advocate (in argument, debate, persuasion) begins with a proposition and persuades groups to his point of view. Discussion as deliberation is thus entirely different in spirit and method from argument. The advocate is typically a debater or persuader. The discussant, somewhat like the scientist, is typically an inquirer. Note below how discussion temporarily ends as advocacy takes over.

We are not here condemning debate; we only want to point out that its purpose and method are different from those of discussion. Once the group arrives at a point where discussion is no longer fruitful, debate may take over in the attempt to secure parliamentary action. Once the debating conclusions are arrived at, discussion may again ensue. Below are listed the major steps in a problem-solving discussion. Discussion may end during any one of these and debate ensue. The steps which are most likely to be points of disagreement, conflict, and so of debate are indicated by asterisks.

1. Explanation of terms*
2. Goals in analyzing and solving the problem*
3. Analysis of the "felt difficulty" or problem—including description of the disturbing phenomena, their causes and results*
4. Statement of hypotheses or probable solutions to be listed *
5. Weighing of solution A
6. Weighing of solution B
7. Weighing of solution C
8. Validation of the preferred solution (A or B or C)
9. Determination of a program to implement the solution preferred

■ 5. *Discussion is an oral form of communication.* Discussion is group experience in socialization of thinking accomplished by oral communication. Although oral communication is cheaper and more expedient than written communication, it is often less carefully thought out. Its advantages are nevertheless obvious for occasions where decisions must be made quickly. Even more important is the opportunity it gives the participants to test ideas, get immediate feedback, adjust, try revised ideas, etc., until one's ideas are honed to a sharp and effective point—or lead to a group decision.

Values and Problems of Discussional Procedures

Discussion and Reflective Thinking

Discussion primarily aims at orderly thinking. Such ordered analysis and solution are the method of reflective thinking suggested by John Dewey; it is "thought in process."[5]

Harry Sharp, Jr., and Joyce Milliken in a study at Purdue University concluded that the reflective thinking ability of discussion group members and the quality of their group's solution to a complex social problem are positively related."[6]

Discussion and Group Leadership

John Brilhart investigated three techniques for communicating a problem-solving pattern to members of a discussion group and concluded that this study showed "only limited support for the recommendation, common in discussion textbooks, that a designated leader should announce the discussion pattern in advance."[7]

William Utterback and Wallace C. Fotheringham in their "Experimental Studies of Motivated Group Discussion" concluded "that better judgment was displayed without a designated moderator than in fully moderated discussion."[8]

Discussion and Personality

John Shepherd, Thomas Scheidel, and Laura Crowell investigated the possible relationships of personality and discussion behavior. Their conclusion was: "The analysis . . . revealed no such relationship of personal characteristic with the other two behavioral dimensions, 'Group Goal Facilitation' and 'Group Sociability.' "[9]

In another study, Crowell and Scheidel examined the relation of member satisfaction with process and product to (1) peer-rating discussion behaviors and (2) personality value structures. They concluded that "except for one positive result, all significant correlations were negative."[10]

According to Gordon Wiseman and Larry Barker, research in discussion has provided "at least five general conclusions that appear to be reliable":

---

[5] John Dewey, *How We Think*, D. C. Heath & Company, Boston, 1910, p. 71.
[6] Harry Sharp, Jr., and Joyce Milliken, "Reflective Thinking Ability and the Product of Problem Solving Discussion," *Speech Monographs*, 31:124–127, 1964.
[7] John Brilhart, "An Experimental Comparison of Three Techniques for Communicating a Problem-solving Pattern to Members of a Discussion Group," *Speech Monographs*, 31:168–177, 1968.
[8] *Speech Monographs*, 25:268–277, 1958.
[9] "Personality and Group Behavior," *Speech Monographs*, 25:220–227, 1958.
[10] "A Study of Discussant Satisfaction in Group Problem-Solving," *Speech Monographs*, 30:56–58, 1963.

1. Attitudes toward social problems do change because of discussion.
2. People tend to become close on an impersonal level because of discussion.
3. As a result of discussion people tend to develop more sound and acceptable ideas.
4. The greatest influence in discussion is exerted by the person with the greatest competency and ability.
5. The make-up of the group is very important in its success. One member can enhance a group far beyond his numerical weight. The more objective the individual members of the group are, the better the group will be.[11]

Discussion and the Scientific Method

The successful discussant, as we have stated above, adopts the mood and method of experimentation. The scientist and the discusser both (1) state and define a problem, (2) start with facts, (3) stress evidence and logic, (4) minimize emotionality, (5) preserve objectivity, and (6) state conclusions limited by the preceding analysis and evidence.

The discussant who applies such systematic methods should increase his ability to analyze himself, his subject, and his audience; he should develop open-mindedness and should be better trained for stating verifiable conclusions.

Gerald Phillips advocates discussion program planning to include a "quasi-mathematical" procedure called PERT (Program Evaluation and Review Techniques). PERT provides the problem-solving group with a method of developing a workable operations plan. This method presumably adds to the standard procedure of checking a program decision before the final action step is completed.

Discussion and Psychological Adjustment

Discussion, because it represents socialized thinking and speaking, fosters teamwork and group solidarity. The egocentric talker soon abandons his dominant tendencies, or he retires to more congenial regions. When he remains, he learns more about his own personality and finds new sources of satisfaction. As he discusses, he tends to share more in the mental explorations of the group and in their ultimate satisfactions. He learns to be more sensitive to other people and their responses to him. In mental hospitals and in other psychiatric and psychological practices, discussion has been widely used for the treatment of a variety of mental or personality disorders. Certain kinds of interactions of the individual with others who

---

[11]Gordon Wiseman and Larry Barker, *Speech—Interpersonal Communication,* Chandler Publishing Company, San Francisco, 1967, p. 193.

have similar problems have been found to have important therapeutic value. Those with problems allegedly feel better when they share their attitudes and conditions with fellow sufferers. Alcoholism, drug addiction, speech disorders, and an endless list of other deviations from normal behavior have been treated by small-group therapy.

Therapy discussion, of course, differs from the traditional type: "It is the reinforcement of identity through interaction that includes personal change, whereas in other types, interaction influences group consensus. The identity of the member may be so threatened that he needs to discover himself." [12]

Academic Study of Current Problems

Because discussional problems usually grow out of a current situation, you will find yourself grappling with the important controversial issues of your day. As this paragraph is written the issues of the early 1970s are uppermost—balancing the national budget, controlling inflation, federal and local taxation problems, the draft for overseas duty, policies on South Vietnam, Korea, Middle East, abortion, arms control, space flights, drugs, the revolution on college campuses, the rise of black power. Thus, materials in contemporary history, sociology, politics, religion, and related fields provide subject matter for discussion and for your development in general education.

Discussion in the Service of Democracy

Discussion, because it provides a climate for self-realization through self-directed mental activity and because it motivates its participants to grow in social consciousness, becomes an ally of democracy. The functioning of our representative republican government depends on popular participation and many kinds of group decisions. The secret ballot, universal suffrage, frequent elections, the large number of legislative and administrative offices—national, state, and local—to be filled, the growing opportunities for quick and full communication, the many provisions for general and integrated education, Constitutional safeguards to ensure freedom of assembly, speech, and writing, the protection of minorities, and legal dissent— all these factors combine to make possible effective talk and discussion and, hence, make our American democracy work. The assumption underlying our form of government is that we as citizens are sufficiently well informed and intelligent to work out our political program and to apply sound judgment to the solution of our affairs.

The programs of democracy and discussion are the same. You who

---

[12] Gerald Phillips, *Communication and the Small Group,* Bobbs-Merrill, Indianapolis, 1966, p. 57.

investigate and apply the techniques of discussion are engaged in the furtherance of democracy. Probably the chief contribution of discussion is its enforcement of this technique characteristic of the American character. If in a democratic country the deliberative processes of discussion, debate, and the orderly resolution of common issues are rejected, there is little hope for a later restitution of free thought, free speech, and social progress. Those who would substitute terror and intimidation and violence for free and open discussion must be made aware of the long-range consequences of these methods of resolving conflicts. No humane and democratic society can long exist if its methods of resolving problems are not humane and democratic. Important among these methods are those proposed in this chapter—honest and intelligent deliberation, discussion, and debate.

Typical Forms of Discussion

As we suggested above, discussions occur everywhere—in schools, colleges, churches, business meetings, community clubs, and over the air—and the term is popularly used to refer to casual conversation as well as to formal group exchanges. In formulating our definition of discussion, however, we have made a distinction between casual talking and discussion. Now we shall describe seven specific types of discussion with which you should be familiar and in which you will often engage.

■ 1. *Round-table or informal discussion.* A discussion in which perhaps five to ten people participate without a contributing audience and in an atmosphere of casualness can be a round table. Although there may be a chairman, he does not function formally. The participants should understand discussion techniques and the purpose of the specific discussion.

Round tables include study groups, the purposes of which are varied: to gain a better understanding of "great books"; classes in schools or colleges; professional groups convening systematically and regularly for "workshops," with the aim of improving their methods of getting practical results; business and other briefing sessions not unduly dominated by a chairman.

■ 2. *Committee discussion.* Committee discussions usually have a specific purpose, such as to prepare a report to a larger organization. The discussion is conducted like a round table, but for the purposes of its end product, the chairman exercises more control. He sees that the agenda is closely followed, that a secretary records the proceedings, and that the report itself is completed and accepted by the members of the committee. At times he has the members of the group vote in order to determine group wishes.

■ 3. *Panel discussion.* A panel is made up of a chairman and a small group who carry on a discussion before an audience. Unless the panel is being broadcast, the members of the audience should be seated close enough to the panel for them to hear well. After the panel has completed its main discussion, the audience should participate by asking questions and making

Howard Sochurek.

Ralph Crane, Life Magazine © Time Inc.

The student rebellion has given rise to extraordinary new modes of dialogue. Teach-ins and march-ins (the demonstration at right protests the policies of the Pacific Gas and Electric Company) are only two contemporary settings in which ideas can be freely exchanged.

Students of all persuasions find more and more frequent occasion to exercise as much eloquence as they can command.

Sam Falk, New York Times.

Wayne Miller, Magnum.

comments. At least half of the total time usually should be given to remarks and questions from the floor, but each of these contributions and its reply by a member of the panel should be brief. At the end, the chairman summarizes. The success of the occasion will depend partly on the extent to which the audience is stimulated to participate in group thinking.

■   4. *Dialogue.* In a dialogue, two communicators have a discussion. Informal conversation prevails, but the format is well planned in advance. Again the audience contributes, as in a panel discussion.

■   5. *Symposium.* A symposium consists of three or four speakers, each of whom is given at least five minutes in which to deliver a prepared speech on a specific phase of a problem. Each speaker must adjust his prepared remarks to the preceding contributions. The purpose of the speakers is chiefly to contribute information and to analyze the issues. After this relatively prepared part of the program is concluded, the chairman and discussion leader will engineer the meeting so that the audience, as in the panel situation, dominate the thinking and discussion.

■   6. *Public forum.* The panel and the symposium are conducted with small audiences of perhaps 100 or 200. The public forum may have an audience of as many as 2,000 or 3,000. It is difficult to maintain a public discussion with this number of people. The speaker must be an energetic and experienced public speaker who lectures for perhaps thirty minutes, creates an atmosphere of open inquiry, and then invites analysis by the audience (although the chairman may offer the actual invitation) of the issues on which he has lectured. The speaker must create an atmosphere of discussion; if he is a rabid protagonist for a cause or if he propagandizes, the discussion will probably not be very fruitful.

A program consisting of a lecture forum, panel, and audience participation period was held at the University of Iowa in Iowa City on December 8, 1968. The occasion was observance of the twentieth anniversary of the Declaration of Human Rights by the General Assembly of the United Nations. Former Ambassador Arthur Goldberg, chief representative of the United States at the United Nations, was the lecture speaker before an overflow crowd of some 2,500 in the Iowa Union.

After his one-hour formal and extempore lecture, the speaker responded to a series of questions posed by a select faculty panel; then he replied to many questions or brief comments from the audience. Mr. Goldberg impressed the hearers by his fairness, tact, and sincerity, as well as high intelligence concerning the record and problems of the United Nations. He demonstrated all of these qualities as he listened carefully and analyzed the questions from the audience, some of them scathing denunciations of the United Nations and of his personal role there. The performance throughout was one of efficient discussion.

■   7. *Radio and television discussion.* Discussions over the air are not distinct in form or content from the types of discussion we have described;

they may take the form of the round table, symposium, panel, or interview. Even the forum can be televised to show the "live" audience in action. However, broadcasting mechanisms and techniques impose limitations and require adaptations that modify the spirit of the discussion. Time limitations, the selection of audience participants in some cases, and preliminary rehearsals if they are held tend to remove the element of spontaneity from the discussion.

Selecting and Wording the Discussion Question

Subjects for discussion should be of interest and concern to all the discussants. Since the object of discussion is to reach a group decision or to further group thinking, the subject should concern a problem about which the participants must eventually reach a decision. Remember the following principles in selecting subjects:

■   1.   *Select an important question.* For a learning group the educational problem is that of choosing a question that will both interest and educate. Most of us do not want to waste hours of talk on a trivial topic. Discussions on dormitory hours or the merits of a "dry" night club are hardly worth the time and energy involved. College and university students will profit more by grappling with the major issues of war, peace, civil rights, and pollution.

■   2.   *Select a controversial question.* Be sure that there are at least two defensible points of view connected with the problem. Subjects on which no real difference of opinion exists are expository and hardly make for interesting or fruitful discussions. Avoid also those topics about which debaters and citizens in general long ago made up their minds unanimously.

■   3.   *Select a question either of fact or of policy.* If we argue a question of an event or situation, we aim to establish in our minds the truth or falsity of the alleged fact. Otherwise, our inquiry may be an attempt to develop a program for solving a given problem. In the first case, our interrogation is obviously one of fact; in the second, one of policy. Questions of fact are of two types: those susceptible of proof through objective evidence and those based largely on subjective judgment. "To what extent do various halucinatory drugs have permanent physiological and psychological effects on those who use them regularly?" is a problem settled by gathering and interpreting reliable data. When the investigators penetrate into the political-social-philosophical realm, however, the answers often rest upon value judgments. The significance of alleged evidence and inference will depend upon each discussant's evaluation of justice and injustice, expediency and inexpediency, or right and wrong.

Questions of fact are concerned with the meaning of terms ("What is black power?"), comparisons or relationships ("Is congressional government better adapted to a democratic Anglo-Saxon nation than the parliamentary type?"), or cause and effect ("Is the threat of Chinese nuclear power producing stepped-up antiballistic defense programs in the United States?").

Questions of policy are of two types: those focusing on general policy-forming principles ("Is the proposal based on sound principles?" "Is the proposal theoretically advisable?"), and those which by general agreement deal with the specific action ("Shall the United Nations be presided over by a three-member administrative committee?" "Should we abandon all personal property taxes?").

■ 4. *Select a question adapted to the learning level and interests of the group.* Creative writers usually consider problems of composition; committees of the General Assembly of the United Nations consider problems assigned to them for analysis and recommendation; college discussants often deal with a problem determined for them by an intercollegiate forensic association. A unit of the armed forces, a state legislature, or a high school forensic group—all select problems closely related to their interests.

■ 5. *The question should be capable of solution.* "Should the Student Senate allocate $2,000 to the debate team?" cannot specifically be settled on the basis of concrete evidence, but a decision can be arrived at. Because of our general curiosity and our long-range view of political and other problems, we are justified at times in evaluating problems that are less tangible— those more clearly in the realm of value judgment. "Should the grading system at my college be modified?" may well be changed to the more specific, "Should the grading system at my college be limited to 'pass' and 'fail' grades?" The question "What should be the role of the United States in South America?" might well be limited to "Should the United States abandon its control over the Panama Canal Zone?"

■ 6. *Select a problem that the group itself can help solve.* Subjects that result in proposed solutions or in action have a great deal of appeal for discussants. If the students believe that college mathematics should be an elective and if the issue confronts the faculty, then a committee of the student council, after deliberation, might frame its opinions as a proposal and consult the faculty curriculum committee. Subjects that result only in extended analysis and talk seem to be less important to most discussants and to most audiences.

■ 7. *Limit the question.* Many discussions are futile because the issue is too broad or is vaguely stated. The factor of time may limit the choice of a problem. Narrower subjects require more specific information, but they produce better results in discussion.

■ 8. *Always state the issue as an impartial question.* The question form is symbolic of the discussion process and sharpens the direction of the thinking.

■ 9. *Phrase the issue clearly.* Vague or ambiguous terms are likely to occur in the phrasing of issues unless an effort at clarity is constantly exercised. Note the vagueness or ambiguity of the italicized words that follow:

"Should all *general education courses* in American colleges be abandoned?" "Should the Iowa legislature pass a law requiring the Board of Regents of the public universities to *discipline* any student or employee who engages in a *campus disturbance?*" "How can the *present system of education* in the United States be improved?" Is the Democratic party *distinctly social-istic* in its political policies?" "Do the Republicans constitute a *rank con-servative party?*" Sometimes the terms even beg the question: "Can we honestly say that smoking cigarettes is harmful to the lungs?" Even carefully worded questions sometimes present a problem in word meaning. Many discussions have failed because the terms, seemingly sensible, led to widely different interpretations.

Outlining the Discussion

The following skeleton outline for a discussion illustrates how a pattern of organization can be applied to a problem of policy.

The question is: . . . .

I.   What explanations are needed?
    A.   What is meant by . . . ?
    B.   What is meant by . . . ?
    C.   What is meant by . . . ?

II. Does this question constitute a major economic, social, or political problem that calls for solution?
    A.   What are the chief facts or events that created the problem?
    B.   What are the chief causes of these disturbing facts or events?
        1.   What are the alleged economic causes?
        2.   What are the alleged political causes?
        3.   What are the alleged social causes?
    C.   What are the alleged economic, political, social results of the problem?

III. What are the proposed solutions?
    A.   What is solution A?
    B.   What is solution B?
    C.   What is solution C?

IV. Are the suggested solutions for dealing with this problem satisfactory?
    A.   What are the alleged advantages and disadvantages of solu-tion A?
        1.   What are the alleged advantages?
        2.   What are the alleged disadvantages?
    B.   What are the alleged advantages and disadvantages of solu-tion B?
        1.   What are the alleged advantages?
        2.   What are the alleged disadvantages?

  C. What are the alleged advantages and disadvantages of solution C?
    1. What are the alleged advantages?
    2. What are the alleged disadvantages?

 V. In view of the discussion above, what solution is on the whole preferable?
  A. What are the advantages of this solution that indicate its superiority over others?
  B. Does the operation of this preferred solution justify its selection on grounds of practicability?

 VI. What program for putting the proposed solution into operation should be set up?

  An individual outline is no doubt of much value to the participant, even though he should modify it much in the discussion itself. A guide for the panel, drawn up in advance, is also of advantage if those involved are free to modify, ignore, or otherwise depart from rigid methods which inhibit group thinking and decision making.

The Chairman of the Discussion Group

Discussion develops from the participation on an equal footing of the individuals who make up the group. Leadership is to be at a minimum. There are no official titles of distinction, no priority in seating arrangements, no set order of speaking, no timing of speeches. Because discussion often requires administration, many groups choose or appoint a leader. Sometimes, a leader or leaders emerge during the course of the discussion.

  The function of the chairman-leader is to guarantee genuine discussion and to prevent any discussant from impeding the free flow of ideas. Actually, every discussant should be qualified to act as moderator. What special qualifications should a moderator have? He should (1) know the subject to be discussed, (2) be familiar with general discussion techniques and the special techniques required for this meeting, (3) know the audience if there is one and understand how small and large audiences behave, (4) have the personal qualities which induce trust and respect, (5) be able to extemporize freely, (6) know the discussants and see that a group outline is in their hands before the meeting, (7) create a favorable climate for the discussion, (8) properly introduce the subject, (9) help develop the discussion pattern, (10) use frequent summaries and transitions, and (11) draw out nontalkers and control overly aggressive discussants. In many "leaderless" groups, we find various individuals carrying out the different functions.

Participation in Discussion

What distinction may we make between the leader and the other discussants? In round tables, the difference is negligible; all are leaders. However, if an audience is created apart from the nucleus of speakers and is definitely separated in seating arrangement from the speakers, then the duties and importance of the leader-chairman become apparent. He is to direct a panel, or introduce a symposium, or control a large audience.

- 1. *Share in the selection and tentative wording of the subject.* As a panel member, committee member, or forum speaker, you will rightly share in deciding what is to be talked about. Use your influence to limit the subject and to reword the issue when necessary.

- 2. *Prepare thoroughly.* Patronize the library; collect and digest several books and many articles on your topic. Take diligent notes that may be read by others, for no substitute yet has been found for the orderly recording on paper of the gist of your systematic reading.

- 3. *Prepare an individual outline and, if your group so proposes, a group outline.* At an early point in your study, crystallize your findings and thinking in the form of an individual outline that conforms to the structure and details illustrated in this chapter. This skeleton pattern should be supplemented by a group outline, the product of the panel rather than of a single spokesman.

- 4. *In the discussion itself, cultivate open-mindedness, tolerance, group sensitivity, and cooperation.* Only in an atmosphere of open-mindedness, free from prejudice and dogmatism, will discussion be profitable. Analyze your own attitude as you enter into a situation and abstain unless you have adopted a mood favorable to genuine discussion.

- 5. *Contribute relevant evidence.* Insist on mustering a sufficient number of pertinent facts to illustrate the point fully and to justify the individual and group generalizations. Check your facts constantly with those of your colleagues. Cite sources adequately but without boring details. Don't flounder among your notes.

- 6. *At every stage reflect principles and methods of sound argument.* Explain why facts and situations are so. Develop your ideas by generalization, analogy, authority, deductive proposition. Question arguments and ideas that seem to you fallacious, but do so with some calmness and tact and with counterevidence. Help to expose propaganda. As the discussion evolves, modify your original stand if you have honestly changed.

- 7. *Contribute to the organization of the discussional thinking.* Like the leader, you will become a sponsor of the logical pattern outlined in this chapter. You, too, will insist upon definitions, statements of goals, tracing causes and effects, and testing panaceas and specific programs—exposing their weaknesses and validating their foundations. You will encourage and help other participants to make their optimum contribution to the discussion. Your summaries, introductory statements, and citation of facts will be an index of your cooperativeness.

■   8. *Adjust your oral style to that of the group.* You may know other members of the group well enough to use first names. How much you incorporate broken sentences, personal pronouns, and interruptions will depend on the occasion. You should avoid poor grammar and mangled syntax, and your language should be free of bromidic triteness or irritating positiveness.

■   9. *Your delivery should be appropriate to the occasion.* Round-table contributors often assume that their discourse is strictly private and that it may be excused from vocal excellence. On the contrary, you should have good voice quality, sufficient loudness, a lively sense of communication, and clear articulation and enunciation; these are the major determinants of desirable delivery. As you move from a private round table to a more public situation—panel, symposium, or larger forum—the demands will be greater. But you will continue to exercise the basic qualities of proper communication before this larger audience.

■   10. *Be a good listener.* Just as fluent speaking is required, so is genuine listening. Listening does not mean silence; it means active cooperation. You are engaged in a dialogue—rather a succession of dialogues—as each member of the group speaks and speaks again. Though you are inaudible, you are constantly "feeding back." You should be able to summarize the discussion at any moment.

■   11. *Ask sensible questions.* Intelligent listening is accompanied by intelligent questioning. Questioning takes place both in the constant give-and-take of a closed discussion session and in the "questions from the floor" by a panel or forum audience. Your interrogations in any case should be short and simply framed. You may call for further information, repetition of a statement, inference from certain data, or additional citation by expert testimony; you may invite a speaker to summarize the state of the controversy; or you may ask specifically, "What should be done about this problem?"

Evaluation of Discussion Performance

How is discussion to be evaluated? What tests do you apply to yourself? How do you judge your skill in analysis, evidence, logic, language, interpersonal relations with the group, and oral communication? How do you measure your general effectiveness? Having a sound knowledge of the problem under discussion, understanding your role as an inquirer after truth and as a cooperative thinker with your colleagues, being able to handle facts skillfully, to reason soundly, and to adjust your delivery and speaking personality to discussion rather than to strong persuasion or debate will make you a satisfactory participant or leader in discussional speaking.

The following evaluation scales are suggested as rough guides for outside critics and for each member as he rates his colleagues and the group chairman.

The group	Low				High		Comments
Knowledge of subject							
Group relationship							
Evidence and reasoning							
Development of the discussion pattern							
Participation by all							
Delivery and personality factors							
Further comments							

The participants	Low				High		Comments
Knowledge of subject							
Relationship to members							
Facts and evidence							
Reasoning							
Development of discussion pattern							
Delivery and personality							
Further comments							

Projects and Problems

PROJECT 1: Collect, from printed sources, five or six representative statements from national leaders—educational, political, religious, or otherwise—concerning the value of discussion. Or solicit from former university students testimony of this type. Present your findings in a four-minute report to the group.

PROJECT 2: Topics for informal classroom discussion: What is the place of discussion in our American political society? Should we prefer debate to discussion? Should we endorse and participate in both? Should we support discussion only?

PROJECT 3: Suggestions for the instructor:

a. Assign four or five members of the group to an informal discussion to demonstrate the principles of group discussion. Allow sufficient time during the hour for class comment on the demonstration.

b. Divide the class into discussion groups of five each. Assign a common topic. Have half the class carry out a full-length discussion; have the others serve as critics. At the following meeting reverse the process so that in two meetings each student will have discussed and will have served as a critic.

c. Have the class prepare to discuss a currently significant problem. Organization should follow a logical framework: The first hour will be given to (1) definitions, goals, and analysis of the problem; the second hour to (2) solution A; the third hour to (3) another representative solution; and the fourth hour to (4) a statement by each student of his solution. The groups will meet simultaneously in several rooms with at least one critic present. A final meeting of the combined groups may be held for application of the "action" step.

d. Have the class organize a forum. Let two members present the problem briefly. Have an experienced moderator (if necessary, the instructor) receive and direct remarks and questions from the floor. Observe the techniques and procedures of a large community forum.

e. Obtain time on the radio and reproduce over the air the best of the discussions in the projects assigned above.

f. Assign a topic to the entire class and have each of six or seven groups prepare an outline. After each group has worked out its outline, have the class confer as a unit and synthesize the outlines. Use the resulting group outline for a classroom forum or panel discussion.

PROJECT 4: Attend a college public-discussion program. Submit to your instructor a 200-word criticism of the leader and of the participants.

PROJECT 5: You have been chosen to organize and prepare a community group for a single discussion on a timely topic. Explain the steps and procedures you would follow.

PROJECT 6: Listen to a radio discussion by your college or university colleagues or by speakers from some other institution. Submit your written criticism to the instructor. Criticize especially the "discussion pattern" of the performance.

References

Baird, A. Craig, *Discussion: Principles and Types.* New York: McGraw-Hill Book Company, 1943.

Barnlund, Dean C. (ed.), *Interpersonal Communication: Survey and Studies*. Boston: Houghton Mifflin Company, 1968.

————, and Franklyn S. Haiman, *The Dynamics of Discussion*. Boston: Houghton Mifflin Company, 1960.

Cartwright, Dorwin, and Alvin Zander, *Group Dynamics—Research and Theory*. New York: Harper and Row Publishers, 1960.

Cathcart, Robert S., and Larry A. Samovar (eds.), *Small Group Communication: A Reader*. Dubuque, Iowa: Wm. C. Brown, 1970.

Crowell, Laura, *Discussion: Method of Democracy*. Chicago: Scott, Foresman and Company, 1963.

Gulley, Halbert E., *Discussion, Conference, and Group Process*, 2nd ed. New York: Holt, Rinehart and Winston, Inc., 1968.

Haiman, F. S., *Group Leadership and Democratic Action*. Boston: Houghton Mifflin Company, 1951.

Hare, A. Paul, *Handbook of Small Group Research*. New York: Free Press of Glencoe, 1962.

Harnack, Victor, and Thorrel B. Fest, *Group Discussion: Theory and Technique*. New York: Appleton-Century-Crofts, 1964.

Howell, William S., and Donald K. Smith, *Discussion*. New York: The Macmillan Company, 1956.

McBurney, James H., and K. G. Hance, *Discussion in Human Affairs*. New York: Harper and Brothers, 1950.

Potter, David, and Martin P. Anderson, *Discussion*. Belmont, Calif.: Wadsworth Publishing Company, 1966.

Phillips, Gerald N., *Communication and the Small Group*. Indianapolis: Bobbs-Merrill Co., 1965.

Sattler, William, and N. Edd Miller, *Discussion and Conference*. Englewood Cliffs, N.J.: Prentice-Hall, Inc., 1954.

Utterback, William E., *Group Thinking and Conference Leadership*. New York: Holt, Rinehart and Winston, Inc., 1964.

Wagner, Russell, and Carroll Arnold, *Handbook of Group Discussion*. Boston: Houghton Mifflin Company, 1965.

Pietro Belluschi explains a model for Lincoln Center in New York.
Katrina Thomas.

informational speaking

One of the most, if not *the* most, important types of speaking is informative speaking. As the world grows increasingly complex, there is an ever-increasing need to know more and more and to be able to do more and more. Colin Cherry has suggested that the accumulation, storage, and retrieval of information may be looked upon as a new kind of capitalism.

Communication is our major tool for the acquisition of information. It is through speech that we help our children learn much of what they need to know and do. It is through speech that we, as students and teachers, help each other learn. It is through speech that we help employees learn their jobs. And it is through speech that we get much of the information about our immediate environment, our society, and our world that helps us to operate intelligently and to make decisions.

Even when one's purpose is primarily persuasion, the communication of information will play an important role. Others often will not accept your belief or waste their energies acting in the way you recommend if they do not clearly understand and remember the information on which your belief or proposed action is based. The novelist, the playwright, even the poet must be concerned with the communication of background information. Groups of individuals who are attempting to solve a problem or develop a plan of action depend upon the sharing of information among the participants. Sometimes your information will be of the very practical type needed for a particular task. At other times, it will supplement other goals you may have, ranging from entertainment to persuasion. You may inform others simply because they want to know, or because they have a right to know. And these are merely a few of the almost infinite variety of examples which we could cite showing the ways in which we are concerned with informative messages.

Much of the information that any individual needs he gets through first-hand experience. This is sometimes called "learning the hard way." However, for almost all individuals—and certainly for anyone living in a highly complex, technological society where one can learn by direct experience only a minute fraction of what he needs to know—informative speeches and other forms of informative communication are vital to existence.

Planning informative speech is quite analogous to a teacher planning a lesson in school. One must begin with objectives. What is it that you want **289** your audience members to know or to be able to do when you get done? What are the situations in which they will need to use that knowledge or those acquired skills? To be certain that you have conceived your goals in a meaningful way, ask yourself how you will know when your speech has been successful. What should you observe your audience do in what situations if your speech is successful? Defining your goals in this way will provide maximum help to you in knowing precisely what to say and do and how to say and do them in your speech.

Once you have determined the goals, it is essential that you consider your audience or probable audience. What do they already know? How is the additional material that you want them to know related to what they know now? Will what they presently know aid or hinder this new learning? How motivated are they to know what you want to tell them? Must you arouse their interest and drive to know, or is it already there waiting? What other sources of information do they already have? The function of speaking is different for a topic about which an audience gets no or little other information and for a topic about which the audience gets a great deal of other information. In the latter case, the major purpose of your speech may be to help the audience learn which sources of information are best for information on this topic or to help them learn to discriminate among and to organize the variety of information that they have gotten and will get in the future.

In much informative speaking, you cannot tell an audience everything it needs to know. For example, no classroom teacher, no matter how expert he is nor how much time he has, can tell you everything that you ought to know about his subject matter. His solution to the problem, and yours, should be to make the audience aware of its need for such information, if it is not already aware, and help it learn ways to acquire such information from other sources. In the teacher's terms, help the audience "learn to learn."

As a result of your definition of goals and your analysis of the audience, you must decide how much information you can include in a single speech. This is a difficult question because the more you include the more the audience will learn, but, conversely, the lower the probability that any particular bit of information will be learned. So, if it is important that certain specific things definitely be learned by the audience, do not include too much. A simple message is said to be a low-definition message. On the other hand, if you want the audience to know as much as possible, and which specific bits of information they learn make little difference, then it is best to "pack" your speech with as much information as possible. Then you have a high-definition message.

If you are to develop a subject in some depth, you need to have a plan for going about it. One such plan suggested by George Gerbner involves the asking and answering of such questions as: "What is?" "What is important?" "What is right?" and "What is related to what?"

Ben Bloom and some colleagues have suggested another pattern involving such levels of information as:

Knowledge [A level of identification and vocabulary.]
Comprehension [A deeper understanding.]
Applications [Examples, illustrations.]
Analysis [Parts and functions.]
Synthesis [Sources, extensions and relationships.]
Evaluation [Worth, significance, ethics.][1]

In any speech in which the audience is to learn to do something, the importance of practice cannot be stressed too much. During the course of your speech, consider the possibility of having your audience repeat certain things that you say, answer questions silently or aloud, or even practice whatever you are demonstrating while you are demonstrating it. If they are encouraged to ask questions of you, it will help.

Whatever it is that the audience should learn from your speech, you can increase the probability of its being learned by planning for appropriate reinforcement. This reinforcement might be something as simple as letting audience members know whether their responses are correct when you ask them to respond aloud to questions or praising those who are doing a new task correctly.

You can also increase audience learning by creating the proper "set" in the audience—making them aware of precisely what it is that they are to learn. In some classroom situations, the most effective way to create this "set" is to give the group a pretest on the material. This cues them to what you expect them to learn and they will then be able to focus upon those relevant aspects of your speech. Such pretests prior to the showing of instructional films, for example, have been shown to increase relevant learning from the film quite sharply. Though you cannot always give a pretest, the introduction to your speech may be able to serve a comparable function if it clearly specifies what the audience is to get from the main portion of the speech or what they ought to be able to do afterwards.

If you are trying to teach a skill or communicate information which is to be applied in a variety of different situations, or even in one situation different from that in which it is being learned, you should try to help the learners overcome the problem of "transfer." For example, if you are explaining to an audience how to recognize fallacious reasoning, you will probably cite some examples. You will want the audience to learn to recognize fallacies not only in the kinds of examples you cite, but also in any other kind of reasoning. That is to say, you want them to be able to transfer the acquired skill to a wide variety of problems. In this case, you could

---

[1]Benjamin S. Bloom (ed.), *Taxonomy of Educational Objectives,* Longmans, Green & Co., New York, 1956, Vol. I, pp. 62–200.

probably increase the probability of transfer by using as wide a range of examples as possible and by explaining to the audience the range of communication situations in which the principles can be applied.

Educational psychologist Robert Gagne's summary of the functions of communication in instruction may help you to remember the major things that you must do in any informative or instructional speech:

Controlling attention
Informing the learner of required performance
Recalling previously learned capabilities [reminding the audience of what they already know that is relevant]
Guidance of learning [suggesting, through statements or questions, the kinds of things the audience ought to be thinking about while they listen, so that they do not get sidetracked]
Presenting the stimulus [or information]
Providing feedback [or reinforcement]
Promoting transfer of learning[2]

Types and Principles of Informative Speaking

Informative communication takes place in many circumstances other than formally organized speeches. Although the descriptions below tend to be of formally organized speeches, the principles are equally applicable to discussions, informal conversations, and almost any other mode of communication.

Description

Effective description depends upon evoking in the mind of the listener the image which is in the mind of the speaker, or one as close to that image as possible.

The material to be included in a description depends upon the purpose to be served by the information rather than upon the many characteristics of the object or event to be described. If you are describing a river for someone planning a canoe trip down it, you will describe it differently than if you are describing it for someone who needs to determine the location of a dam or a bridge, or someone who wants to find a good fishing spot, or someone who wants drinking water, a good beach, scenic beauty, or irrigation, or who fears flood. Some descriptions may serve several purposes; none can serve all of them. This is another reason that you must have a clear idea of the specific purpose or purposes to be served by information before you select and organize it.

---

[2]Robert M. Gagne, "Learning and Communication," in Raymond V. Wiman and Wesley C. Meierhenry (eds.), *Educational Media: Theory into Practice,* Charles E. Merrill Publishing Co., Columbus, Ohio, 1969, p. 110.

The purposes will help you to determine whether the information must be exact or only approximate. If the river is to be dammed, it must be measured exactly. If the purpose is to know whether it is deep enough for high-diving, a bit less precision is necessary. If the purpose is to know the location of a good beach, a rough approximation is adequate to lead swimmers to the right place.

In locating objects or events in space or time, it is important for audience comprehension that you have a clear system, an obvious reference point or starting point, and an understandable order from that point. Thus, for example, in a group photograph the person in the lower left-hand corner is often identified first and then others in the first row, going from left to right, second row left to right, etc. On the other hand, if there is an especially prominent person in the center, he might be identified first and then those to his left and right. The obvious way to describe events that have occurred over a space of time so that the audience can follow the description easily is to describe them in the order in which they occurred. Thus, if describing the scoring in a football game, you would probably describe the touchdown plays in the order in which they occurred.

The vividness of the details included is as important as the general outline or organization of the description. Vividness can be achieved by using specific, discriminative, image-evoking words, voice patterns, and visual cues. The action in the statement "He moved" is made more concrete and more vivid in such statements as "He ambled," "He glided," "He wormed his way," "He shoved," "He slid," "He paced," "He scuttled," "He weaved in and out," "He zigzagged," and "He dived forward."

Suggestive descriptions, as opposed to exact descriptions, make use of figurative language to impute specific qualities to objects. Consider, for example, the cool shadow, the protective shadow, the sinister shadow, and the waning shadow. Use a thesaurus regularly to help build the varied vocabulary necessary for vivid descriptions.

Some descriptions are incomplete until the mood that unifies the scene or event is presented. Consider, for example, the line from Poe's "The Raven," "Long I stood there, wondering, fearing," or the lines from Wordsworth's "The Daffodils,"

And then my heart with pleasure fills,
And dances with the daffodils.

or, in quite a different mood, the words of Malcolm X, "It's got to be the ballot or the bullet." All these follow extended descriptions of the details of a situation. They are intended to summarize the situation and suggest the speaker's reaction to the situation as a whole. The reactions of the observer add an important element to the description.

The informative speaker who makes use of description will find it helpful to understand some principles of the psychology of observation.[3] Two people looking at an object do not necessarily see the same details or even the same number of details. Skill in observation can be developed; the student of art sees more in a picture than the artistically uninformed. The bird-lover or hunter will observe life in a woodland which goes unnoticed by others. Effective description not only presents a picture; it also calls attention to features to be observed. It interprets the significance of features of the scene to the listener. Because the attitudes of observers toward an object or situation often affect what they see, you must beware of these attitudes among your auditors and adjust the treatment of your subject accordingly.

Analysis, Classification, and Definition

Since analysis is principally a process of dividing and classifying the data used in the development of the subject, many principles which apply to classification of data as we studied it in Chapters Eight and Ten also apply to explanation through analysis. We analyze a topic to discover its elements. We classify elements in order to make them easier to understand and remember.

Follow these four principles in classifying data logically: First, the units must treat the subject comprehensively. Second, the units should be distinct, free from overlapping. Third, they should be classified upon the basis of a single principle. (For example, it would be illogical to classify students as freshmen, engineers, or women, because a different principle is illustrated by each of these three nonparallel categories. Such categories as class, major, and sex would be logical, however.) Fourth, classified items should be arranged in some suitable order for comprehension, such as size, sequence of events, cause and effect, functions of parts, or types—for example, the classification of the functions of government as legislative, executive, and judicial; or the classification of music as vocal and instrumental; or the instruments used in an orchestra as string, brass, woodwind, and percussion.

Many subjects about which we make informative speeches do not lend themselves readily to the rigid requirements of logical classification. In treating such subjects, we may classify data topically, rather than logically. As an example, consider some of the part titles of this book: "General Processes and Aims," "The Communicator," "Audience Adaptation," "The Message," "Symbol Systems," "Channels of Communication." Clearly, the principles of logical classification cannot be applied to these topics in any meaningful way. This topical organization, rather, follows a pattern for the

---

[3] See Jonas F. Soltis, *Seeing, Knowing, and Believing*, Addison-Wesley, Reading, Mass., 1966.

study of speech in units which much experience has shown to work well for a reader who wants to understand the nature of communication and to improve his speaking skill. Therefore, this classification system fits our purpose. You will often need to develop topical classifications to fit particular subjects and purposes.

To clarify the nature of specific features of data, after they have been analyzed and classified, we use definition. Definition circumscribes, localizes, and makes specific the meaning of a word or phrase. Its function is not to provide an authoritarian interpretation of a word; rather, it is to indicate the meaning with which a word is used at the time. Its purpose is to provide a common ground of understanding between speakers and auditors.

Illustration, Example, and Analogy

In informative speaking, examples serve many purposes. They clarify principles, general statements or trends, and types of classifications. Since few people develop the mental habits necessary for following abstract thinking, general and abstract statements should be illustrated abundantly. Examples not only help to clarify meaning, they add drama and human interest. They also arouse the curiosity of listeners and interest them in following the story to its conclusion.

There are many types of examples used for informative purposes. General and specific illustrations are two of these types. The speaker who is discussing cooperation, for example, may offer "socialism" as a general illustration of cooperation. If he goes on to say that publicly owned utilities are socialistic, he is offering a general illustration of the operation of socialism. But if he discusses the publicly owned waterworks or municipally owned light plant in a specific town, he is providing not general illustrations but specific instances or examples.

Hypothetical illustrations ordinarily begin with a phrase such as, "Suppose we had a case . . ." or "Imagine a situation in which. . . ." Some real examples could be given fictitious elements to make them more typical, to disguise them, or to protect personalities.

Examples should fit the subject under discussion. When they are not to the point, they confuse rather than clarify. Examples should suit the audience in terms of interest, experience, and level of complexity. Examples from a common area of experience are ordinarily better than examples selected from the experiences of the few. Well-known examples may be referred to briefly; unfamiliar examples should be elaborated. In one of Churchill's speeches, a brief reference to the battle of Gettysburg was as effective as a detailed recounting of another battle.

The more fitting the story, the less the speaker needs to say about its application to the subject. Elaborate pointing of the moral may spoil its effectiveness. Although the details of the example should be vivid, they should not be so spectacular that the story overshadows the point.

Historical Narrative

Our concept of history should be broad enough to include the story of the development of any subject worthy of our attention. Historical exposition is used primarily to throw light on the background of a subject. The method is best exemplified in the doctor's tracing the symptoms of his patient's illness. The account should be accurate and interesting, but it must also be brief, designed primarily to impart information rather than to entertain, and adapted to the purpose of a particular speaking situation. Successful student speeches on the following subjects might well include an explanation by historical narrative: The development of jet aircraft, the history of hybrid corn, changes in the game of basketball, the struggle for civil rights. This form of exposition has some of the characteristics of the extended example.

This type of explanation should generally follow all of the principles of historical study: utilizing original sources where possible rather than the less reliable secondary sources, corroborating questionable facts by using two or more sources, clearly identifying sources so that the audience can assess validity and reliability, and including sufficient data to provide a continuous narrative of the significant events.

Tracing Causal Relationships

Two of the questions we often attempt to answer in informative speech are "What causes it?" and "What can be done about it?" The tracing of causal relationships is an attempt to answer such questions. It seeks to clarify a situation by identifying the causes which have produced a known effect, or the effects which may result from known causes. When our purpose is to identify causes, we will trace events backward in time; when it is to identify effects, we will trace events forward. We seek to identify causes and effects primarily for the purpose of predicting or controlling future events; and we can control events either by modifying causes or by blocking their normal effects.

In explaining causes, limit the discussion to important events in the sequence. Describe and analyze each step with great care. Complex phenomena have complex or multiple causes; therefore, do not oversimplify. Beware of mistaking for the cause of a given effect what may be merely another effect of a common cause. The student who has difficulty in speech may report that he does not.like speech. It is easy to ascribe his difficulties to lack of interest. Both difficulty and lack of interest are probably more accurately attributable to the fact that he has not had a favorable opportunity to learn to speak effectively. (See Chapter Ten for an analysis of causal reasoning.)

Informative Speaking with Visual Aids

Virtually anything may be used for a visual aid, if you have the imagination to see the various things which can clarify your ideas for your particular audience, which can attract their attention and maintain their interest. Even your body, through stance and gestures, provides an important visual aid to communication in most speech situations, as we explain in some detail in Chapter Thirteen.

The Informative Speech of Operation

The operations speech is designed to give precise directions on how to perform an action or carry out a process. You may give instructions for driving a car, working a mathematical formula, building scenery, or editing a film. If your listeners are not familiar with the activity, you may need to create interest in the process. Define terms with which your listeners are not familiar. Describe objects to be used, explain their functions, and give directions for using them. Compare and contrast objects and steps with similar materials and processes that are familiar.

Explain the steps in the order in which they are to be carried out. Make the significance of each step clear as you proceed. Demonstrate as well as describe the action. Sometimes the listeners can carry out the action along with you—computing a rank-order correlation, for example. Observe and correct the mistakes they make. Indicate acceptable variations in procedure. Anticipate difficulties and explain how they can be overcome. Present a clear picture or description of expected results.

The Critical Interpretation

This type of speech activity may appear to you to be argumentative rather than informative. Certainly, a simple statement of like or dislike is argumentative. But this is criticism on an emotional rather than an intellectual basis. We are concerned here with intellectual criticism, that criticism which is the essence of teaching and, hence, a type of informative speaking. Criticism in this sense is the interpretation of a product or process in terms of acceptable standards of achievement. If the listener does not agree on what is to be criticized, or on the standard by which the elements are to be evaluated, and if differences of opinion develop on the subject and its evaluation, then the exposition passes into the field of argument. If both speaker and listener agree during the process of instruction on the elements of the act or product, the standard to be applied, and the application of the standard to the act, then critical interpretation is identical with informative speaking.

The steps in a critical interpretation include (1) the selection of elements or parts of an object to be criticized, (2) the accumulation of information on the object to be evaluated, (3) the application of appropriate standards in interpreting the facts, and (4) the presentation of the evaluation.

Criticism should take into account the specific purpose of the activity. A piece of work performed for one purpose should not be criticized for failing to accomplish another. Do not elaborate the obvious or dwell upon minor slips or petty flaws. Exercise judgment in arriving at a fair interpretation of the work as a whole, remembering that the critic must accept responsibility for his criticism. Your status as a critic does not grant you license to be irresponsible. (See Chapter Seventeen for a more extensive treatment of one type of criticism.)

Combinations of Methods in Informative Speaking

The types and principles of informative speaking have been presented in some detail. As you study these types, remember that they can be combined in a variety of ways. Many aspects of one type can be useful in making speeches of other types.

It may have occurred to you that discussion is also a type of informative speaking. The techniques of sharing information in discussion are presented in Chapter Nineteen.

Projects and Problems

PROJECT 1: Develop and present to the class an informative message in which you present knowledge about a subject at each of the levels of information suggested by Bloom.

PROJECT 2: Develop a visual which you might use in presenting an informative message on some subject. Hold a visual fair in which you explain the visual aid. Have the class vote on a display of these aids and award first and second place recognition.

PROJECT 3: Performance of a process.
Purposes of this assignment: The ability to direct others in the specific operations or activities required in carrying through some process is a useful skill. Can you present such directions clearly and effectively? If not, this project should help you improve your skill in making this type of informative speech.

Suggested subjects for this assignment:

Hybridizing a plant	Making a blueprint
Flying by instrument	Using the library
Preparing a speech	Fly casting
How to study	Running a political convention
Designing a stage set	How to float on the water
Making a steel casting	Skin diving
Artificial respiration	Blowing glass
Digging clams	

PROJECT 4: Description of scenes, objects, and events.

Purposes of this assignment: Can you make yourself clearly understood when you describe a house or a room? Can you look at a contour map and describe the country represented? How well do you describe such objects as a piece of machinery, a kitchen or workbench tool, a slide rule, a subway, a car, or a boat? Can you describe sounds, tastes, odors, movement, and moods? Do you describe persons precisely? Work on description should help you analyze and talk about such matters more clearly.

Suggested subjects for this speech:

A radio studio	Judo
A wet-bulb thermometer	The scene of the crime
The South Sea Island native	A famous battle in history
My dream air flivver	Night life in the jungle
A power lathe	The art of Alexander Calder
The Alcan Highway	The surveyor's transit
Standards for judging purebred horses	A jet engine
An urban housing project	Space flight
A traditional family farm	A moon landing ship

PROJECT 5: The historical narrative.

Purposes of this assignment: The historical narrative informs and explains by presenting the background and development of a principle, institution, or object. It answers the questions: What is the origin and development of this idea? Have you wondered about the development of protective armor, the modern college, public health measures, the professions of medicine, law, or personnel management? Do you know the history of railroads, the Flying Fortress, free speech, the mining of iron ore, Percheron horses, or realism in the theater? Such subjects are appropriate for learning to use the historical narrative in informative speaking.

Suggested subjects for this assignment:

The fight against yellow fever	The use of electricity
Group medicine	The liberal arts college
The cultivation of wheat	The modern novel
The study of speech	Democratic government
Popular music	The practice of dentistry

The rise of Hitler
The production of quinine
Conquest of space
The black man in America
The microscope

Educational television
The Berlin crisis
A protest demonstration
Women's suffrage

PROJECT 6: Analysis, classification, and division.

Purposes of this assignment: Occasionally you will find it necessary to use words which are new or which may mean different things to different people. These words must be defined. To formulate effective definitions requires practice. The new is explained by relating it to the familiar. One method of relating a new idea to an old one is to classify the new idea. In what class does the new idea belong? How does it differ from other ideas in the same class? The processes of definition and classification serve to analyze the subject, to break it down into its significant parts so that you may think about one at a time. This assignment should help you explain your ideas through definition, classification, and analysis.

Suggested subjects for this speech:

Communication models
Weather
Words and their meaning
Synthetic rubber
The pioneer movement
The skyscraper
Conservation of natural resources
The four freedoms

ABMs
Lincoln's ideas of the evil of slavery
Developing concepts of democracy
Dictatorships
The idea of human rights
Imperialism
Theories of communication
Theories of learning

PROJECT 7: Illustration, example, and analogy.

Purposes of this assignment: Informative speaking often involves the consideration of general ideas, principles, and abstractions. When we explain the concepts of speech standards, illustrations probably do more to clarify principles than do general statements. We use examples and analogies to get the audience's attention, keep their interest, crystallize abstractions, demonstrate the working of principles, and facilitate memory for facts. The speech student should learn how to explain his ideas by the use of this method.

Suggested subjects: a. A principle of government illustrated by examples from history. *b.* A principle of the development of industry. *c.* A principle of military action. *d.* A social problem or trend. *e.* Application of historical examples to current events.

PROJECT 8: Tracing causal relationships.

Purposes of this assignment: The answers to many requests for information begin with the word "because." The importance of causal relationships justifies careful study of this type of informative speaking. If causes or effects cited are complex or difficult to trace, you should understand the methods by which causal relationships are traced and how such relationships are tested. This assignment should help you to improve your causal explanations.

Suggested topics for this assignment:

Nonverbal communication

Causes of the Vietnam war

The effects of soil erosion

Causes of juvenile delinquency

Subsidized industry

Effects of the Versailles Treaty

The significance of free enterprise in the United States

The rise of the Ku Klux Klan

Cross-cultural communication

Foreign aid programs

The failure (or the success) of the United Nations

The effects of bureaucratic government

Words are weapons

Why we behave like human beings

The values of education

The new wonder drugs

References

Bloom, Benjamin S. (ed.), *Taxonomy of Educational Objectives,* Volume I, "Cognitive Domain." New York: Longmans, Green & Co., 1956.

Bruner, Jerome, *Toward a Theory of Instruction.* Cambridge, Mass.: Harvard University Press, 1966.

Chisholm, Roderick M., *Theory of Knowledge.* Englewood Cliffs, N.J.: Prentice-Hall, Inc., 1966.

Kibler, Robert J., Larry L. Barker, and David T. Melis, *Behavioral Objectives and Instruction.* Boston: Allyn & Bacon, 1970.

Krathwohl, David R., Benjamin S. Bloom, and Bertram B. Masia, *Taxonomy of Educational Objectives,* Volume II, "Affective Domain." New York: Longmans, Green & Co., 1964.

Larabee, Harold A., *Reliable Knowledge.* Boston: Houghton Mifflin Company, 1964.

Lewis, C. I., *An Analysis of Knowledge and Valuation.* LaSalle, Ill.: Open Court, 1962.

MacDougall, Curtis D., *Interpretative Reporting.* New York: Macmillan, 1968.

Marx, Melvin H. (ed.), *Learning,* 2 volumes. New York: Macmillan, 1969.

Meetham, Roger, *Information Retrieval.* Garden City, N.Y.: Doubleday & Company, Inc., 1970.

Olbricht, Thomas H., *Informative Speaking.* Glenview, Ill.: Scott Foresman and Company, 1968.

Payne, Stanley L., *The Art of Asking Questions.* Princeton: Princeton University Press, 1951.

Powell, Len S., *Communication and Learning.* London: Pelman, 1969.

Singer, T. E. R., *Information and Communication.* New York: Reinhold Publishing Corporation, 1958.

Skinner, B. F., *The Technology of Teaching.* New York: Meredith Corporation, 1968.

Estimates and Projections of the Population of the
United States 1900 to 2015

persuasion: cognitive domain

Persuasive speaking goes on endlessly. In classrooms, among friends, acquaintances, and strangers, we all join in controversial challenges and replies. Our positions, pro or con, concern the nucleus of endless trivial or important subjects. We debate whether this summer is unseasonably hot; or whether hurricane Camille of August, 1969, was the most powerful and devastating ever to hit the United States. A universal argument during this same period concerned whether Senator Edward Kennedy of Massachusetts was negligent in reporting on the death of Mary Jo Kopechne at Martha's Vineyard; whether the withdrawal of thousands of American troops and their equipment from Southeast Asia would imperil our national security; whether the federal government should share tax returns with the fifty states; whether Congress should establish wage and price controls to regulate the business cycle.

What is persuasive speaking? According to the *Century Dictionary and Encyclopedia Lexicon,* "Persuasion is the act of influencing or winning over the mind or will to some conclusion, determination, or course of action, by argument of the presentation of suitable reasons, and not by the exercise of authority, force, or fear."

Other more recent definitions reflect somewhat the same concept. For example, Brembeck and Howell say, "Persuasion is the conscious attempt to modify the thought and action by manipulating the motives of men toward predetermined ends."[1] James McCroskey quotes and endorses James Winans' statement that "Persuasion is the process of inducing others to give fair, favorable and undivided attention to propositions."[2] Gary Cronkhite quotes the definition of persuasion in the Merriam-Webster *New Collegiate Dictionary* as the "act of influencing the mind by arguments and reasons." Cronkhite qualifies this definition by three specifications: "(3) persuasion is an act, (2) it influences the mind, (1) it does so by means of arguments and reasons."[3]

These various approaches have in common concepts of persuasion that

---

[1] W. L. Brembeck and W. S. Howell, *Persuasion,* Prentice-Hall, Inc., Englewood Cliffs, N.J., 1952, p. 24.

[2] James McCroskey, *An Introduction to Rhetorical Communication,* Prentice-Hall, Inc., Englewood Cliffs, N.J., 1968, p. 165.

[3] Gary Cronkhite, *Persuasion,* Bobbs-Merrill Company, Inc., Indianapolis and New York, 1969, pp. 3–4.

include emphasis on the sources, character, functioning, and results of this type of rhetorical communication.

1. Persuasion is a rhetorical-communicative act. It involves the speaker or agent, the audience, the occasion, and the message itself.
2. It aims to influence an audience, one or more, especially through language symbols.
3. Its rhetorical purpose is to move the listener or listeners to adopt evaluated behavior, attitude, and action, which can be analyzed and appraised specifically.
4. The medium is symbolic behavior, usually language as communicated through spoken or sometimes written discourse.
5. If the speaker's purpose succeeds, the resulting beliefs and behavior of the audience conform to the purpose of the speaker or speakers.
6. The speaker's basic ways of influencing these listeners are through both logical (reasoning) and psychological (motivative) means.
7. He is dealing with attitudes, values, beliefs, and related behavior.[4]
8. He may rely mainly on logical techniques (facts, inferences, examples, analogy, causality, testimony, deductive and classificational patterns).
9. He will also influence their beliefs and behavior through psychological forms of communication (appeals to drives, motives, habits, attitudes, sentiments, stereotypes, and personal character).
10. The speaker's persuasive process avoids the use of force, fear, or coercive authority. His communicative activity is to achieve some harmony between his attitudes and his conduct. The means are thus within the method of communication proper—by voice, audiovisual aids, language and the techniques by which ideas and appeals may affect audiences without military, autocratic, or other coercive means hostile to genuine communication. The expectancy of the persuasive outcome is that a new equilibrium between purposes and intellectual psychological attitudes of speaker and audience may be affected.[5]

In this chapter we concentrate on persuasion that chiefly relates to reasoned discourse, including forms of argumentative speaking and debating. In the chapter following we will discuss in detail the nature and application of psychological techniques in persuasion. *It is understood, however, that these aspects constitute a single unified system of the total organism,* and this organism strives to maintain a working consistency and harmony of these cognitive and affective subsystems.

Charles Woolbert declared more than fifty years ago that the mind was an organic unit performing the function of reasoning, feeling, willing, "as

---

[4]Cf. Cronkhite, *op. cit.,* chaps. 1 to 4.
[5]See Jesse G. Delia, "Logical Fallacy, Cognitive Theory and the Enthymeme," *Quarterly Journal of Speech,* 56:143, 1970.

may be demanded by the situation." In general speech authorities have adopted his position.[6]

Techniques of the Cognitive System in Persuasion

Effective persuasion in its logical argumentative development depends upon (1) persuasive purpose of the speaker, (2) adjustment to and cooperation with the audience at every turn, (3) analysis of the specific problem as indicated by the speaker and audience orientation, (4) tentative overview of the structural factors in relation to the hearers, (5) framing tentative propositions in line with rhetorical goals, (5) evaluation of the facts, data, evidence (again as interpreted by audience concepts), (7) evaluation of the inferences that support or reject the tentative propositions, (8) language composition that attempts to frame the persuasive content, cognitive and affective, to give audience comprehension, stimulation, and behavior, and (9) delivery to express effectively the communicative aims.

Some of the highest achievements of man have their foundations not in cold and closely reasoned logic, but in attitudes, loyalties, sentiments, and aspirations. Many roads lead to the good and the true. They are exemplified in the persuasion of drama, poetry, painting, and religion. Persuasion provides a means of ordering motives, a means not open to the narrowly logical mind.

- *Persuasive aim.* Decide what is your persuasive aim and concentrate on its techniques and desirable outcome. For example, you will provide necessary information, but your discourse will be other than primarily informational. The added knowledge you impart will be used to affect opinions, beliefs, attitudes, and conduct of the hearers. Those that you believe hold positions favorable to your proposal, you will try to influence further. Those who are indifferent or neutral, you will attempt to shake out of their neutrality and move in your direction. Those opposed—if they are strong in their attitudes—you will concentrate on and so hope for a consensus of endorsement of your proposal.[7]
- *Speaker-audience cohesion.* All communication, including persuasion, is based upon speaker-audience cohesion or identification. All listeners and observers will continue to have their mind sets, their prejudices, their individual drives and motives for resisting or accepting suggestions that differ from their habits, attitudes, and conduct. Your problem always is to

---

[6] Charles Woolbert, "Persuasion; Principles and Method," *Quarterly Journal of Speech Education,* 5:101–119, 1919.

[7] Cf. Maurice Natanson, "Rhetoric and Philosophical Argumentation," *Quarterly Journal of Speech,* 48:24–30, 1962; Halbert E. Gulley, *Essentials of Discussion and Debate,* Henry Holt and Company, Inc., New York, 1955, chap. 1; James G. McBurney and Kenneth G. Hance, *Discussion in Human Affairs,* Harper & Row, Publishers, Inc., New York, 1950, chap. 1.

understand the general and specific attributes of those you would influence, to modify your own attitudes and beliefs so as to appeal to the audience's cognitive-affective traits. You are attempting to apply constructive rather than destructive communicative implementation and to rely at every turn on your understanding of the attitudes and behavior of individuals and audiences.[8]

■ *Analysis of the specific problem.* A controversial situation is one in which the speaker and audience are disturbed by factors that threaten their immediate and larger interests. The equilibrium of internal stability, of place and surroundings, seems to topple.

Whatever beliefs, attitudes, desires, and conduct the communicator may have about a specific experience or situation, the disturbances that encroach on his internal reactions become the basis of his effort to understand and perhaps regain psychological equilibrium. His inquiries are also social, for the threats also invariably affect the group. The problem is to analyze the specific facts that threaten or disturb. Are these difficulties chiefly economic, social, political, ethical, or religious? More specifically, is the condition a concrete one of long standing or of recent development? For example, during the summer of 1969, the railroads were transmitting deadly phosgene gas from Denver, Colorado, to Lockport, N.Y., via the Northwestern Railroad through Iowa. The governor and the citizens of Iowa suddenly became aroused over the danger of accidents and wide destruction in the state from the gas. Later this method for shipping phosgene gas was cancelled. The issue was specific. As in all other problems, the prospective speaker explored the causes of the irritation, the extent of its operation, the results if unimpeded, and alternative lines of action that would dispel the threat. This problematic situation, transferred into language, becomes the controversial elements and the exploratory answers of your rhetoric.

In the analysis of a problem, its central questions usually arise. Philosophical or not, each of us, as ourselves and as one of our fellows, asks why. Also, we ask, what will be the results if other affecting situations do not impede? Will the bad situation taper off and harmful effects cease? Will the difficulties continue until death and other disasters result? These questions involve several apparent subquestions: (1) What factors call for some action to correct the situation? (2) Will the proposal for specific corrective or alternative courses of action properly meet the need? Will the difficulties be removed? Will positive benefits or satisfactory conditions follow? (3) Is a preferred course of action practicable? Can the proposed machinery or organization necessary for its operation be established? Has the proposed solution been demonstrated as successful in other places and in other disturbed areas?

---

[8] See Douglas Ehninger, "Argument as Method: Its Nature, Its Limitations and Its Uses," *Speech Monographs*, 37:101–110, 1970.

Such questions are the so-called "stock issues" familiar to most students of argumentative discourse. Such inquiries are mechanical, but they do help to focus on the outstanding lines of investigation. They are by no means all the pertinent questions, but they suggest a type of survey helpful in any preview of the problematic situation.

■ *Arguments and propositions.* Persuasion in argumentative and related forms of speaking (and writing) is based upon tentative propositions. These statements or propositions convey in essence what the speaker has in mind as his audience objective. They are framed as simply and clearly as possible to guide the speaker in his composition and the audience in its reception.

The analysis of the problem leads to major and minor questions. These in turn may become the speaker's affirmations, whether or not he reveals them directly in his talk. For example, his analysis may raise main and subquestions centering on the issue, "shall congress establish a system of universal military training? " The discussant might well leave the problem as a question to be pursued in detail from one inquiry to another. The persuader, however, reduces the matter to a concrete declarative sentence: "Congress should establish universal military training." If the talk is given in a legislative deliberative situation the word *Resolved* is prefixed to the sentence and thus a parliamentary resolution is under way.

The scope of the major statement is to be limited. If your speaking time is limited to a few minutes (and we hope so), you will correspondingly concentrate on one phase of a larger issue. For example, your stand and that of your group (or some members of it) may be that the American public will (or will not) support any movement toward such military training.

Phrase the proposition in a simple rather than a compound sentence. Free it from ambiguous, vague, or question-begging terms. If the problem is phrased for school or college debate, construct it so as to give the affirmative the burden of proof. This term means simply that those who propose the resolution should advocate a change from the status quo, or, in rare cases, a defense of the established position if the audience supports a contrary line of thinking and behavior on this subject. In general, word the statement so that it proposes a change or a policy counter to audience opinion.

Propositions are usually listed as of three kinds: those of fact (the moon is without "life"); those of desirability or undesirability (liberal arts training is desirable for all professional students); and propositions of policy (a national Liberal political party should be established in the United States). Persuasion, as we have defined it, aims at a change in audience behavior rather than a mere modification of audience knowledge. We assume that the change in knowledge will affect attitudes and subsequent behavior. All persuasion includes information and implies the desirability of a given proposition. But the end is the modification of behavior.[9]

---

[9] See Cronkhite, *op. cit.,* pp. 14–15.

■   *Structural pattern of the given argument.* The tentative view of the
ground of the specific argument and of the argumentative aim will be
tangibly furthered if the structural elements are viewed and assembled.

The analysis of issues leads directly to the selection, unity, order, and
proportion of the materials covering the speaking transaction. The propositions that incorporate this structure are of course conditional and often
modified, dismissed, or otherwise dealt with as audience identification
indicates. Nevertheless the principles of structural relevance and rhetorical
efficacy are basic to an effective production.

What propositions and subpropositions are to be included? This selective
process proceeds not by chance but by a methodical survey of the problem.
Similarly the order in which the phases are unfolded—whether an extended
argument or one limited to a few minutes—becomes important in view of
the audience's attitudes toward the issue. Furthermore, the prominence of
materials and the weight of the speaker's logic are also strong determinants
of the persuasive excellence. We are not implying that this final implementation of organization and structure is hard and fast and that it precedes
the development itself. As every creative speaker or writer knows, the
modification of arrangement parallels the composition itself and *structure
is never complete until the speaker and his audience have completed the
message.*

Follow a Logical Cognitive Pattern of Development

Your speaking purpose in argumentative development means that you will
rely heavily on the materials of reasoning and supporting fact. The set of
your talk is that of reflective thinking and the minimization of random
emotionalism.

The details of this reflective process consist of facts, the inferences from
these facts, and the conclusions. Reason and inference occur when the
mental exploration leads to some tentative position with respect to the facts
and related details. Inference, in a sense, is guessing, but it is also theoretically a methodical, cautious, and critical examination of the facts and
connections. It is based on a critical survey of the probabilities and hazards
that accompany a new stand. We hope that the leap of the gap from facts
to conclusions is justified.

When you infer or reason you do so in one or more of several ways. You
may view details that have similarities, then generalize concerning the
■   whole array (*inference from specific facts*); you may limit your description
and inference to a comparison between specific objects or relationships
■   (*inference from analogy*); you may focus on two or more particular events
■   that seem to have an invisible but definite connection (*inference from
causality*); you may view the statements of others who speak with assurance

- and experience on an event or theory (*inference from authority*); you may
- draw specific conclusions from general statements (*inference by deduction and classification*).

These typical modes of logic are the practical substance of your argumentative talk. They are not rigid forms to be followed in sequence, but are to be flexibly introduced at points that call for their application. These logical forms are a unit in the description of the mental process, but they are usually described separately by logicians and students of communication for purposes of detailed explanation and application. These logical considerations, as we have stated, are not sharply differentiated from the motivative modes of development. Each logical segment is intertwined with appeals to self-respect, pride, fair play, love and friendship, sympathy, conformity, or other types from the long list of appeals. *We here stress the dominant techniques that characterize argumentation, discussion, debate* and other types of persuasive speaking that chiefly employ reason and logical supports.[10]

For our purpose in this chapter we begin with facts as the foundation for every inference.[11]

1. Evidence (Facts)

The foundations of all experience, including communication, must rest on alleged facts. This term loosely covers all details of experience as recorded by observation and all other reactions to the world of reality. What are facts? The events may be important or insignificant for each life and for the associated lives. They are the records of personal testimony, statistics, experiment, chronicles, authoritative utterances, and ultimatums. The experiences may be the reactions of a population to violent rampages of nature, such as hurricane Camille or the Peruvian earthquake of June, 1970.[12] Or the crises may be man-made, such as the Soviet missile buildup in Cuba in 1962 which caused President Kennedy and the United States to demand Russia withdraw the missiles or run the risk of a nuclear war.

Facts, as we have often stated, are the objects or events as conceived by the audience. Such a datum may be an isolated item or a more general fact comprising an entire discourse in its character as knowledge. It may

---

[10]See Stephen Toulmin, *The Uses of Argument,* Cambridge University Press, London, 1958, chap. 3; Wayne Brockriede and Douglas Ehninger, "Toulmin on Argument: An Interpretation and Application," *Quarterly Journal of Speech,* 46:44–53, 1960; James C. McCroskey, *An Introduction to Rhetorical Communication,* Prentice-Hall, Inc., Englewood Cliffs, N.J., 1968, chaps. 5, 7; Cronkhite, *op. cit.,* chaps. 3–5; Douglas Ehninger and Wayne Brockriede, *Decision by Debate,* Dodd, Mead and Company, New York, 1963, chaps. 7–10.
[11]See Chapter Nine, "Sources of Message Materials."
[12]See McCroskey, *op. cit.,* pp. 135ff.

be later revealed as completely erroneous, but for the time and audience
it is "true."

McCroskey defines evidence as "factual statements originating from a
source other than that of the speaker, objects not created by the speaker,
and opinions of persons other than the speaker, which are offered in support
of the speaker's claims." [13] Such facts, technically examined and labelled
in a scientific laboratory or courtroom, are "evidence." According to Webster's *New World Dictionary,* the legal view of evidence is that it is "something legally presented before a court, as a statement of a witness, an object
etc., which bears on or establishes the point in question."

Facts are obviously to be well verified and represent the genuine beliefs
of the "audience" or at least the knowledgeable audience. Obviously, too,
the speaker has no justification at any point to distort or otherwise misrep-
resent data.

Test your supporting materials by asking yourself these questions: Are
the facts in my argument stated clearly and concisely? Have we included
enough facts? Do acceptable authorities subscribe to them? Are the sources
of these facts or the authorities cited specifically identified? Are these
authorities unprejudiced, intellectually honest, competent to testify? Do they
have special knowledge? Are the facts from a primary source? Is the source
corroborated by other sources? Are the facts acceptable to the audience?
Are the facts reasonable according to the tests of causation? [14]

2. Inference from Causality

A basic form of inference is reasoning from causation. We conclude that
assumed facts effect alleged results (cause-to-effect reasoning). Or we focus
our attention on these same instances or cases and attempt to describe other
factors, cases, or situations that may have produced them (effect-to-cause
reasoning). Like analogy, inference attempts to establish relationships between particulars.

What are the tests of such reasoning? In every case logical causality must
come from audience beliefs and attitudes. Almost every argument will
contain inferences from causal relations—either specific arguments within
a section or large arguments encompassing the entire proposition. How shall
we analyze their validity? We may ask four principal questions: (a) Does
a genuine connection appear between the antecedent (prior fact, event,
situation) and the consequent (subsequent fact, event, situation)? (b) If so,
is the alleged cause adequate to produce the alleged effect, or is the alleged
effect determined by the alleged cause? (c) Even if an alleged cause is

---

[13] James C. McCroskey.
[14] See Gerald Miller, "Questions of Fact and Value: Another Look," *Southern Speech
Journal,* 28:116–122, 1962; McCroskey, *op. cit.,* chaps. 5, 7; Cronkhite, *op. cit.,* chaps.
3, 4.

sufficient to determine the character of an allegedly related event or situation, are not intervening factors at work to cancel or minimize the controlling influence of the connection or relationship? (d) Have the alleged facts in this case been properly verified? (e) Does such reasoning harmonize with our positions concerning such inferences? Does it avoid fallacious inference?

To illustrate inference by cause-to-effect, note the following example: *Proposition to be proved:* The base of the federal income tax should be readjusted to eliminate provisions that permit some individuals and groups with large incomes to pay little or no taxes.

Inference: There is need for such readjustment, for (cause to effect).

Evidence: Many individuals and groups now escape their fair share of federal taxes.

Subevidence: Many foundations, universities, and churches now use their tax-free status to prosper in business and commerce.

Note that the causal argument here to be valid would need to be extensively qualified and questioned ("reservations" according to Toulmin[15]), for many audiences would extend the types and illustrations to those who avoided federal taxes (e.g., those well-to-do who invest in state and local bonds, real estate operators, "big" farmers, investors in the oil and gas business).

Note also that the sources and accuracy of the evidence underlying each type of inference should be checked.

3. Inference from Specific Instances

Your logical method here is to reason from specific instances to a general conclusion. This method is probably more widely resorted to than any other, because it encourages quick expansion of observation to cover and include cases not directly seen and experienced. One case of a student breaking into the president's office on a university campus may lead to a hasty conclusion that all the students of this university are violent and defiant of law and order. Your problem here is to harmonize with audience beliefs. But those beliefs, if the problem is important to them, will call for divided opinions and conjectures and so necessitate proper application of reservations, qualifications, and negative positions to be investigated and dealt with.

In the example above of causal reasoning the proper framing of a sound argument for dealing with individuals and groups in their relation to federal taxation calls for a citation of cases of the wealthy who pay little or no federal tax. Schools, churches, and foundations were cited above. But other cases need to be included, such as industrial and agricultural groups that

---

[15]Toulmin, *op. cit.,* chap. 3.

also have special tax exemptions. Thus only the generalization that "We need to correct the unfair levelling of federal taxes, because representative groups of the wealthy in representative aspects of American Industrial life are exempt from their share of taxes" can be justified.

After examining a representative number of cases or instances, you draw up a statement that covers the general field of the topic, excluding those cases that you may not have had opportunity to inspect.

How can you check your own thinking and that of others as you generalize from instances? You will note that the cases are sufficient in number. You will question whether the cases are representative or typical. If you wish to prove that the leaders of the Republican party are on the whole conservatives, you will in all fairness not limit your instances to the "old guard," or to those over seventy; you will include the obviously younger Republican governors and congressmen and study a cross section of the party leadership. Furthermore, you will look closely at the sources of your facts, at yourself as observer and collector, and at official or unofficial sources in print from which you quote. You will check the character, authority, reliability, and corroborative value of your sources. In the interest of your audience and of sound logic and communication, you will also test the causal factors involved.

4. Inference from Analogy

A third type of inference is from analogy (inference by comparison). The isolated facts, cases, objects, or relationships between such objects are compared with similar facts, cases, objects, or relationships about which our information is relatively hazy. From such matching and contrast you may draw conclusions concerning these relatively unknown situations, facts, objects, or relationships. By analogy we Americans can compare our democracy with that of the British, about whose democratic ways we are less sure, and conclude that the British support democratic principles similar to those we adhere to.

The worth of your analogies or comparisons will obviously depend on the accuracy with which the factors of similarity are carried out. We ask: Do the objects or relationships under comparison actually have a considerable number of items in common? If so, have these items significance or importance with respect to the conclusion we would draw? Do important differences exist? Are the alleged facts on which the comparisons are based fully established and clearly stated? Can the alleged comparison or conclusion be in turn verified by argument from generalization, by causal reasoning, by testimony of experts? False analogy should be avoided.

We continually utilize analogies and comparisons in our experience, thinking, and speaking. The astronauts, Neil Armstrong, Edwin Aldrin, and Michael Collins, preparing for their moon flight, were hailed as launching a voyage more impressive than that of Columbus discovering America. Prior to the actual event, when the comparison was first made, we knew something about the Columbus discovery, but practically nothing about what might happen on a moon landing. The inferences, however, were that the two events had much in common in terms of preparation, intelligent leadership, and so on, so that the unknown element of the astronautic flight would in effectiveness duplicate the known items of the 1492 precedent. Although the details of each transaction were entirely different, making comparisons dramatic rather than logical, the comparisons were impressive.

Much of analogous reasoning is figurative rather than literal comparison. It forms the background and content of poetry and other literature; it is imaginative and descriptive and without logical quality. Nevertheless, as the comparisons approach similarity in points that affect results and audience attitudes, the cases become more obviously inferential.

Thus we have compared national defense and a dike ("national armaments keep out invaders just as the Holland dikes keep out the sea—or did so before World War II"). Or consider this one: "The present system of declaring war only by consent of Congress is sound and strong, like the trestle over which twenty trains have passed."

5.   Inference from Authority

Still another method of inference is to cite authorities or expert sources for verification of an idea. The gist of such inference is that "so-and-so is true, because Mr. X so states." Here an authority is identified with an alleged conclusion. The reasoning really amounts to the assumption that whatever Mr. X has to say on this subject is sound. This kind of assumption may be tested by means of these questions: Is the source accurately quoted? Are the facts (if facts are given) properly reported? Is the source especially qualified on this subject? Is he unbiased? Is the testimony offered contrary to the interests of the authority? In general, is the source accepted by the audience? Does reasoning from causal relation, analogy, generalization, and specific instances confirm this conclusion or assumption?

The design of such an inference is as follows:

Proposition: The short-term licenses for radio-television stations should be replaced by long-term (twenty-year) licenses, for
Inference: competent authorities endorse such policy, for
Evidence: a prominent senator who endorses the policy has competency.

Note that this example has obvious logical weaknesses. The conclusion should be based not only on authority, but on examples, analogies, and causal connections. Furthermore, in this example the senator is not named. The testimony of supporters of the Federal Communications Commission would represent more valid evidence.

6. Inference from Classification (General Propositions and Assumptions)

Inference by generalizations, as we noted above, assumes that what is true of cases or samples from a class is also true of other cases or samples from the same class. Often we treat such type of inference as induction. This classificational thought pattern also assumes that what is true of the class is also true of the cases or examples within that class. Such pattern is traditionally labeled "deduction."

Inferences based upon the assumption of classification and homogeneity of the cases or details that comprise a unit of thought or scrutiny are not different from the inferences based upon generalization, causation, analogy, and other types of logical examination.

The logic of deduction assumes that the category has certain characteristics that identify the class. The inference attempts to establish that each member has characteristics typical of the general class. The data are used to buttress the inference.

The general statements, uttered or not, are assumptions, hypotheses, principles, or even unwarranted "hunches." Practically every speech or other rational procedure is related to or implies these kinds of basic concepts that give logical solidity to what it says. In any case the inferential development should conform to the beliefs and attitudes of the audience (in this case, approval of the general propositions or assumptions).

To the logician, deductions are sometimes framed as *syllogisms,* in which the first proposition is labeled the major premise; the related or more specific propositions, the minor premise; and the connecting proposition, the conclusion.[16]

To illustrate:

Persuasive purpose: To "prove" that Howard Hummerfield has been or will have lung cancer.

Inference: Cigarette smoking produces lung cancer.

Assumption, or hypothesis or facts and inferences from authority, generalizations, causation, analogy, etc.

Data or evidence: Howard Hummerfield smokes cigarettes.

The general field is lung cancer. Within that field is cigarette smoking. Hummerfield is by evidence grouped among the cigarette smokers.

Note the logical testing to be applied to general propositions:

a.   Speeches are hardly ever framed as syllogisms. You will recognize these general statements and so examine your own thinking and that of other speakers.

b.   These major statements, whether stated or implied, are to be carefully proved rather than assumed. The major premise of the categorical illus-

---

[16] See Walter R. Fisher, "The Uses of the Enthymeme," *Speech Teacher,* 13:197–203, 1964; Samuel L. Becker, "Research in Emotional and Logical Proofs," *Southern Speech Journal,* 28:208–218, 1963.

tration above, for example, calls for further scientific establishment. Cigarette smoking needs definition. Is it a package a week, or three packages a day? Are the cigarettes equipped with fiber tips? Does the smoker inhale? Thus, we need to qualify the major proposition in terms of sometimes and some people and so to harmonize with whatever research justifies.

c. All deductive statements, whether or not they are framed as *enthymemes* (major premises or equivalents in syllogistic constructions of major premise, minor premise, and conclusion), are to be understood and applied as the joint construction of speakers and their audiences.[17]

d. All general statements are probabilities rather than certainties. Use the word "some" or an equivalent qualifying term in all-inclusive statements. Avoid unqualified assertions like those applied above to cigarette smoking. Avoid sweeping statements such as "Americans are democratic." The implication here that all Americans are believers in democracy is obviously invalid. There are at least some who oppose democracy.

e. Thorough testing of the premises and conclusions of all examples usually reveals obvious statements that need full proof and much revision. Use evidence and arguments from causation, analogy, and generalization from specific cases to verify each proposition.

f. All facts need to be verified and all terms explained and defined.

g. All of the above are guidelines for thinking and planning; you will seldom use formal syllogisms in your actual speeches.

Removing Audience Inhibitions and Applying Refutation

All argumentative speaking is both constructive and refutatory. All logical positions and conclusions are comparisons on a continuum from valid to invalid. Refutation is the process of producing arguments and evidence that substantiate your own statements. If you are the sole speaker, you are to understand such possible undeclared arguments and to remove the inhibitions that an audience may have to your ideas and conclusions. In a question period you may also reply to arguments you have heard. See also the next chapter for psychological factors in persuasion. Here are a few suggestions for your refutatory methods:

1. Before you begin your argument or your reply to another's, arm yourself on the subject.
2. In your own speech or in your reply to another's, begin with a clear statement of the opposing position. Represent fairly and fully what an alternative position and argument have been—or would be if expressed.
3. Express your refutational position clearly and fairly without pugnacity or dogmatism.

---

[17]Cf. Delia, *op. cit.,* p. 147: "The enthymeme constitutes the substance of persuasion because it builds directly upon universal psychological processes."

4. Test a rival argument, whether expressed or not, by examination of its underlying assumptions, its hasty generalizations, its weak analogies, its false causal relations.

Conducting a Debate

To ensure that both sides of an argumentative discourse are given, a debate may be presented.[18] One speaker or more on each side speaks. Debating is thus persuasion by argument conducted under strict parliamentary rules, as is done in legislative, courtroom, or other situations conforming to law. The rules in theory at least ensure equal treatment of both sides of an issue. This is the procedure of democratic government.

Discussion and debate, as we explained in Chapter Nineteen, are complementary. Discussion implies analysis and objective review of arguments and evidence. Debate emerges when special arguments at any stage indicate the temporary abandonment of cooperative reflection. Discussion is not to be dismissed as impracticable; we should use it as much as we can. Debate, however, is justified in certain conditions. When well-grounded convictions prevail, democratic action requires that the various positions be argued with votes and action to follow. But the minority vote is not trampled on. Debate, properly handled, contains the elements of good discussion. "The Advocates," a weekly program produced for educational television in 1970, is an excellent example.

What is the relation of debate to argumentative speaking? In debate (1) time limits are observed, (2) the argument is under parliamentary rules, (3) each side has an equal number of speakers and an equal amount of time, (4) the subject is framed in resolution form, (5) an equal amount of time is given to each side for rebuttal, and (6) a vote is taken at the end to decide the merits of the question.[19]

Let us assume that you are to take part in a debate—to argue according to specific rules. What are the rules and regulations of formal debates?

Time limits are very important. Intercollegiate debates, for example, usually last one hour. During this time, according to the conventional plan, each of the four speakers speaks twice. Each speaker makes a constructive speech ten minutes long, and each is allowed five minutes for rebuttal to ensure review of the arguments presented. In rebuttal the order is usually first negative, first affirmative, second negative, second affirmative.

For classroom debates the number of speakers and time limits may be shortened. Four speakers may each have seven and three minutes. If two speakers only make up the debate, each may have a total of fifteen, ten and five minutes. The parliamentary rules guarantee to the two sides equal

---

[18] See Chapter Nineteen, "Discussional Communication."
[19] See Douglas Ehninger, "Decision by Debate: A Re-examination," *Quarterly Journal of Speech,* 45:282–287, 1959; Douglas Ehninger and Wayne Brockriede, *Decision by Debate,* Dodd Mead, New York & Toronto, 1963, chaps. 19–21.

protection and opportunity. The affirmative opens and closes the debate; the negative speaks first in rebuttal, even though in a two-speaker program, he has just completed his first speech.

The purpose of debating is to arrive at and record a decision. In student debates, undertaken for learning purposes, a critic-judge decides in favor of the team that does the most effective debating. A distinction is thus made between debating in realistic life situations and debating by students who are trying out logical techniques in persuasion.

As a student of communication, you will work under the close supervision of your instructor. With your fellow speakers, select a topic that is of interest to you and word it carefully. Prepare or secure a list of references on your topic, and take careful notes on the material you read. Develop your argument with constant reference to the logical techniques outlined above. Draw up a tentative brief and submit it to your instructor or adviser for criticism. Revise this brief repeatedly as your command of your material develops.

In preliminary sessions with your teammates (unless you are the sole speaker for your side) report to one another on your readings, analyze the problems, and frame the issues. Decide upon your team case—the series of propositions that you want the judges and the audiences to accept in your argument. For example, the case for an affirmative proposition of policy might follow closely the stock issue propositions.

First Affirmative
- I. The present situation is unsatisfactory.
- II. Defects are inherent in the present system. (These two contentions prove the contention of the second affirmative that the proposition advocated is necessary.)

Second Affirmative
- I. The proposal will remedy these defects.
- II. It is a practicable proposal.
- III. It is preferable to other remedies. (These three contentions allegedly prove the advantages and practicality of the proposal.)

For the negative, the case might be exactly reverse:

CASE A
First Negative
- I. The present situation is satisfactory.
- II. The alleged defects can be corrected without destroying the present policy.

Second Negative
- III. The proposal will be detrimental.
- IV. The proposal is impracticable.

The negative may vary these cases by some such plan as the following:

CASE B
First Negative
I. The proposal is impracticable.
II. The proposal is detrimental.

Second Negative
III. The proposal is not needed.

CASE C
First Negative
I. The plan is unworkable.
II. The plan is detrimental.

Second Negative
III. A better plan is proposed.

Other choices of case are also open to the negative. The case for a proposition of fact resolves itself into a series of statements that usually reflect (1) causes and results or (2) classification of the arguments or evidence.

Write your debate speech as a means of achieving effective condensation, clarity, and persuasiveness. But leave your written speech at home. Good debating must be extempore.

The outline above, we agree, is oversimplified and mechanical. We are merely suggesting some orderly way to get at the essential problem and develop it fairly and cooperatively with your colleague.

Judging Debate

How good or bad is a given debate? What standards shall we apply? One method of judging is to get audience response. If most of the hearers vote for your position either by show of hands or by ballot, you have succeeded. But what should be the basis for judgment beyond merely "I like you" or "I like your argument and delivery"?

The critic-judge and you as listener-observer or member of the audience usually base an evaluation on the following: (1) skill in defining and analyzing the subject (selecting the proper issues), (2) skill in the use of evidence, (3) skill in the use of inference, (4) excellence in organization, (5) skill in audience adaptation, including the use of persuasive techniques (see also next chapter), (6) skill in refutation (to be noted especially in the second or rebuttal speech), (7) effective language, (8) effective delivery, and (9) general effectiveness. These items overlap; they do not have equal weight, and not all are to be strongly noted in each given speech. But they do cover quite thoroughly the field of criticism.

Critic-judges use them or similar criteria for their decisions in the learning situations, "on the merits of the debate."

To measure a debate in a life situation, opportunities for the audience to vote on the merits of the question itself are provided. These votes on a shift-of-opinion ballot record audience attitudes on the question before the debate begins and a second vote afterward to note whether a shift takes place from favorable to neutral or opposed, or in the reverse direction.[20]

Projects and Problems

PROJECT 1: Effectiveness in argumentative speaking.
Purpose of this assignment: To demonstrate the effective use of analysis, organization, evidence, argument, refutation, and delivery in a five-minute speech.
Procedure: Each member will select and limit his topic for a five-minute argumentative speech. Prepare and present to the instructor a brief to accompany your oral argument. (See Chapter Eleven on "Organization.") In the presentation, define terms and state the issues (make this introduction not more than one minute long); develop a point or two with accompanying evidence and inference; conclude with a summary and a brief appeal for audience acceptance of your thesis or proposition.

PROJECT 2: Individual debate.
Purpose of this assignment: To give class members some information about the conduct of a debate and to provide experiences in this type of speech.
Procedure: The class will select and word an important local or regional topic for debate. Assign to each member the presentation of the affirmative or negative side. Attempt to give each his choice of sides. Divide the time equally; for example, allow the affirmative seven minutes each for the constructive speech, the negative ten minutes each, and the affirmative three minutes for the rebuttal.

PROJECT 3: Two-speaker team debate. If more convenient for the instructor and class, a two-speaker team can be organized for each side. Each debater should prepare and present to the instructor a brief of his constructive argument. The class and instructor will comment briefly on each debater. The following are possible topics for debate for Projects 1, 2, or 3 above. Each may be rephrased by the group to make the issue more concrete.

a. Farm price supports should be discontinued.
b. The United States should withdraw all military forces from the European continent, including West Germany.
c. The dissemination of birth control information should be legalized.

---

[20] See Chapter Seventeen, "Measures of Effectiveness."

d. Students who protest with violence at my university should be immediately expelled.
e. The United States and Russia should adopt a joint program for prohibiting the worldwide proliferation of hydrogen bombs.
f. College and university grades should be abolished—except for "pass" and "fail."
g. The federal government should regulate all interstate trucking rates.

References

Anderson, Richard C., and David P. Ausubel, *Readings in the Psychology of Cognition.* New York: Holt, Rinehart and Winston, Inc., 1966.

Brembeck, W. L., and W. S. Howell, *Persuasion.* Englewood Cliffs, N.J.: Prentice-Hall, Inc., 1952. Chapters XI and XII.

Campbell, George, *The Philosophy of Rhetoric,* ed. Lloyd Bitzer. Carbondale, Ill.: Southern Illinois University Press, 1963.

Cronkhite, Gary, *Persuasion: Speech and Behavioral Change.* Indianapolis and New York: The Bobbs-Merrill Company, 1969.

Crowell, Laura, *Discussion: Method of Democracy.* New York: Scott Foresman and Co., 1963.

Dewey, John, *How We Think.* Boston: D. C. Heath, 1933.

Ehninger, Douglas, and Wayne Brockriede, *Decision by Debate.* New York: Dodd, Mead and Company, Inc., 1963.

Ellingsworth, Huber, and Theodore Clevenger, *Speech and Social Action.* Englewood Cliffs, N.J.: Prentice-Hall, Inc., 1967.

Glazer, Edward M., *An Experiment in the Development of Critical Thinking.* New York: Teachers College Press, Columbia University, 1951.

Gulley, Halbert E., *Discussion, Conference, and Group Process.* New York: Holt, Rinehart and Winston, Inc., 1968.

McBurney, James H., and Glen E. Mills, *Argumentation and Debate,* 2nd ed. New York: The Macmillan Company, 1964.

McCroskey, James C., *An Introduction to Rhetorical Communication.* Englewood Cliffs, N.J.: Prentice-Hall, Inc., 1968.

Mill, John Stuart, *Philosophy of Scientific Method,* ed. Ernest Nagel. New York: Hafner Publishing Company, 1950. Pp. 211–233.

———, *A System of Logic,* 8th ed. London: Longmans, Green, Reader and Dyer, 1872. 2 volumes.

Miller, Gerald R., *Speech Communication, A Behavioral Approach.* Indianapolis: The Bobbs-Merrill Company, 1966.

———, and Thomas R. Nilsen (eds.), *Perspectives on Argumentation.* Chicago: Scott, Foresman and Co., 1966.

Mills, Glen, *Reason in Controversy,* 2nd ed. Boston: Allyn Bacon and Co., 1968.

Minnick, Wayne, *The Art of Persuasion.* Boston: Houghton-Mifflin Co., 1968.

Toulmin, S. E., *The Uses of Argument.* New York: Cambridge University Press, 1968.

UPI.

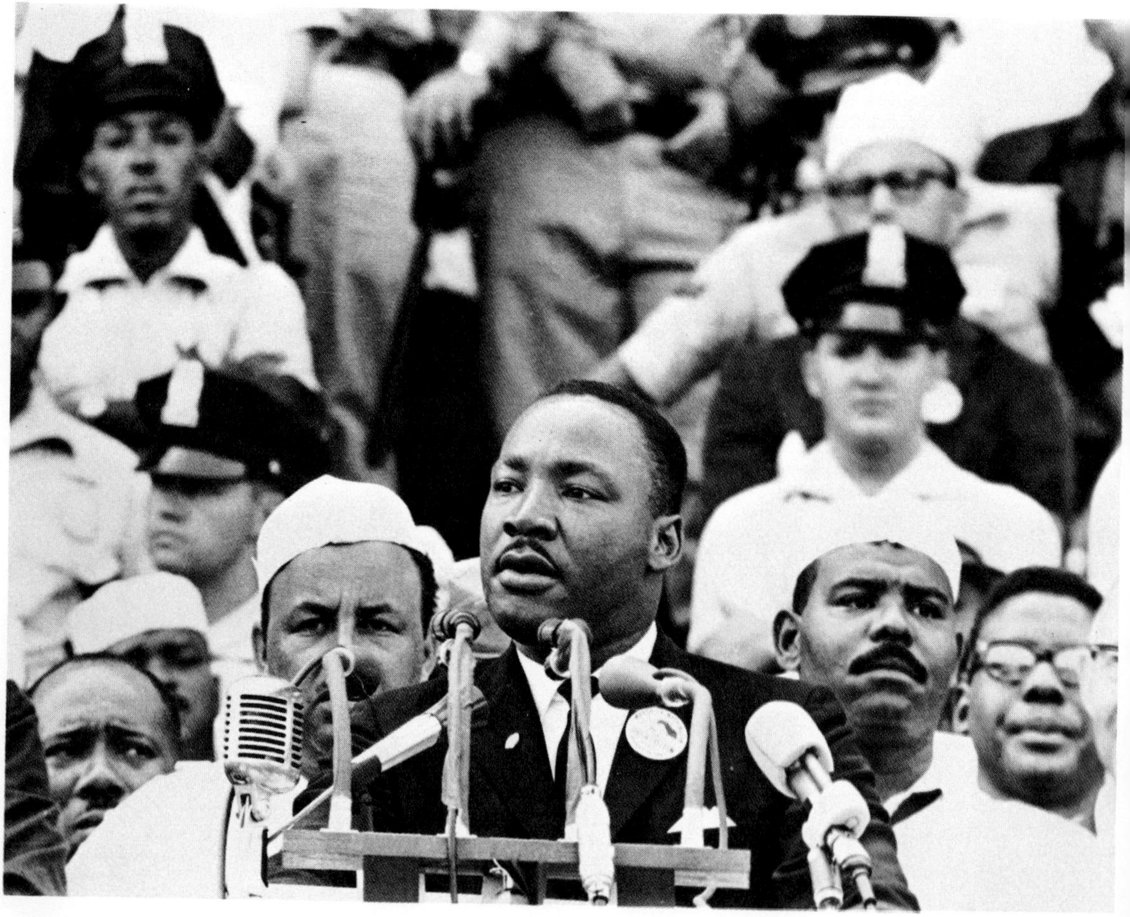

persuasion: affective domain

In the last chapter we were concerned with persuasive speaking as a cognitive process. Here we concern ourselves with affective and motor processes. We give them independent consideration because they can be best understood in their roles as variables in communication behavior if we take the time and space to give each of them the consideration they require by students of communication. Classical rhetoricians recognized the conceptual value of differentiating *ethos* and *pathos* from logos. Modern psychologists also have found distinctions between cognitive, affective, and motor response behavior to be concepts of convenience. Information and attitude development and change may be identified as instrumental goals and changes in overt behavior as consummatory goals or purposes in persuasive communication.

Emotive Behavior

Ogden and Richards make use of a concept of *emotive language* which directs and arouses to action in one's self and others. This language function is differentiated from a referential function which is manipulative and reflective. The consideration of thought, stock issues in argument, and learning theory all make use of participants' concepts of need. Needs and concepts of need have a direct relationship to human motives as explanations of behavior. Man's value systems, real and choice-selected, are also related to his motives. Attitudes are a form of human response behavior different from knowledge or comprehension and can be identified with motives and value systems. An emotive approach to persuasion can thus be considered a modern and reliable as well as a traditional approach to communication.

It is a mistake to assume that logical and emotive elements are mutually exclusive, that they are opposite ends of a single continuum, or that a speech usually consists of only one of these elements, although it may be preponderately one or the other. We can illustrate ways in which these two elements are interrelated by indicating them on two continua which cross at some point, as illustrated in the following diagrams. Number 1 on each continuum indicates the near absence of that factor, and number 7 indicates its presence in the highest degree.

In the diagrams, one line represents logic and the other emotive processes. **323**

Speech I, therefore, is weak: Although it is strong in value, it is weak in logic, since the point of intersection comes at 7 on the emotive continuum and 1 on the logic continuum. Speech II is a relatively useless speech: it is weak both in emotive appeal (1) and in logic (1). Speech III is strong in logic (7), but highly deficient in emotive persuasion (1)—an ineffectual speech. Speech IV is best in that both the logical (7) and emotive values (7) are strong. Of course these continua could cross at other points.

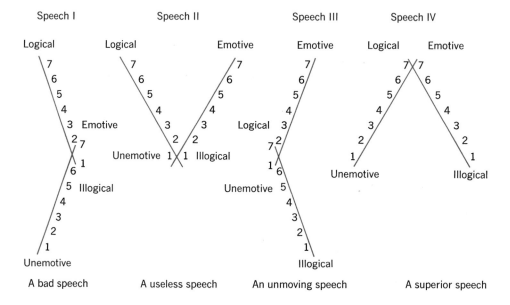

In speech making, as in our daily lives, we must establish a balance between logic and value judgments. John Dewey has given us an excellent description of the place of emotion in our lives.

The conclusion is not that the emotional, passionate phase of action can be or should be eliminated in behalf of a bloodless reason. More "passions," not fewer, is the answer. To check the influence of hate there must be sympathy, while to rationalize sympathy there are needed emotions of curiosity, caution, respect for the freedom of others—dispositions which evoke objects which balance those called up by sympathy, and prevent its degeneration into maudlin sentiment and meddling interference. Rationality, once more, is not a force to evoke against impulse and habit. It is the attainment of a working harmony among diverse desires.[1]

Most of us are aware of the value in our lives of motives which stabilize and help our society to maintain our value systems. It is important to realize

[1]John Dewey, *Human Nature and Conduct,* Holt, New York, 1922, pp. 195–196.

that man's values in any culture tend to be both stable and variable. Change occurs, but the basic patterns of cultures tend to change slowly. Some needs are subject to cyclical changes; at a satiation stage they are lower in the operational hierarchy of motives than at a need stage. But what has this to do, we ask, with our use of emotional appeals? The words "emotion" and "motivated" come from the same root as the word "motion." An emotionally stimulated response is an energized response, at least for all the emotions associated with approach to or withdrawal from the stimulus object. When the organism responds emotionally, glycogen is released from the liver into the blood stream. The energy provided in this way prepares the individual for action. It is therefore no mere accident that the persuasive speaker has found the appeal to the emotions as a practical device for stirring the listener to action. It is only when the listener's emotions have been conditioned to his logical-thinking behavior that the logical appeal results in action. Thus even the use of logic to produce action is dependent ultimately upon the emotions.

Evaluation of Persuasive Appeals

We have already pointed out the importance to intelligent listening of evaluation of emotive appeals. From the point of view of validity, there are three types of persuasive appeals: valid, marginal, and bogus.

■   1. *Valid appeals.* Valid appeals to action are directed toward worthy motives which have a reasonable prospect of satisfaction in the action proposed. Few satisfactions are absolutely certain, but only those which are free from reasonable doubt should be proposed. An example of such an appeal was the request by President Nixon for government budget cuts in the interest of controlling inflation.

■   2. *Marginal appeals.* Marginal appeals are proposals in which the satisfactions suggested may be real but are of minor or incidental value. These short-term appeals to action may be accepted as appropriate for needs to which they appeal; they can scarcely be approved for use in connection with the satisfaction of more permanent and important needs. For example, "Buy this insurance policy and receive a new billfold free."

■   3. *Bogus appeals.* Appeals which foment hasty and ill-considered action or which offer false and improbable claims of satisfaction through the action proposed are bogus. They include appeals which frustrate the higher codes of society by arousing the baser emotions. Most of the abuses of persuasion belong to this class. Patent-medicine advertisements are an example: "Restore your health with a bottle of Zixolon."

Establishing Goodwill and Credibility

The goodwill of the speaker toward the audience is essential in persuasive speaking. But it is not sufficient that the speaker be a person of goodwill;

he must communicate his attitude to his audience. He must avoid inconsistency of expression that would make him seem incredible.[2] The discussion of the speaker's personality in Chapter Four will be helpful in connection with persuasive speaking. Here we shall discuss some of the habits which a speaker should cultivate for effective persuasive speaking.

■   1. *Know your audience; plan and word your appeals to take into account the audience's known experience, interests, value systems, and attitudes.* Recognition of the right to disagree must be the basis of any attempt at persuasion, for the persuaded person must be won, not pushed, to agreement. Recognition of this right is part of your respect for your listeners and their ability to make a wise decision. Even though you will disagree with them on major issues—if you did not you would not be making a persuasive speech—you must yield to their views in some respects. Sometimes you can do this by praising what the listener approves or condemning what he hates. But if you cannot do these things in honest respect, you should not do them at all.

■   2. *Demonstrate your mastery of your subject.* Evidence of your knowledge of and ability to handle the materials of your subject—to interpret soundly and organize well—will influence your audience strongly.[3] When talking to an educated and capable audience it is helpful to give evidence that you know different sides of an argument.[4] There may be two sides, you know, or even three or more. You must be fair and just even to those arguments you reject. If you can demonstrate your ability to solve problems and resolve conflicts through unusual insight, you will win your audience's respect and admiration. Avoid dogmatism, often a defensive attitude suggesting weakness. Evidence that your experience has contributed successfully to the needs of others in similar situations is highly persuasive.

■   3. *Give evidence that you are a worthy communicator.* The record of your achievements, if it is well presented, will add to your prestige. It is difficult to prove your ability to your audience tactfully, but if you solicit the support of others, you must indicate to them that you are a credible person. Courage to fight for your convictions, the ability to meet tests, and evidence of past successes are evidence to your audience of your capacity for future successes. Learn to use your record without a vulgar parade of egotism and conceit.

■   4. *Your character will influence your audience.* In the opinion of your listeners, character means a record of conformity with the virtues they recognize. As a persuasive speaker, you must identify your character with the just and virtuous, with deeds of altruism and magnanimity. Where character is in doubt, other qualities of personality are useless.

---

[2] See Carl I. Hovland et al., *Communication and Persuasion*, Yale University Press, New Haven, Conn., 1953, chap. 2.
[3] See Carl I. Hovland et al., *The Order of Presentation in Persuasion*, Yale University Press, New Haven, Conn., 1953.
[4] See Hovland et al., *Communication and Persuasion*.

Certain personality traits can be depended upon to contribute to persuasive speaking. Modesty, restraint, understatement, and temperate demands are to be preferred to egotism, lack of control, exaggeration, and unreasonableness. Develop the ability to adapt your moods to listeners—to be earnest, to be good-humored, to see any humor in the situation, to be forgiving, or to be uncompromising concerning certain ideals.[5]

Goodwill toward your subject may be created by showing its altruistic nature, the personal benefits it will provide to your listeners, and its practical advantages. Although the other sides of the argument must be taken into account and duly eliminated, they should not be heavily stressed. Keep the true strength of the proposal in focus by emphasizing its benefits. Lead your listeners to the desired conclusion by placing the necessary information in their hands and encouraging them to make their own decisions.

Getting Attention and Creating Interest

William James's theory of persuasion was that what holds attention determines action.[6] When this theory is true, your ability to hold your audience's attention may influence your success as a persuasive speaker. You must keep the attention of the audience focused upon the job to be done. The relevance of the attention devices to the critical issues and information under consideration has long been known to be important in communication. This variable has recently been reemphasized by both Norman and Crane. Man's attention span is limited, because attention involves tension which must be relaxed occasionally. If the speaker does not give his listeners opportunity to relax occasionally, they may cease to follow him. The speaker must make it easy for his audience to be attentive.

■ 1. *Show the significance of the proposal.* Presenting an idea as something vital to the listener is the most important way of maintaining interest. The listener must be well motivated to be attentive. Your proposal must appeal to important wants, desires, and needs. By focusing your audience's attention upon the personal benefits to be derived from your proposal, you can arouse responses of anticipation, acceptance, and approach—responses which are only a short step from action.

■ 2. *Make use of conflict resolution concerning your proposal.* When man's values and goals are threatened, his energies are renewed. To direct this energy through your persuasive speech, show the dangers which threaten the listeners' understanding, ideals, and standards if they do not accept your proposal. If members of your audience feel that their cherished ideals are threatened and that your proposal will protect those ideals, they are more apt to identify themselves with you as a person and endorse your proposal.

Behavioral science research in the field of persuasion has centered heavily

---

[5] *Ibid.,* chap. 6.
[6] See William James, *Psychology, Briefer Course,* Holt, New York, 1900, p. 448.

during the last few years on several variations of balance, dissonance, and conflict resolution. The work of Festinger has given strong impetus to this program. Feldman, Fishbein, and Insko have all critically reviewed this work. In general, we can accept the idea that persuasive impact can be facilitated by message systems which arouse dissonance over the inconsistencies in the subject of concern, and proceed to relieve this dissonance by encouraging the acceptance, approval of, and action toward a solution which relieves the disturbing inconsistency.[7]

■   3. *Shock the listener.* If the listener accepts his goals as a matter of course, he may need to be jolted out of his complacency. Pearl Harbor was a shock which awakened many Americans to the need to fight to preserve our way of life. Many drivers are more careful after witnessing an automobile wreck. The introduction of surprise has in it elements of the shock response. Use this technique carefully in order to avoid creating resentment which will damage your cause rather than help it.

■   4. *Arouse curiosity.* It is human nature to want to complete an attractive or habitual pattern once the act has been begun. Arouse the curiosity of the listener by telling a story which has a conclusion that is pertinent to your cause. Expound causes which will arouse the audience's curiosity concerning the effects. An unexpected pause attracts attention. When you use these techniques, be sure to show the significance for your speech of the materials in which you use them.

■   5. *Make your speech easy to follow.* A proposal which puts a strain on attention will meet with resistance. Make attention easy for your listeners by appealing to the various senses—visual, auditory, kinetic, olfactory, gustatory, and others. Organize your proposal so that main points are arranged in a natural and easy-to-remember sequence. Repeat and restate your ideas so that there can be no chance of confusion. Provide adequate transition from point to point.

■   6. *Use variety.* A speech in which the new is balanced with the familiar is more interesting than a speech in which all the materials are completely new or completely familiar. Movement which appeals to the eye; variations in rate, loudness, pitch, and quality of voice which appeal to the ear; and changes in sentence length and form are methods of achieving variety which we have discussed in earlier chapters.

Attention can be contagious and cumulative in an audience, and it can be increased by the deliberate use of the methods we have suggested. But beware of attention-getting devices which call attention to themselves; "ham" acting is not good speaking. To acquire skill in the use of attention-getting techniques requires a finesse not ordinarily achieved without much practice.

---

[7]See Chapter Six for a further discussion of cognitive dissonance and its operation in behavior change.

Stimulating Favorable Feelings and Emotional Energies

■   1.   *Appeal to dominant motives, attitudes, and values.* Good persuasion is in effect the successful appeal to motives. This appeal must achieve a close harmony between the proposal and the dominant motives of the listener. Motives are usually complex and variable. Behavior is organized through an arrangement of the motives of the moment in a hierarchy of values; motives dominant at one time may play a subordinate role in influencing behavior at a later time. Different persons do the same thing for different reasons.

Many attempts have been made to catalogue human motives, and the various classifications differ greatly with regard to the nature and value of the motives. We do not maintain that the following classification is complete. The student may add to this list as his knowledge and experience warrant. The four different types of motives, which overlap in some degree, are (a) the biological motives, (b) the ego motives, (c) the social motives, (d) the motives of habit.[8]

Many of the *biological* motives may be called "hungers." They are cyclical in nature, and their force depends upon the state of the organism. The desire for food and shelter is basic to life. Our efforts to acquire and retain these necessities consume much of our energy. The particular forms in which we satisfy these motives are largely matters of habit. These are among the strongest of the motives. Closely related to them is the desire to avoid danger. The sex drive, also a strong motive, may or may not, depending upon the person, be identical with the desire to care for and rear children. The desire for freedom from restraints on action appears to be of biological origin: The newborn babe struggles when held too tightly; the adult seeks personal freedom of belief and action. There appears also to be a motive for ease and economy of action. We strive to release emotional tension in the exercise of pleasant sensations and emotions, and we attempt to avoid unpleasant sensations and emotions. Our biological motives are stronger and more primitive than most others. They are commonly considered the baser motives to action.

Desires for self-respect, pride, and dignity can be classified as *ego* motives. Professor Wendell White has called these motives the desire for a feeling of personal worth.[9] Men commonly seek to excel, to gain power, to control, to create, to meet the challenges to their abilities. Property is one of the ways in which this motive finds expression at an early age. The care of one's appearance is no doubt a function of the desire for self-respect. The attainment of self-images and ideals is a process involving great struggle. These motives are also subject to modification by experience and learning,

[8]Hovland et al., *Communication and Persuasion*, chaps. 3 and 4.
[9]Wendell White, *The Psychology of Dealing with People*, The Macmillan Company, New York, 1936, chap. 4.

and they constitute a type of motive which combines the biological and the social.

Social motives are to a great extent the product of experience. They may be largely habitual. They appear in the desire for conformity, favorable attention, and status. We like to be approved by our associates. As a result, we are stimulated by praise and reproof, by social sanctions and taboos. The self may be sublimated to serve the social virtues of trust, integrity, loyalty, precedent, fair play, good sportsmanship, and justice. Someone has said that everyone wants an audience, and the kind of person he is reflects the type of audience he wants. These drives tend to be more altruistic and unselfish than some others. For this reason they are sometimes called the "higher motives." They offer long-term appeals to enlightened selfishness.

The motives of *habit* include the desire for maintenance of tastes, interests and preferences, work habits, and intellectual and emotional habits. They also involve the search for new experience, adventure, and growth as well as the preferences for the traditional, the familiar, and the maintenance of the status quo. We often retain for years habits that have ceased to serve their original purpose.

Word the main ideas of your persuasive speech so that they contain appeals to the dominant motives of your audience, and use supporting materials which show the relationships of the proposition to the motive.

■   2.   *Meet objections.* Persuasion cannot be expected to work where action is inhibited by conflicting drives. The causes of objection to action may be met by strengthening favorable drives and reducing the strength of competing drives. Competing drives can be eliminated by showing that they do not apply to the proposal or that they may be satisfied in other ways. If the drives that inhibit action are successfully removed, a proposal for action which stimulates a dominant motive develops and releases the energy necessary for action.

■   3.   *Adapt to the situation.* Make use of the total situational context to support action. Rhetoric was originally defined as "finding within a subject the available means of persuasion." If we substitute the word "situation" for "subject" we have a good definition of this theory. We must recognize that people respond to many stimuli in every situation. Some of these factors are their memory of the past of the stimuli; their hopes, interests, desires, or wishes for the future; the resources for responses from which a choice is made; the environment in which a stimulus is presented, including the people present; their cultural patterns, including conventions, customs, and mores; the degree of their frustration or conflict of motives; their attachments to particular stimuli; their habits; their transient and more permanent emotional conditions; the depth of their understandings; and many other factors. Although there is no inevitable stimulus for action for most people, the greater the stimulus conforms to all potential conditions for action the greater the probability of response.

Conciliation and Restraint of Action

Conciliation as a type of persuasion differs from persuasion as we have described it in this chapter in that, instead of stimulating interest, conviction, or action, conciliation seeks to create disinterest, doubt, and the cessation of action. Many of the principles we have discussed apply in reverse to conciliation, because the purpose of conciliation is to stop action, to create doubt, and to diminish opposition. To achieve these things, the speaker seeks to reduce the intensity of motivation. Persuasion cannot be expected to work where action is inhibited by conflicting drives. The causes of objection to action may be met by strengthening favorable drives and reducing the strength of competing drives. Competing drives may be eliminated by showing that they do not apply to the proposal or that they may be satisfied in other ways. If the drives that inhibit action are successfully removed, a proposal for action which stimulates a dominant motive develops and releases the energy necessary for action.

As a conciliatory speaker, you must create goodwill. An objective and impersonal manner provides little opportunity for positive emotional response. Keep the attention of the listener pleasantly distracted and focused on inaction. Delay action by appealing to motives that conflict with those which are aroused. Pit motive against motive to create doubt, uncertainty, frustration. Concede on some issues as an appeal to pride and tolerance, and emphasize pertinent grounds of agreement. Show that similar ventures were frustrating and unsuccessful. Reduce tension and strain by finding harmless opportunities for action. Otherwise the repression of active drives may intensify them, making their release more explosive. Make immediate action difficult, and initiate minor patterns of action inconsistent with the dominant trend. Break up larger groups into smaller ones. Show better ways of satisfying the motives for action, and appeal to the higher and more critical motives.

Present a Practical Plan of Action

The persuasive speech derives much of its force from the presentation of a practical plan of action. The plan may be the deciding element in persuasion when powerful motives and drives are closely associated with the proposal in the mind of the audience but lack direction and organization. Emphasis on the benefits to be derived from carrying out the plan serves to strengthen the relationship between desire and method.

We have considered persuasion as techniques of motivation added to the evidence and logic of argumentation in appeals to action. The persuasive speaker should carefully consider his appeals to motives to assure himself of their validity. The techniques of persuasion involve such processes as creating goodwill, getting attention and maintaining interest, and showing the relationship of the proposal to the dominant motives of listeners. Although most persuasion is designed to release the energies in action, occasionally the situation calls for inhibition or cessation of action. Under these circumstances appeals are directed to conciliation and demotivation.

Projects and Problems

PROJECT 1: Find five advertisements in a newspaper or magazine which are based on theories of persuasion. Explain each in class.

PROJECT 2: What persuasive strategies can you find in a campaign or action speech of a candidate for office or a public official? Explain these strategies in class.

PROJECT 3: Development of interest in the subject.
Purposes of this assignment: (a) to develop knowledge of the techniques of making speeches interesting; (b) to develop skill in arousing interest. *Procedure:* Select a topic, word a central idea for an informative speech, and outline two or three main points to support the central idea. Develop your main points by using material which applies one or more of the principles for making material interesting (see the section "Getting Attention and Creating Interest" in this chapter). Plan the appropriate methods of delivery for making your speech interesting.
Methods of creating interest: Create interest through selection and development of materials. Show how your subject and materials are important to your audience. Put your material in a narrative form which arouses curiosity about the outcome of the conflicts. Use illustrations in which you can draw vivid word pictures for your audience. Relate the unknown to the known by sharp comparison and contrast. Tell your listeners just enough to suggest the idea with the implication that they can reach the proper conclusion without being told. Use language forms which express feelings and emotions as well as intellectual ideas. Find a humorous side to your material. Keep the development of the main idea obviously moving forward.

Use methods of delivery for creating interest. Be alert, active, and direct. Dramatize, illustrate, visualize with or without use of blackboard and chalk, and be easily understood. Use a voice which responds to the specific moods of your material. Show your own interest in the ideas you are presenting.

Make use of general principles for the development of interest. No topic is inherently dull; speakers sometimes do not take the trouble to help themselves. Never use an interest technique which calls more attention to itself than to the idea to be developed. Audiences may pay attention to sheer noise, anticlimax, highly personal reference in public speeches, unfairness, discourtesy, and other evidence of bad taste or manners, but they will also be irritated. Do not be obvious, trivial, repetitious, or ponderous, and do not go into endless detail.

PROJECT 4: The persuasive appeal to action.
Purposes of this assignment: The persuasive appeal to action adds the use of emotional appeal to evidence and logic. Although illogical appeals to

action are sometimes made in argument, there is no justification for use of illogical emotional appeals or for the assumption that emotional appeals must be illogical. Emotional appeals add interest to argument and stir up and release the energies necessary for action on propositions of policy. The student not only should know the technique of appeal to the basic human drives and emotions, but should also learn to apply principles for creating interest, the devices for achieving emphasis in argument, and the procedures for using language persuasively. Careful selection of a few persuasive techniques adapted to particular listeners or readers is a better method of persuasion than the attempt to use a large number of such devices in a particular argument.

Subjects for this speech:

Build a fallout shelter	Drive carefully
Buy government bonds	Become a church member
Join a hobby club	Buy a school paper
Sign this petition	Form new study habits
Have an annual health examination	Take a course in psychology
Read this book	Make government service a
Keep a budget	lifework
Buy Christmas seals	Contribute to the Red Cross
Keep to the campus walks	Write your letters with
Learn to swim	Scripture ink

PROJECT 5:   The speech to restrain action.

Purposes of this project: The speech designed to inhibit or restrain action operates on principles which are quite dissimilar to those which arouse action. It seeks to quiet emotion, create doubt, distract attention, arouse awareness of difficulty, release energies through other channels than that already proposed, and postpone action. It is essentially the refutation of the emotional appeal. Work on these techniques in a three-minute speech.

Subjects for this assignment:

Break the smoking habit	Don't take advantage of the
Beware of drugs	little fellow
Learn to control your temper	Don't walk on the grass
Don't spend money foolishly	Curb a licentious tongue
Don't speed	Stop drifting
Some don'ts of human relationships	

PROJECT 6:   The speech of conciliation.

Purposes of this project: The techniques of conciliation in argument are aimed at the attention of the antagonistic listener or reader or the person who has a closed mind on the subject. In the development of the idea and its support, these techniques function not as a substitute for evidence and reasoning, but as a method of handling evidence for a particular type of purpose.

Subjects for this assignment:

Some demands of college students are unrealistic.

Demonstrations are to be condemned as a method of persuasion.

Southerners are responsible for the plight of the Negro in the South.

Racial prejudice against minority groups is to be deplored.

Compulsory teacher oaths will not produce better democracy.

The rights of labor must be preserved.

Modern society demands some governmental control of business.

Civil liberties do not excuse citizens from social responsibilities.

Conscientious objectors are not necessarily cowards.

American democracy can be improved.

Religious freedom does not include the right to prevent compulsory vaccination of children.

War crimes cannot be punished as ordinary crimes are punished within a nation.

Progressive education is not a panacea.

New ideas and practices do not always mean progress.

The various Christian denominations have much to learn from one another.

Someone in a position of authority over you has emphatically denied a request. You do not consider the case closed. How would you get a hearing?

A friend takes offense because of some imagined insult. Straighten out the misunderstanding.

You are accused unfairly and maliciously of an act you did not commit. How will you square yourself?

As a committee chairman, you are to present a request to a group in which there is tension and irritation toward the proposal. How will you get a favorable hearing?

Facts and principles you should know to succeed in this assignment: Some of the principal means of arguing in this situation are indicated by the following rules. First, take special care to present your argument in an objective and impersonal manner. Argue calmly, frankly, and simply. These are the facts and this is the way to reason about them to reach this conclusion. Personal interests and wishes are unimportant. Limit your objectives. It is a mistake to try to accomplish too much at once. If a man's mind is closed, the attempt to yank it open may only result in wedging it more tightly shut. Show understanding of and respect for opposite opinions and the persons who hold them. There is no place in this type of argument for blame or censure. Be calm, patient, friendly, and agreeable. Make use of humor if you can without being flippant. Finally, find an indirect way to present your argument. Use arguments which suggest rather than state your conclusion directly. Show personal benefits for your listener which he may have overlooked. Select your subject or situation and proceed to prepare your material. Know your procedure thoroughly and present the speech in a fair and effective manner.

References

Arnold, Magda B. (ed.), *The Nature of Emotion.* Baltimore: Penguin Books, 1968.

Bettinghaus, Erwin P., *Persuasive Communication.* New York: Holt, Rinehart and Winston, 1968.

Bindra, Dalbir, and Jane Stewart (eds.), *Motivation*. Baltimore: Penguin Books, 1966.

Brown, J. A. C., *Techniques of Persuasion*. Baltimore: Penguin Books, 1963.

Cofer, Charles N., and Mortimer H. Apley, *Motivation: Theory and Research*. New York: John Wiley & Sons, Inc., 1967.

Crane, Edgar, *Marketing Communication*. New York: John Wiley & Sons, Inc., 1965.

Cronkhite, Gary, *Persuasion, Speech and Behavioral Change*. Indianapolis: The Bobbs-Merrill Company, Inc., 1969.

Dewey, John, *Human Nature and Conduct*. New York: Holt, 1922.

Edelman, Murray, *The Symbolic Uses of Politics*. Urbana, Ill.: University of Illinois Press, 1964.

Feldman, Shel, *Cognitive Consistency*. New York: Academic Press, 1966.

Festinger, Leon, *A Theory of Cognitive Dissonance*. Evanston, Ill.: Row, Peterson and Company, 1957.

Fishbein, Martin (ed.), *Attitude Theory and Research*. New York: John Wiley & Sons, Inc., 1967.

Fotheringham, Wallace C., *Perspectives on Persuasion*. Boston: Allyn and Bacon, 1966.

Hovland, Carl I., et al., *Communication and Persuasion*. New Haven: Yale University Press, 1953.

———, *The Order of Presentation in Persuasion*. New Haven: Yale University Press, 1957.

Insko, Chester A., *Theories of Attitude Change*. New York: Appleton-Century-Crofts, 1967.

Klapp, Orrin E., *Symbolic Leaders*. Chicago: Aldine Publishing Company, 1964.

Langer, Susanne K., *An Essay on Human Feeling*. Baltimore: The Johns Hopkins Press, 1967.

Minnick, Wayne C., *The Art of Persuasion*. Boston: Houghton Mifflin Company, 1968.

Murray, Edward J., *Motivation and Emotion*. Englewood Cliffs, N.J.: Prentice-Hall, Inc., 1964.

Norman, Donald A., *Memory and Attention*. New York: John Wiley & Sons, Inc., 1969.

Ogden, C. K., and I. A. Richards, *The Meaning of Meaning*. New York: Harcourt, Brace and World, Inc., 1923.

Rokeach, Milton, *Belief, Attitudes, and Values*. San Francisco: Jossey-Bass, Inc., Publishers, 1968.

Scheidel, Thomas M., *Persuasive Speaking*. Evanston, Ill.: Scott, Foresman and Co., 1967.

Sherif, Muzafer, and Carolyn W. Sherif, *Reference Groups*. New York: Harper and Row, Publishers, 1964.

Thurstone, L. L., *The Measurement of Values*. Chicago: The University of Chicago Press, 1959.

Vernon, M. D., *Human Motivation*. Cambridge: Cambridge University Press, 1969.

PART NINE

Special Speech Types

James Dickey reading at The Poetry Center of the YM and YWHA in New York City.

Diane Dorr-Dorynek.

oral reading

Oral reading differs from other types of communication activity in some important ways. It may seem comparatively simple. You already have the ideas to be expressed and the language to represent them. You should not let this fact deceive you. To be a good oral reader is something of an art that may not have been mastered even by those who are good silent readers. Because it often depends upon the selection of literature to be read, it is also something of a humane study.

Oral reading is both an act of interpretation and a form of communication. Like the reporter and the editor, the oral reader stands between the sources of his ideas and their destination. It may be used less frequently than some other patterns of communication behavior, but it is nevertheless too important to be taken for granted. You will find many occasions when you need to read aloud. We all read a bit of something we wish to share with a member of the family or friends. Much formal speaking and discussion calls for something to be read, as in teaching or religious services. Resolutions, motions, and the minutes of meetings are often read aloud. Unless you are an old hand at broadcasting, you will probably be expected to read such messages. Rituals and ceremonies often call for such reading.

Oral reading can also be an end in itself, an attempt to enjoy yourself through reading aloud and listening to literature. Remember that the purpose of most art is to give pleasure. For most literature—whether poetry, short stories, or drama—the pleasure can be enhanced through oral interpretation.

The constant study of good literature, returning to a work again and again, results in new insights, new experiences. You will continually get new meanings and, hence, new pleasures. Sharing your insights and enjoyment through oral reading can serve to still further enhance them. In addition, your oral performance can serve as a testing ground for your particular understanding or interpretation. When you read a work aloud, you can discover, in a way that is quite difficult in silent reading, whether your interpretation "works."

Oral reading can also be an important and exciting activity for you because not only does it demand an understanding and appreciation of the work by you, but also because it permits you to *share* that understanding and appreciation with others. It is an interesting and often quite different sort of communication problem than that you face in your other communication. A simple test will quickly demonstrate the importance of such performances for the audience. Test the enjoyment which other students get from a Shakespeare play when they *read* it and when they *hear* it from a skilled reader. Three writers on oral interpretation have made this point another way:

It is one thing to know *about* the horrors of war. It is quite another thing to be a member of a fighting unit. In other words, experiencing an event means personal involvement. One of the functions of literature is to bridge the gap so that we know *about* something *through experiencing* it.[1]

For many kinds of oral reading, one of your important jobs will be to make the material you are interpreting so vivid for an audience that their experience approximates the experience depicted in the work.

A final, but no less important, reason for practice at oral reading is that through working with superior works of literature and rhetoric, you can improve your capacity for communication. Familiarity with these works and practice at using them in oral situations should increase your repertoire of stylistic devices and treatments of various kinds of ideas.

Principles of Oral Reading

■ 1. *Study the meaning of the material you are to read.* You must be constantly aware that oral reading is a form of communication. Basic to effective oral interpretation, to achieve the communication purposes described above, is a sound understanding of your material—of its intellectual and emotional content and its imaginative ways of dealing with its content.

In studying a work which you plan to read to an audience, consider *its purpose* (what it is trying to achieve), *its method* (how it is trying to achieve

[1] Keith Brooks, Eugene Bahn, and L. LaMont Okey, *The Communicative Art of Oral Interpretation,* Allyn and Bacon, Boston, 1967, p. 45.

it), and *your purpose* in using it. There are many cues in a work which can help you to discover its purpose. The title of a work is clearly your first cue, though obviously not an infallible one when considered alone. In many works, you can find the theme stated quite clearly in a phrase or sentence or paragraph near the beginning. Think about the symbolism used by the author. Has he used objects or characters or actions to represent something else—some larger group of objects, characters, or actions or some abstract idea? Is the entire work a symbol, as is an Aesop fable? In Aesop's fables, as in a work such as Hemingway's *Old Man and the Sea,* the symbolism is quite obvious if you think about the matter at all. In many literary works, it is much less obvious and you must be sensitive and imaginative in order to appreciate fully the significance. A fourth means of getting at the purpose of a work is to consider its "attitude." Normally we think only of people having attitudes, but a piece of literature or rhetoric does also, and we discover those attitudes in the same way we discover them in people; we see how the work describes the attitude object, the kinds of language used, the other objects with which this one is compared and contrasted.

In addition to discovering the purpose or purposes of a work you are to read, you must also understand the words and the ways in which they are put together. Study each sentence to find the methods of phrasing which make the meaning clear. Phrasing within the sentence is often—but not always—revealed by punctuation. Consider the differences in meaning of the two ways of punctuating or phrasing the following sentence:

The Captain said the mate was drunk today.
"The Captain," said the mate, "was drunk today."

■   2. *Develop "empathy" for the material and your audience.* "Empathy" is probably one of the most abused terms in the English language; it has been used to indicate a wide variety of phenomena. Yet, almost all of the phenomena for which the term has been used are relevant to oral inter- pretation. One scholar, George Gunkle,[2] has examined the literature on theatre and human behavior and has found, among others, the following referents for the term:

1. Sympathizing with another
2. Intellectually understanding or seeing something as someone else sees it
3. Actually feeling the emotions which another person is feeling
4. Overt motor mimicry
5. Covert motor mimicry
6. The ability to predict what other people will do

---

[2]George Gunkle, "Empathy: Implications for Theatre Research," *Educational Theatre Journal,* 15:15–23, 1963.

Whether or not you choose to call all of these "empathy," all are important for certain kinds of oral interpretation. You must certainly have some understanding and sympathy, in the broad sense of that term, for the author of the work being interpreted and for the characters within the work if there are any. You must understand both the author's point of view and the points of view of the audience for whom you must interpret that author. Though you will probably not go as far as some actors do in "feeling the emotions" of the author or the characters in his work, you must be able to put yourself into their shoes to some extent in order to adequately communicate their attitudes and emotions. Closely related to this is the need which you will often have to mimic, either overtly or covertly, the actions of characters within the works you interpret. Covert mimicry will help you to interpret the work. At times, a bit of overt mimicry will help you to communicate that interpretation more effectively to your audience. In every case, though, you must remain in *control* of your instrument of communication, which is your body and your voice. You should never become "lost" in the work you are interpreting; otherwise you risk a complete breakdown of communication between you and the audience. In other words, do not become like those actors of the so-called "mumble school" who claim to truly feel the role, but whom the audience cannot understand. Oral interpretation, like any other form of speech, should be a communicative act, not solely a personal experience for you as the interpreter.

■   3.   *Read ideas, not words.* If you learned to read by words, rather than by ideas, with careful and distinct—pronunciation—of—each—word, you may now have difficulty communicating ideas from the printed page. Familiarity with meaning, as described above, concentration upon this meaning while reading, and practice should help you to overcome this problem.

■   4.   *Be aware of the differences between silent and oral reading.* Silent reading is often a process of skimming a paragraph or page to get the meaning of a passage as a whole. If the meaning of a word or phrase is not readily apparent, you may hurry over it with the hope of getting the meaning from the context. Although the ability to skim material in this fashion is important for many purposes, you must be careful not to let the habits learned for silent reading affect your reading aloud for quite different purposes. These habits are destructive to good oral reading when they cause you to race, run words together, and mumble. Since the listener does not have the benefit of punctuation marks, you must use techniques of phrasing and inflection to take their place. Rapid and monotonous oral reading often fails completely to convey intended meanings.

■   5.   *Develop maximum voice control.* In no other form of oral communication is control of the voice as important as in oral reading. Everything that we have said in Chapter Fifteen about the voice should be reviewed as you work to improve your ability to interpret literature or other material to audiences. Voice quality, pitch, loudness, rate—all can help you to help your audience get the full impact of what you are reading.

■   6.   *Phrase or group words to make the meaning clear.* One of your most effective means of communicating certain meanings when interpreting another's work is silence—doing nothing—the pause. In planning pauses in the material which you are reading, be guided first by the punctuation of the author. However, punctuation is virtually never a perfectly reliable nor adequate controller of the pauses for optimum communication. Your pauses must be controlled ultimately by the variety of meanings which the work has for you and by your sensed need to give the audience additional cues to these meanings, or to give them an opportunity to assimilate an idea, or to give them a sense of anticipation or suspense. Thus, pauses aid understanding.

Pauses are your primary means of phrasing; hence, they are your primary means of communicating meaning through phrases rather than through individual words or sentences. Phrasing or pausing also helps you to maintain adequate control of your breathing for vocalization.

Though the pause is the major means of phrasing, varying the rate, pitch, quality, and loudness of different phrases also helps to differentiate them and to make their meaning clear.

Overphrasing, or the mechanical breaking up of sentences into minor units, is undesirable of course. It confuses rather than clarifies meaning. For most speakers, however, underphrasing is a greater problem than overphrasing.

■   7.   *Acquire skill in emphasizing and subordinating ideas.* In spite of the fact that the ideas in any reading passage vary in importance, one of the common weaknesses or faults of oral reading is monotony. Monotony does not result only from a lack of variation; rhythmical variations in voice which produce a singsong pattern may be just as monotonous as a lack of variation. In addition, arbitrary variations for the sake of arousing attention can be confusing. The variations that you use must be developed from the meaning of the material. Use vocal emphasis to make transitions clear. Indicate a climax by using minor vocal variations in the introduction and more radical variations near the point of greatest emphasis.

■   8.   *Read loudly enough to be heard easily.* The level of intensity of a bedtime story is not adequate for group reading. There is no communication if the audience cannot hear. Note that some sounds in the English language are difficult to hear unless you use sufficient force to project them clearly and sharply. Such unvoiced sounds as *f, t, p,* and initial *th* are especially difficult.

■   9.   *Adjust to the materials and situation.* Learn to hold the reading material up so that you can see it clearly and avoid constriction in your jaw and throat. Do not hold a paper or book in such a way that your face is hidden from your listeners. Be sure that you have adequate light. Practice reading with and without a reading stand. But do not become so engrossed in your materials that you act them out. Respond with facial expression and bodily action to ideas, but avoid distracting mannerisms. Learn to respond effectively to humor without conspicuously laughing at your own jokes. It is possible to read emotionally toned materials in a manner which reveals the mood without immersing yourself in the emotion. Read informative materials sympathetically but objectively; your manner of reading emotionally toned materials will not seem convincing, however, unless you respond to their mood. For example, a ritual will not be effective if read like the routine of a radio comedian.

■ 10. *Adjust the processes of oral reading to your listeners.* The ultimate objective of oral reading is to affect your listeners. Good reading is not exhibitionistic or elocutionary. Keep the social purpose of your reading in mind, and develop the techniques which will achieve it. Think of your work as projection to *listeners* rather than merely reading *from a manuscript.* If your material needs introduction, orient your listeners before you start; do not plunge in and expect them to catch up with you. On the other hand, if some factor in the situation has operated as an introduction and your listeners are ready to hear what you are to read, you do not need an introduction.

Projects and Problems

PROJECT 1: Turn to one of the speeches in the Appendix C and select a portion to read aloud to the class. You should introduce your selection by telling what it is about and why you have chosen to read it. The instructor and class will evaluate your reading.

PROJECT 2: Practice in oral reading.

In consultation with your instructor, choose one or more of the following˙ selections for oral reading before the class. Keep in mind, in preparing and presenting the selection, the exact meaning of the material, the author's philosophy, the background and setting of the reading, the intellectual and emotional mood and purpose of the passage. Be flexible in your rate of reading; phrase the words within sentences to make the meaning clear; properly emphasize and subordinate the ideas; control your loudness level; read fluently and precisely; articulate and pronounce clearly; project rather than merely read; and make the necessary adjustments to the light and other physical conditions.

(a)
The world is too much with us; late and soon,
Getting and spending, we lay waste our powers:
Little we see in Nature that is ours;
We have given our hearts away, a sordid boon!

The Sea that bares her bosom to the moon;
The winds that will be howling at all hours,
And are up-gathered now like sleeping flowers;
For this, for everything, we are out of tune;
It moves us not.—Great God! I'd rather be
A Pagan suckled in a creed outworn;
So might I, standing on this pleasant lea,
Have glimpses that would make me less forlorn;
Have sight of Proteus rising from the sea;
Or hear old Triton blow his wreathed horn.
—William Wordsworth, "The World Is Too Much with Us."

(b)

I am loath to close. We are not enemies, but friends. We must not be enemies. Though passion may have strained, it must not break, our bonds of affection. The mystic chords of memory, stretching from every battlefield and patriot grave to every living heart and hearthstone all over this broad land, will yet swell the chorus of the Union when again touched, as surely they will be, by the better angels of our nature.
—Abraham Lincoln, First Inaugural Address, March 4, 1861.

(c)

The theory of books is noble. The scholar of the first age received into him the world around; brooded thereon; gave it the new arrangement of his own mind, and uttered it again. It came into him life; it went out from him truth. It came to him short-lived actions; it went out from him immortal thoughts. It came to him business; it went from him poetry. It was dead fact; now, it is quick thought. It can stand, and it can go. It now endures, it now flies, it now inspires. Precisely in proportion to the depth of mind from which it issued, so high does it soar, so long does it sing.
—Ralph Waldo Emerson, The American Scholar, August 31, 1837.

(d)

We cannot reconcile Jesus Christ and war—that is the essence of the matter. That is the challenge which today should stir the conscience of Christendom. War is the most colossal and ruinous social sin that afflicts mankind; it is utterly and irremediably unchristian; in its total method and effect it means everything that Jesus did not mean and it means nothing that He did mean; it is a more blatant denial of every Christian doctrine about God and man than all the theoretical atheists on earth ever could devise. It would be worthwhile, would it not, to see the Christian Church claim as her own this greatest moral issue of our time, to see her lift once more, as in our fathers' days, a clear standard against the paganism of this present world and, refusing to hold her conscience at the beck and call of belligerent states, put the Kingdom of God above nationalism and call the world to peace? That would not be the denial of patriotism but its apotheosis.

Here today, as an American, under this high and hospitable roof, I cannot speak for my government, but both as an American, and as a Christian I do speak for millions of my fellow citizens in wishing your great work, in which we believe, for which we pray, our absence from which we painfully regret, the eminent success which it desires. We work in many ways for the same end—a world organized for peace. Never was an end better worth working for. The alternative is the most appalling catastrophe mankind has ever faced. Like gravitation in the physical realm, the law of the Lord in the moral realm bends for no man and no nation: "All they that take the sword shall perish with the sword."
—Harry Emerson Fosdick, *A Christian Conscience about War,* September 13, 1925.

(e)

If we must choose an arbitrary beginning to our contemporary world, my choice would be July 16, 1945. If you go to the library and search out the newspapers for that date, you will find no earth-shaking headlines, no world-shattering news story. For our age began in the shadow of a great and guarded secret.

And yet the earth was shaken on that day; and the conventional world we had grown accustomed to was shattered and, perhaps, forever ended. Certainly, in a profound sense, a new age dawned on that date.

For it was the first date in the history of mankind on which, at dawn, not one sun rose over the horizon—but two.

One was the sun that God had made, the other, a sun that man had made, alive in the full blaze for only a split instant, but a sun nevertheless, fired with the same source of ultimate, primordial energy.

As the scientists turned to leave their observation post on the mesa that morning in 1945, they noted with irony that the forty-thousand-foot mushroom cloud had been shaped by the random desert winds into a gigantic and grotesque question mark.

Today . . . that question mark still hangs high over our horizon.
—Carl T. Rowan, "Our Contemporary World," October 14, 1965.

(f)

The black nationalists, those whose philosophy is black nationalism, in bringing about this new interpretation of the entire meaning of civil rights, look upon it as meaning, as Brother Lomax has pointed out, equality of opportunity. Well, we're justified in seeking civil rights, if it means equality of opportunity, because all we're doing there is trying to collect for our investment. Our mothers and fathers invested sweat and blood. Three hundred and ten years we worked in this country without a dime in return—I mean without a dime in return. You let the white men walk around here talking about how rich this country is, but you never stop to think how it got rich so quick. It got rich because you made it rich.

This is our investment. This is our contribution—our blood. Not only did we give of our free labor, we gave of our blood. Every time we had a call

to arms, we were the first ones in uniform. We died on every battlefield the white man had. We have made a greater sacrifice than anybody who's standing up in America today. We have made a greater contribution and have collected less. Civil rights, for those of us whose philosophy is black nationalism, means, "Give it to us now. Don't wait for next year. Give it to us yesterday, and that's not fast enough."
—Malcolm X, "The Ballot or the Bullet," April 3, 1964.

(g)

O Lord our Lord, how excellent is thy name in all the earth: who hast set thy glory above the heavens!

Out of the mouths of babes and sucklings hast thou ordained strength because of thine enemies: that thou mightest still the enemy and the avenger.

When I consider thy heavens, the work of thy fingers: the moon and the stars, which thou hast ordained;

What is man, that thou art mindful of him: and the son of man, that thou visitest him?

For thou hast made him a little lower than the angels: and hast crowned him with glory and honour.

Thou madest him to have dominion over the works of thy hands: thou hast put all things under his feet;

All sheep and oxen: yea, and the beasts of the field;

The fowl of the air, and the fish of the sea: and whatsoever passeth through the paths of the seas.

O Lord our Lord: How excellent is thy name in all the earth!
—Psalm 8

(h)

What is education? Above all things, what is our ideal of a thoroughly liberal education?—of that education which, if we could begin life again, we would give ourselves?—of that education which, if we could mold the fates to our own will, we would give our children? Well, I know not what may be your conceptions upon this matter but I will tell you mine, and I hope I shall find that our views are not very discrepant.

Suppose it were perfectly certain that the life and fortune of every one of us would, one day or other, depend upon his winning or losing a game at chess. Don't you think we should all consider it to be a primary duty to learn at least the names and the moves of the pieces; to have a notion of a gambit, and a keen eye for all the means of giving and getting out of check? Do you not think that we should look with a disapprobation amounting to scorn upon the father who allowed his son, or the state which allowed its members, to grow up without knowing a pawn from a knight? . . .

Well, what I mean by education is learning the rules of this mighty game. In other words, education is the instruction of the intellect in the laws of nature, under which name I include not merely things and their forces, but men and their ways; and the fashioning of the affections and of the

*will into an earnest and loving desire to move in harmony with those laws.
For me education means neither more nor less than this.*
—Thomas Henry Huxley, "What is Education?" from *A Liberal Education
and Where to Find It,* 1868.

(i)
*They tell us, sir, that we are weak; unable to cope with so formidable
an adversary. But when shall we be stronger? Will it be the next week,
or the next year? Will it be when we are totally disarmed, and when a
British guard shall be stationed in every house? Shall we gather strength
by irresolution and inaction? Shall we acquire the means of effectual
resistance by lying supinely on our backs, and hugging the delusive phantom of hope, until our enemies shall have bound us hand and foot? Sir,
we are not weak, if we make a proper use of the means which the God
of nature hath placed in our power. Three millions of people, armed in
the holy cause of liberty, and in such a country as that which we possess,
are invincible by any force which our enemy can send against us. Besides,
sir, we shall not fight our battles alone. There is a just God who presides
over the destinies of nations; and who will raise friends to fight our battles
for us. The battle, sir, is not to the strong alone; it is to the vigilant, the
active, the brave. Besides, sir, we have no election. If we were base enough
to desire it, it is now too late to retire from the contest. There is no retreat
but in submission and slavery! Our chains are forged! Their clanking may
be heard on the plains of Boston! The war is inevitable—and let it come!
I repeat, sir, let it come!*
—Patrick Henry, "Liberty or Death," March 23, 1775.

(j)
*"Christmas Day began in London nearly an hour ago. The church bells
did not ring at midnight. When they ring again, it will be to announce
invasion. And if they ring, the British are ready. Tonight, as on every other
night, the rooftop watchers are peering out across the fantastic forest of
London's chimney pots. The anti-aircraft gunners stand ready. And all
along the coast of this island, the observers revolve in their reclining chairs,
listening for the sound of German planes. The fire fighters and the ambu-
lance drivers are waiting, too. The blackout stretches from Birmingham
to Bethlehem, but tonight over Britain the skies are clear.*

*"This is not a merry Christmas in London. I heard that phrase only twice
in the last three days. This afternoon as the stores were closing, as shoppers
and office workers were hurrying home, one heard such phrases as 'So long,
Mamie' and 'Good luck, Jack' but never 'A merry Christmas.' It can't be
a merry Christmas, for those people who spend tonight and tomorrow by
their firesides in their own homes and realize that they have bought this
Christmas with their nerve, their bodies and their old buildings. Their nerve
is unshaken; the casualties have not been large, and there are many old
buildings still untouched. Between now and next Christmas there stretches
twelve months of increasing toil and sacrifice, a period when the Britishers
will live hard. Most of them realize that. Tonight's serious Christmas Eve*

is the result of a realization of the future, rather than the aftermath of hardships sustained during the past year. The British find some basis for confidence in the last few month's developments. . . . So far, shelter life has produced none of the predicted epidemics. The nation's health is about as good now as it was at this time last year. And above all they're sustained by a tradition of victory."
—Edward R. Murrow broadcast from London, December 24, 1940.

(k)
    All the world's a stage,
And all the men and women merely players:
They have their exits and their entrances;
And one man in his time plays many parts,
His acts being seven ages. At first the infant,
Mewling and puking in the nurse's arms.
Then the whining school-boy, with his satchel,
And shining morning face, creeping like snail
Unwillingly to school. And then the lover,
Sighing like furnace, with a woeful ballad
Made to his mistress' eyebrow. Then a soldier,
Full of strange oaths and bearded like the pard,
Jealous in honor, sudden and quick in quarrel,
Seeking the bubble reputation
Even in the cannon's mouth. And then the justice,
In fair round belly with good capon lin'd
With eyes severe, and beard of formal cut,
Full of wise saws and modern instances;
And so he plays his part. The sixth age shifts
Into the lean and slipper'd pantaloon,
With spectacles on nose and pouch on side,
His youthful hose well sav'd, a world too wide
For his shrunk shank; and his big manly voice,
Turning again toward childish treble, pipes
And whistles in his sound. Last scene of all,
That ends this strange eventful history,
Is second childishness and mere oblivion,
Sans teeth, sans eyes, sans taste, sans everything.
—William Shakespeare, Soliloquy of Jacques from *As You Like It*, II, vii.

(l)
    My friends: No one, not in my situation, can appreciate my feeling of sadness at this parting. To this place, and the kindness of these people, I owe everything. Here I have lived a quarter of a century, and have passed from a young to an old man. Here my children have been born, and one is buried. I now leave, not knowing when or whether ever I may return, with a task before me greater than that which rested upon Washington. Without the assistance of that Divine Being who ever attended him, I cannot succeed. With that assistance, I cannot fail. Trusting in Him who

can go with me, and remain with you, and be everywhere for good, let
us confidently hope that all will yet be well. To His care commending you,
farewell.
—Abraham Lincoln, Farewell Address at Springfield, Illinois, February 11,
1861.

(m)

   . . . You owe a duty to the public, as well as to the prisoner at the bar.
You cannot presume to be wiser than the law. Your duty is a plain,
straightforward one. Doubtless we would all judge him in mercy. Towards
him, as an individual, the law inculcates no hostility; but towards him,
if proved to be a murderer, the law, and the oaths you have taken, and
public justice, demand that you do your duty.

   With consciences satisfied with the discharge of duty, no consequences
can harm you. There is no evil that we cannot either face or fly from, but
the consciousness of duty disregarded. A sense of duty pursues us ever.
It is omnipresent, like the Deity. If we take to ourselves the wings of the
morning, and dwell in the uttermost parts of the sea, duty performed, or
duty violated, is still with us, for our happiness or our misery. If we say
the darkness shall cover us, in the darkness as in the light our obligations
are yet with us. We cannot escape their power, nor fly from their presence.
They are with us in this life, will be with us at its close; and in that scene
of inconceivable solemnity, which lies yet farther onward, we shall still
find ourselves surrounded by the consciousness of duty, to pain us wherever
it has been violated, and to console us so far as God may have given us
grace to perform it.
—Daniel Webster, *Address to the Jury,* Knapp-White Murder Case, August
8–20, 1830.

(n)
Speak gently, Spring, and make no sudden sound;
For in my windy valley yesterday I found
New-born foxes squirming on the ground—
                    Speak gently.
Walk softly, March, forbear the bitter blow;
Her feet within a trap, her blood upon the snow,
The four little foxes saw their mother go—
                    Walk softly.
Go lightly, Spring—oh, give them no alarm;
When I covered them with boughs to shelter them from harm,
The thin blue foxes suckled at my arm—
                    Go lightly.
Step softly, March, with your rampant hurricane;
Nuzzling one another, and whimpering with pain,
The new little foxes are shivering in the rain—
                    Step softly.
—Lew Sarett, "Four Little Foxes."

(o)

A vision of the future rises:

I see our country filled with happy homes, with firesides of content,—the foremost land of all the earth.

I see a world where thrones have crumbled and where kings are dust. The aristocracy of idleness have perished from the earth.

I see a world without a slave. Man at last is free. Nature's forces have by Science been enslaved. Lightning and light, wind and wave, frost and flame, and all the secret, subtle powers of earth and air are the tireless toilers for the human race.

I see a world at peace, adorned with every form of art, with music's myriad voices thrilled, while lips are rich with words of love and truth; a world in which no exile sighs; no prisoner mourns; a world on which the gibbet's shadow does not fall; a world where labor reaps its full reward, where work and worth go hand in hand, where the poor girl trying to win bread with the needle—the needle that has been called "the asp for the breast of the poor"—is not driven to the desperate choice of crime or death, of suicide or shame.

I see a world without the beggar's outstretched palm, the miser's heartless, stony stare, the piteous wail of want, the vivid lips of lies, the cruel eyes of scorn.

I see a race without disease of flesh or brain—shapely and fair—the married harmony of form and function—and as I look, life lengthens, joy deepens, love canopies the earth; and over all, in the great dome, shines the eternal star of human hope.

—Robert G. Ingersoll, *Decoration Day Address*, May 30, 1888.

(p)

While American labor will continue to foster and maintain a frankly critical spirit and constructive attitude towards our own political, social, and economic weaknesses and shortcomings, and we have them, and we intend to fight against them, we will at the same time intensify our activities to help strengthen the ranks of free labor and of other democratic forces abroad. We not only welcome the recent setbacks to Communism in Italy, India, Germany, and in other countries, but will continue every possible effort to still further advance this process of disintegration now taking place there and elsewhere.

It is our firm conviction that only America is strong enough to discourage, to defeat, and to destroy the aggressors and enemies of world peace. It is our definite belief that this is the historical mission of America to the human race. It is our determination to hold ourselves in readiness at all times to make available American know-how in health, industry, and self-government on a world scale to the economically underdeveloped countries and regions of the world, and to render every service possible to humankind.

In the field of ideology, the A. F. of L. and the American labor movement will redouble its efforts to advance the ideals of democracy and peace as against dictatorship and war, of freedom of enterprise as against state *control, of freedom of expression and worship as against fear of persecution and intolerance.*

Our enemy is strong, shrewd, and ruthless. Our enemy has a global approach. We will meet and defeat this enemy, not only by military force, but by all other economic, social, cultural, and political measures and weapons at our command and thus hold secure and advance human freedom and human well-being.

American labor has full confidence in the ability of our country and its people to provide dynamic and inspiring leadership in this world struggle for human freedom. In that struggle, the trade and labor organizations of our land will contribute more than their share to help our nation to perform its historical mission, and rally world labor for the triumph of freedom, of democracy, and of peace over tyranny, despotism, and war.

One final observation, and that is this: No matter what avocation we may follow, no matter what trade or occupation we may be engaged in, as Americans let us be happy that we are here, whether as native or foreign-born, for no other nation the world has ever known has offered the great heritage that is yours and mine—the heritage of freedom, the heritage to express ourselves as we please, the heritage of working out our problems as God intended they should be worked out, by the exchange of opinions, by understanding, by mutual cooperation. May that ever be so! God bless America, and may its blessings extend all over the world in the not far distant future!

Thank you, indeed, for this opportunity of presenting these few observations to you.

—Philip Murray, *Labor's Role in Higher Education.*

(q)

. . . Science seems ready to confer upon us, as its final gift, the power to erase human life from the earth.

At such a time in history, we who are free must proclaim anew our faith.

This faith is the abiding creed of our fathers. It is our faith in the deathless dignity of man, governed by eternal moral and natural laws. This faith defines our full view of life. It establishes, beyond debate, those gifts of the Creator that are man's inalienable rights, and that make all men equal in His sight.

In the light of this equality, we know that the virtues most cherished by free people—love of truth, pride of work, devotion to country—all are treasures equally precious in the lives of the most humble and of the most exalted. The men who mine coal and fire furnaces and balance ledgers and turn lathes and pick cotton and heal the sick and plant corn, all serve as proudly, and as profitably, for America as the statesmen who draft treaties or the legislators who enact laws.

This faith rules our whole way of life. It decrees that we, the people, elect leaders not to rule but to serve. It asserts that we have the right to choice of our own work and to the reward of our own toil. It inspires the initiative that makes our productivity the wonder of the world. And it

*warns that any man who seeks to deny equality in all his brothers betrays
the spirit of the free and invites the mockery of the tyrant.*
—Dwight D. Eisenhower, *Inaugural Address*, January 20, 1953.

(r)
Let us remember also that the first of the seven deadly sins is spiritual
pride: the sin which assures me that I know and you don't, so that I give
myself permission to use any dubious or dishonest means to discredit your
opinion. Because we have always thought of government as friendly, not
as brutal, character assassins and slanderers in the Congress of the United
States have a free hand in the methods they use. We never foresaw that
the cult of thought-control and of the big lie would come to America. So
if their conscience permits, they can say almost anything. And if my
opponent's conscience permits, he can try to help all of them get re-elected.
But will he have strengthened or weakened the American idea?

For this is no small thing, this remorseless attack upon freedom of
conscience, freedom of thought. A few peddlers of hate and fear would
be of little consequence if they had not been welcomed as satellites by
Senator Taft and included in the leadership of this strange crusade. And
none of them would be significant if the General—who was implored to
come home by Republican leaders so that they might be quit of Senator
Taft—had not yielded to the demands of his beaten foe. But because of
that surrender, because of those strange allies in his queer crusade, our
role in world history, our faithfulness to the men who made the United
States, is challenged in this election.

Finally, then, let us recall that our basic faith in liberty of conscience
has an ancient ancestry. We can trace it back through Christian Europe,
and through pagan Rome, back to the Old Testament prophets. It is by
no means exclusive with us. It is in fact our bond of unity with all free
men. But we are its ordained guardians today.

Let us lift up our hearts, therefore—glad of our strength, proud of the
task it imposes. So far from being half-defeated, half-divided, half-
bankrupt—while we are true to ourselves we can never be defeated; while
we accept the honorable burden of leadership, we can never be divided.
And in the name of that burden we shall find the means and the determination to spend in money and in labor and in hard thought whatever is
needed to save ourselves and our world.
—Adlai E. Stevenson, *America's Role*, Address at Salt Lake City, October
14, 1952.

(s)
*To-morrow, and to-morrow, and to-morrow,
Creeps in this petty pace from day to day,
To the last syllable of recorded time;
And all our yesterdays have lighted fools
The way to dusty death. Out, out, brief candle!
Life's but a walking shadow; a poor player*

That struts and frets his hour upon the stage
And then is heard no more: it is a tale
Told by an idiot, full of sound and fury,
Signifying nothing.
—Shakespeare, *Macbeth*, V, v.

(t)
This message, Mr. President, comes to you from consecrated ground. Every foot of the soil about the city in which I live is sacred as a battleground of the Republic. Every hill that invests it is hallowed to you by the blood of your brothers, who died for your victory, and doubly hallowed to us by the blood of those who died hopeless, but undaunted, in defeat— sacred soil to all of us, rich with memories that make us purer and stronger and better, silent but staunch witnesses in its red desolation of the matchless valor of American hearts and the deathless glory of American arms—speaking an eloquent witness in its white peace and prosperity to the indissoluble union of American states and the imperishable brotherhood of the American people.
—Henry Grady, *The New South*, December 22, 1886.

References

Aggertt, Otis J., and Elbert R. Bowen, *Communicative Reading*, 2nd ed. New York: Macmillan Company, 1963.

Bacon, Wallace, *The Art of Interpretation*. New York: Holt, Rinehart, and Winston, Inc., 1966.

Bacon, Wallace A., and Robert S. Breen, *Literature for Interpretation*. New York: Holt, Rinehart and Winston, Inc., 1961.

Beebe, Maurice, *Literary Symbolism: An Introduction to the Interpretation of Literature*. Belmont, Calif.: Wadsworth Publishing Co., Inc., 1960.

Brack, Harold A., *Effective Oral Interpretation for Religious Leaders*. Englewood Cliffs, N.J.: Prentice-Hall, 1964.

Brooks, Keith, Eugene Bahn, and L. LaMont Okey, *Literature for Listening: An Oral Interpreter's Anthology*. Boston: Allyn and Bacon, Inc., 1968.

———, *The Communicative Art of Oral Interpretation*. Boston: Allyn and Bacon, Inc., 1967.

Campbell, Paul N., *Oral Interpretation*. New York: Macmillan Company, 1966.

Geeting, Baxter M., *Interpretation for Our Time*. Dubuque, Iowa: Wm. C. Brown Co., 1966.

Lee, Charlotte I., *Oral Interpretation*, 3rd ed. Boston: Houghton Mifflin Co., 1965.

Lowrey, Sara, and Gertrude Johnson, *Interpretative Reading*, rev. ed. New York: Appleton-Century-Crofts, 1953.

Mattingly, Althea Smith, *Interpretation: Writer-Reader-Audience*, 2nd ed. Belmont, Calif.: Wadsworth Publishing Co., Inc., 1970.

Sessions, Virgil D., and Jack B. Holland, *Oral Interpretation Drill Book*. Boston: Holbrook Press, Inc., 1968.

————, *Your Role in Oral Interpretation.* Boston: Holbrook Press, Inc., 1968.

Sloan, Thomas G. (ed.), *The Oral Study of Literature.* New York: Random House, 1966.

Smith, Joseph F., and James R. Linn, *Skill in Reading Aloud.* New York: Harper & Row, Publishers, 1960.

Veilleux, Jere, *Oral Interpretation: The Re-Creation of Literature.* New York: Harper & Row, Publishers, 1967.

Woolbert, Charles H., and Severina E. Nelson, *The Art of Interpretative Speech: Principles and Practices,* 5th ed. New York: Appleton-Century-Crofts, 1967.

NBC Photo.

radio and television speaking

Radio or television speaking is not basically different from any other form of speaking. Any speech begins with an idea in someone's brain. For television, this idea is translated into aural (and visual) symbols, transmitted and received. It is then translated from the aural and visual symbols back into an idea. There are many points where this communication process can break down. The idea may be poorly defined. A faulty translation into aural symbols may be due to a limited vocabulary or misperception of the audience. A poor translation into visual symbols may be caused by lack of imagination. The message may be distorted if you use the medium improperly. Reception may be poor due to unclear speech or gestures. The symbols may be translated into an idea other than the original one because the symbols do not mean the same thing to the audience that they do to you. These problems are important for almost any sort of speaking: thus all of the material in this book is relevant to effective radio and television speaking. The material in this chapter should help you to cope with the few special problems of electronic communication.

Mass Media Differences

The major differences that exist between face-to-face communication and radio or television communication are due not so much to the machinery of the media as to the context in which the audience hears you. When you speak at a political caucus or a P.T.A. meeting, the audience members are usually there because they want to hear you speak. The audience is relatively homogeneous and, because they are in close proximity as they listen to you, the reaction of one tends to affect others; there is a type of crowd effect. Very often they know beforehand the kind of thing that you will say and they tend to be interested already and to agree with you; if they did not agree with you or if they were not interested they most likely would not have come. When you speak on radio or television, on the other hand, whether you are giving a fifteen-minute speech or a twenty-second speech or commercial, a very large proportion of your audience is listening only because they happened to be listening to the program that preceded you and they left their receivers tuned to the same station. Thus, you have an audience with less initial interest in you or what you have to say and, if they are interested, they have a higher probability of being in disagreement with you when you start speaking.

Equally important, your television or radio audience is not gathered in a group to listen to you; each member of your audience is listening alone or with one or two other members of his family. This is the reason we believe it to be misleading to speak or think of a "mass audience." Instead of an audience of thousands or millions of people, it is more accurate and useful to think of thousands or millions of audiences, each made up of one, two, or three persons.

The third important difference between the audience of the broadcast speech and the audience of the platform speech is that the latter is doing little else generally but concentrating upon what you are doing and saying; it is unusual for people to be engaged in other activities while listening to you. The broadcasting audience, on the other hand, is almost always doing other things while listening to you. This is especially true of the radio audience. Rare is the member of your radio audience who will be simply sitting and listening. Some will be driving cars while they listen; some will be washing the dishes or cleaning the house; some will be reading or doing homework. Though not many members of your television audience will be driving automobiles while watching you, many will be doing other things. If you can imagine yourself in someone's house, trying to give a speech to two or three members of the family while they are reading the newspaper, talking to each other, doing homework, and wandering in and out of the room, you will have a reasonably accurate notion of the problems you will face when you speak on radio or television.

These differences in the audience situation have both advantages and disadvantages. The major advantage is that radio and television give you a much better chance of reaching people who are unconcerned or who disagree with you. Thus, if you are a political candidate, the media provide your best opportunity to reach the apathetic voter and the voter who is not affiliated with your party. The media also give you your best chance of reaching him when he is in a receptive mood (that is, assuming that he isn't angry because your speech has preempted one of his favorite programs).

The major disadvantage of radio and television is that it is difficult to catch and hold the attention of the audience members. As far as most members of your audience are concerned, radio and television are *entertainment* media. You are competing for the attention of your audience with rock groups, plays, and comedians. There is a much greater need to interest the audience immediately, before they walk into another room or before they switch to another station or before they switch you off psychologically. As with any audience which is uninterested or not in agreement with you at the beginning, you must immediately establish need; you must immediately give them a good reason for listening to you—either because you are interesting or because you have something to say which will help them or, ideally, both.

The Technique of Radio and Television Speaking

In speaking on radio or television, keep in mind that you are sitting in someone's car with him or in his family room. You must adjust your manner of speaking to these types of situations. The style you would use at Convention Hall in Chicago, or at a political rally, or even in front of a class is not appropriate when you are invited into someone's family room or when you are sitting beside him in his automobile. These situations, whether you are there in person or have been "invited" via the electronic media, demand a conversational style; don't speak *at* your audience, converse *with* them.

Though you cannot see your radio or television audience and therefore do not get some of the cues from them which help your audience adaptation in a face-to-face situation, audience adaptation in radio or television speaking is far from impossible. Obviously, you can make certain predictions about the nature of the audience from the subject matter, the format, and the method of presentation of the program. You can predict the nature of the audience even more precisely if you take into account the time of day, the program which is on the station preceding your appearance, and the programs which are on other stations during your appearance. Media audiences are fluid, but they change in predictable ways. Knowing these ways will help you to pinpoint the nature of your audience quite accurately, so that you can adapt.

From 7:00 to 8:00 in the morning and from 6:00 to 7:00 and 10:00 to 12:00 in the evening, you can expect a fair balance between men and women because these are the hours in which they turn on the media for information and, late in the evening, for entertainment. During the mid-morning and mid-afternoon weekday hours, you will get primarily housewives. Late afternoons are the children's hours. From 7:00 to 10:00 in the evening are the family-viewing hours when you will get the most heterogeneous audience. Saturdays and Sundays are more difficult to predict; on these days you should probably pay greater attention to the kind of program preceding yours and to the competition.

Because of the way in which most people use the media, you can tell a great deal about the audience you will get from the kind of program which preceded yours. If it is a children's program, you can expect few adults in your audience when your program starts. If it is a sports program, you can expect a heavier than usual proportion of men, and so on. The viewers or listeners to the preceding program generally stay tuned in long enough to discover whether your program will be interesting to them. If they are the sort of audience you want, it is extremely important that you catch their interest immediately, before they turn the dial. Similarly, if you are competing with a popular sports event, you must plan on losing a large proportion of the males in your audience and, hence, must concentrate on the women. Or if the competition is of the sort that will appeal more to women, you can take advantage of the opportunity to win and hold the male audience.

Radio versus Television

The obvious difference between radio and television speaking is the importance of the visual dimensions of your message in the latter. We will talk about that below. A less obvious difference for the listener, but most obvious for the speaker, is the amount and kind of distraction which confronts the speaker. When speaking on the radio, you will probably feel relatively isolated. Quite often, you will be alone in the studio in which you are speaking, isolated even from the engineer in his glassed-in booth. Since even he will not appear to be listening to you sometimes, you will often get the uncomfortable feeling that you are isolated from the world and speaking only to yourself. When speaking on television, on the other hand, you will often be performing in the midst of what appears to be complete chaos. The cameramen will be pushing their cameras about while you are speaking, the floor manager may be standing between the cameras giving you signals, someone else may be swinging a microphone boom over your head, and other people may be wandering around the studio out of sight of the cameras but well within your range of vision. The lights will be uncomfortably bright and warm. Looking into the terrifying depths of the television camera lens will make remembering what you wanted to say almost impossible. You may decide at that point that it is a completely impossible situation in which to try to speak. If you stick with it though, you will be amazed how quickly you can become accustomed to the situation and virtually oblivious to the chaos, so that you can just talk intimately and informally with those people who have invited you into their homes.

Though the technical problems of radio and television speaking are simple, they can interfere with good communication if you are not aware of them. When speaking on either radio or television, your voice level will be tested beforehand and microphone "levels" set so that you can maintain an easy conversational tone and yet be clearly heard. Once these levels are set, you should not increase or decrease your loudness too abruptly during your speech without warning the engineer or you will blast your audience off their seats or fade out so that they cannot hear you. If it is important to be louder in one section, move slightly back from the microphone; if it is important to speak more softly in a section, move slightly closer to the microphone. Otherwise, try to maintain the same distance from the microphone throughout your speech. In addition, because microphones are so sensitive, they pick up many sounds which are not heard in the usual speaking situation. One of the most irritating and distracting to audiences is the sound of scripts rattling or pages turning. Therefore, if you use a manuscript, be extremely careful that you turn pages silently.

Preparing Messages

It will usually be necessary in radio to work from a script, but in writing the script keep in mind at all times that it is to be delivered orally. It must sound extemporaneous and it must be easily understood. Use simple rather than complex sentences. Use short sentences, but vary their internal structure. Use periodic sentences and parallel constructions; use questions and exclamations, and occasionally the imperative mood. Your style should be colorful, clear, and concise. Avoid abstract, hackneyed, and pedantic terms; use figurative and connotative language. Avoid cliches: "each and every," "it may interest you to know," "our boys," "man in the street," "average American," "give their all," and many other such expressions will cause your audience to turn you off. Personalize your style. Don't talk about "listeners" or "people"; talk about "us" and "you."

Prepare your manuscript for easy reading. See that the copy is typed in capitals and double-spaced, and that almost every sentence is a paragraph. Be sure it is free from cancellations or other marks that may confuse you. Use only one side of each sheet of paper, and do not clip or fold them. Arrange the pages in order and number them.

Study the effects of intonation on individual words and phrases. Underline phrases that you wish especially to stress. You need not follow the manuscript word for word. Experienced speakers interpolate phrases and omit or change the phrasing to conform to the mood or requirements of the moment. This can give your speech added spontaneity.

In television, if you are to be seen while you are speaking, it is best not to have a manuscript or even notes in your hand. If needed, your notes or script should be on large cue cards or on teleprompters which are placed near the camera lens at which you will need to look. In radio, even with a manuscript, one can and should sound as though he is extemporizing. In a face-to-face public speaking situation, audiences generally accept the fact that speakers use note cards or manuscripts. In television, audiences do not seem to accept these aids except when used by newscasters. They have become accustomed to the illusion that television speakers of all other sorts simply look them in the eye and talk. If you do otherwise, you risk the audience concluding that you do not know what you are talking about.

The Camera

For the cameras in the studio in which you work, you will need to learn where the "take" lens is—the lens at which to look to give each audience member the illusion that you are looking him directly in the eye. Some cameras have only a single lens (a "zoom" lens with adaptable focal length), so there is no problem. Other cameras have three or four different lenses, and you must know at which to look. In addition, if you are speaking for more than a few seconds, the director may use more than one camera on you. In this case, you will need to watch for the floor director's signals or the red tally lights on the camera which indicate which camera is "on the air" at any given moment. You will also need to learn to shift your glance easily from one camera to another when the director cuts from one camera to the other. Generally, the easiest thing to do when a cut is made is to glance down and then up at the new taking camera, rather than simply jerking your head from side to side.

Timing

Because time generally is so critical in radio or television, you will need to plan the timing of your speech for one of these media much more carefully than you do for other situations. Often, it is a good idea to have a "cushion"—material near the end which can be added or deleted to help you finish right on time without losing the impact of your closing because of unplanned cuts or additions or without your needing to slow down or speed up your speaking rate to an unnatural level. In radio, there will usually be a studio clock which you can watch and to which you can adjust your presentation. In television, the floor manager or one of the cameramen will probably give you signals. Check beforehand on the kind of signals which he will give you and at what points in time they will be given.

Very often, of course, your speech will be prerecorded on audio or videotape. In such cases, timing is less significant because if your speech does not run the right length the first time, you can record it again or edit the tape.

Television and Your Personality

Television, of course, is a visual medium. This does not mean simply that the audience is able to see as well as hear you. It also means that you must plan the *visual* portion of your presentation as carefully as you plan the oral portion. The visual portion includes your appearance, what you do, and what you show.

Unlike the usual situation in which you speak to a relatively large group of people at a meeting or in a classroom, audiences are able to scrutinize closely every facet of your appearance, the slightest expression of your face, the smallest gesture. This is why those who work in television refer to it as an "intimate" medium. Because of the searching nature of the television closeup, which can cast your face into people's living rooms not only in "living color" but also larger than life-size, you must be sure that your grooming, your dress, your gestures and facial expression contribute to—or at least do not distract from—your speech.

Unless you are an extremely skilled actor, do not try to be anything but yourself. Then, if you are confident of your material, believe in what you are saying, and care about the audience, these attributes should come through in your facial expressions, in your voice, and in your gestures.

Dress

As in any other type of speech, dress in a way that is appropriate to the situation. In a sense, proper clothing is like good scenery in a play; it should not call attention to itself. You know you have dressed appropriately, just as you know you have the right sort of scenery, if no one afterward can describe it—if it was so right for the situation that no one thought of paying any special attention to it. For television, of course, you must avoid certain kinds of things, especially shiny jewelry and black and white clothing. For most purposes, it is best to wear various shades of gray, or colors which will appear as various shades of gray on monochromatic (black and white) receivers. You will generally want to use relatively bright colors for visuals and for clothing, since a large proportion of viewers now have color receivers, but the colors must be such that they provide some contrast when seen in monochrome. Otherwise, you will appear to be wearing just one gray blob. It is a good idea to check what you plan to wear with a director at the television station. Similarly, you should check the colors to be used in the visuals that you will show.

Use of Visuals

In planning your visuals for television presentation, keep in mind the aspect ratio of the television screen; the height is three-forths of the width. Whenever possible, your visuals should be made in this three-by-four aspect ratio. In addition, you should leave ample border around the main part of the visual so that none of the critical portion will be cut off of anyone's home screen. A good rule of thumb to follow in planning the amount of border is the rule of one-sixth. If you divide the width of the visual into sixths and the height into sixths, the top and bottom and side sixths should be left as border—or at least should contain none of the critical material. This is illustrated below:

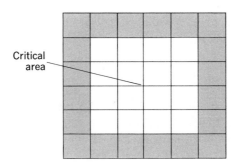

Critical
area

Careful planning of the way in which the visuals will be integrated with your speech is even more important for a television presentation than it is for other types of speeches. You must plan precisely when each visual is to be on the screen and for how long. You must also consider carefully what you will be saying while a visual is being shown. What you say during this period must be integrated with what the visual is saying, so that what you say does not distract the audience from the visual, and so that the visual does not distract the audience from your words. One should be consistent with or supplementary to the other.

When you plan your radio or television speech, although it is important to understand the medium for optimum impact, never forget that the most important and interesting programs on either medium are those in which there are interesting people talking in interesting ways about important subjects. Finally, never forget that, although one must clearly adapt to the medium, speaking on radio or on television or in a face-to-face situation is like Gertrude Stein's rose; good speech is good speech is good speech. To make a good speech on one of the media, it is first necessary to be able to make a good speech.

Projects and Problems

PROJECT 1: Watch one of the President's speeches or news conferences on television. Report to the class on your assessment of his skill at using the medium and the ways in which you believe his presentation on television differs from the presentation that he would make in a conventional platform speech.

PROJECT 2: Listen to a variety of radio commercials and select one or two which you believe epitomize good radio communication and one or two which epitomize what you believe to be poor radio communication. Describe them to the class and explain the reasons that you have categorized them as you have.

PROJECT 3: If your school has a videotape recorder which your class can use, record a brief persuasive presentation which would be suitable for broadcast on your local television station. After viewing it, write a detailed critique in which you assess the strengths and weaknesses of the presentation for television. Or, using an audio tape recorder, do the same for a radio broadcast.

PROJECT 4: Rewrite three minutes of copy from your local newspaper, adapting it to an aural radio style. Read it to the class to see whether you have achieved the sort of conversational style desirable for radio. Report to the class on the kinds of changes which you found to be necessary to change your stories from newspaper to radio or oral style.

PROJECT 5: Read some of Edward R. Murrow's broadcasts in the book *In Search of Light,* edited by Edward Bliss, Jr. Report to the class on the ways in which Murrow made his broadcasts sound conversational, even intimate. What in the broadcasts seems to account for the strong personal feelings which many listeners developed for Murrow?

References

Becker, Samuel L., and H. Clay Harshbarger, *Television: Techniques for Planning and Performance.* New York: Holt, 1958.

Bliss, Edward, Jr., *In Search of Light: The Broadcasts of Edward R. Murrow, 1938–1961.* New York: Knopf, 1967.

Head, Sydney W., *Broadcasting in America.* Boston: Houghton Mifflin, 1956.

Hilliard, Robert L. (ed.), *Radio Broadcasting: An Introduction to the Sound Medium.* New York: Hastings House, 1967.

Hyde, Stuart W., *Television and Radio Announcing.* Boston: Houghton Mifflin, 1959.

Lewis, Bruce, *The Technique of Television Announcing.* New York: Hastings House, 1966.

Lewis, Colby, *The TV Director/Interpreter.* New York: Hastings House, 1968.

Millerson, Gerald, *The Technique of Television Production,* 6th ed. New York: Hastings House, 1968.

Stasheff, Edward, and Rudy Bretz, *The Television Program: Its Direction and Production,* 4th ed. New York: Hill & Wang, 1968.

Summers, Robert F., and Harrison B. Summers, *Broadcasting and the Public.* Belmont, Calif.: Wadsworth, 1966.

Zettl, Herbert, *Television Production Handbook.* Belmont, Calif.: Wadsworth, 1961.

House of Commons.
London Portrait Gallery.

parliamentary procedure

Debating is the characteristic method by which organizations (clubs, courts, legislatures) conduct affairs, and parliamentary procedure provides the rules that govern debates. Group action can be regarded as legal and binding on the organization only if discussion proceeds according to parliamentary regulations.

Principles

Parliamentary rules exist to facilitate orderly procedure rather than to encourage vocal and legal sparring. It is the responsibility of the chairman of the assembly to see that the rules are administered impartially; that the majority vote decides the issue; that minority rights are safeguarded; that every proposition is fully discussed before a decision is registered; that all members have equal rights and responsibilities; that motions are introduced and disposed of in a definite and logical order; and that only one question is considered at a time.

Creating an Organization

How are organizations created? A group comes together under the stimulus of some common purpose. In order to work toward their common goal, the members must delegate responsibility and establish procedures.

Electing temporary officers. A member rises and says, "The meeting will come to order. I nominate Mr. X as temporary chairman." Or he may call for nominations for temporary chairman. If more than one nomination is made, he will put the names to a vote by voice or by show of hands. The nominee receiving a majority of the votes cast is declared temporary chairman. This temporary officer then presides over the election of a temporary secretary.

Stating the purpose of the meeting. The chairman then calls upon some member or members to state the purpose of the meeting. Informal discussion follows, presided over by the chairman.

Forming a permanent organization. A member rises upon recognition and presents a resolution which authorizes the formation of a permanent organization: "Mr. Chairman, I move that the meeting form a permanent organization, to be known as the State University of Iowa Forensic Association."

If this motion receives a majority vote, a member then moves that the chairman appoint a committee to draft a constitution and bylaws. If these have already been prepared, the drafting committee is asked to report then and there. If not, a drafting committee is appointed or elected, and the meeting adjourns to reconvene at a time specified by the assembly vote.

The constitution should be brief and clear. The articles usually include (1) the name of the organization, (2) the purposes and scope of the organization, (3) membership qualifications, (4) a list of officers, their duties, and procedure for electing them, (5) the time and place of meetings, (6) the number constituting a quorum, and (7) methods of amending the constitution.

Bylaws. Bylaws usually cover such subjects as (1) details governing membership; (2) a list of committees and their duties; (3) finances, including dues, fines, fees, credits, etc.; (4) the duties and powers of each officer; (5)

provisions for meetings; (6) methods of election; (7) order of business; (8) official parliamentary code; (9) methods of voting; (10) quorums; and (11) method of amending the bylaws.

Adoption of the constitution and bylaws. The chairman of the committee on constitution and bylaws moves that the document be adopted. The presiding officer then puts the motion: "It has been moved and recorded that this constitution be adopted."

The secretary records the constitution as a whole if it has already been read to the group; if not, he proceeds section by section. As each section is read, the chairman calls for discussion. Amendments are proposed, discussed, and approved or rejected. After all the sections are thus disposed of, the chairman asks, "Is further discussion on the constitution as a whole or further amendment proposed?" If there is no further discussion, the chairman calls for a vote on the original motion to adopt the document. A majority vote in favor will mean adoption.

The bylaws are discussed and adopted in the same way as the constitution. Then the organization is ready for its permanent business.

Conducting a Meeting

Parliamentary law and most organizational bylaws suggest the following order of business: (1) call to order; (2) reading and disposition of minutes of the previous meeting; (3) statement of agenda; (4) reports of officers and standing committees; (5) reports of special committees; (6) unfinished business; (7) new business; (8) adjournment.

The Presiding Officer

It is the responsibility of the presiding officer to see that the meeting moves forward efficiently—that the debate does not bog down in useless filibustering; that parliamentary rules are used only to further the group's discussion and decisions; that the facts being considered are clear to all; and—in general—that the assembly gets results.

The presiding officer should be tactful and impartial; he should never adopt a dictatorial attitude; and he should make the members feel at ease. He should be familiar with the rules of parliamentary procedure and their application; but instead of depending upon memory, he should keep a chart of these rules before him at each meeting. Since members will often veer away from the subject under discussion or introduce other subjects which should not be dealt with at the same time, it is the duty of the presiding officer to keep clearly in mind the business of the meeting and the order in which it is to be presented and to remind the members of this order. The presiding officer will recognize each speaker by name, or ask him to give his name; state each motion clearly and be sure it is properly recorded, having the secretary record it and helping him to repeat it accurately if necessary. He must keep the discussion of the motion and be sure that all who wish to speak have the opportunity to do so. Before a vote is taken, he should state the exact question to be voted on; afterward, he should announce the outcome and explain its consequences.

He must see that the secretary records each step of the meeting and has present a copy of the constitution and bylaws and other material that might serve the purposes of the meeting. In a formal meeting, he must ensure the appointment of a sergeant at arms, whose duties are to attend to the physical arrangements of the meeting and supervise the behavior of the members. In some organizations a parliamentarian should be designated to advise the presiding officer.

Voting and Quorum

Most motions are settled by a majority vote. Usually this term refers to a majority of the qualified votes cast; however, the constitution, bylaws, or rules of the organization should define the term. Voting is done by one of the following methods: *voice* ("Those in favor, say 'aye.' Those opposed say 'no.'"); *rising ballot; show of hands;* and *roll call* (The secretary calls the roll. Those in favor answer "yes" as their names are called; those opposed, "no.").

A quorum is necessary for a legal decision. The quorum, the minimum number of members that must be present in order to make the transactions of the meeting legal, is a majority of the members, unless otherwise stated in the constitution and bylaws.

Handling Motions

Business is carried on by motions (resolutions, proposals, propositions, or questions). A member rises and addresses the chairman, and the procedure is as follows:

Member: "Mr. Chairman."
Chairman: "Mr. Blair."
Member: "I move that we vote $50 to provide for a freshman party."
Chairman: "Is there a second?"
Another member: "I second the motion."
Chairman: "You have heard the motion as made and seconded. Is there any discussion?"
[Discussion proceeds.]
Chairman: "Are you ready for the vote?" [Hearing no dissent, he continues:] "Those in favor say 'aye.' ["Ayes" are given.] Those opposed say 'no.' The motion is carried." [Or "The motion is lost."]

There are four types of motions: *main, subsidiary, incidental,* and *privileged.* In order of this proposal (priority) these are arranged as follows (incidental motions may be made at any point):

1. Main motions
2. Subsidiary motions
3. Privileged motions

In order of their disposition, these motions rank as follows:

1. Privileged motions
2. Subsidiary motions
3. Main motions

More specifically, the order of disposal of these motions is:

I. Privileged motions
    1. Fix time to adjourn
    2. Adjourn
    3. Recess
    4. Question of privilege
    5. Call for order of the day

II. Subsidiary motions
    6. "Lay on the table"
    7. "Previous question" (immediate vote)
    8. Limit debate
    9. Postpone to a specific time
    10. Refer to a committee
    11. Amend
    12. Postpone indefinitely

III. Main motions
    13. Any "general" main motion, and such "specific" main motions as (*a*) reconsider, (*b*) rescind, (*c*) resume consideration (take from the table)

IV. Incidental motions (may be proposed and disposed of at any time)
    1. Appeal
    2. Point of order
    3. Inquiry
    4. Suspend rules
    5. Withdraw a motion
    6. Object to consideration
    7. Division of the question

This order of handling motions means that when a motion is before the assembly, any motion of higher rank takes precedence and may be proposed, but not a motion of lower rank. The motion to adjourn takes precedence over all others, and the "main motion" comes last. The last motion proposed should be disposed of first, and so on until the first motion is arrived at and disposed of.[1] In this way, procedure in dealing with motions listed above would be as follows:

I. MAIN MOTION

13. *Original Motion*

PURPOSE: To propose original business.

FORM: "Mr. Chairman, I move that we approve President Nixon's proposal for international control of atomic material."

COMMENT: Requires a second, is debatable, can be amended, requires a majority vote; if lost cannot be revived at the same meeting.

13a. *Resume Consideration (Take from the Table)*

FORM: "Mr. Chairman, I move we resume consideration of the motion to approve Mr. Nixon's proposal."

COMMENT: Requires a second, is not debatable, is not amendable, requires a majority.

13b. *Reconsider*

FORM: "Mr. Chairman, I move that we reconsider the vote to approve President Nixon's proposal."

COMMENT: Requires a second, is not amendable, and requires a majority; is debatable if motion to which it applies is debatable.

13c. *Rescind (Repeal, Annul)*

PURPOSE: To nullify or void a motion previously passed.

FORM: "I move to rescind (or repeal) the motion passed on December 5, which motion approved Mr. Nixon's proposal."

COMMENT: Requires a second, is debatable, cannot be amended, requires a majority vote, applies to main motions previously adopted.

II. SUBSIDIARY MOTIONS

12. *Postpone Indefinitely ("Kill" or "Suppress")*

PURPOSE: To suppress a question pending before the meeting.

FORM: "I move that the motion be postponed indefinitely."

COMMENT: Debatable, requires a second, cannot be amended, requires majority vote, applies to main motions only.

11. *Amend*

PURPOSE: To change or modify a motion before the assembly.

FORM: "I move to amend (by adding, striking out, substituting). . . ."

COMMENT: Cannot interrupt a speaker, requires a second, is debatable, can be amended, requires a majority vote, takes precedence over main motion.

---

[1] For the plan outlined above and as a general authority on parliamentary procedure, the authors are indebted to Alice Sturgis, *Learning Parliamentary Procedure,* McGraw-Hill Book Company, Inc., New York, 1953.

10. *Refer to a Committee*

PURPOSE: To transfer a proposal from assembly to a smaller group working under the assembly.

FORM: "I move to refer the motion to a committee."

COMMENT: Requires a second, debatable, can be amended, requires a majority vote.

9. *Postpone to a Specific Time*

PURPOSE: To postpone consideration or decision to a specific time.

FORM: "I move to postpone consideration of the motion until the next regular meeting."

COMMENT: Requires a second, is debatable and amendable; requires a majority vote, applies to main motions only.

8. *Limit Debate*

PURPOSE: To limit amount of time for discussion of a question.

FORM: "I move to limit debate on this question to one hour."

COMMENT: Requires a second, is not debatable, can be amended, requires a two-thirds vote, applies to all debatable questions.

7. *Previous Question (Immediate Vote)*

PURPOSE: To end discussion and bring motion to immediate vote.

FORM: "I move the previous question."

COMMENT: Requires a second, is not debatable, cannot be amended, requires a two-thirds vote, applies to any debatable motion.

6. *"Lay on the Table"*

PURPOSE: To postpone the motion for an undetermined time.

FORM: "I move that the motion be laid on the table."

COMMENT: Requires a second, is not debatable, cannot be amended, requires a majority vote.

III. PRIVILEGED MOTIONS

5. *Call for the Order of the Day*

PURPOSE: To remind the chairman and assembly to take up certain business at a fixed hour, when that business and hour have been previously agreed upon, and when the chairman has overlooked the scheduled event.

FORM: "Mr. Chairman, I call for the order of the day." Chairman: "If there is no objection, we will proceed to the business as scheduled."

COMMENT: No second required, not debatable, not amendable, in order when another has the floor, cannot be reconsidered.

4. *Questions of Privilege*

PURPOSE: To secure action on a motion related to "comfort rights, or privileges of the organization or of its members."

FORM: "Mr. Chairman, I rise to a question of privilege."

COMMENT: Can interrupt a speaker, requires no second, is not debatable, cannot be amended, requires no vote, is decided by the presiding officer.

3. Take Recess

PURPOSE: To permit a temporary break in the meeting.

FORM: "I move that we recess for one hour."

COMMENT: Requires a second, is not debatable, requires a majority vote, applies to no other motion.

2. Adjourn

PURPOSE: To end a meeting.

FORM: "I move we adjourn."

COMMENT: Requires a second, is not debatable, cannot be amended, requires a majority vote, takes precedence over all other motions, applies to no other motion, can be renewed at the same meeting when a new parliamentary situation develops.

1. Fix Time to Adjourn

PURPOSE: To fix time for the next meeting.

FORM: "Mr. Chairman, I move that we adjourn to meet tomorrow at 1 P.M."

COMMENT: Requires a second, not debatable if made when another motion is before the assembly, amendable, majority vote, not in order when another has the floor, can be reconsidered.

IV. INCIDENTAL MOTIONS

1. Appeal

PURPOSE: To decide by assembly vote whether the chairman's ruling is to be upheld.

FORM: "Mr. Chairman, I appeal from the decision of the chair."

COMMENT: Can interrupt a speaker, requires a second, is debatable, cannot be amended, requires a majority of the vote to sustain the chairman's position.

2. Point of Order

PURPOSE: To call attention to a violation of the rules.

FORM: "Mr. Chairman, I rise to a point of order."

COMMENT: Can interrupt a speaker, requires no second, is not debatable, cannot be amended, requires no vote.

3. Parliamentary Inquiry

PURPOSE: To enable a member to obtain information from the chairman.

FORM: "I rise to a parliamentary inquiry."

COMMENT: Requires no second, is not debatable, requires no vote.

4. Suspend Rules

PURPOSE: To allow assembly to act in some manner forbidden by parliamentary rules.

FORM: "I move to suspend the rules in order that . . . ."

COMMENT: Cannot interrupt a speaker, requires a second, is not debatable, cannot be amended, requires a two-thirds vote.

5. Withdraw a Motion

PURPOSE: To enable a member to withdraw a motion he has made.

TABLE OF PARLIAMENTARY MOTIONS

Motions	Need of second	Amendable	Debatable	Vote required	May be postponed	May be reconsidered	May be laid on table	May interrupt speaker
I. Privileged Motions								
1. Fix time to adjourn	Yes	Yes	No	Majority	No	No	No	No
2. To adjourn	Yes	No	No	Majority	No	No	No	No
3. To take a recess	Yes	Yes	No (usually)	Majority	No	No	No	No
4. Question of privilege	No	No	No	Chairman	No	No	No	Yes
5. Order of day	No	No	No	Chairman	No	No	No	Yes
II. Subsidiary Motions								
6. To lay on table	Yes	No	No	Majority	No	No	No	No
7. Previous question	Yes	No	No	Two-thirds	No	If lost, no	Yes	No
8. To postpone to a definite time	Yes	Yes	Yes	Majority	No	Yes	Yes	No
9. To commit, refer, recommit	Yes	Yes	Yes	Majority	No	Yes	Yes	No
10. To amend	Yes	Yes	Yes	Majority	Yes	Yes	Yes	No
11. To postpone indefinitely	Yes	No	Yes	Majority	Yes	Yes	Yes	No
12. Limit debate	Yes	Yes	No	Two-thirds	Yes	Yes	Yes	No
III. Main Motions								
13. Any main question	Yes	Yes	Yes	Majority	Yes	Yes	Yes	No
13a. Specific main question								
(13a) Reconsider	Yes	No	Yes	Majority	No	No	Yes	No
(13b) Rescind	Yes	No	Yes	Majority	No	No	Yes	No
(13c) Resume consideration	Yes	No	No	Majority	No	Yes, after change in procedure	Part	No
IV. Incidental Motions								
1. To appeal from chair	Yes	No	Debate limited	Majority	No	Yes	No	Yes
2. Point of order	No	No	No	Chairman	No	No	No	Yes
3. Parliamentary inquiry	No	No	No	No vote	No	No	No	Yes
4. To suspend a rule	Yes	No	No	Two-thirds	No	No	No	No
5. To withdraw a motion	No	No	No	Majority	No	Yes	Yes	No
6. To object to consideration	Yes	No	Yes	Two-thirds frequently	No	No	Yes	No
7. Division of a question	No	No	No	No vote	No	No	No	No

SOURCE: Adapted from A. Craig Baird, *Argumentation, Discussion, and Debate*, McGraw-Hill Book Company, Inc., New York, 1950, Appendix C, pp. 400–402.

FORM: "I wish to withdraw my motion."

COMMENT: Requires no second, is not debatable, cannot be amended, requires no vote, granted only by unanimous consent.

6. *Object to Consideration*

PURPOSE: To suppress a motion.

FORM: "Mr. President, I object to consideration of this question."

COMMENT: Can interrupt a speaker, requires no second, is not debatable, cannot be amended, requires a two-thirds negative vote, applies to main motion only.

7. *Division of Question*

PURPOSE: To divide a motion so that each section can be considered and voted on separately.

FORM: "I request that the motion just stated be divided into two parts . . . ."

COMMENT: Cannot interrupt a speaker, requires no second, is not debatable, cannot be amended, requires no vote.

Projects and Problems

PROJECT 1:   The class will organize a "Forensics Club." A preliminary meeting will be called to establish such a club. A temporary leader will be selected in advance to open the session and conduct the election of temporary officers. Motions will be presented and discussed concerning the purpose and scope of the organization. If the proposed organization is approved, a committee will be elected to draft a constitution and bylaws.

PROJECT 2:   The class will hold a preliminary session under the temporary chairman and temporary secretary to read and discuss the proposed constitution (copies of which have been prepared for each member). The document will be read section by section with discussion and possible amendments. The constitution is then read in its complete and amended form for final passage. The same procedure is followed for the bylaws. Permanent officers for the group are then elected and possible agenda for the next meeting suggested.

PROJECT 3:   The Forensics Club will meet, following the order of business suggested in this chapter. A resolution, selected in advance by a committee approved at the previous meeting, will be debated and approved or rejected. By agreement, the chairman and secretary may be changed at the middle of the session. Parliamentary procedures will be observed. By agreement, each speech may be limited to two minutes. The instructor will serve as the parliamentarian. Parliamentary complexities and confusion will be discouraged.

PROJECT 4:   Each member will be prepared to explain, without notes, each of the following terms: (*a*) appeal, (*b*) chair, (*c*) division of assembly, (*d*) division of question, (*e*) floor, (*f*) incidental motions, (*g*) lay on the table,

(h) main motion, (i) majority vote, (j) object to consideration, (k) order of the day, (l) plurality, (m) point of order, (n) previous question, (o) reconsider, (p) rescind, (q) withdraw.

PROJECT 5: Explain each: (a) What is the precedence of motions? (b) What motions require a second? (c) What motions may be amended? (d) What vote is required for typical motions?

PROJECT 6: A member says, "I move the previous question." What procedures may the chairman follow?

PROJECT 7: As chairman, explain how you will handle the following parliamentary situation: A motion has been made and seconded that this club endorse the Student Council proposal for a higher student-activity fee to include free admission to all campus theatre programs (or some similar campus program).

An amendment to the motion has been proposed to read, "and to all campus operas and student musical shows."

A member moves to lay the entire motion on the table. Another member moves to amend the amendment by striking out all words in the resolution beyond "higher student-activity fee."

PROJECT 8: A member questions the decision of the chairman and says, "I appeal from the decision of the chair." What situations then may confront the chairman, and how does he proceed?

References

Auer, J. Jeffery, *Essentials of Parliamentary Procedure,* 3rd ed. New York: Appleton-Century-Crofts, 1959.

Bosmajian, Haig A., *Readings in Parliamentary Procedures.* New York: Harper and Row, 1968.

Gulley, Halbert E., *Discussion, Conference, and Group Process.* New York: Holt, Rinehart and Winston, Inc., New York, 1960. Chapter 16.

O'Brien, Joseph F., *Parliamentary Law for the Layman.* New York: Harper & Brothers, 1952.

Robert's Rules of Order, rev. ed. Glenview, Ill.: Scott, Foresman and Company, 1969.

Sturgis, Alice F., *Standard Code of Parliamentary Procedure.* New York: McGraw-Hill Book Company, Inc., 1950.

———, *Learning Parliamentary Procedure.* New York: McGraw-Hill Book Company, Inc., 1953.

appendix A

MAIN SYMBOLS OF THE PHONETIC ALPHABET, FOR ENGLISH

Pho-netic symbol	Dictionary symbol	Example	Pho-netic symbol	Dictionary symbol	Example
i	ē	be	t	t	lit
ɪ	ĭ	hit	d	d	lid
ɛ	ĕ	bed	k	k	wick
æ	ă	tan	g	g	wig
ə	à	about	r	r	rice
ʌ	ŭ	but	l	l	lice
ɑ	ä	far	f	f	fine
ɔ	ô	law	v	v	vine
ʊ	o͞o	foot	θ	th	both
u	o͞o	fool	ð	th	bathe
e	ā	ape	s	s	lace
iu	ū	mute	z	z	lazy
ou	ou	coal	ʃ	sh	rush
au	ou	ouch	ʒ	zh	rouge
aɪ	ī	light	h	h	hit
ɔɪ	oi	oil	ʍ	hw	whine
m	m	men	w	w	wine
n	n	new	j	y	yes
ŋ	ng	sing	tʃ	ch	char
p	p	pin	dʒ	j	jar
b	b	bin			

appendix B

Sources of Information and Opinion

General Encyclopedias

Encyclopedia Americana, 30 vols., Americana Corporation, 1969; Americana Annual, 1918 to date.

Encyclopaedia Britannica, 24 vols., 1970; 11th ed., 1910–1911, 32 vols., generally considered most scholarly of all. Britannica Book of the Year, 1938 to date.

Special Encyclopedias

Encyclopedia of Philosophy, 8 vols., Paul Edwards (ed.), The Macmillan Company, New York, 1967.

Encyclopedia of Religion and Ethics, 13 vols., James Hastings (ed.), Charles Scribner's Sons, New York, 1959.

International Encyclopedia of the Social Sciences, 17 vols., David L. Sills (ed.), The Macmillan Company, New York, 1968.

Yearbooks

American Yearbook, Thomas Nelson & Sons, New York, 1925 to date.

American Annual, Encyclopedia Americana, since 1923.

Britannica Book of the Year, Encyclopaedia Britannica, since 1938.

Collier's Yearbook, P. F. Collier & Sons Corporation, New York, since 1939.

New International Year Book, Funk & Wagnalls Company, New York, since 1907.

Yearbook of the United Nations, United Nations, Department of Public Information, New York, 1947 to date.

Statesman's Yearbook, The Macmillan Company, New York, 1864 to date.

World Almanac, Newspaper Enterprise Association, New York, 1868 to date. Contains a list of organizations in the United States many of which publish material in their special fields.

Directories and Biographical Dictionaries

Who's Who (English), A & C Black, Ltd., and The Macmillan Company, New York, annual, 1849 to date.

Who's Who in America, The A. N. Marquis Co., Chicago, Ill., 1899 to date. **381**

Additional volumes of the Who's Who series are available in special fields,
e.g., *Who's Who in American Women, Who's Who in Art, Who's Who
in Engineering, Who's Who in the Theatre.*

Current Biography, The H. W. Wilson Company, New York, monthly, annual
cumulation, 1940 to date.

Dictionary of American Biography, 20 vols., Allen Johnson and Dumas
Malone (eds.), Charles Scribner's Sons, New York, 1928–1937; with later
supplements.

Dictionary of National Biography, 22 vols., Leslie Stephen and Sidney Lee
(eds.), Smith, Elder, London, 1908–1909; regular supplements.

Directory of American Scholars, 4th ed., R. R. Bowker Company, New York,
1964.

Leaders in Education, 5th ed., Jaques Cattell and E. E. Ross (eds.), Science
Press, Lancaster, Pa., 1960.

Magazines

Reader's Guide to Periodical Literature, H. W. Wilson Company, New York,
1900 to date. See also Special Indexes, including *Agricultural Index, Art
Index, Biography Index, Education Index, Index to Legal Periodicals,
Industrial Arts Index, Social Sciences and Humanities Index.*

Psychological Abstracts, American Psychological Association, Inc., Washington, 1927 to date.

*Table of Contents of Quarterly Journal of Speech, 1915–1964, Speech Mon-
ographs, 1934–1964,* and *The Speech Teacher, 1952–1964,* Franklin H.
Knower (comp.), Speech Association of America, 1965.

*Index and Table of Contents of Southern Speech Journal, 1935–1965. West-
ern Speech Journal, 1937–1965, Central States Speech Journal, 1949–1965,*
and *Today's Speech, 1953–1965,* Robert Dunham, L. S. Harms, and Richard
Gregg (comps.), Speech Association of America, 1966.

Public Affairs Information Service Bulletin, 1915 to date. Weekly.

Newspapers

New York Times Index, 1913 to date.

Index to the Times [London], 1907 to date.

Government Documents and Bibliographies

Bureau of the Census, *Statistical Abstract of the United States,* Government
Printing Office, annual, 1878 to date.

Bureau of Foreign and Domestic Commerce, *Survey of Current Business,*
Government Printing Office, monthly, 1921 to date.

Department of Agriculture, *Agricultural Statistics,* Government Printing
Office, annual, 1936 to date.

Department of State, *Bulletin,* Government Printing Office, Official Record of United States foreign policy; issued weekly by the Office of Public Services, Bureau of Public Affairs, since 1939.

United States Superintendent of Documents

Numerical Lists and Schedule of Volumes of the Reports and Documents of the 73rd Congress, Government Printing Office, 1934 to date. Continued for successive sessions of Congress.

United States Congress, *Congressional Record,* Government Printing Office, 1873 to date.

Bureau of Labor Statistics, *Subject Index of Bulletins,* 1915–1959, Bulletin No. 1281, United States Department of Labor.

United States Bureau of the Census, *Census Publications,* catalog and subject guide, Government Printing Office, quarterly, annual cumulation, 1945 to date.

United States Superintendent of Documents, *United States Government Publications: Monthly Catalog,* Government Printing Office, 1895 to date, supplements, 1941–1942, 1943–1944, 1945–1946.

Nongovernmental Documents and Pamphlets

Brookings Institution, *Brookings Publications,* Washington, D.C. A checklist issued annually. Material especially useful in the field of economics, politics, and foreign affairs.

National Association of Manufacturers, Research Department, *National Fact Book,* Washington, D.C. Current statistical service.

Foreign Policy Association, *Headline Series,* Washington, D.C. Summaries and analyses of all aspects of United States foreign policy (74 pamphlets to 1966).

See also publications of other professional organizations (addresses in *World Almanac* and other sources).

Bibliographies, Book Indexes

Bibliographic Index: A Cumulative Bibliography of Bibliographies, H. W. Wilson Company, New York, 1938 to date.

Book Review Digest, H. W. Wilson Company, New York, 1905 to date.

Conover, Helen F.: *Guide to Bibliographic Tools for Research in Foreign Affairs,* Library of Congress, Washington, D.C., 1958.

Cumulative Book Index, H. W. Wilson Company, New York, 1898 to date. A world list of books in the English language; supplements the United States Catalog.

Essay and General Literature Index, H. W. Wilson Company, New York, 1900 to date.

Foreign Affairs Bibliography, Harper and Brothers, New York, 1933 to date.

Public Affairs Information Service Bulletin, Public Affairs Information Service, 1915 to date, weekly, annual cumulation. Indexes books, pamphlets, documents, and periodicals in political and social sciences.

Publishers' Weekly, 1872 to date. American trade book journal, lists currently published books.

United States Catalog, H. W. Wilson Company, New York, 1899–1928, supplements, 1906, 1912–1917, 1918–1921, 1921–1924. A list of all books in print in the English language. Kept up-to-date by the *Cumulative Book Index.*

Vertical File Index, H. W. Wilson Company, New York, 1932–1934. Monthly, annual cumulation. Annotated subject catalog of pamphlets, booklets, leaflets, circulars, folders, maps, charts, and mimeographed bulletins.

Winchell, Constance (ed.): *Guide to Reference Books,* 8th ed., American Library Association, Chicago, 1967, and frequent supplements since.

Facts on File, News Digests, with cumulative index, since 1940.

appendix C

Examples of Speech Communication

Some outstanding speeches have become examples that suggest proper methods for the student in his own speech development. This is not to suggest, however, that excellent talks, short or long, are to be closely imitated or copied. But the experiences and methods of successful public communicators give clues and principles that guide the learner in his own effective creativity.

How, then, are we to profit by the illustrative examples in this book, including the speeches in the section below?

Your judgment of a speech and its speaker can well be guided by the principles and methods that make up this book.

The speech process that you judge is composed of the speaker, the speaking situation, the audience, the speech itself, and the overall combination of these factors that make up the communication act. (See again Chapters Three and Four.)

Pertinent questions that may help the reader to explore a given speech are thus suggested:

1. *Did the speaker compose the speech attributed to him?* We need to question whether a ghost writer produced the document.
2. *Did the text as produced duplicate what the speaker actually said?* If an electrical or other recording of the actual remarks uttered is available, we can compare it with the written text of the speech.
3. *What was the speaking situation?* Was the speaker talking in the midst of a war, economic depression, or another event, large or small, that might have affected what he said? (See Chapter Six.)
4. *What was the nature of the specific audience?* What was its race, education, economic level, or other characteristics? (See Chapter Six.)
5. *What was the purpose of the speaker?* Was it mainly to inform, persuade, inspire, entertain? (See Chapters Eight and Twenty through Twenty-three.)
6. *What were the chief ideas of the speech?* Were they worthwhile? (See Chapters Nine and Ten.)
7. *What evidence or other details supported the central ideas?* (See Chapters Eight, Nineteen through Twenty-two.)
8. *What motivative elements in addition to the logical substance of the* **385**

    speech were apparent, and were they effectively developed? (See Chapters Eighteen, Twenty-one, and Twenty-two.)

9. *Was the speech well organized?* (See Chapter Eleven.)
10. *Was the language effective?* Was it original, interesting, clear, accurate, adapted to the occasion and audience? (See Chapter Twelve.)
11. *Can we determine the effectiveness of the speaker's delivery?* The written speech, to be sure, provides no clues about the speaker's voice, rate, quality, and other vocal features. These can obviously be checked by the testimony of those who heard the speaker. (See Chapters Fifteen and Sixteen.)
12. *Can we judge the total effectiveness of the speech?* Your judgment here will involve a study of separate details and of the overall effect. You may judge a speech on the basis of its ideas, its structure, its appeals, or its language—or some synthesis of these factors. (See Chapter Seventeen.)

You will need a norm by which to judge these speeches. A review of the principles of this book should help you.

Campus Revolutionaries

Richard M. Nixon, *President of the United States**

Freedom. A condition and a process. As we dedicate this beautiful new library, I think this is the time and place to speak of some basic things in American life. It is the time, because we find our fundamental values under bitter and even violent attack; it is the place, because so much that is basic is represented here.

    Opportunity for all is represented here.

    This is a small college: not rich and famous, like Harvard or Yale; not a vast state university like Berkeley or Michigan. But for almost 90 years it has served the people of South Dakota, opening doors of opportunity for thousands of deserving young men and women.

    Like hundreds of other fine small colleges across the nation, General Beadle State College—has offered a chance to people who might not otherwise have had a chance.

    The pioneer spirit is represented here, and the progress that has shaped our heritage.

    In South Dakota we still can sense the daring that converted a raw frontier into part of the vast heartland of America.

    The vitality of thought is represented here.

    A college library is a place of living ideas—a place where timeless truths

*Delivered at General Beadle State College, Madison, South Dakota, June 3, 1969. *Vital Speeches of the Day*, 35:546–548, July 1, 1969. By permission of this publication and President Nixon.

are collected, to become the raw materials of discovery. In addition, the Karl E. Mundt Library will house the papers of a wise and dedicated man who for 30 years has been at the center of public events. Thus, more than most, this is a library of both thought and action, combining the wisdom of past ages with a uniquely personal record of the present time.

As we dedicate this place of ideas, therefore, let us reflect on some of the values we have inherited, which are now under challenge.

We live in a deeply troubled and profoundly unsettled time. Drugs, crime, campus revolts, racial discord, draft resistance—on every hand we find old standards violated, old values discarded, old precepts ignored. A vocal minority of the young are opting out of the process by which a civilization maintains its continuity: the passing on of values from one generation to the next. Old and young across a chasm of misunderstanding—and the more loudly they shout, the wider the chasm grows.

As a result, our institutions are undergoing what may be their severest challenge yet. I speak not of the physical challenge: the forces and threats of force that have wracked our cities, and now our colleges. Force can be contained.

We have the power to strike back if need be, and to prevail. The nation has survived other attempts at this. It has not been a lack of civil power, but the reluctance of a free people to employ it, that so often has stayed the hand of authorities faced with confrontation.

The challenge I speak of is deeper: the challenge to our values, and to the moral base of the authority that sustains those values.

At the outset, let me draw one clear distinction.

A great deal of today's debate about "values," or about "morality," centers on what essentially are private values and personal codes: patterns of dress and appearance, sexual mores; religious practices; the uses to which a person intends to put his own life.

These are immensely important, but they are not the values I mean to discuss here.

My concern today is not with the length of a person's hair, but with his conduct in relation to his community; not with what he wears, but with his impact on the process by which a free society governs itself.

I speak not of private morality but of public morality—and of "morality" in its broadest sense, as a set of standards by which the community chooses to judge itself.

Some critics call ours an "immoral" society because they disagree with its policies, or they refuse to obey its laws because they claim that those laws have no moral basis. Yet the structure of our laws has rested from the beginning on a foundation of moral purpose.

That moral purpose embodies what is, above all, a deeply humane set of values—rooted in a profound respect for the individual, for the integrity of his person and the dignity of his humanity.

At first glance, there is something homely and unexciting about basic values we have long believed in. We feel apologetic about espousing them; even the profoundest truths become cliches with repetition. But they can be live sleeping giants: slow to rouse, but magnificent in their strength.

Let us look at some of those values—so familiar now, and yet once so revolutionary:

Liberty: recognizing that liberties can only exist in balance, with the liberty of each stopping at that point at which it would infringe the liberty of another.

Freedom of conscience: meaning that each person has the freedom of his own conscience, and therefore none has the right to dictate the conscience of his neighbor.

Justice: recognizing that true justice is impartial, and that no man can be judge in his own cause.

Human dignity: a dignity that inspires pride, is rooted in self-reliance and provides the satisfaction of being a useful and respected member of the community.

Concern for the disadvantaged and dispossessed: but a concern that neither panders nor patronizes.

The right to participate in public decisions: which carries with it the duty to abide by those decisions when reached, recognizing that no one can have his own way all the time.

Human fulfillment: in the sense not of unlimited license, but of maximum opportunity.

The right to grow, to reach upward, to be all that we can become, in a system that rewards enterprise, encourages innovation and honors excellence.

In essence, these all are aspects of freedom. They inhere in the concept of freedom; they aim at extending freedom; they celebrate the uses of freedom. They are not new. But they are as timeless and as timely as the human spirit because they are rooted in the human spirit.

Our basic values concern not only what we seek but how we seek it.

Freedom is a condition; it also is a process. And the process is essential to the freedom itself.

We have a Constitution that sets certain limits on what government can do but that allows wide discretion within those limits. We have a system of divided powers, of checks and balances, of periodic elections, all of which are designed to insure that the majority has a chance to work its will—but not to override the rights of the minority or to infringe the rights of the individual.

What this adds up to is a democratic process, carefully constructed and stringently guarded. It is not perfect. No system could be. But it has served the nation well—and nearly two centuries of growth and change testify to its strength and adaptability.

They testify, also, to the fact that avenues of peaceful change do exist.

Those who can make a persuasive case for changes they want can achieve them through this orderly process.

To challenge a particular policy is one thing; to challenge the government's right to set it is another—for this denies the process of freedom.

Lately, however, a great many people have become impatient with the democratic process. Some of the more extreme even argue, with curious logic, that there is no majority, because the majority has no right to hold opinions that they disagree with.

Scorning persuasion, they prefer coercion. Awarding themselves what they call a higher morality, they try to bully authorities into yielding to their "demands."

On college campuses, they draw support from faculty members who should know better; in the larger community, they find the usual apologists ready to excuse any tactic in the name of "progress."

It should be self-evident that this sort of self-righteous moral arrogance has no place in a free community. It denies the most fundamental of all the values we hold: respect for the rights of others. This principle of mutual respect is the keystone of the entire structure of ordered liberty that makes freedom possible.

The student who invades an administration building, roughs up the dean, rifles the files and issues "non-negotiable demands" may have some of his demands met by a permissive university administration. But the greater his "victory" the more he will have undermined the security of his own rights.

In a free society, the rights of none are secure unless the rights of all are respected. It is precisely the structure of law and custom that he has chosen to violate—the process of freedom—by which the rights of all are protected.

We have long considered our colleges and universities citadels of freedom, where the rule of reason prevails. Now both the process of freedom and the rule of reason are under attack. At the same time, our colleges are under pressure to collapse their educational standards in the misguided belief that this would promote "opportunity."

Instead of seeking to raise lagging students up to meet the college stand-ards, the cry now is to lower the standards to meet the students. This is the old, familiar, self-indulgent cry for the easy way. It debases the integrity of the educational process.

There is no easy way to excellence, no short-cut to the truth, no magic wand that can produce a trained and disciplined mind without the hard discipline of learning. To yield to these demands would weaken the institu-tion; more importantly, it would cheat the student of what he comes to a college for: his education.

No group, as a group, should be more zealous defenders of the integrity of academic standards and the rule of reason in academic life than the faculties of our great institutions. If they simply follow the loudest voices, parrot the latest slogan, yield to unreasonable demands, they will have won not the respect but the contempt of their students.

Students have a right to guidance, to leadership, to direction; they have a right to expect their teachers to listen, and to be reasonable, but also to stand for something—and most especially, to stand for the rule of reason against the rule of force.

Our colleges have their weaknesses. Some have become too impersonal, or too ingrown, and curricula have lagged. But with all its faults, the fact remains that the American system of higher education is the best in this whole imperfect world—and it provides, in the United States today, a better education for more students of all economic levels than ever before, anywhere, in the history of the world.

This is no small achievement.

Often, the worst mischief is done by the name of the best cause. In our zeal for instant reform, we should be careful not to destroy our educational standards, and our educational system along with them; and not to undermine the process of freedom, on which all else rests.

The process of freedom will be less threatened in America, however, if we pay more heed to one of the great cries of the young today. I speak now of their demand for honesty: intellectual honesty, personal honesty, public honesty.

Much of what seems to be revolt is really little more than this: an attempt to strip away sham and pretense, to puncture illusion, to get down to the basic nub of truth.

We should welcome this. We have seen too many patterns of deception:

In political life, impossible promises.

In advertising, extravagant claims.

In business, shady deals.

In personal life, we all have witnessed deceits that ranged from the "little white lie" to moral hypocrisy; from cheating on income taxes to bilking insurance companies.

In public life, we have seen reputations destroyed by smear, and gimmicks paraded as panaceas. We have heard shrill voices of hate, shouting lies, and sly voices of malice, twisting facts.

Even in intellectual life, we too often have seen logical gymnastics performed to justify a pet theory, and refusal to accept facts that fail to support it.

Absolute honesty would be ungenerous. Courtesy compels us to welcome the unwanted visitor; kindness leads us to compliment the homely girl on how pretty she looks. But in our public discussions, we sorely need a kind of honesty that has too often been lacking; the honesty of straight talk; a doing away with hyperbole; a careful concern with the gradations of truth, and a frank recognition of the limits of our knowledge about the problems we have to deal with.

We have long demanded financial integrity in public life; we now need the most rigorous kind of intellectual integrity in public debate.

Unless we can find a way to speak plainly, truly, unselfconsciously, about the facts of public life, we may find that our grip on the forces of history is too loose to control our own destiny.

The honesty of straight talk leads us to the conclusion that some of our recent social experiments have worked, and some have failed, and that most have achieved something—but less than their advance billing promised.

This same honesty is concerned not with assigning blame, but with discovering what lessons can be drawn from that experience in order to design better programs next time. Perhaps the goals were unattainable; perhaps the means were inadequate; perhaps the program was based on an unrealistic assessment of human nature.

We can learn these lessons only to the extent that we can be candid with one another. We face enormously complex choices. In approaching these, confrontation is no substitute for consultation; passionate concern gets us nowhere without dispassionate analysis. More fundamentally, our structure of faith depends on faith, and faith depends on truth.

The values we cherish are sustained by a fabric of mutual self-restraint, woven of ordinary civil decency, respect for the rights of others, respect for the laws of the community, and respect for the democratic process of orderly change.

The purpose of these restraints is not to protect an "establishment," but to establish the protection of liberty; not to prevent change, but to insure that change reflects the public will and respects the rights of all.

This process is our most precious resource as a nation. But it depends on public acceptance, public understanding and public faith.

Whether our values are maintained depends ultimately not on the Government, but on the people.

A nation can be only as great at its people want it to be.

A nation can be only as free as its people insist that it be.

A nation's laws are only as strong as its people's will to see them enforced.

A nation's freedoms are only as secure as its people's determination to see them maintained.

A nation's values are only as lasting as the ability of each generation to pass them on to the next.

We often have a tendency to turn away from the familiar because it is familiar, and to seek the new because it is new.

To those intoxicated with the romance of violent revolution, the continuing revolution of democracy may seem unexciting. But no system has ever liberated the spirits of so many so fully. Nothing has ever "turned on" man's energies, his imagination, his unfettered creativity, the way the ideal of freedom has.

Some see America's vast wealth and protest that this has made us "materialistic." But we should not be apologetic about our abundance. We should not fall into the easy trap of confusing the production of things with the worship of things. We produce abundantly; but our values turn not on what we have, but on what we believe.

We believe in liberty, and decency, and the process of freedom. On these beliefs we rest our pride as a nation; in these beliefs we rest our hopes for the future; and by our fidelity to the process of freedom, we can assure to ourselves and our posterity the blessings of freedom.

Environmental Pollution: A National Problem

John E. Swearingen, *Chairman, Standard Oil Company (Indiana)**

As we enter the concluding chapters of the 20th Century, we find the United States in a mood of uncertainty and self-doubt which has few parallels in our history. While the Civil War was the high water mark of our national division, it was at least division into two broad camps, each of which was convinced of the eternal rightness of its position.

Today, however, nearly every aspect of our national life is under attack for one reason or another. Considerable numbers of the young appear convinced that our whole society is rotten to the core, and in need of rebuilding from the ground up. At the other end of the age spectrum are eminent adults who are equally convinced that fatal threats to our well-being lie in the conduct of foreign policy, defense, taxation and spending, or some other policy area. In between we are confronted by a host of crusaders for various causes, enthusiastically abetted by the mass media, reminding us of an endless list of deficiencies demanding immediate correction if the nation is to survive. Many of the crusaders have drastic, and sometimes peculiar, solutions to the problems which have caught their attention.

In the course of this national psychoanalysis, we have rediscovered a number of problems—such as poverty, inferior education, inequality of opportunity, and urban decay—which are as old as civilization itself. The scale of this self-criticism has reached such proportions that it threatens to turn us into a nation of hypochondriacs—along with giving aid and comfort to our enemies, who delight in the deliberate exaggeration of anything which puts the United States in an unfavorable light.

A good deal of the hand-wringing that is going on is unproductive of anything but a mood of fatalism and despair. Certainly we have a formidable list of very real problems crying for solution. As I have suggested, however, none of these is new, and all of them happen to exist to a greater degree outside the United States than they do here.

---

*Address at Annual Meeting of the Indiana State Chamber of Commerce, Indianapolis, November 6, 1969.

In addition, the heat and extent of the debate going on—whether the subject is pot in the schools or the war in Vietnam—is ample evidence of vitality within our society. It is also a daily reminder that our system allows considerably more room for dissent than is to be found in the systems erected by the followers of Marx, Lenin, Che Guevara, Comrade Mao and the other heroes of the militant Left.

More to the point is the fact that we are trying to eradicate some of these age-old evils. This is clearly in the pioneering and egalitarian tradition of America. Thanks to the tremendous productive capacity of our economy, such a goal may indeed be within our reach. No other sizeable country in the world could seriously begin to consider such an undertaking, on economic grounds alone.

There is hardly a problem area you can name which has not been the target of increasing expenditures and efforts in recent years, and—measured by historical standards—considerable progress has been registered on many fronts. With our characteristic impatience, however, we want to see the job done tomorrow, and more attention gets focused on the shortcomings than on the gains.

Along the way, we have made the painful discovery that some of these problems are a good deal more complex and intractable than had been generally realized. It has also been discovered that it takes more than grants of money, however large, and the enactment of legislation, however well-intended, to bring about the desired changes.

The most recent of our problems to assume national priority—and the one to which I am going to address my remarks today—is air and water pollution. I think this is an appropriate forum in which to raise the subject, since we have represented here the principal elements of our society which are currently engaged in the effort to arrest pollution. While individuals and groups of every persuasion have an interest in cleaner air and water, the assignment of doing something about the matter is in the hands of the governmental and business leadership of which this audience is composed.

While pollution has been a subject of concern in many quarters for some time, it is only in recent years that the public has given it real note. However, according to national opinion surveys, over 50 per cent of the public now considers air and water pollution to have reached serious levels. The concern of the forward-looking conservationist has been communicated to the public, and has provided the leverage for legislation and other action to combat the problem.

Within the past few years, approximately 500 bills and amendments dealing with pollution control have been introduced in Congress. Even admitting the sure-fire political appeal of standing foursquare on the side of clean air and water, this is a truly remarkable concentration of Congressional attention in so short a period.

The most significant outcome of this concentration to date has been the

Air Quality Act of 1967, a blueprint for dealing with air pollution on a regional basis by establishing concurrent state and federal jurisdictions and enforcement requirements. In turn, this act has provided a springboard for corollary legislation at the state and local levels. Equally far-reaching proposals to deal with water pollution are nearing approval.

Running through the bills and amendments at the national level is a determined effort to extend federal jurisdiction into many areas traditionally reserved to the states. The basis of the demand by federal agencies for a greater role in decision making is the contention that the states have not been vigorous enough in using their control authority, and that many state programs are either nominal or inadequate, or both. Friction and jurisdictional disputes extending down to local governmental levels have been among the byproducts of this process, and more can be expected. Meanwhile, business and industry are called upon to devote increasing amounts of time and money to comply with progressively stricter standards applying to their operations.

Apart from the question of who's in charge, there is no mistaking the gravity of the challenge posed by pollution. Individually and collectively, we have defied the laws of intelligent housekeeping for so long as to impair the quality of our environment to a serious degree. Before the situation is further compounded by the projected new waves of population about to crash down upon us, concerted action is imperative.

One of the accomplishments of the space program has been to give us a better perspective of our situation here on earth. Scientists have been pointing out for years the relative frailty of the envelope of atmosphere and water which sustains life on this planet. Now that we have had a closer look at the desolate landscapes of some of our neighbors in the solar system—along with a view of this lush earth from outside—the importance of preserving our environmental heritage has been driven forcibly home.

However, there is a danger that national concern over arresting pollution is going to lead us into repeating some of the same mistakes that have hobbled efforts to combat problems in other social areas. Lesson number one is that you can't successfully solve a problem unless you understand it—and there is considerable evidence that we have not yet reached this point.

The rhetoric, the television shows, the magazine and newspaper articles, the campaign speeches, the committees and the demonstrations that have awakened the public to the spread of pollution have made a positive contribution by calling attention to a situation in need of correction. To the extent that this barrage has tended to concentrate on industrial pollution, on the other hand, it has been somewhat misleading.

There is a danger that the public is being led into a belief that most of the problem can be eliminated simply by imposing strict controls on industry. Unfortunately, the problem is far too complex to be legislated out of existence, and crash programs aimed at symptoms rather than underlying causes are more likely to lead to economic waste than to environmental improvement.

We are not likely to make much headway in the fight against pollution unless we recognize that:

Environmental pollution is both a social and an economic problem.

It must be approached and solved on a practical basis—in terms of costs versus benefits.

In one manner or another, the costs must inevitably be borne by the consuming public—which means all of us.

A rational and effective approach to pollution control is impossible without genuine understanding of what the problem is, why it has developed, and what the roles of industry, government, and the individual should be in meeting the problem. In short, there is urgent need for an overall perspective—a philosophy of pollution control.

The central question is not whether we should have cleaner air and water, but how clean, at what cost, and how long to take to do the job.

The fact that these considerations are frequently ignored in popular discussions of the problem does not diminish their validity. No one can argue with the premise that wherever pollution can be scientifically demonstrated to be a genuine hazard to human health, it should be eliminated immediately and regardless of expense.

Beyond question, pollution has increased hand in hand with growth and concentration of population and with the introduction of technology. Some degree of pollution is part of the cost involved in achieving the benefits made possible in a technological society. Our challenge is to identify the complex sources of pollution and keep them within socially and economically tolerable limits.

There are a good number of people around who are convinced the curses of technology outweigh its blessings. My own view is closer to that expressed in the findings of a major study of the progress of technological societies, whose authors concluded: "Without its progress since the 19th Century, most men alive today would not have been born; those alive would have been sentenced to disease, filth, and even greater misery than exists in the world today. We are in better shape because of it."

Another long study of technology and society by a different group of scholars has concluded that the effect of technology has been to promote individualism—to give Americans a greater range of personal choice, wider experience, and a more highly developed sense of self-worth that any people in history.

Even the detractors of modern technology are hard put to portray it as the source of all our difficulties. Both air and water pollution have been around for a long time. Strong complaints were lodged by the patricians of ancient Rome because soot was smudging their white wool togas. Residents of the Los Angeles Basin who may think smog is a recent local invention might be interested to know that early Spanish explorers noted the haze from Indian campfires already hanging over the area.

As for water pollution, the battle against silt—which is still the leading pollutant—began some 8,000 years ago in Mesopotamia not long after the Sumerians invented irrigation. Babylon and Ninevah were brought down primarily because silt overcame the irrigation system on which the first great civilization was built. The same problem ruined Rome's famed sewer system and created the disease-breeding Pontine Marshes.

Our present situation is largely a function of ancient forces at work in an urban society of unprecedented size, and in which insufficient attention has been given to the changes this combination was bringing about in our environment.

Now that we are belatedly aware that the supply of pure air over a number of our cities is diminishing and that contamination of our water supplies has risen alarmingly, we are setting out to do something about the threat. Laws have been passed, new regulatory bodies have been established, funds appropriated, and research accelerated.

But the prospects for successful action to arrest pollution cannot be ranked very high until there is greater awareness that all members of society have created the problem and that all will have to be parties to the solution. Any serious examination of the situation indicates that there are three major sources of pollution: the public, governmental agencies, and industry. Of these three, I might note, responsible elements of industry were the first to recognize their contributions to pollution and to initiate remedial measures.

However, public criticism is levelled chiefly at industry as the major cause of both air and water pollution. The contributions to air pollution of public incinerators, garbage dumps, and the heating of homes and buildings are largely disregarded. When it comes to water pollution, the public singles out factory and plant wastes as the major offender, and assigns only a minor role to the silting of rivers and streams, to private septic tanks, or to wastes from other private sources such as power boats. In addition, the surveys also suggest that public enthusiasm for pollution control is matched by a reluctance to pay even a modest share of the cost.

This attitude will have to change. While industry presents one identifiable source of pollution, the unhappy fact remains that a problem of national magnitude would still be with us if pollution were somehow completely eliminated from all industrial operations. As one leading government enforcement official has noted, an underlying cause of water pollution is that all over the country we have municipal sewage systems that are inadequate for the loads imposed on them in the past few years. The cost of providing adequate municipal sewage treatment facilities has, by itself, been estimated at over $30 billion through the year 2000.

Or let us consider agriculture. Agriculture withdraws twice as much water from streams and wells as public water utilities and manufacturing industry combined. Much of this water finds its way back into rivers and streams, and we really know very little about the condition in which it is returned—although there are grounds for definite concern.

Any public illusions that the problem will be solved simply by applying strict controls on industry, and at little public cost, are going to be shattered before very long. The public can recognize its direct financial involvement when called upon to vote on a local bond issue or tax increase to underwrite improved sewage treatment or incineration facilities. But the same principle applies when it comes to pollution-control expenditures by industry. These are merely an additional cost of doing business, and—like all other costs—must ultimately be passed on to the consumer. As for government grants to control pollution, that bill will be rendered to us all by the Internal Revenue Service.

Along with many others, the petroleum industry is making strenuous efforts to minimize its contributions to the problem. Oil company expenditures for air and water conservation last year reached an estimated $382 million, as against $271 million two years earlier, and are expected to continue to increase. More than half of these pollution control expenditures are being devoted to capital equipment.

In arriving at decisions in this area, I should note that any corporate management faces a dual responsibility—to conserve not only natural resources, but also social and economic resources, such as capital. Even in designing a new facility, it usually becomes apparent at an early stage that, while significant improvement in pollution control can be made at reasonably modest cost, further additional investments will achieve smaller and smaller improvements.

Finally one reaches a point beyond which prohibitive incremental investments are required for small incremental improvements. Some place along the line, economic penalties outweigh social benefits, and management—along with society at large—must determine where that occurs in evaluating the cost and benefits involved.

In arriving at proper solutions to environmental control problems, it is essential that decisions be based on facts, not on suppositions or suspicion. Urgent situations create a responsibility to develop facts speedily, but not the responsibility to act before facts are determined. In its planning for conservation, industry needs reasonable assurance that a proposed solution is not motivated solely by a desire to solve the problem, but is backed up by enough facts to insure that is the best solution available.

The only sound bases for legislation and regulation are scientific knowledge and a sense of social responsibility, along with a series of definite goals. Without clear objectives, crash programs rather than planned ones are likely to result. This leads to a situation in which everyone is sure to lose, but not at all certain to win.

In our attempts to find the best available solution, I think it is clear from experience that pollution problems are not monolithic; they vary widely according to geographical conditions. There are, for example, different types of smog. London-type smog occurs chiefly where coal is the principal fuel used, and blankets the area at night or on cold foggy days when the air is stagnant. Photochemical smog, on the other hand, is prevalent around Los Angeles and some other sunny, poorly ventilated urban centers—and remains a big city, rather than a nationwide, problem. The same is true in regard to water pollution. Watersheds are defined by nature, and different geographical and ecological conditions call for different solutions.

When it comes to regulatory responsibility, the soundest principle is to place responsibility to take the necessary action on the level of government best able to cope with specific conservation problems. Such action should be tailored to local conditions. Mere copying of regulations adopted by other governmental units fails to recognize the diversity of local needs—and it is part of industry's responsibility to work to help clarify these local needs.

I think it is clear that the responsibility to act in defense of our essential natural resources, such as air and water, extends across the entire social structure of the nation—individuals, industry, plus local, state, and federal governments. In addition to its internal efforts to minimize pollution stemming from its operations, and research to improve conservation technology, industry has a responsibility to cooperate actively with government.

It is equally important that the public understands its role in the process, and comes to recognize the importance of balancing the inevitably large costs involved. The range of cost-versus-benefit choices is already extremely wide, and will grow wider as federal, state, and municipal programs for pollution control are put into effect. Only if the economic facts are widely understood can the public make an informed decision in each case, based on its willingness to pay for a stated degree of environmental cleanliness.

The cost-versus-benefit approach will not result in a Utopia, with an environment as pure as our first pioneers found it; rather, it points toward air and water quality that is acceptable, and compatible with the multiple needs of a technology-centered society.

In conclusion let me suggest that it is time we left the stage of finger-pointing, reciting past sins, and viewing with alarm and moved on to the vastly more difficult matter of solving some of our pollution problems. If a problem could be talked to death, pollution would have long since been lowered into its final resting place.

In today's climate, there are probably more people who are against pollution than are for motherhood, and a number of them are extremely vocal about where they stand. In their zeal, some of them verge on fanaticism. Just as in other areas, true fanatics at least merit our understanding. In my judgment, there is not much to be said for a much larger group of people who have been cynically and systematically using public concern over pollution as another platform from which to attack the business community and its motives.

Despite the positive harm these people do through fogging the issues, however, the best course appears to be to ignore them and to try to get on with the job.

In the words of John W. Gardner, "We have plenty of debaters, plenty of blamers, plenty of provocateurs, plenty of people who treat public affairs as an opportunity for personal catharsis or glorification. We don't have plenty of problem-solvers."

American industry at least has a high percentage of people in its ranks who have experience in solving problems, and, as I have noted, responsible segments of industry were the first to recognize their contribution to pollution and to launch costly and extensive measures to try to remedy the situation. That these efforts are going to accelerate is unquestionable, and they are one of the most promising signs on the horizon that something concrete is going to get done about our collective problem.

The roadblocks in our path lie more in the realm of sociology than technology. A society capable of interplanetary travel can surely devise the technology to control its own wastes. But broad public support of the necessary steps and a willingness to share the costs are indispensable. This is one more counter at which no free lunch is available, and the sooner the public faces up to that fact the sooner we will be on our way.

Eulogy on Dr. Martin Luther King, Jr.

Benjamin E. Mays, *President Emeritus, Morehouse College**

On April 9, 1968, Dr. Martin Luther King, Jr. was buried in Atlanta. The funeral services in his memory began shortly after 10:30 A.M. at Ebenezer Baptist Church, where he and his father had shared the pulpit. The Rev. Ralph D. Abernathy, successor to the presidency of the Southern Christian Leadership Conference, conducted the services at which short tributes were delivered by the Rev. Ronald English, assistant pastor of Dr. King's church, and Dr. L. Harold DeWolfe, dean of Wesley Theological Seminary in Washington, D.C.

A cortege headed by the mule-drawn wagon bearing the coffin of Dr. King, and followed by thousands of mourners, then moved through the streets of the city to the campus of Morehouse College, where Dr. King received his bachelor's degree in 1948. In an impressive ceremony attended by many of America's most distinguished citizens, Dr. Benjamin H. Mays, president emeritus of Morehouse College, delivered the formal eulogy on Dr. King.

*Morehouse College, Atlanta, Georgia, April 9, 1968. Text furnished by Dr. Mays, with permission for this reprint. Reprinted from the text in Lester Thonssen (ed.), *Representative American Speeches: 1967–68*, H. W. Wilson Co., New York, 1968, pp. 161–168.

*He belonged to the world and to mankind [said Dr. Mays]. Now he
belongs to posterity. . . .*

*If physical death was the price he had to pay to rid America of prejudice
and injustice, nothing could be more redemptive. And, to paraphrase the
words of the immortal John Fitzgerald Kennedy, permit me to say that
Martin Luther King, Jr.'s unfinished work on earth must truly be our own.*

To be honored by being requested to give the eulogy at the funeral of
Dr. Martin Luther King, Jr. is like asking one to eulogize his deceased son—so
close and so precious was he to me. Our friendship goes back to his student
days at Morehouse College. It is not an easy task; nevertheless I accept it,
with a sad heart and with full knowledge of my inadequacy to do justice
to this man. It was my desire that if I predeceased Dr. King, he would pay
tribute to me on my final day. It was his wish that if he predeceased me,
I would deliver the homily at his funeral. Fate has decreed that I eulogize
him. I wish it might have been otherwise; for, after all, I am three score
years and ten and Martin Luther is dead at thirty-nine.

Although there are some who rejoice in his death, there are millions across
the length and breadth of this world who are smitten with grief that this
friend of mankind—all mankind—has been cut down in the flower of his
youth. So, multitudes here and in foreign lands, queens, kings, heads of
governments, the clergy of the world, and the common man everywhere,
are praying that God will be with the family, the American people, and
the President of the United States in this tragic hour. We hope that this
universal concern will bring comfort to the family—for grief is like a heavy
load: when shared it is easier to bear. We come today to help the family
carry the load.

We have assembled here from every section of this great nation and from
other parts of the world to give thanks to God that He gave to America,
at this moment in history, Martin Luther King, Jr. Truly God is no respecter
of persons. How strange! God called the grandson of a slave on his father's
side, and the grandson of a man born during the Civil War on his mother's
side, and said to him: Martin Luther, speak to America about war and peace;
about social justice and racial discrimination; about its obligation to the
poor; and about nonviolence as a way of perfecting social change in a world
of brutality and war.

Here was a man who believed with all of his might that the pursuit of
violence at any time is ethically and morally wrong; that God and the moral
weight of the universe are against it; that violence is self-defeating; and
that only love and forgiveness can break the vicious circle of revenge. He
believed that nonviolence would prove effective in the abolition of injustice
in politics, in economics, in education, and in race relations. He was convinced, also, that people could not be moved to abolish voluntarily the
inhumanity of man to man by mere persuasion and pleading, but that they

could be moved to do so by dramatizing the evil through massive nonviolent resistance. He believed that nonviolent direct action was necessary to supplement the nonviolent victories won in the Federal courts. He believed that the nonviolent approach to solving social problems would ultimately prove to be redemptive.

Out of this conviction, history records the marches in Montgomery, Birmingham, Selma, Chicago, and other cities. He gave people an ethical and moral way to engage in activities designed to perfect social change without bloodshed and violence; and when violence did erupt it was that which is potential in any protest which aims to uproot deeply entrenched wrongs. No reasonable person would deny that the activities and the personality of Martin Luther King, Jr. contributed largely to the success of the student sit-in movements in abolishing segregation in downtown establishments; and that his activities contributed mightily to the passage of the Civil Rights legislation of 1964 and 1965.

Martin Luther King, Jr. believed in a united America. He believed that the walls of separation brought on by legal and de facto segregation, and discrimination based on race and color, could be eradicated. As he said in his Washington Monument address: "I have a dream."

He had faith in his country. He died striving to desegregate and integrate America to the end that this great nation of ours, born in revolution and blood, conceived in liberty and dedicated to the proposition that all men are created free and equal, will truly become the lighthouse of freedom where none will be denied because his skin is black and none favored because his eyes are blue; where our nation will be militarily strong but perpetually at peace; economically secure but just; learned but wise; where the poorest—the garbage collectors—will have bread enough and to spare; where no one will be poorly housed; each educated up to his capacity; and where the richest will understand the meaning of empathy. *This* was his dream, and the end toward which he strove. As he and his followers so often sang: "We shall overcome someday; black and white together."

Let it be thoroughly understood that our deceased brother did not embrace nonviolence out of fear or cowardice. Moral courage was one of his noblest virtues. As Mahatma Gandhi challenged the British Empire without a sword and won, Martin Luther King, Jr. challenged the interracial wrongs of his country without a gun. And he had the faith to believe that he would win the battle for social justice. I make bold to assert that it took more courage for King to practice nonviolence than it took his assassin to fire the fatal shot. The assassin is a coward: he committed his dastardly deed and fled. When Martin Luther disobeyed an unjust law, he accepted the consequences of his actions. He never ran away and he never begged for mercy. He returned to the Birmingham jail to serve his time.

Perhaps he was more courageous than soldiers who fight and die on the battlefield. There is an element of compulsion in their dying. But when

Martin Luther faced death again and again, and finally embraced it, there
was no external pressure. He was acting on an inner compulsion that drove
him on. More courageous than those who advocate violence as a way out,
for they carry weapons of destruction for defense. But Martin Luther faced
the dogs, the police, jail, heavy criticism, and finally death; and he never
carried a gun, not even a knife to defend himself. He had only his faith in
a just God to rely on; and the belief that "thrice is he armed who has his
quarrels just." The faith that Browning writes about when he says:

One who never turned his back but marched breast forward,
  Never doubted clouds would break,
  Never dreamed, though right were worsted, wrong would triumph,
  Held we fall to rise, and baffled to fight better,
    Sleep to wake,

Coupled with moral courage was Martin Luther King, Jr.'s capacity to
love people. Though deeply committed to a program of freedom for Negroes,
he had love and concern for all kinds of peoples. He drew no distinction
between the high and the low; none between the rich and the poor. He
believed especially that he was sent to champion the cause of the man
farthest down. He would probably say that if death had to come, I am sure
there was no greater cause to die for than fighting to get a just wage for
garbage collectors. He was supra-race, supra-nation, supra-denomination,
supra-class, and supra-culture. He belonged to the world and to mankind.
Now he belongs to posterity.

But there is a dichotomy in all this. This man was loved by some and
hated by others. If any man knew the meaning of suffering, King knew.
House bombed; living day by day for thirteen years under constant threats
of death; maliciously accused of being a Communist; falsely accused of
being insincere and seeking the limelight for his own glory; stabbed by a
member of his own race; slugged in a hotel lobby; jailed thirty times;
occasionally deeply hurt because friends betrayed him—and yet this man
had no bitterness in his heart, no rancor in his soul, no revenge in his mind;
and he went up and down the length and breadth of this world preaching
nonviolence and the redemptive power of love. He believed with all of his
heart, mind, and soul that the way to peace and brotherhood is through
nonviolence, love, and suffering. He was severely criticized for his opposition to the war in Vietnam. It must be said, however, that one could hardly
expect a prophet of Dr. King's commitments to advocate nonviolence at
home and violence in Vietnam. Nonviolence to King was total commitment
not only in solving the problems of race in the United States but in solving
the problems of the world.

Surely this man was called of God to do this work. If Amos and Micah
were prophets in the eighth century B.C., Martin Luther King, Jr. was a

prophet in the twentieth century. If Isaiah was called of God to prophesy in his day, Martin Luther was called of God to prophesy in his time. If Hosea was sent to preach love and forgiveness centuries ago, Martin Luther was sent to expound the doctrine of nonviolence and forgiveness in the third quarter of the twentieth century. If Jesus was called to preach the Gospel to the poor, Martin Luther was called to give dignity to the common man. If a prophet is one who interprets in clear and intelligible language the will of God, Martin Luther King, Jr. fits that designation. If a prophet is one who does not seek popular causes to espouse, but rather the causes he thinks are right, Martin Luther qualified on that score.

No! He was not ahead of his time. No man is ahead of his time. Every man is within his star, each in his time. Each man must respond to the call of God in his lifetime and not in somebody else's time. Jesus had to respond to the call of God in the first century A.D., and not in the twentieth century. He had but one life to live. He couldn't wait. How long do you think Jesus would have had to wait for the constituted authorities to accept him? Twenty-five years? A hundred years? A thousand? He died at thirty-three. He couldn't wait. Paul, Galileo, Copernicus, Martin Luther the Protestant reformer, Gandhi and Nehru couldn't wait for another time. They had to act in their lifetimes. No man is ahead of his time. Abraham, leaving his country in obedience to God's call; Moses leading a rebellious people to the Promised Land; Jesus dying on a cross; Galileo on his knees recanting; Lincoln dying of an assassin's bullet; Woodrow Wilson crusading for a League of Nations; Martin Luther King, Jr. dying fighting for justice for garbage collectors—none of these men were ahead of their time. With them the time was always ripe to do that which was right and that which needed to be done.

Too bad, you say, that Martin Luther King, Jr. died so young. I feel that way, too. But, as I have said many times before, it isn't how long one lives, but how well. It's what one accomplishes for mankind that matters. Jesus died at thirty-three; Joan of Arc at nineteen; Byron and Burns at thirty-six; Keats at twenty-five; Marlowe at twenty-nine; Shelley at thirty; Dunbar before thirty-five; John Fitzgerald Kennedy at forty-six; William Rainey Harper at forty-nine; and Martin Luther King, Jr. at thirty-nine.

We all pray that the assassin will be apprehended and brought to justice. But, make no mistake, the American people are in part responsible for Martin Luther King, Jr.'s death. The assassin heard enough condemnation of King and of Negroes to feel that he had public support. He knew that millions hated King.

The Memphis officials must bear some of the guilt for Martin Luther's assassination. The strike should have been settled several weeks ago. The lowest paid men in our society should not have to strike for a more just wage. A century after Emancipation, and after the enactment of the Thirteenth, Fourteenth, and Fifteenth Amendments, it should not have been necessary for Martin Luther King, Jr. to stage marches in Montgomery, Birmingham, and Selma, and go to jail thirty times trying to achieve for his people those rights which people of lighter hue get by virtue of their being born white. We, too, are guilty of murder. It is time for the American people to repent and make democracy equally applicable to all Americans. What can we do? We, and not the assassin, represent America at its best. We have the power—not the prejudiced, not the assassin—to make things right.

If we love Martin Luther King, Jr., and respect him, as this crowd surely testifies, let us see to it that he did not die in vain; let us see to it that we do not dishonor his name by trying to solve our problems through rioting in the streets. Violence was foreign to his nature. He warned that continued riots could produce a Fascist state. But let us see to it also that the conditions that cause riots are promptly removed, as the President of the United States is trying to get us to do. Let black and white alike search their hearts; and if there be prejudice in our hearts against any racial or ethnic group, let us exterminate it and let us pray, as Martin Luther King, Jr. would pray if he could: "Father, forgive them for they know not what they do." If we do this, Martin Luther King, Jr. will have died a redemptive death from which all mankind will benefit.

Morehouse College will never be the same because Martin Luther came by here; and the nation and the world will be indebted to him for centuries to come. It is natural, therefore, that we here at Morehouse and President Gloster would want to memorialize him to serve as an inspiration to all students who study in this Center.

I close by saying to you what Martin Luther King, Jr. believed: If physical death was the price he had to pay to rid America of prejudice and injustice, nothing could be more redemptive. And, to paraphrase the words of the immortal John Fitzgerald Kennedy, permit me to say that Martin Luther King, Jr.'s unfinished work on earth must truly be our own.

Moon Rendezvous

Neil Armstrong, Col. Edwin E. Aldrin, and Lt. Col. Michael Collins*

The SPEAKER. My distinguished colleagues of the Congress, we are honoring today three men who represent the best in America and whose coordinated skill, fantastic daring, and visionary drive have made history that constitutes a turning point of paramount importance in the journey of mankind. I have the high honor and official and personal pleasure of presenting to you the

*Delivered to a Joint Session of Congress, September 16, 1969. By permission of Armstrong, Aldrin, and Collins. Reprinted from *Congressional Record*, Vol. 115, #148, September 16, 1969, H 7937-7938.

crew of Apollo 11, who successfully made the historic journey to the moon, Neil A. Armstrong, Col. Edwin E. Aldrin, Jr., and Lt. Col. Michael Collins.

The Chair recognizes Mr. Armstrong.

Mr. ARMSTRONG. Mr. Speaker, Mr. President, Members of Congress, distinguished guests, we are greatly honored that you have invited us here today. Only now have we completed our journey to land on and explore the moon, and return. It was here in these Halls that our venture really began. Here the Space Act of 1958 was framed, the chartering document of the National Aeronautics and Space Administration. And here in the years that followed the key decisions that permitted the successive steps of Mercury and Gemini and Apollo were permitted.

Your policies and the marvels of modern communication have permitted people around the world to share the excitement of our exploration. And, although you have been informed of the results of the Apollo 11, we are particularly pleased to have this opportunity to complete our work by reporting to you and through you to the American people. My colleagues share the honor of presenting this report. First, it is my pleasure to present Col. Edwin Aldrin.

Colonel ALDRIN. Distinguished ladies and gentlemen, it is with a great sense of pride as an American and with humility as a human being that I say to you today what no men have been privileged to say before: "We walked on the moon." But the footprints at Tranquillity Base belong to more than the crew of Apollo 11. They were put there by hundreds of thousands of people across this country, people in Government, industry, and universities, the teams and crews that preceded us, all who strived throughout the years with Mercury, Gemini, and Apollo. Those footprints belong to the American people and you, their representatives, who accepted and supported the inevitable challenge of the moon. And, since we came in peace for all mankind those footprints belong also to all people of the world. As the moon shines impartially on all those looking up from our spinning earth so do we hope the benefits of space exploration will be spread equally with a harmonizing influence to all mankind.

Scientific exploration implies investigating the unknown. The result can never be wholly anticipated. Charles Lindbergh said, "Scientific accomplishment is a path, not an end; a path leading to and disappearing in mystery."

Our steps in space have been a symbol of this country's way of life as we open our doors and windows to the world to view our successes and failures and as we share with all nations our discovery. The Saturn, Columbia, and Eagle, and the extravehicular mobility unit have proved to Neil, Mike, and me that this Nation can produce equipment of the highest quality and dependability. This should give all of us hope and inspiration to overcome some of the more difficult problems here on earth. The Apollo lesson is that national goals can be met where there is a strong enough will to do so.

The first step on the moon was a step toward our sister planets and ultimately toward the stars. "A small step for a man," was a statement of fact, "a giant leap for mankind," is a hope for the future.

What this country does with the lessons of Apollo apply to domestic problems, and what we do in further space exploration programs will determine just how giant a leap we have taken.

Thank you.

Mr. ARMSTRONG. Now I should like to present Col. Michael Collins.

Colonel COLLINS. Mr. President, Members of Congress, and distinguished guests: One of the many things I have very much enjoyed about working for the Space Agency, and for the Air Force, is that they have always given me free rein, even to the extent of addressing this most august assemblage without coaching, without putting any words in my mouth. Therefore, my brief remarks are simply those of a free citizen living in a free country and expressing free thoughts that are purely my own.

Many years before there was a space program my father had a favorite quotation: "He who would bring back the wealth of the Indies must take the wealth of the Indies with him." This we have done. We have taken to the moon the wealth of this Nation, the vision of its political leaders, the intelligence of its scientists, the dedication of its engineers, the careful craftsmanship of its workers, and the enthusiastic support of its people. We have brought back rocks. And I think it is a fair trade. For just as the Rosetta stone revealed the language of ancient Egypt, so may these rocks unlock the mystery of the origin of the moon, of our earth, and even of our solar system.

During the flight of Apollo 11, in the constant sunlight between the earth and the moon, it was necessary for us to control the temperature of our spacecraft by a slow rotation not unlike that of a chicken on a barbecue spit. As we turned, the earth and the moon alternately appeared in our windows. We had our choice. We could look toward the Moon, toward Mars, toward our future in space—toward the new Indies—or we could look back toward the Earth, our home, with its problems spawned over more than a millennium of human occupancy.

We looked both ways. We saw both, and I think that is what our Nation must do.

We can ignore neither the wealth of the Indies nor the realities of the immediate needs of our cities, our citizens, or our civics. We cannot launch our planetary probes from a springboard of poverty, discrimination, or unrest. But neither can we wait until each and every terrestrial problem has been solved. Such logic 200 years ago would have prevented expansion westward past the Appalachian Mountains, for assuredly the eastern seaboard was beset by problems of great urgency then, as it is today.

Man has always gone where he has been able to go. It is that simple. He will continue pushing back his frontier, no matter how far it may carry him from his homeland.

Someday in the not-too-distant future, when I listen to an earthling step out onto the surface of Mars or some other planet, just as I listened to Neil step out onto the surface of the Moon, I hope I hear him say: "I come from the United States of America."

Mr. ARMSTRONG. We landed on the Sea of Tranquillity, in the cool of the early lunar morning, when the long shadows would aid our perception.

The sun was only 10° above the horizon. While the earth turned through nearly a full day during our stay, the sun at Tranquillity Base rose barely 11°—a small fraction of the month-long lunar day. There was a peculiar sensation of the duality of time—the swift rush of events that characterizes all our lives—and the ponderous parade which marks the aging of the universe.

Both kinds of time were evident—the first by the routine events of the flight, whose planning and execution were detailed to fractions of a second—the latter by rocks around us, unchanged throughout the history of man—whose 3-billion-year-old secrets made them the treasure we sought.

The plaque of the Eagle which summarized our hopes bears this message:

Here men from the planet earth first set foot upon the moon July 1969 A.D.

We came in peace for all mankind. Those nineteen hundred and sixty-nine years had constituted the majority of the age of Pisces, a 12th of the great year. That is measured by the thousand generations the precession of the earth's axis requires to scribe a giant circle in the heavens.

In the next 20 centuries, the age of Aquarius of the great year, the age for which our young people have such high hopes, humanity may begin to understand its most baffling mystery—where are we going?

The earth is, in fact, traveling many thousands of miles per hour in the direction of the constellation Hercules—to some unknown destination in the cosmos. Man must understand his universe in order to understand his destiny.

Mystery however is a very necessary ingredient in our lives. Mystery creates wonder and wonder is the basis for man's desire to understand. Who knows what mysteries will be solved in our lifetime, and what new riddles will become the challenge of the new generations?

Science has not mastered prophesy. We predict too much for next year yet far too little for the next ten. Responding to challenge is one of democracy's great strengths. Our successes in space lead us to hope that this strength can be used in the next decade in the solution of many of our planet's problems. Several weeks ago I enjoyed the warmth of reflection on the true meanings of the spirit of Apollo.

I stood in the highlands of this Nation, near the Continental Divide, introducing to my sons the wonders of nature, and pleasures of looking for deer and for elk.

In their enthusiasm for the view they frequently stumbled on the rocky trails, but when they looked only to their footing, they did not see the elk. To those of you who have advocated looking high we owe our sincere gratitude, for you have granted us the opportunity to see some of the grandest views of the Creator.

To those of you who have been our honest critics, we also thank, for you have reminded us that we dare not forget to watch the trail. We carried on Apollo 11 two flags of this Union that had flown over the Capitol, one over the House of Representatives, one over the Senate. It is our privilege to return them now in these Halls which exemplify man's highest purpose—to serve one's fellow man.

We thank you, on behalf of all the men of Apollo, for giving us the privilege of joining you in serving—for all mankind.

[Applause, the Members rising.]

(Thereupon, the flags were presented to the Speaker and to the Vice President.)

The SPEAKER. I think we would be remiss on this occasion if we did not, in paying the highest honor that the Congress can pay to any person—to invite them and receive them in joint meeting—also honor what might be termed the unseen astronauts, the wives of our distinguished friends. I am going to ask the wives of the Astronauts to rise: Mrs. Armstrong, Mrs. Collins, Mrs. Aldrin.

[Applause, the Members rising.]

The VICE PRESIDENT. On behalf of the Members of the Senate, we are very grateful for the presentation of this flag. We watched with great interest the Apollo program proceed and are conscious of the thrust of the need, in the words of the gentleman who spoke here this morning, the primary need being balance and the need to meet the problems of our society wherever they arise.

I can assure you that this memento will not fall into that category but will be kept and appreciated with the dignity that it deserves.

Thank you very much.

The SPEAKER. On behalf of the House of Representatives I want to express our sincere thanks to the members of the Apollo 11 for the thought and for the action in carrying this flag, presented to the House, to the moon and flying it on the moon. These two flags are probably two of the most precious flags, not only of our own country, but of any other country. We extend to you the deep thanks of the Members of the House of Representatives and assure you that every care and caution will be taken, because this will be forever one of the most treasured possessions of this great Chamber.

[Applause, the Members rising.]

The Astronauts on the Moon

Edmund Muskie, *United States Senator**

During most of the past two weeks, our people have been unified in a way that only great moments of triumph or tragedy seem to produce.

In the affluent suburbs; in the steaming inner cities; in our troubled universities, and in neighborhoods where the schools are inadequate and overcrowded; in mountain and seashore resorts, and in homes where families cannot afford a summer vacation; beside clear lakes, and on the shores of polluted rivers; whether we were white or black, rich or poor, young or old, supporters or critics of the war in Vietnam, Democrats or Republicans, New Left or Old Right—the magnificent adventure of Apollo XI gripped us all.

The image of Neil Armstrong's foot swinging down from the Eagle, and onto the surface of the moon, is a permanent part of our consciousness. No matter where we saw that television screen—in a rec room, or in a tenement—its fantastic image last Sunday night belongs to all of us. Time cannot erase it, nor in any way diminish its power. For a while, it made us one people.

And our unity was based on something deeper than national pride. Armstrong and Aldrin were representing all of us—all mankind—reaching out into the cosmos.

How long will that sense of unity last?

I'm afraid the answer is not long, if you consider the history of other great events that have drawn us together, in exultation or sorrow.

Because sooner or later the television sets go off, and we return to the earth and the heat of summer. To high prices. A weak stock market. To traffic congestion. Rising crime. Cities hard-pressed for funds, and public services deteriorating. The air we breathe dark with chemical waste. Mistrust between the races. Mutiny in the hearts of many young people. The war dragging on.

That, it can be said, is the real world. Our vicarious participation in the moon mission is just that—vicarious—though we did pay for it.

But I want to suggest tonight that at least one aspect of the moon mission is part of our real world, too—or could be.

I don't mean all the technological advances, the by-products, that are supposed to come from space science. I assume they are real. But by themselves, they are not likely to do much to relieve the problems we live with here on earth.

As a matter of fact, the science and technology, the national resources,

---

*Address at Jeffersonville, Indiana, July 25, 1969. The text is from the *Congressional Record*, Vol. 115, July 31, 1969, Appendix E 6515ff. Reprinted by permission of Senator Muskie.

and even the bravery that went into Apollo 11 could not in themselves have lifted that rocket a foot off the launching pad.

It took something more, something that could put all those elements together and give them coherence and power. It took a unifying goal, understood by all, and the will and determination to reach it.

In the case of the space program, the goal was simple. It was to enable a human being to walk on the moon's surface by the end of this decade. Achieving it was a terrifically complicated business. But the goal was clear and understandable and it inspired and unified our efforts, and we made it.

What if we decided that there were some goals here on earth that were no less important to us, no less urgent?

Now that we have seen that man can operate successfully in the lunar environment, what if we decided to help him operate successfully in the urban environment?

Now that we have shown ghetto children that a dream of sophisticated science may come true, I think it's about time to teach them to read.

Now that we have protected the health of three astronauts hundreds of thousands of miles away, I think we ought to find a way to give all our people good medical care at reasonable cost.

Now that we have built machines that can sustain great journeys in space, I think it's time to solve the problem of transporting people to and from work, without turning the countryside into concrete and the air into carbon and sulphur compounds.

Now that we've seen men cooperate to unite two machines in orbit at terrific speeds around the moon, let's find out how to get white men and black men to cooperate in improving city life.

I recognize that there is a difference between a physical triumph like putting a man on the moon, and a social triumph like putting a poor teenager on his way to a successful and responsible life.

With the one, we've been dealing with brilliant, highly educated men and women. We've had the use of the most advanced scientific equipment. We've been able to measure our progress exactly. When we've failed, when there was a tragic fire that set us back, we've pressed on, undaunted. We've had the funds that let us call on the vast resources of private industry. And most of all, we've had a simple goal.

But dealing with our human problems is another matter. We've found that we could not simply put together a few ingredients—a little money to improve the schools, a year of Head Start, a job training program, and some good intentions—and heal the lives of people who have known nothing but poverty and deprivation from the beginning. We don't know yet how to measure the effect of most of what we are doing—how much a billion dollars of aid to education can do for school children, for example.

Every failure—every grant to some group that mis-spends it—is the occasion for cries of outrage and calls for stopping the program. We've talked a lot about getting private industry involved, but we haven't found the key—the incentive—to bring that about in sufficient quantity. And most of all, our goals have been very general—and very rhetorical.

I think it's time we delivered some simple goals and some firm target dates for our problems here in America.

Like improving the reading skills of high-school graduates in the ghetto from the ninth grade level to at least the eleventh grade level by 1976.

Like meeting the goal of the National Housing Act—26 million new units—in the next nine years.

Like cleaning every American river of unacceptable pollution by 1976.

Like assuring that no American family goes hungry by 1971.

Like reducing the delays in our courts of criminal jurisdiction by $-\%$ within five years.

There are plenty of other goals—in higher education, in mass transportation, in cleaning the air, in reducing infant mortality.

And it is up to the political leadership of this country to set those goals and to provide some target dates for reaching them—dates that are just as demanding as putting a man on the moon in the sixties was, when John Kennedy set it in 1961.

You don't provide that kind of leadership if you back-pedal before every reactionary breeze.

And whatever your Gallup poll rating, you can't lead from a low silhouette. You've got to stand up. You've got to invest some of your political capital in making this a more human and hopeful country. You've got to help your people understand how critical our problems are—and how we can marshal our energies, as we did in the space program, to solve them.

Because the real issue is not who wins in 1970 or 1972. It's what happens to the country in the next four years—whether it regains its old determination, its old optimism and hope, or whether it divides still further into frustrated, despairing factions.

I hope our President has a successful trip in Asia and Eastern Europe. But when he returns—as when Armstrong and Aldrin and Collins returned—he will find an America very much as it was when he left it: In need of political leadership that identifies our problems realistically, and that describes some human goals within our reach.

It may be that this is too much to ask from Republicans. They are better at turning the clock back, or making it stand still, than they are at anticipating what could be in the hours and days to come.

It has been our democratic role to identify national needs, and to set the forces in motion that will meet them. We have done that before. We shall do it again. And between now and 1972, let us press this administration to stand up and lead. Let us—speaking as the majority party representing the people—try to exert more forward pressure than Strom Thurmond can brake.

Let us take heart from the spectacular achievement on the moon, and set ourselves some goals here in America. And let us bring together the resources and the will we need to reach them, and press on, through whatever disappointments and delays, until we do. That is the way, and the only way, by which we regain the union we knew last weekend. And, despite the glory of Apollo XI, that is what really counts.

On Understanding Society

Walter Lippmann*

Public opinion has been the third force that really changed American policy on the Vietnam war. How did that come about?

Well, the war was very distant, nobody was interested in it, and the Johnson method of handling the war was to conceal it from the American people. In the first year of the fighting, this was the Johnson escalation, because before that it was not really a war in the sense that it is now. It was concealed by the fact that the Army which was sent to Vietnam to do the fighting was really a professional army. It was not a drafted army. What Johnson did was to cannibalize the American forces all over the world, and build up probably the best army the United States has had in the world. But that army could last only about a year, until its term expired. During the next year or two Johnson more and more couldn't hide the fact that we were drafting men to fight that war.

Now, drafting men to fight a war 10,000 miles away is something that no sensible great power has ever attempted. The British, in all their period of imperial rule in the nineteenth century, never conscripted Englishmen to fight in Asia. They always relied on volunteers, professional soldiers, and on mercenaries. They hired the Indians, the Gurkhas; regiments of Iranians and other people from the Middle East, and so on; but there were no Englishmen conscripted to fight around the world. Johnson, who knows no history, didn't realize what a thing he was doing when he began to conscript an army to fight a war that nobody believed in particularly anyway— nobody had ever had it explained to them, nobody could explain the reason for it—10,000 miles away. It was that that began to arouse the American

---

*Some weeks before his eightieth birthday, at the invitation of Prof. Fred W. Friendly of the Columbia journalism faculty, Mr. Lippmann held a seminar with a small group of graduate students to discuss the contemporary applicability of this and other observations from his long and distinguished career. The text below is excerpted from the three-hour dialogue which resulted. Reprinted from the *Columbia Journalism Review* (fall, 1969), by permission of Alfred Balk, editor, and by Walter Lippmann.

people to realize what this was. And Johnson kept getting one general after another to come forward and say we were winning it when we were not winning it. Finally the Tet Offensive came, and he tried to get generals to say we would only take 35,000 men. But finally it was leaked out from Washington that Westmoreland wanted 206,000 men. And that figure broke Johnson's back. That was when public opinion revolted. That's why Johnson had to retire.

One of the reasons for all the turmoil in the country the last few years has been the feeling of a lot of young people that our governmental institutions are not responsive to the needs and feelings of the people. But apparently you do believe that at least in an informal way our government is responsive to public opinion?

Well, it's responsive to the kind of thing that I was talking about, which is being for the war or against it. The fact that the country came to be against the war is very important. Whether you can get a public opinion sharpened and attuned and made accurate to more specific reforms, I'm not sure. And I think that one of the difficulties—the difficulty with television, the difficulty with this turmoil—is that you cannot refine public opinion and educate it to very detailed and complicated things. I don't expect that any large audience, for instance, could ever really understand the problem of decentralizing the schools in New York City. I think it's just too complicated and difficult. It just won't catch in the net. So I don't want to sound too optimistic about public opinion.

How many problems do you think this country can digest at one time without breaking at the seams? We have Vietnam, the cities, the race problem. Are these likely to create a permanent cleavage?

Well, that's a problem I've been worried about all my life, but I have begun to realize, since I wrote *Public Opinion* and also while I was writing it, that the capacity of the general public—on which we're dependent for votes—to take on many problems is very limited. I wrote a book called *The Phantom Public* [1925], arguing that really what public opinion in the end could do was to say yes or no. It couldn't do anything very much more complicated than that. It couldn't say three-quarters or five-sixths but not two-sevenths—it isn't able to do that. That's what a scientist has to do. That's what an administrator has to do, what a public servant has to do. But public opinion as a mass can't do that. And it's one of the great unsolved problems of democracy: how are you going to make popular government—because it's always going to be popular, in the sense of involving a great many people—how are you going to make that work in the face of the problems which have become infinitely complicated even in the last twenty years?

In that regard, how do you see the role of the mass media, if in fact public opinion is not responsive to very sophisticated and very subtle problems? Is the role of the media to oversimplify them in the hopes of mobilizing some force?

Well, undoubtedly the mass media oversimplify. The American people are very simplistic, they want to be told that things are absolute, that they're black or white. They don't want to be bothered very long.

So what should the mass media do?

That is the question, I admit, but first of all, I don't know enough about the mass media. I know something about journalism, but I know very little about broadcasting. I listen to broadcast journalism, but for the news at night; I don't get the news from it. I feel utterly dissatisfied almost always. Of course, I'm very interested to see a picture of something happening. That's very interesting—a splashdown, that's wonderful. But as for the problems which are very difficult, urban problems and all, you can't find out about them. You can get a smell of them. You know a little bit about what they're like, and then you can read about them, or somebody can lecture to you about them. But broadcast journalism has not only a terribly simplifying effect, but a distorting effect, I think, because it makes everything more dramatic than it should be, more interesting, more amusing. And the world of life isn't that. It's prosaic.

The current controversy over advertising of cigarettes seems to raise a central question about the relationship between public opinion and social policy. If the scientists and doctors who have no economic involvement in the industry are correct, and they seem to be, then there should be some public outcry about this; it's not just a problem of public opinion's not getting to the legislators.

But there's a good deal of feeling. You see, this pressure has worked. Public opinion doesn't always work through big mass meetings or demonstrations.

How much do you think public opinion has become synonymous with public relations?

Well, these professionals at public relations are too much for me. There is an awful manipulation of public opinion going on all the time, no doubt about it. It's not the whole thing, though. Public relations was unable to do anything about the Vietnam war. They tried to. Johnson tried all the techniques he could to hide that war, and then to make it acceptable. And it didn't work.

How is public opinion best measured? Is the Gallup Poll, for instance, an effective measure of public opinion?

The Gallup Poll is pretty good, if it's very broadly taken. But 96.3 per cent, that's foolishness. The taxicab poll that most people take when they ride in a taxi and find out what the driver thinks—that has some validity. My wife comes home and tells me about the hairdressers and what they think. Very reactionary, I assure you. They're afraid to go out at night.

If you're a public man—say, a President or a candidate or a good journalist—you suddenly know what the public feeling is. Why did Johnson retire, do you think? He knew that he was beaten. And where did he get that? He got it from polls, a little bit, but mostly he just knew, as a public man very well trained in public affairs—he assumed it. I don't think you can measure everything.

Public opinion isn't instantaneous. You can't take flashlights of public opinion and get it right every time. But a man like Johnson, who is made to hear an awful lot, and the representatives in Congress who are representative in the sense that they're like the others—you talk to them and you know what people in their districts are thinking or feeling, and what they're prejudiced against or for.

You once wrote that the hardest thing to report is chaos, even evolving chaos. That was in 1922. Now, 1968 was a very chaotic year; how do you think journalism performed then?

Well, if I remember what I said in 1922, the world actually—and I think I used the phrase of William James—is a "blooming, buzzing confusion," and the mind's eye has to form a picture out of really a very chaotic thing. And that's done by the creation of stereotypes, which are ways of looking at things; and then after a while when you have these, that's all you see—what the stereotype says to you. That's all that comes through.

Now, I think that today the good reporters, both electronic and newspaper, are much more sophisticated and educated men than reporters were in 1922 when I was writing. They're much more aware of the dangers of superficiality and so on. And they strike me as extremely intelligent. I think on the whole 1968 left us rather confused. Everybody was confused, including the newspapermen, because they were dealing with a situation for which they had no preparation.

Does it seem to you that political writers of the country are swinging to the right? If so, how far to the right do you think they will go?

Well, there's no doubt that—whether that's age or personal ambition or what—men do that. It's a rule any journalist would know: it's always safer to be conservative than not. You're much less on the defensive. You have much less to explain yourself for. The Left has recently done some very vicious things, I think. But on the whole, in the lifetime of most men who are now fifty or more, the Right is the one that's done the vicious things. Fascism was very vicious. I don't think anybody can predict how far it will go, because it's action and reaction, how the Left acts and how the Right acts.

How would you compare the social rebelliousness of the generation coming of age now with the social rebelliousness of the one that came of age immediately after World War I? And why, in the seven decades we have had in the century, have these two produced the greatest generation gaps, when they seem to be such dissimilar decades?

First, of course, there was rebellion and disillusion at the end of the First World War, and that produced the Twenties, in which a lot of the people who now are extremely Left just expatriated themselves. A whole colony formed in Paris of people who just couldn't stand this country. It was too awful for them. Hemingway belonged to that generation, Archibald MacLeish belonged to it. But what is new that I never knew then is the violence and disruption. They were rebellious, they made speeches, they wrote books, but they didn't come into the classroom and say, "By God, you're not teaching what we like, you're not going to teach." That didn't exist.

This man Herbert Marcuse has written a book, as you know, about the limits of toleration, and he doesn't want to tolerate people who don't agree with him. He says you mustn't tolerate people who are wrong. Those are the people he doesn't agree with. You mustn't tolerate the Right or the middle, you must only tolerate the Left, and the Left must decide whom to tolerate. Now, that philosophy, that is new. That is a revival of a thing that started quite differently about the middle of the nineteenth century and became anarchism, with people like Bakunin, who was the great antagonist of Marx. Bakunin was a Russian nobleman who had a romantic view of the Russian serf, and if only he were in charge of things all evil would disappear from the world.

But it was an amiable and decent thing. It was impracticable, of course, and it disappeared, and now it has revived, and that is the significant and dangerous thing about the recent times. We saw it abroad. We saw it in Berkeley. We see it all around: this feeling that you must stop things from happening that you don't agree with, and that liberalism is the great enemy.

But the power of the economic system is so vast, and yet so destructive and unaware of its destructiveness, that the people who see that power and that destructiveness are frustrated, and feel they can't work within traditional lines to counter the power, and so the question really is: is the society capable of change?

It is changing all the time. It is changing much more rapidly than we know how to understand it. But can it be remade to your heart's desire? I would say no, it cannot. And that isn't because the Right is in control, it is because this is the way of life in which we are embedded. Just as primitive man was embedded in his system of tribes and so on, we're embedded in this, and we can't get out of it. It's like jumping out of your skin.

It is possible that the rebellion of the young may be a product of technology's getting out of our hands, so that we really have produced a generation that is more different from their parent generation than ever has been the case before. Could you point to a time in history, perhaps, when you believe the same thing happened?

I think you're absolutely right, and I think it's fundamental. The technological gap and the generation gap are the same thing. And the young people today are coming into a world for which there was no preparation in custom. There never was a world like this. Not that any revolutionist made it. It was created by technology and science. They don't know what to do about it, and the older people don't know what to do about it, either. They don't understand it themselves. That is absolutely the core of our problems. How will we be able to create a capacity to govern this enormously new and enormously complicated and very rapidly changing social environment? That is the problem. And there's no answer. We may not solve it in a generation. That's the problem today. The revolutionary—all that business—is of no importance except as a byproduct of that.

Of course, one of the most revolutionary technological inventions of our time—much more revolutionary I think than people realize generally—is contraception: The Pill. It absolutely knocked the family to pieces. The old reasons for creating and holding families together have been knocked out by this technological interference in the relationship between procreation and sexual life. And that is felt everywhere. There's no family, there's no neighborhood, there are no clans.

But how do you get around the problem of being ruled by a generation brought up in a time of slower change? Really, the problem seems to be re-educating Congressmen and Senators and the like, and this is the media's responsibility. But how do you get at them?

Well, this is an autobiography for me. I have lived through this. I feel it. I have felt it for years. And I have lived right in the midst of this change, never really understanding it very well and knowing I didn't understand it very well, not knowing what to do about it. I don't feel able to say what I'm going to tell a Congressman to do. I myself don't know what to do. We might as well be honest about it with ourselves: we are not in a position yet to re-educate the masses because we don't know what to teach them. And that is one of the critical conditions of our time.

Is it more important for us to educate the Congressmen or to educate the Middlewestern farmer?

First of all, it's most important to educate ourselves. And that is really absolutely fundamental. We know what to do about a particular thing, but about the general situation we don't know. And the fact that we don't know is perhaps the beginning of wisdom. We're going to have to create the general knowledge that we don't know.

Yale University Commencement Statement on Peace

Text of Statement at Yale University Commencement, June 9, 1969, Delivered by William McIlwaine Thompson, Jr., Class Secretary of the Yale Class of 1969, at The Request of the Majority of the Class.

Last month an overwhelming majority of the Senior Class requested by petition that their commencement be dedicated to an expression of opposition to the war in Vietnam. Furthermore, they asked that some provisions be made for the public expression of that sentiment here today.

As part of that expression a petition was circulated among members of the class opening with the following paragraph:

We, members of the Yale Class of 1969, strongly oppose the current United States policy in Vietnam. We feel that the war is a tragic waste of life and resources, both American and Vietnamese, which completely outweighs any possible gains. We also see it as detrimental to the solutions of the urgent domestic problems our nation faces. The war must be ended now. We plead with the leaders of this country to bring about an immediate end to the war.

It closed with this paragraph: "We now, at the time of our commencement from Yale College, state our determination that we will act in our public and private lives to assure that the tragic mistakes of Vietnam will not be repeated in our country's future." *725** or *77** per cent of the class signed that petition. In addition *135** members of the class signed a petition indicating that if confronted with the draft they would refuse induction, thereby risking jail sentences and jeopardizing careers to oppose the war. And finally a majority of the class has pledged to contribute to a legal defense fund established to help with the legal fees of those members of the class refusing induction.

---

*These are approximate figures only. [Thompson's note.]

Certainly the importance of these statements, especially the first, is not merely their expression of strong opposition to the war in Vietnam. Expressions of opposition have been made before. The real significance of these statements involves the percentage of the class which signed them. No longer can it be said that opposition to the war is limited to a radical minority or even to a liberal majority. Opposition to the war in Vietnam covers a much broader spectrum including concerned students of all political persuasions.

Graduation is traditionally a joyous occasion; a time of great celebration; a time for hope. But today despair outweighs hope; mourning outweighs celebration. This is not a tradition commencement; it cannot be. In a time of crisis tradition must be broken.

For the past four years we at Yale have witnessed a war justified by false assumptions and sustained by an unwillingness to accept new ones. It is a distant war, a war that is despised. And yet it cannot be forgotten or ignored. Because of the draft the war is brought close to all of us. Most of us are plagued by the pain of an uncertain future and the prospect of fighting in a war which cannot be supported. As a solution to this anxiety, the present administration has proposed that the draft be modified. Changes in the draft, however, will not change our opposition to the war. Our opposition is based on more than self-interest; it is based on a deep and overriding concern with the welfare of this country. The vast majority of Yale seniors want to serve and protect their country. Patriotism is not dead on the college campus today. Patriotism at its best has never been the blind obedience to the policies of a nation. It is the constant search for good and better policies. And when old policies are shown to be wrong, patriotism generates efforts to implement new ones. Today the war in Vietnam is almost unanimously regarded as a national tragedy. The leaders of our nation have admitted that the old policies of military escalation have been wrong and that new ones of de-escalation must be employed. And yet today the new seem no different from the old. Americans are still charging up isolated hills in senseless military actions, the lives of thousands are lost to win supposed diplomatic advantage at the negotiating table. We are told that the pride of the nation is at stake. Pride is expendable, lives are not. Within the next year some of us will die, others will be maimed, in a war which has been declared a mistake. And yet it continues.

Equally devastating have been our miscalculations at home. The war is destroying not one nation but two—the Vietnamese and our own. Our cities are in decay; our universities are in chaos; our poor are hungry. And yet our money and our energies are expended upon war and the perpetuation of war.

Today as we leave Yale a sense of frustration and despair overwhelms us. On some campuses this frustration has erupted into a violence which has shocked the American public. And yet that same public silently condones violence abroad in senseless military action killing thousands of Americans and Vietnamese. The connection between the violence here and abroad must be made: the violence at home will not end while the violence abroad continues. The one feeds the other. To understand the frustrations causing violence, however, is not to condone it. The great majority of students would not advocate violent confrontation. But we do demand a confrontation with reason. The death and destruction in Vietnam have not been explained adequately because they cannot be explained. Then why does the war continue?

For the past four years our leaders have attempted to soothe us with predictions of peace. We are tired of their rhetoric—of promises to act without action; of a willingness to take risks without risks. False rhetoric is no longer acceptable. Nor will token action such as the withdrawal of small numbers of troops without a decrease in the current level of fighting, be greeted with more than dismay. We will not be appeased by cynical attempts to silence public criticism of the war. As long as the fighting continues at its present level, our opposition to the war will also continue. Immediate action must be taken to extricate us from the disaster that is Vietnam. The war must end now; and the fight for our cities, for our nation, for our people must begin.

index